D1357252

C334387797

THE
RAILWAY
HATERS

THE
RAILWAY
HATERS

OPPOSITION TO RAILWAYS
FROM THE 19TH TO 21ST CENTURIES

DAVID BRANDON *and* ALAN BROOKE

PEN & SWORD
TRANSPORT

AN IMPRINT OF PEN & SWORD BOOKS LTD.
YORKSHIRE – PHILADELPHIA

First published in Great Britain in 2019 by
PEN & SWORD TRANSPORT
An imprint of
Pen & Sword Books Ltd
Yorkshire - Philadelphia

Copyright © David Brandon and Alan Brooke, 2019

ISBN 978 1 52670 020 9

Typeset in 10.5/13.5 pt Palatino
Typeset by Aura Technology and Software Services, India
Printed and bound in the UK by CPI Group (UK) Ltd., Croydon, CRO 4YY

Pen & Sword Books Ltd incorporates the Imprints of Pen & Sword Books Archaeology, Atlas, Aviation, Battleground, Discovery, Family History, History, Maritime, Military, Naval, Politics, Railways, Select, Transport, True Crime, Fiction, Frontline Books, Leo Cooper, Praetorian Press, Seaforth Publishing, Wharncliffe and White Owl.

For a complete list of Pen & Sword titles please contact

PEN & SWORD BOOKS LIMITED
47 Church Street, Barnsley, South Yorkshire, S70 2AS, England
E-mail: enquiries@pen-and-sword.co.uk
Website: www.pen-and-sword.co.uk

Or
PEN AND SWORD BOOKS
1950 Lawrence Rd, Havertown, PA 19083, USA
E-mail: Uspen-and-sword@casematepublishers.com
Website: www.penandswordbooks.com

Contents

Introduction

The period during which most of Britain's railways were built was one of unprecedented change. From say 1830 to 1900, many of Britain's towns and substantial parts of the countryside were transformed as railway lines carved their way over, through, and under them. The scars they made generally healed quickly. The sight and sound of trains was considerably less intrusive than today's trunk roads and motorways with their permanent pandemonium and incessant cacophony. Their impact at the time was considerable, however.

Although there were places that did not want anything to do with railways, at least in the early years, it was generally felt that to be located on a railway was necessary for beneficial connection with the wider world. Not to be connected could mean economic stagnation or decay. There are parallels with current debates predicting the economy seriously losing out if this or that airport is not allowed to have an extra runway, if motorways are not widened or if HS2 is not built. Over the nineteenth century, it became obvious that railways usually assisted economic growth and most people wanted the benefits of that growth. Some disruption was a small price to pay.

When a railway opened, people had immediate access to a far wider world and the opportunity greatly to extend their horizons. The railways provided dramatic evidence of the economic, social and political impact of the Industrial Revolution. In *Dombey and Son* this was recognised by Charles Dickens in relation to London, not without a muted critical element:

> 'There were railway patterns in its drapers' shops, and railway journals in the windows of its newsmen. There were railway hotels, coffee-houses, lodging-houses, boarding-houses; railway plans, maps, views, wrappers, bottles, sandwich-boxes and timetables; railway hackney coach and cabstands; railway omnibuses, railway streets and buildings, railway hangers-on and parasites, and flatterers out of all calculation. There was even railway time observed in clocks, as if the sun itself had given in.'

From their earliest days, steam-hauled railways incurred hostility. Those with interests in existing forms of transport wanted railways to fail; landowners resented their physical intrusiveness and legal powers of compulsory purchase; many people were scared of their appearance, noise, weight and speed. For some, railways were vulgar and brash, evidence of a new age in which established practices were being ruthlessly shouldered aside by changes based on blatantly materialist values. It damaged the emerging image of the railways when William Huskisson, former President of the Board of Trade and Colonial Secretary was run down by a steam locomotive at the opening of the Liverpool & Manchester Railway in 1830. What better demonstration could there be, some asked, of the destructive effect of railways?

Few written criticisms of the new-fangled railways were quite as splenetic as this excerpt from an edition of *John Bull* in 1835:

'We denounce the mania as destructive of the country in a thousand particulars – the whole face of the Kingdom is to be tattooed with these odious deformities – huge mounds are to intersect our beautiful valleys; the noise and stench of locomotive steam-engines are to disturb the quietude of the peasant, the farmer and the gentleman … Railroads will in their efforts to gain ground do incalculable mischief. If they succeed they will give an unnatural impetus to society, destroy all the relations which exist between man and man, overthrow all mercantile regulations, overturn the metropolitan markets, drain the provinces of all their resources, and create, at the peril of life, all sorts of confusion and distress. If they fail nothing will be left but the hideous memorials of public folly.'[1]

Another tirade was launched by an anonymous MP in the early 1830s:

'…the whole country was to be traversed and dissected by iron roads, and whenever there was a hamlet or a cattle track, a market or a manufactory, there was to be a railroad; physical objects and private rights were stamped under the chariot wheels of the Fire King. Mountains were to be cut through; valleys were to be lifted, the skies were to be scaled; the earth was to be tunnelled; parks, gardens and ornamental estates were to be broken into; the shrieking engine was to carry the riot of the town into the sylvan retreat of pastoral life; sweltering trains were to penetrate solitudes hitherto sacred to the ruins of antiquity; hissing locomotives were to rush over the tops of houses.'[2]

Less lyrically, in 1838 a writer named 'Phoenix' lampooned the experience of railway travel:

'A railway conveyance is a locomotive prison. At a certain period you are compelled to place your person and property in the custody of a set of men exceedingly independent, and who have little regard for your accommodation. Till your journey is accomplished, you are completely subservient to their commands. You pass through the country without much opportunity of contemplating its beauties; you are subjected to the monotonous clatter of its machinery, and every now and then to the unpleasant grating of the brake. To all these things must be added the horribly offensive smells of rancid oil and smoky coal.'[3]

While there have always been people apparently indifferent to them, railways have inspired emotions as varied as excitement, awe and reverence; fear, aversion and utter loathing. The radical politician John Bright, referring to the first train he ever saw, said that for ever after he could never view them without wonder and admiration. Others, by contrast, were horrified and scared on seeing their first moving train and hoped that this sighting would be their last. Sir Thomas Masterman Hardy, Nelson's friend and flag-captain on the *Victory* at the Battle of Trafalgar, was capable of nonchalantly moving around the quarterdeck when under fire from enemy cannon and snipers' bullets, but tense and anxious whenever travelling by train, fearful of some awful catastrophe occurring and preferring any other form of land transport if it was available. The Duke of Wellington appreciated the utility of the railways but greatly disliked travelling on them. When he had to do so, he, like others of the rich, travelled in his own personal carriage mounted on a flat wagon so as to avoid being forced to share accommodation with people he had no wish to meet. He feared that the ability to move about by train would encourage the common people to get above themselves.

Railways contributed greatly to the profound changes taking place in Britain in the nineteenth century. It could be said that the modern world began with the coming of the railways. They stimulated demand for building materials, coal, iron and, later, steel. Excelling in the bulk movement of coal, they provided the fuel for the furnaces of industry and for domestic fireplaces. Millions of people were able to travel who had scarcely ever travelled before. Railways enabled mail, newspapers, periodicals and cheap literature to be distributed easily, quickly and cheaply allowing a much wider and faster dissemination of ideas and information. They had a significant impact on improving diet, especially in the towns and cities as the price of meat, fresh vegetables and fish fell because of the cheap transport they provided. They contributed to the process whereby a proportionately smaller agricultural industry was able to feed a much larger urban population. They helped to keep down the cost of the fertilisers and other supplies that farmers needed. They employed huge quantities of labour both directly and indirectly. They helped Britain to become the 'Workshop of the World' by reducing transport costs not only of raw materials but of finished goods, large amounts of which were exported. The building and operation of railways required occupations such as surveying and civil engineering to be far more professional while encouraging the emergence of new ones like mechanical engineering and accountancy. It could be said that today's global corporations originated with the great limited liability railway companies of the nineteenth century such as the Midland, the London & North Western and the Great Western. Railways profoundly contributed to but did not, of themselves, initiate the complex of inter-related changes which we associate with the Industrial Revolution. By the third quarter of the nineteenth century, there was scarcely any person living in Britain whose life had not been altered in some way by the coming of the railways. Railways contributed to the transformation of Britain from a rural to a predominantly urban society.

The growth of the railway network widened the available market for large-scale businesses based in the bigger towns. They could now gain access to the consumers in the rural areas and country towns. Such businesses often enjoyed significant economies of scale and could undercut the prices of small-scale local producers. Railways were blamed as the distinctive styles of these producers began to be edged aside by manufacturers using the railways and operating on a regional or even a national basis. Local styles of clothing and building materials, for example, began to retreat in the face of cheap, standardised and mass-produced items. Retail chain outlets began to spread across the country at the expense of small family-run local shops. Ancient trades went into decline and by the end of the nineteenth century, the world of small local craftsmen, manufacturers and retailers was in retreat. Many of them must have rued the day they had sat down to a celebratory banquet when their local railway line opened. Railways were even blamed for emphasising class differences as they assisted the development of suburbs, distinguished by the occupations and incomes of their occupants. The quality of service provided by the railways was very dependent on ability to pay.

Eric Hobsbawm neatly sums up the impact of the railway:

> '... the railway locomotives...were part of the most dramatic innovation of the century, undreamt of – unlike air travel – a century earlier when Mozart wrote his operas. Vast networks of shining rails, running along embankments, across bridges and viaducts, through cuttings, through tunnels...the railways collectively constituted the most massive effort of public building as yet undertaken by man. They employed more men than any other industrial undertakings. They reached into the centre of great cities, where their triumphal achievements were celebrated in equally triumphal and gigantic railway stations, and into the remotest stretches of the countryside...'[4]

Now, speed of personal movement was no longer restricted to the capacity of a horse. Moving people and information more quickly than was previously possible, especially with the associated invention and application of the electric telegraph, railways helped to initiate a revolution in the high-speed transmission of information which has continued ever since.

Railways were at the forefront of changes in business organisation, not least because they separated ownership and day-to-day control and encouraged the development of managerial elites and rigid hierarchical structures. Most railway employees were required to wear uniforms and were subjected to a discipline not unlike that of the military. The seniority of railway employees, significantly described as 'servants', was evident by the insignia they displayed. A station master was the tribune of the railway company and a major figure in the community. At a major station like Paddington, King's Cross or Edinburgh Waverley, he was a grandee.

Railways played a key role in the development of British trade unionism as the employees fought for some degree of control over their working terms and conditions against employers who may have regarded themselves as paternalistic but were often highly autocratic. The Labour Party was created partly out of a desire to obtain a secure legal basis for trade unionism in the face of considerable hostility from the employers, parliament and the judiciary. Issues particularly around strikes and union membership had caused much bitterness and many trade unionists felt that their own 'Labour' MPs could help to expedite legislation that would give unionism a firmer foundation. Disputes on the railways had been among the most acrimonious features of labour relations from the late 1890s through to the First World War.

What can arguably be described as the first modern railway, the Liverpool & Manchester, set a trend with its gala-like ceremonial opening but also its sense of theatre; its determination to set its stamp on the districts it traversed. We think of the Moorish Arch at the Liverpool end, the dramatic Olive Mount Cutting carved through solid rock and the spectacular Sankey Viaduct. The trains on the opening day left Liverpool to the accompaniment of cheering crowds. At the Manchester end the mood was very different where large numbers of sullen working people had assembled keen to let the Duke of Wellington and other politicians aboard the inaugural trains know about their many grievances. On one hand, a celebration of this monumental achievement; on the other, evidence of bitter social and political divisions.

L.T.C. Rolt wrote:

> '…the railways are with us still and we should see them and value them for what they are, the greatest achievement of the nineteenth century. They represent a colossal outpouring of creative energy unmatched by any other age; the embodiment of the pride, the hope, and the aspiration of a pioneer generation expressed in the cyclopean masonry of arch and pier and in the smoke-blackened architectural splendour of great stations.'[5]

More modestly, George Macaulay Trevelyan in his *English Social History* (1944) described railways as 'England's Gift to the World'. H.G. Wells in 1902 said that if he was asked to produce a symbol which best characterised the nineteenth century, it would almost certainly depict a steam locomotive running on a railway.

Railways attracted interest from earliest times and spectacles such as the Rainhill Trials of 1829 drew huge and fascinated crowds.

Early impressions were often affirmative, people being filled with interest and wonderment at the scale and boldness of such works as viaducts and tunnels and, of course, at the sight and sound of working steam locomotives. The railways were much more than that. In the words of Michael Freeman:

> 'The railway was deeply embedded in the evolving structures of Victorian society. It both echoed those structures and interacted with them. It had educational, intellectual, emotional and psychological dimensions. It was enmeshed in the spirit of the age, an undiminishing zest for bigger and better, for an all-pervasive machine technology and, in concert, a perpetual fascination with a sense of becoming, of living in an age of transition, in anxious and sometimes fearful contemplation of what the future held.'[6]

Towards the end of the 'Railway Age', the positive role that railways were establishing in the life of the nation was shown by the appearance in 1897 of the first railway periodical for enthusiasts as opposed to investors. This was *The Railway Magazine* and it was followed in 1899 by the pioneering organisation for railway enthusiasts, the Railway Club.

The particular interest of the authors lies with the economic, social, political and cultural impact of Britain's railways. We proudly admit to a great respect for the work of Professor Jack Simmons whose research and writing particularly in the 1980s and 1990s provided fascinating insights into what were then largely unexplored aspects of British railway history, his writings always firmly contextualised. His work was a model of erudition and lucidity leavened with understated humour and evident enthusiasm. It was a model for any railway historian to emulate.

The current work is the outcome of the authors' perception that comparatively little work has been published specifically examining the responses of the landed aristocracy to the coming of the railways in the nineteenth century. The authors live near the delightful stone-built town of Stamford in the south-western extremity of Lincolnshire. For long, Stamford was cited as an example of a significant town which failed to be located astride a major long-distance railway route. This was ascribed to the aversion to railways of the powerful Marquess of Exeter from nearby Burghley House. Although he was never omnipotent, it was frequently averred that that he used his very considerable local influence to ensure that the direct line from London and Peterborough to the north, later known as the East Coast Main Line, avoided the town by being built on an alignment a few miles to the east and largely away from his land. According to this account, it was the abuse of his power by the marquess that then caused Stamford to suffer decades of relative economic stagnation in the nineteenth century. Stamford stood on the Great North Road and had become a very important coaching town, enjoying considerable prosperity as a result. Most of this business disappeared when the Great Northern Railway opened its 'Town Line' from Peterborough through Grantham and Newark-on-Trent to Doncaster and points north. The marquess bears most of the blame according to this narrative. The reality was different and more complex.

The case of Stamford and the Marquess of Exeter led the authors to consider how other influential landowners responded to the issues raised by the coming of the railways. History is about the interconnectedness of conditions, ideas and events. It was therefore natural to move on to examine other individuals and organisations that displayed hostility to railways *per se*, to particular railways or to specific activities with which railways were associated. We concluded that any consideration of this hostility needed to be balanced by some evidence of the welcome and support extended to the railways. Is it possible to identify continuities and differences in attitudes to railways over two centuries? Railways have continued to evoke both criticism and approbation. Some of the controversies surrounding railways especially since their nationalisation after the Second World War are discussed.

We make no pretence that this is a comprehensive treatment of a complex and multi-faceted subject and hope that these introductory efforts will stimulate more research and writing in this field. We would hope to reach people interested in the changes brought about by the railways in the context of British social and economic history and history in general.

The authors would like particularly to thank Sean McCartney and Ed Brandon, Christian Woolmar and Janet Brookes for their help and encouragement. An attempt has been made to contact copyright holders but if any have been missed, the authors apologise and suggest they contact the publisher.

CHAPTER ONE

The Impact of Industrialisation and Urbanisation on Britain

From approximately 1830 to 1900, many of Britain's towns and substantial tracts of her countryside were transformed as railway lines carved their way over, through and under them, their appearance and character changing radically.

It is necessary to appreciate the sheer dynamism of the economic forces being applied in this period as Britain became, for a few decades in the mid-century, the leading economic and industrial power in the world. Railways were both a product of and a great contributor to this dynamism.

The process of developing an economy dominated by manufacturing industry required, among other things, a disciplined workforce able to comply with the new, demanding and highly uncongenial requirements of factory and workshop employment. Railways in particular, with their essential emphasis on safety, needed an almost military-style discipline from the workforce. The work regimes desired by management could not be imposed simply by authoritarian methods. It was necessary to try to win, or at least control, the hearts and minds of the workforce by ideological means. The churches, chapels, mechanics' institutes, the concept of self-help and the provision of controlled, commercialised leisure were counterpoised to the old folkways of anarchic sports, heavy drinking, 'St Monday' and bawdy, potentially riotous communal entertainment. A new popular culture had to be created to obtain the consent, often given grudgingly, of the workforce required by the emerging industrial society.

Although there were places that did not want anything to do with railways, at least in the early years, a general feeling emerged that to be connected to the railway was also to be connected to the wider world. Not to be connected could mean economic stagnation or decay. There are parallels with current debates which predict dire consequences for the economy if HS2 is not built. It became obvious from the 1830s that, overall, railways contributed to economic growth. Most people wanted to benefit from that growth.

Some disruption, even annoyance, was a small price to pay. If existing companies displayed little interest in providing a railway connection, local business people and others might raise funds to promote and build a line that was nominally independent, at least to start with. This was done for various reasons, not the least of which was the fear that their local economy would stagnate or even go into decline if it did not have railway links to the wider economic world.

There might be quite dramatic reductions in the price of coal in certain towns after a railway had been opened. Local farmers might be able to get livestock quickly and easily to larger and more lucrative markets. Examples of the beneficial impact of new railways on specific places and their economies could be given. Equally, examples could be provided of other, less beneficial effects of the coming of the railways on various aspects of town and country economic and social life. The development of the railway network gave access to large producers from the bigger towns. They could now penetrate established rural and country-town markets. Big producers often enjoyed significant economies of scale. The creation of a comprehensive railway network, providing a reasonably cheap transport infrastructure, assisted the tendency towards local types and styles of commodities made by small-scale local producers being edged aside by manufacturers operating on a regional or even a national basis and on an increasingly large scale. Local styles of clothing and of building materials, for example, began to disappear. Retail chain outlets spread across the country at the expense of small, family-run local shops. Occupations such as those of wheelwrights, blacksmiths and thatchers went into gradual decline unless they could carve out a specialist niche in the market. Over a period of only a few decades the world of the small local craftsman, producer and retailer was to be transformed and many of them must have rued the day when they had supported the local railway project or even sat down at the celebratory banquet when the line opened.

Railways were blamed for creating dull, monotonous suburbs. Street after street of largely uniform houses were laid down in the late nineteenth century. Wood Green and Hornsey in North London are often cited as examples but the accusation is a false one. It was the presence of the railway which encouraged speculative builders to erect housing for clerical and better-off artisans who could afford to commute short distances but required relatively cheap housing. Such people were in regular work and did not need to tout for hire on a daily basis like so many manual workers, notoriously but by no means exclusively those seeking work in the docks. These new-build districts were characterised as lacking a sense of community with each family being wrapped up in its own domestic bubble and the paterfamilias being out all day earning his crust in the City or Central London. Even if such a view of the nature of these districts was true, blaming the railways was a bit like blaming the messenger. Such an accusation might have been more accurate had the railway companies had been legally permitted to buy land for development close to projected railways. Few companies obtained such powers.

It was also alleged that railway development was exacerbating or at least emphasising class differences. The medieval town, it was alleged, and medieval London in particular, saw rich and poor live cheek-by-jowl. Now whole districts were given over to occupation by members of the same class partly at least because they liked to cluster with their own kind. The poor had little option. Suburbs developed, the character of which closely reflected the income of their inhabitants. Close to the centre were the dwellings of the poor, whose impoverishment and often casual employment, meant they needed to be near their employment. Lower middle-class people lived in the likes of Wood Green, more affluent middle-class elements lived in Surbiton or Sidcup and the rich could live where they chose, usually in the sylvan and healthier outer districts. Of course, this is a pattern rather than an immutable formula. By no means all the main-line companies that served London initially showed much interest in developing short-haul traffic in the capital's environs. The London & North Western and Great Western were examples. Others, admittedly, saw a potential market in suburban traffic. The building of a line through largely rural terrain in outer London was, however, no guarantee that rapid residential development automatically followed, the Fairlop Loop of the Great Eastern Railway being evidence of this. Comments on 'monotonous' suburbs and the existence or otherwise of class divisions evidenced by the growth of such suburbs are, after all, subjective.

The one early railway company that will always be associated with property development was the Metropolitan Railway. It gained legal entitlement to do so in 1874. It started granting building leases and selling ground rents at Willesden Green and by the 1900s was actively building houses as far out from the centre as Pinner. After the Great War, the Metropolitan established the Metropolitan Railway Country Estates which engaged in large-scale development of housing for middle-class commuters all the way into leafy Buckinghamshire. 'Metroland' as this became known provoked accusations that the railway was engaged in building residential districts lacking character but, over time, some of these have come to be regarded with affection and the gentle, not unkind mocking that was so characteristic of John Betjeman.

Care needs to be exercised when making statements that the opening of a particular railway led to such and such economic change in a specific location. Many assertions may be true but hard quantitative evidence to support them is often hard to produce, being partial, unreliable or non-existent. An example of a tendency which lacks quantifiable evidence can be provided by changes that occurred in Northumberland. There, much arable land was being converted to pasture for sheep farming in the nineteenth century. This benefitted farmers but because livestock rearing required less labour than arable farming, the effect was to make farmworkers redundant and intensify rural depopulation with a drift away to the industrial towns. The railways were welcomed by the farmers because they could get their stock quickly and easily to a wider range of markets. Carriage by rail ended the loss of weight that took place when livestock was driven long distances overland. Clearly, the railways benefitted many of the local farming fraternity but forced the rural proletariat to seek employment and housing elsewhere. This may have been a traumatic experience at the time, but the likelihood was that those who drifted to the towns benefitted materially from the generally higher wages that were paid for industrial work even if they also had to experience the horrors of urban overcrowding and environmental pollution.

CHAPTER TWO

Inland Transport Before
the Railway Age

When stagecoach services started between Liverpool and Manchester in the latter part of the eighteenth century, coaches took up to twelve hours for the journey but, in response to increased demand, by 1825 there were coaches using turnpikes (improved roads charging a toll for usage) and completing the journey in just three hours. This was a reckless pace and with the roads being crowded with other users, accidents were very frequent. Demand continued to grow so that increased numbers of coaches were laid on but with horses as the motive power, any further increase in speed was impossible. A more powerful form of traction was needed.

Long-distance stagecoach travel was expensive, uncomfortable and often dangerous. Fares were high and the traveller was expected to disburse tips to all and sundry, adding considerably to the cost. Coaches were unheated but marginally more comfortable (and certainly more expensive) for those travelling inside. Passengers perched precariously on top risked sunstroke, a soaking or a freezing depending on the caprices of the weather. There was always the possibility of armed robbery and also of accidents. It was not unknown for outside passengers to fall from their perch, sometimes with fatal consequences.

Between two such important commercial centres as Liverpool and Manchester, with traffic building up by the mid-1820s, it was clear that a better means of transport was needed to take full advantage of developing business opportunities. The surfaces of the turnpikes were being damaged by so much use and the cost of repairs was reflected in higher charges for the coaches passing along them and higher fares for their passengers. Businessmen were constantly complaining about the rates charged by the three waterways which connected the two towns. Small wonder that thoughts were turning towards the almost unthinkable – a railway line linking the two centres.

Turnpike trusts and coaching were significant industries. In the mid-1830s there were over 1,100 turnpike trusts in England and

Wales between them controlling around 22,000 miles of road. In 1835, 700 mail coaches and 3,300 stage coaches were in regular use in Great Britain. The standard of the roads maintained by turnpike trusts was variable. The trustees of some turnpikes simply used the income for their own purposes rather than for maintaining the road in a decent condition. Turnpikes, however, were almost always better than roads not controlled by trusts, of which there remained significant stretches in varying degrees of disrepair. These had to be endured on most lengthy coach journeys. Turnpike trusts were unpopular as local people objected to having to pay to use roads they had previously traversed for free. Another source of acrimony was that it took time for a turnpike trust to generate enough income to embark on the improvements which were supposed to be its *raison d'etre*. Users understandably objected to having to pay to travel a road that was not yet improved. Animosity to the turnpikes led in some places to the Rebecca Riots, when gates, fences and tollhouses were attacked. The authorities took such riots very seriously and those convicted could face a death sentence. Turnpike trustees deplored the fact that the opening of a competing railway meant that they would still have to pay for the upkeep of the road with much less income when traffic had been extracted by the railway.

Turnpike trusts, stage coach owners, hoteliers, ostlers and all others who derived their living from road transport had good reason for viewing the coming of the railways with concern. However, railways did not simply destroy the livelihoods of all those earning their living from road usage. Economic activity was increasing through the nineteenth century and more people and more goods were on the move requiring the services of hauliers and waggoners, farriers and others needed to service the draught animals and the vehicles involved. Laments were penned for the fate of the horse. No one needed to concern themselves because the horse was not destined for extinction. Plenty of work was available for horses hauling wagons feeding goods to and from the railways.

Railways certainly administered the kiss of death to the long-distance coaching industry. Coaches could not compete on speed, comfort or fares with the railways. The very last regular stage coach was withdrawn in 1874 when the Highland Railway opened up a line in the north of Scotland. Even on the four-mile route between London and Greenwich served by London's first railway, the train cut fifty minutes off the time taken by coaches on

EFFECTS of the RAIL ROAD on the BRUTE CREATION.

The industry that supported road travel obviously saw threats in the coming of the railways. This contemporary satire bemoans the fate of the horses whose livelihood was bound up with road traffic. As a train passes in the distance, these horses are reduced to beggary. (Authors' collection)

the turnpike. It was a measure of the impact of the railways that the Liverpool & Manchester Railway received a contract from the Post Office to carry the mails as early as November 1830. In 1838, the Railways (Conveyance of Mails) Act empowered the Postmaster-General to require all existing and future railways to carry the mail. This was official recognition of the merits of the railways as a means of transport.

In 1835, no fewer than 350 stage coaches and Royal Mail coaches were leaving Birmingham daily, evidence of the sheer intensity of the coaching system but things were changing very rapidly. In the summer of 1838, there were still fifty-nine mail coaches in England and Wales and sixteen in Scotland. Four months later, one of many similar advertisements appearing in

The Times showed the way things were moving. It announced the sale by auction at the *King's Arms*, Bagshot, Surrey, of:

> 'Forty superior, good-sized, strangthy, [sic] short-legged, quick-actioned fresh horses and six sets of four-horse harness, which had been working the Exeter 'Telegraph', Southampton and Gosport Fast Coaches and one stage of the Devonshire Mail... The above genuine stock for unreserved sale, entirely on account of the coaches being removed from the Road to the Railway!'[1]

The demand for passenger and goods transport by the railways created the need for short-haul road passenger and goods haulage feeding into them. The turnpike trusts went into decline with the arrival of the railway age and most went out of business very quickly once a competing railway was opened. The last turnpike closed in 1895. The impact of the railways caused hardship for many of those involved in the turnpike trusts and all aspects of long-distance coaching, including hospitality services, and this generated protests which were largely ineffectual because 'the force', as they say, was with the railways. However, the leading coach proprietor who told a Parliamentary Select Committee that his business and those of others like him was being 'annihilated' by the railways was guilty of exaggeration. Even on turnpike trusts, passenger traffic could increase at least in the short term. The revenue of the Peterborough and Wellingborough Turnpike Trust, for example, increased sharply as coaches brought passengers to stations along the London & Birmingham Railway's Blisworth to Peterborough line.[2] On occasion, the opening of a railway prompted interested local parties to build a brand new turnpike acting as a feeder to the railway. An example was that built from Chirk on the Shrewsbury & Chester line to Llanarmon. Sometimes road and rail communication could complement each other. Starting in May 1840, a new coach service was put on from Derby to Manchester. This was advertised as enabling the coach passenger to get to Manchester in time to catch the 4 o'clock train to Liverpool.

George Shillibeer was an enterprising businessman who, in 1829, started a horse bus service from the 'Yorkshire Stingo' public house in Lisson Grove, Marylebone, eastwards towards the City and eventually reaching the Bank. He experienced competition and decided instead to operate a service between London, Greenwich and Woolwich. He was therefore less than pleased when the

London and Greenwich Railway opened in 1836. This was at a time when there were many railway accidents and some wag penned a song which briefly became popular, called 'Shillibeer's Original Omnibus versus the Greenwich Railroad'. One verse went thus:

These pleasure and comfort with safety combine,
They will neither blow up nor explode like a mine;
Those who ride on the railroad might half die with fear,
You can come to no harm in the safe Shillibeer.

Early railway travel was distinctly hazardous. 1840 was a year when there was a marked spate of accidents. Some coach proprietors took advantage and advertised the superiority of the service they still offered, albeit conveniently forgetting the not unblemished safety record of the coaching industry. Thus, a coach proprietor reminded passengers contemplating a journey from Derby to Nottingham of the advantages of 'going by coaches combining safety and expedition with comfort' and boasting that it 'must be evident to all that the Old Mode of Travelling is still the most preferable, and the only one to escape the Dreadful Railway Accidents, too awful to describe.'

The generally acknowledged superiority of railway over road transport was not always borne out in practice. The Eastern Counties Railway had the reputation of being something of a shocker with its slowness, timekeeping and general inefficiency. Coach proprietors and other road operators in the district where the company operated were able to make much of the item in a Norwich newspaper, which reported with some relish that fine Norfolk turkeys which, had been despatched from Norwich for sale in London did not arrive in the capital until many hours after they would need to have been cooked for Christmas dinner. A story about the Eastern Counties Railway which may be apocryphal but gives some idea of its reputation concerns a hulking great youth who had been apprehended travelling feloniously on a child's ticket. The case was dismissed in court when the magistrate readily accepted the miscreant youth's plea that he had been underage when he had started out on his journey.

In very flat parts of Britain like the Fens of Cambridgeshire and Lincolnshire and the Broads of Norfolk, a network of waterways existed, either altered or created by man, which predated the railways. Even in the Railway Age, small craft navigating these could undercut the railways at least for traffic which did not perish quickly and where time taken in transit was not a major issue. For other kinds of traffic, railways might constitute a serious rival even where large, easily navigable rivers were concerned. There was a long-standing tradition of Glaswegians commuting or pleasure-cruising from the city westwards along the Clyde to the salubrious districts downriver. It was perfectly understandable that the shipping interests involved were extremely hostile to the proposals to build railways along the banks of the Clyde to places like Gourock and Helensburgh because it was clear that trains could perform such journeys far more quickly.

The problem with rivers, no matter how much they were 'improved' as a means of providing cheap inland transport, was that their use was restricted to those directions in which the topography directs the rainfall to the sea. Britain's rivers generally flow from the higher terrain which is mostly in the north and west in directions which are not necessarily those in which merchandise and minerals need to travel. Canals allowed the opening up of completely new routes enabling waterborne traffic to meet the needs of producers and customers far more effectively than rivers. Canals can be made considerably straighter than rivers with more consistent depth and water flow which enhances the efficiency of their waterborne traffic. It is worth noting that the Bridgewater Canal Company was vociferous in its opposition to the Liverpool & Manchester Railway, having conveniently forgotten that only about fifty years earlier the Duke of Bridgewater and his engineer James Brindley had been lambasted by the local river navigation companies for the unfair competition presented by the canal.

The canals made a significant contribution to Britain's industrial development. They were the product of the uncoordinated activities of numerous independent companies and investors. Between them, they created a network of canals ('system' is probably too strong a word) also embracing river navigations. This network was most comprehensive in the north-west, around the Humber, the Fens, the West Midlands and the Thames Basin. Of the seventy largest British towns in 1841, only Luton then had no river or canal links to the sea.

Most of the canals were built over a period of just seventy years between 1760 and 1830. The consensus seems to be that the Sankey Canal near St Helens in south Lancashire was the first modern canal. It opened in 1755. With the growth of industry there was an increasing demand for the transporting of bulk goods. The roads were ill-suited to this kind of traffic and the canals so much more efficient for heavy, bulky consignments where speed was not an essential requirement. They were also far better for the carriage of lighter but fragile goods such as the products of the pottery industry around Stoke-on-Trent. Soon, increasing numbers of canals were being promoted, obtaining parliamentary sanction and mostly, but by no means exclusively, serving collieries and moving coal, iron ore and finished metal goods. One hundred and sixty-three Canal Acts were passed between 1758 and 1803, the process reaching a peak in the 1790s in what was known as the 'Canal Mania'.

Canals reduced the cost of inland transport and brought down the price of coal, iron, bricks and building materials and cotton and grain in the industrial areas. The network connected most industrial centres of importance to an emerging national market and provided links to rivers and ports and thereby to a wider national and international market. They contributed to the acceleration of economic growth, which was a feature of most of the 1780s and 1790s, but it became clear that continued growth required a form of transport faster, more efficient and more flexible than the canals. It was the function of the railways to fulfil this need.

Canals and inland waterways provided much employment and large numbers had been engaged in their construction. This work had seen the appearance of the notorious 'navvies' or 'navigators', the hard-working, hard-drinking and hard-living men who, during the railway-building era, went on to strike fear into rural communities with stories about how fathers had to secrete their poultry and lock up their daughters when these anarchic horny-handed sons of labour were in the neighbourhood.

While the canals offered an improvement over roads, they had their limitations. Horses moving along the towpath could haul barges with much heavier loads but only slowly. When steamboats were introduced, their speed was limited by the need to prevent their wash eroding the banks. Canalised rivers and canals might experience water shortages, floods or freezing. The Oakham Canal, for example, was closed for five months in 1844 owing to water shortage. Some canals, especially in the Midlands where water supplies were relatively scarce, were narrow but since that area was the hub of the canal network, boats using wider canals elsewhere could not navigate much of the network in that region. Boats that could navigate the narrow canals were necessarily small with limited carrying capacity which made them less economical to use when operated on the wider canals. This lack of a standard gauge was a serious shortcoming. Canals were largely built to address local needs with little thought being given to the creation of a national system. Additionally, where canals tried to follow contour lines as much as possible, their alignments could be very circuitous and journeys time-consuming. Where they tackled gradients through the use of locks, such as the staircase of thirty locks at Tardebigge on the Worcester & Birmingham Canal, the rate of progress was extremely slow. Tunnels might be driven as a means of avoiding locks but the expense of building them meant that they were usually only wide enough to take boats going in one direction at a time. This inevitably slowed traffic and increased the cost of transportation. An ever-present problem was the pilfering of cargoes either from the vessels themselves or from quays and warehouses.

Railways had their advocates as early as the beginning of the nineteenth century. In 1801, a Dr Anderson told anyone who would listen that it was scarcely possible to envisage any institution that would expedite more social progress than would follow from the introduction of the railways.

Countering Anderson's enthusiasm for railways were some of the wild allegations made about the likely effect of a railway between Liverpool and Manchester by those who had interests in the existing waterways between the towns. These were in response to the first prospectus canvassing support for the line, published in 1824. In the words of Francis:

'Every report that could promote a prejudice, every rumour that could affect a principle, was spread. The country gentleman was told that the smoke would kill the birds as they flew over the locomotive. The public were informed that the weight of the engine would prevent its moving; and the manufacturer was told that the sparks from its chimney would burn his goods. The passenger was frightened by the assertion that life and limb would be endangered. Ladies were alarmed at the thought that their horses would take fright. Foxes and pheasants were to cease in the neighbourhood of a railway. The race of horses was to be extinguished. Farmers were possessed with the idea that oats and hay would no more be marketable produce; cattle [sic] would start and throw their riders, cows even, it was said, would cease to yield their milk in the neighbourhood of one of these infernal machines.'[3]

By the 1830s, the canals had probably reached the limit of their capabilities given the available technology. They represented a considerable advance on road transport but had limitations which were thrown into sharp relief when the railways appeared on the scene. Manchester and Liverpool were about fifty miles apart by either the Bridgewater Canal or the Mersey & Irwell Navigation. On rare occasions when conditions were ideal, a consignment might take as little as twenty-four hours by one or other of these routes. Longer times were far more usual. Two weeks was not unknown. It was not uncommon for those in the Manchester cotton business to complain that the raw material took longer to get from Liverpool to Manchester than to cross the Atlantic from America. It soon became obvious that railways were capable of far greater speeds, of carrying heavier loads and providing a much more comprehensive coverage across the country. Railways were also much cheaper to build than canals. In 1824 it was estimated that it would be seventy-five per cent cheaper to build a railway than a canal from Newcastle to Carlisle.

It was only to be expected that the canals would rightly see railways as serious potential rivals and mount a campaign of opposition. An early example was the Mersey & Irwell Navigation which published a broadsheet inveighing against the L&M in which it said:

'That the advantages held out by means of a Railway are fallacious, and are not warranted by any one circumstance. Neither in speed, cheapness or accommodation can a Railway, even with locomotive engines, compete with water conveyance.'

Generalisations to the effect that railways destroyed the canals simply do not stand up to scrutiny. Canals and railways often developed symbiotic rather than competitive relationships, especially where the former were taken over by railway companies. Railways might utilise the carrying capacity of canals in the industrial districts and ran them as adjuncts to their own business. A very comprehensive and complex network of canals developed in the Birmingham and Black Country districts. Many of the businesses they served were located close to or by the canals and where much of the traffic was short-haul, low value and bulky, it made sense to leave the canals to do what they did best. The quantity of goods carried by some canals did not reach a peak until the late 1840s, well into the railway era. The Leeds and Liverpool, the Leicester Navigation and the Kennet and Avon Canals were examples. In certain areas such as south Lancashire and the West Riding of Yorkshire, canals were still a viable transport option well into the 1870s and 1880s despite those areas having intensive railway networks.

Some canals used their pre-railway position of monopoly to generate considerable profits. In 1830 the seven most profitable canals paid dividends in excess of twenty-five per cent which explains why such canals were so opposed to the construction of railways that would provide them with formidable competition. Possibly the shareholders of many canals were their own worst enemies. They put their eagerness for dividends before the investment in the infrastructure which might just have enabled them to compete more effectively once the railways had arrived on the scene.

It was possible for canals to dovetail neatly with railway operations. The North Staffordshire Railway took over the Trent & Mersey Canal and diverted suitable traffic along the canal to reduce the need for it to pay exorbitant running powers costs where its trains ran over the metals of the London & North Western Railway. Other canals were struggling financially before the railways arrived. In the case of the Oakham and Carlisle Canals, the railways probably did the canal companies a favour by buying them out and using parts of their formation, suitably filled in, for their own alignment. In 1865, there were still 109 canals totalling 2,552 miles and 49 river navigations amounting to 1,339 miles. Thirty-seven of these undertakings were amalgamated with railways, five had actually been converted into railways and two others had been leased by railways. Twelve companies had waterway interests headed by the LNWR with 498 route miles and the GWR with 225. Canals did not simply roll over and die with the coming of the railways. Some carried on simply doing what they did well while others went into slow decline. The best of them offered rates that undercut the railways, but they suffered from a negative image when compared with the modernity, speed and controlled power of the railways.

Such a relationship sometimes existed between companies running coaches and newly opened railways. When the Leeds & Selby Railway was opened in 1834, a daily coach was put on to and from Bradford to the Leeds terminus of the line, then at Marsh Lane. This allowed early travellers to catch the first train of the day to Selby where river packets plied to York and Hull and coaches were available to Doncaster and the south. A coach ran in the opposite direction in the evening.

Kingston-on-Thames was bypassed by the London & Southampton's main line. It was a town with extensive coaching operations. Once a station was built on the fringe of Kingston at what became Surbiton, enterprising people in the town put on coaches connecting into and out of trains at the railway station. These trains ran to and from the then London terminus of the line at Nine Elms from where boats or coaches connected for central London. Clearly the railway provided potential alternative work for coach proprietors.

The bulk of the railway network was completed by 1870. A number of towns, sometimes of some importance, were isolated from the network at that time. An example was Stony Stratford in Buckinghamshire. This was a major calling point for coaches on Watling Street, the trunk route from London to Holyhead. Its high street was noted for the number of its inns. The town's economy plummeted with the opening of the London & Birmingham Railway (L&B) bypassing it by about two miles. The decision not to serve the town was taken for engineering reasons. Instead, the line passed through Wolverton, then no more than a hamlet. It was chosen as the site for the L&B's engineering works whereupon it mushroomed into a railway town. This helped to save Stony Stratford because many local people became employed at the works and a strange steam-powered tram connected the two places.

We have seen that both road and inland water transport continued to serve a useful purpose even when the railways extended into most parts of Britain. Mention should also be made of coastal shipping which had much success in fighting off the challenge posed by the railway especially in the transportation of coal from ports serving the Northumberland and Durham coalfields down the east coast to the huge market represented by London.

Railways helped to keep down freight charges which were rising when the canals enjoyed some level of monopoly, but their major contribution was probably to speed up the transport of bulk consignments and extend efficient transport to areas beyond the reach of canals. Whatever the effect of railways on the transport of goods, it was, however, in the carriage of passengers that they had their greatest impact. Here the speed, convenience and comfort offered by the railway immediately rendered other modes undesirable and out of date. Predictably, people engaged on commercial and other forms of business quickly found railways a boon, but it was in travel for pleasure that the railways tapped into an unpredicted but huge market. In 1851 Britain's railways carried eighty million passengers, not including season-ticket holders. By 1881 they carried over 600 million and in 1901 a phenomenal 1.1 billion.

Chapter Three

The Railway Age – An Outline of Railway Developments 1820-1914

By 1800, the pace of industrialisation was accelerating as the power of steam was applied to a widening range of productive processes and, tentatively, to haulage, especially on railways. Political and economic power was starting to edge away from the landed classes towards the industrial and commercial capitalists. An industrial proletariat was being created as vast numbers of working people migrated from the rural areas, including Ireland, to the environmentally blighted manufacturing and mining settlements in search of economic betterment. This proletariat, in conjunction with elements of the middle class, would in the nineteenth century demand a greater share of the wealth it created and the right to take some part in the political decision-making processes. Grievances accumulated and were manifest in such mass movements as the Chartists. The level of political dissidence, particularly from 1815 to 1850, was such that the establishment felt extremely insecure and concluded that the concession of some reforms was necessary to cut across demands for more radical and thoroughgoing change.

From around 1850, Britain entered that period of twenty-five to thirty years during which she was unquestionably the dominant economic nation in the world, often being described as 'The Workshop of the World'. This, briefly, was the background to the Railway Age. The railways and their associated steam locomotives were both a product of the vast range of inter-related changes of the period and a major contributor to those changes.

Although canal promotion and construction reached a peak in the 1790s, thought was already being given to the ways in which steam power could be harnessed for railway transportation. Those of a cautious nature believed that stationary steam engines could provide the power for cable haulage on rails. Bolder spirits envisaged the development of existing primitive steam locomotives on short railways to haul heavy minerals in particular from quarries or mines to the nearest navigable waterways. By the 1820s, some piecemeal development of railways had taken place. A number of these were public railways requiring sanction by Acts of Parliament. Others were private projects. All were of a fairly local nature and mostly used the horse as motive power. The world was waiting to be convinced that railways and steam locomotives could unite to offer an enhanced form of transportation over longer distances than was possible with those transport modes already in existence.

The Surrey Iron Railway was arguably the pioneer public railway in Britain because it was the first to be incorporated by parliament for the conveyance of general public traffic although, not officially including the conveyance of passengers. It was opened in 1803 and its trains were hauled by horses. The first fare-paying passengers were conveyed on the Oystermouth Railway near Swansea in 1807, also with haulage by horses. For many historians, mechanical traction is the essence of a railway. It could be argued that two schemes were crucial in the development of mechanically operated railways in Britain. While various short industrial lines were employing steam traction with at least some success in the 1810s, the Stockton & Darlington (S&D) which opened in 1825 was a longer-distance facility. Although it was intended primarily to move coal from pithead to navigable water and it used steam locomotives for this purpose, it also ran passenger trains although, until 1833, these were usually hauled by horses. Like the canal companies, the S&D owned the infrastructure and allowed what we would now call 'train operators' to use its facilities. This proved to be an anomaly because it became usual for railway companies to own and manage the infrastructure and operate the services. Other small, local railway projects followed without there being at this stage any vision of a future national network of railways.

Opposition to railways had manifested itself when the first bill for the S&D had been presented to parliament. Lord Darlington protested that the proposed line would pass through one of his fox-coverts. For landowners like him, it was simply unthinkable that the pleasure he derived from hunting on his own property should be challenged by commercial interests whose only purpose was self-enrichment. Like many of his kind, he thought that the powers of compulsory purchase were an affront to his property rights and that those rights were synonymous with the rights and interests of society as a whole. He unsuccessfully tried to persuade the promoters to consider an alternative alignment. They decided to go ahead with their original alignment and chose their moment to inform His Lordship, doing so while he was actually riding to hounds. The air went blue with His Lordship's expletives. He then departed post haste to Westminster where he used his influence to have the S&D Bill defeated. When a second bill was presented to parliament, the promoters recognised *realpolitik* and proposed a substantial deviation so as to avoid his opposition. Lessons were being learned. The change in attitude of many landowners from instinctive opposition in the 1820s to a more self-interested pragmatism based on realising how much compensation could be negotiated became evident and was noted in parliament in the early 1840s:

> '…the greatly increased favour and support which, as compared with the property of former years, these undertakings now receive from the owners of Landed Property in the districts through which they pass.'[1]

Fox-hunting was an integral part of the prestige and lifestyle that went with landownership. Railways were resented by the hunting fraternity because they might interfere with the 'sport'. This picture was painted by Alken in 1866. (Authors' collection)

The ground-breaking project was unquestionably the Liverpool & Manchester Railway (L&M). It opened in 1830 and was designed to use high-speed steam haulage and convey both passenger and freight traffic. It linked two of Britain's most important towns, one a leading seaport and the other a burgeoning commercial centre. Its construction involved unprecedented civil engineering works and the company controlled both the infrastructure and the traffic. The L&M represented a major qualitative advance in railway practice and demonstrated that a railway outside the mining areas could provide a profitable investment for people across Britain while benefitting the economy of south Lancashire by breaking the stranglehold held by the canals on transportation between Liverpool and Manchester. The L&M was soon bringing an annual return of over nine per cent for its investors. Its spectacular success led to much longer routes soon being planned and promoted. These included London to Brighton, to Southampton, to Bristol and to Birmingham and from there to Liverpool and to Manchester.

In the early 1830s, those investing in railway schemes were mainly businesspeople local to the places concerned as well as cash-rich Quaker financiers, prominent country solicitors and speculators from Lancashire frequently referred to as 'the Liverpool Party'. The latter spread their bets by being prepared to invest wherever there were schemes they thought promised a useful return. There was unease about the dominance of northern capital being invested in the early trunk routes, including many of those into London. The natural aversion of country landowners to the compulsory purchase powers enjoyed by the railway companies was compounded by the fact that behind these companies was the spectre of 'new rich' and brash northern manufacturers.

Railways had arrived. At the end of 1835, just 338 miles of public railway were open but by the end of 1837 another 1,500 miles had been sanctioned by parliament. The lines that had been built were all the creation of private enterprise. Britain was unusual among the countries of north-west Europe in not involving the state in the financing and construction of major infrastructure such as the railways. France already had an extensive canal system built and paid for by the state. The railway systems being developed in France and Belgium, while encouraging private investment, went ahead with the government having a considerable say in how the money was used, something not seriously considered in Britain.

The Belgian government built the main line system and thereafter controlled it. Minor lines were constructed by private enterprise.

The political economy of the time in Britain was never going to permit active government involvement in drawing up and implementing a comprehensive plan for the development of Britain's railway system by individuals seeking personal profit. Here lies the key paradox. The railway companies were business enterprises financed with private capital. Their success depended primarily on the return they could provide for their shareholders. Despite their private character, they were, however, the beneficiaries of two unusual legal privileges. These were corporate form and status and the power to acquire the private property of others by compulsory purchase. This marked them out from the private partnerships and family businesses so typical of enterprise in early nineteenth-century Britain. It accorded them joint stock incorporation, recognising that they were large-scale undertakings whose financing, like those of public utilities, canals and docks, for example, was beyond the resources of a small number of business partners. The privilege they enjoyed was based on the understanding that the services they provided would accrue benefits not just for their own shareholders but to the wider economic and social communities. It was not unfair to expect that in exchange for this very real privilege they should accept a degree of regulation by government. This issued a challenge to the prevalent values of the age of *laissez-faire* which regarded private property as sacrosanct. In turn, property owners whose interests were affected directly by railway schemes were given the legal right, *locus standi,* to object and appear before and give evidence to the parliamentary bodies that were established to adjudicate on such schemes. However, as a solicitor for the South Eastern Railway made clear, such a concession was of little use to those small proprietors who could not afford the cost of petitioning parliament.[2]

Early government intervention in Britain was limited to preventing railways doing certain things thought to be against the public interest. It would put an upper limit on fares and charges; would protect landowners from damage to their property and 'loss of amenity' and require compensation from railway companies where these were proven and it would ensure that the construction of railways did not damage the fabric of existing roads and canals without compensation. Governments would not provide capital for the construction or operation of railways or any responsibility for their everyday management. From early on, however, some politicians were expressing their disapproval of the way that governments shrank from taking active steps to guard against monopoly and mismanagement on the part of the railway companies.

In the early days, important financial and commercial centres such as London, Liverpool, Manchester, Bristol and Birmingham provided much of the capital for major railway projects. Their business communities stood to gain from such investment. Over seventy-eight per cent of the initial capital of the Manchester & Leeds Railway, opened in 1841, was provided by people in Lancashire, Yorkshire and Cheshire. On occasions, prominent landowners invested heavily in local schemes. The Duke of Buccleuch and the Earl of Burlington between them subscribed over fifty per cent of the initial capital for the Furness Railway. This was not altruism. They owned land and mineral rights whose exploitation the Furness could expedite. As the network spread, so the sources of investment widened. People put their money into railways while perhaps having nothing to do with the locality served by the company involved. They did so hoping to obtain a rate of return as good, if not better, than any other investment would provide. A wide range of people with varying amounts of spare money were drawn into investing in railway projects, some of these proving to be of dubious integrity. By the early 1840s, railways were seen as a solid and sound investment but not at this stage generally attractive for those who wanted to get rich quickly. It was acknowledged that they were stimulants to wider commercial and industrial activity but, after several years of sluggish economic activity, many people considered that the viable railway network was, by this time, virtually complete. This perception was to change with astounding rapidity. In 1844, it was clear that there was an economic upturn. Food prices were falling and there were good harvests. With interest rates declining and gold reserves rising, banks were keen to put their reserves to good use by lending. It was as if investors believed that they could only get richer and richer. An economic 'bubble' was about to be created. Between 1844 and 1847, parliament approved no fewer than 650 bills pertaining to railways. With such feverish promotional activity, it is not surprising that the phrase 'Railway Mania' was coined. In 1845 the *Manchester Guardian* estimated that 357 projected railways with an aggregate capital of £332,000,000 had been advertised in one month alone. In 1844, parliament authorised 805 miles of railway; 2,700 miles in 1845 and no less than 4,538 miles in 1846. The momentum then fell away rapidly with 1,354 miles approved in 1847, 371 miles in 1848 and only eight miles in 1850.

Economic booms and recessions do not fall from the sky. Each is the product of a conjuncture of factors which gestate over the preceding period but which, at a certain stage, take on critical mass and become elements of decisive historical change in a set of unique circumstances. One of the factors at this time was the impact of the policies implemented by William Gladstone, President of the Board of Trade. To encourage railway development, in 1844 he reduced the percentage of the proposed cost of a new line which had to be deposited when a bill was placed before parliament. This deposit was intended to deter ridiculous or pointless schemes from wasting parliamentary time. Now, the figure was reduced from ten per cent to five per cent and was implemented by Gladstone because he thought that new railway schemes would stimulate the economy. Simultaneously, he ended the requirement that three-quarters of the shareholders should contribute to this deposit.

Gladstone's measures provided the intended stimulus to investment in railway schemes. An economic bubble was being created and even investors with small amounts of cash were finding themselves tempted to have a flutter. In something of an understatement, *The Economist* commented in 1845, 'Railway property is a new feature in England's social economy which has introduced commercial feelings to the firesides of thousands'.

Confidence tricksters came on the scene, some making a quick fortune from promoting new lines which they had no intention of building and inveigling the gullible into buying shares in these schemes. Other men appeared, enriching themselves from buying and selling railway shares and from promoting new lines. They employed methods which may not have been illegal but were often distinctly unethical. The doyen of these was George Hudson, who rose rapidly from obscurity working in a shop in York to being one of the richest and most powerful men in Britain. His spectacular rise, if not his equally spectacular fall, encouraged others, usually considerably less energetic and focussed, to try to make their fortunes. Some did so but a lot more fell by the wayside. *Punch* went for Hudson, often portraying him as 'The Great Railway Guy', either a stuffed effigy sitting in a barrow or a fat man with a gross paunch, sitting astride a railway locomotive. His efforts brought him a huge personal fortune, a seat in parliament, widespread if short-lived adulation verging on hero-worship, bankruptcy, and disgrace. Hudson, however, was more than a mere knave. He embodied the energy and spirit of his age but saw more clearly than most the economic and social possibilities of railways and he left an indelible stamp on the early railway network of England. The railways were as powerful a force as free trade in hastening the urban and industrial development of modern Britain and Hudson contributed significantly to their development.

As happens with all such bubbles, those with spare cash thought they could get rich quick. Charlotte and Emily Brontë for example,

During his spectacular rise to the position of the first railway tycoon, George Hudson made many enemies. Therefore, there was much rejoicing in certain circles when he overreached himself and, with equally spectacular speed, fell from grace. The fall of 'King Hudson' is satirised in this Punch cartoon.

invested rather injudiciously in the York & North Midland Railway. It was a headlong feeding frenzy of greed, not unlike the South Sea Bubble of 1720 and the dot.com bubble of the late 1990s and early 2000s. Some of the most absurd schemes were launched, aimed at the gullible. One such was titled 'The Direct Great Western. From the GWR at Reading in as near a straight line to Land's End'. Thousands of speculators paid the legally required deposit of ten per cent of the face value of the shares they bought intending to sell them quickly at the most opportune time in what they thought would be a continuously rising market. As early as January 1846, *The Times* newspaper was expressing concern about whether there was sufficient money available to meet all the claims on funds being made at that time.

On 16 October 1845, the Bank of England raised the bank rate by half a per cent. This had the effect of decelerating the 'Railway Mania' as share values plummeted. The repercussions were felt immediately. Many people had borrowed money in order to buy shares and, now finding their shares virtually worthless, were financially embarrassed because they still had to pay interest on the money they had borrowed to provide a deposit on the shares. Events outside the railway world brought the mania to an abrupt end. The failure of the Irish potato crop coupled with Peel's repeal of the Corn Laws meant heavy imports of food; and in the autumn of 1847 wheat prices fell drastically, ruining many corn dealers. At the same time, the price of cotton rose sharply because of the shortage of supply from America. The increased costs of these imports placed a heavy strain on bullion reserves. As the Bank of England's reserves fell, there was a fear that further advances and discounts would have to be refused; the panic ended abruptly with the suspension of the Bank Charter Act.

As always when the greed encapsulated in free enterprise overreaches itself, no one wanted to accept responsibility although there was an inevitable search for scapegoats. Some argued that there was nothing wrong with the system, but it was a few 'bad eggs' who had taken advantage of peoples' gullibility. The fault lay deep in the economic system and the practices which sprung from it. Many people were left financially ruined. 'The financial losses, damaged prestige and vast litigation caused by the panic all contrived to debilitate the (railway) industry not months but years after the event.'[3]

George Hudson was made into a scapegoat and many rejoiced in his fall from grace, but the Mania was the product of a system which permitted and even encouraged people of energy but questionable principles to operate in similar ways. As A.J. Arnold and S. McCartney (2004) said of George Hudson:

'...his energy and enterprise generated vast new wealth during the heady days of the railway construction era. The "get-rich-quick" ethos of the railway mania period, which he exemplified, generated huge sums for those who invested in stocks and shares, including many from the new middle classes who had developed a taste for railway speculation. The representatives of old wealth took their share of these spoils but they were also nervous of so much new money and disapproved of the brash new world of commerce that no longer knew its place...The exposure of his failings was attended by the most enormous public interest and there was a vigorous debate in the press. Hudson was of course the author of his own misfortune but some of his contemporaries recognised that many of his shortcomings were also failures of the system, the predictable outcome of the "get rich quick, money for nothing" mentality that had become so pervasive.'

Certainly, there had been 'bad eggs'. These included the people who produced flashy prospectuses containing what were known as subscription lists. These might include people well-known for their apparent probity who actually had absolutely nothing to do with the scheme being advertised, did not know they were lending their 'support' and were most unhappy when they found out how their names had been used.

One scheme touting for support claimed the financial support of four subscribers, all of whom had died before the scheme was even drawn up! Some schemes were totally fraudulent. In *Blackwood's Magazine* for October 1845 there was a satirical article contributed by a Professor Aytoun called 'How we got up the Glenmutchkin Railway; and how we got out of it'. It showed how easy it was for fraudsters to promote fictitious railway schemes, persuade the gullible public to buy shares and then abscond with the resulting funds. An example of a hare-brained and presumably fraudulent scheme was 'The Direct Sheffield and Manchester Railway' which was registered in 1845 with the ostensible intention of its plan being deposited with parliament in 1846. It would have passed through very sparsely-populated and exceptionally hilly terrain and involved extremely steep gradients unless a number of long and expensive tunnels had been built. From Sheffield, the line would have followed the valley of the River Rivelin and climbed to around 1,000 feet at Moscar Moor, only about eight miles from Sheffield. The project was never presented to parliament and was eventually wound up acrimoniously but not without a number of investors having parted permanently with good money. *Punch* in 1846 poked fun at some of the madcap schemes that were floated and invented

THE MOMENTOUS QUESTION.

"Tell me, oh tell me, dearest Albert, have you any Railway Shares?"

The fallout from the collapse of the 'Railway Mania' entangled a wide spectrum of society. Here a *Punch* cartoon shows an anxious Queen Victoria pressing Prince Albert to reveal whether he has any railway shares.

some of its own including the 'John O'Groats and Land's End Junction with branches to Ben Lomond and Battersea Railway'.

In the absence of being able to bring to justice most of the swindling fraternity, pressure was put on politicians to give governments closer control over the financial activities of the railway companies. A number of select committees were established to investigate and report on the factors that came together to cause the 'Railway Mania' and to examine its effects. However, radical legislation to control activities, many highly unethical as well as those which were definitely illegal, was not to be expected by politicians devoted to notions of *laissez-faire* and the free play of market forces. The 'Railway Interest' played an important role in defusing anger at what had happened. They wanted to ensure that only the very lightest of regulatory control, if any, would be exercised. Some of them had probably been involved in the nefarious activities which had been taking place. In the late 1840s, many railway companies appointed some kind of body to investigate alleged frauds, scandals and abuses or to prove that they themselves had not been party to anything dubious. Whatever the impact of such moves, the public standing of railway companies as businesses and as investments had been greatly damaged.

Herapath's Journal, whose eponymous owner and editor had his fingers burnt in the Mania, was highly indignant and wanted heads to roll. He claimed that:

'Members had not merely been canvassed to support a bill, but that large sums had been spent among them, to secure their support, and that Members of Parliament had been known to go from office to office and hawk their support as a pauper would his wares.'[4]

The 'Railway Mania' left a legacy which associated railway promotion with sharp practice. The collapse of the Mania contributed to the financial crisis of 1847-50 and many of those who had been badly affected wanted to blame the railway projects in which they had invested rather than thinking that they themselves had been guilty of greed and misjudgement. However, a negative impression was created which the railways found hard to shake off even though they were not really to blame.

At the height of the feverish activity around railway promotion, the services of surveyors were at a premium and they could command a very high price for their services. In the rush to draw up schemes, many people were employed in surveying work who were inexperienced, poorly trained or simply incompetent. Inevitably many blunders were committed not all of which could be kept quiet. Textbooks, basically 'Surveying for Dummies' sold well. People tried to pass themselves off as surveyors who did not even know what a theodolite was. This shed further bad light on the world of railway promotion.

In the reception accorded to railways, contractors were frequently portrayed unfavourably despite, or perhaps because, some of them rose from very humble origins to position of great wealth and power. A few, indeed, started their careers as labourers on railway schemes. A fictional contractor called Roger Scatcherd features in Anthony Trollope's 1858 novel *Dr Thorne*. He fits the stereotype of a graceless *parvenu*, who graduates from being a stonemason to become a knighted MP and a man of wealth and influence. Apart from driving ambition, Scatcherd has little to recommend him. He finds himself isolated from those who shared his humble origins while those born to higher social status tend to look down on him. He takes refuge in the bottle and eventually falls from grace. Contemporary railway periodicals did not have much time for contractors. As the *Railway Times* of 27 November 1852 put it:

> 'No one can have failed to observe the active movements of our wealthy and enterprising contractors, gentlemen who have made large fortunes within a short time, and who now seem bent on losing them as quickly. Having completed as they consider their work at home, and having given us an almost perfect system of railways here, they have started on a kind of knight-errantry to supply railway deficiencies all over the world.'

William Gladstone in his time at the Board of Trade displayed great perceptiveness about the harmful implications of allowing virtually uncontrolled competition in the promotion and building of railways. He saw the potential clash of interests between the private profit-making activities of the railway companies and the wider public interest. He wanted some official provision that would allow for the developing network to be brought under state control in the future if, in governmental opinion, it was not developing to the advantage of the public. More immediately, he established an

Advisory Board of five members to scrutinise every railway scheme presented to parliament in 1845 and to produce a report providing guidance for the Select Committee which would be examining each scheme. This body was known as 'Lord Dalhousie's Board'. It proved successful in its remit but powerful individuals, including members of the Lords and Commons, wanted the enrichment that might result from unrestricted railway promotion. They brought pressure to bear and the board, whose work might ultimately have saved incalculable amounts of money by supporting the creation of a logical railway system, was disbanded. It was a clear case of short-term individual economic gain taking preference over the long-term benefit of the economy and wider society.

It was a measure of the successful growth of the railways that with amalgamations some very large-scale enterprises were being created. In the late 1840s, the London & North Western Railway had 10,000 employees and its capital was around £20 million. Outside government departments and the armed forces, enterprises providing so much employment and possessing financial assets on this scale were previously unknown.

The 1850s and 1860s saw expansion which created a genuine nationwide network and most towns of significance were served by a railway. Between 1850 and 1870, about 8,000 route miles were built, the extent of promotion and construction reflecting fluctuations in the economy at any particular time. Most of the major routes had been built but branch lines, connecting links and cut-off lines were still being made. In 1870, the only English towns that lacked railway stations were places as small as Tenterden, Shaftesbury, Lyme Regis, Chagford, Burford, Abbot's Bromley and Clun. Some of these never joined the railway map. The larger companies had had their fingers burnt in the aftermath of the Mania and were wary of building extensions and new branches that were of dubious viability. Where people wanted their town to be joined to the railway they might canvass the support of one or more local landowners especially if it was thought that a railway would enhance land values in the vicinity. Hepple (1974) cited the example of the Salisbury and Yeovil Railway which in 1852 formed a Provisional Committee including some prominent local landowners including Lords Westminster, Sherborne and Rivers, the Right Honourable Sidney Herbert and, interestingly, Joseph Locke, the eminent railway engineer, whose contacts had gained him sufficient money to buy an estate of his own at Honiton. Between them, these landowners and other local people put up £550,000 of the £1,100,000 needed for parliamentary approval.[5] A line from Fakenham to Wells-next-the-Sea was given vital support from the Earl of Leicester of Holkham Hall and other interested local landowners who between them subscribed £40,000 of the legal requirement of £70,000. The Dorset Central Railway which later became part of the Somerset & Dorset had financial and moral support from Sir Ivor Guest of Canford Manor, whose father was Sir John Guest, the ironmaster from South Wales. Sir John had bought the Canford Estate in 1846, thereby being an example of a new rich industrialist aping the traditional landed aristocracy by acquiring an estate of his own. Other examples of local landowners having a major input into lines were the Harris family, who had much to do with the line from Chippenham to Calne in Wiltshire and the Marlborough Railway in the same county, promoted by the Marquis of Ailesbury.

The independent lines that were the result of local initiative were often worked by a main line company on the basis that they would receive such a proportion of the revenue as would meet their operating costs. The independent company might find that although it was now relieved of the onus of actually working the line, its income was very limited and it was likely to be receptive to the offer of a takeover by the company. This tactic allowed the latter to expand its system at little capital cost. The South Eastern Railway Company made much use of this ploy.

Even in the 1860s, there were still some landowners who would not be moved on their hostility to all railways. When Lieutenant General Bouverie of Delapre Abbey near Northampton was asked in 1864 for his views on the proposed Bedford, Northampton and Weedon Railway, he made it clear that he did not want it near his estate and he could not resist reiterating his well-known aversion to all railways. His wishes were granted and a new alignment proposed even though he had admitted that the original alignment would not have caused him any residential injury. This gives an indication of the extent to which, even at this relatively late date, railway promoters were prepared to defer to influential landowners. We can only presume the promoters took the pragmatic view that to persist with the original alignment would ultimately cause more trouble and expense.

When the major banking company of Overend & Gurney collapsed in 1866, this constituted a major setback to the promotion of further railways. The bank rate soared to an unprecedented ten per cent which made it exceptionally difficult to raise the stipulated capital when applications were being made to parliament for the authorisation of new projects. Many schemes were abandoned and others perforce delayed indefinitely. Several companies, including the mighty GWR, were in straitened financial circumstances and a delegation of senior railway figures led by Daniel Gooch of the GWR petitioned the Prime Minister, Benjamin Disraeli, with a demand for nationalisation. Disraeli sent them away with a flea in their ear, making it clear that he did not consider it part of the government's remit to interfere in the affairs of railway companies.

The major trunk routes most likely to generate useful profits and attract subscribers had already been built. Increasingly, the lines now being promoted were those where local people wanted their town connected to the railway or were 'imperialistic' gestures whereby a company wanted to play political games by thrusting a line into a rival's territory. The promotion and building of new lines petered out but did not cease completely. In the remaining decades of the nineteenth century and through to 1914, the network continued to be added to in a rather piecemeal way. Michael Robbins (1962) argues that the British railway system, then standing at 13,500 route miles, had probably reached its optimum size in 1870.

Despite the great success of the early Underground lines in shifting passengers and reducing road congestion, by 1871 the Metropolitan Railway was producing a poor dividend for its shareholders and a new chairman, Edward Watkin, recently knighted, was installed. He had considerable experience in railway management and, having made enquiries, it quickly became clear to him that the financial arrangements of the Metropolitan had been culpably lax, leading to fraud. In 1872, shortly after he took up office, he addressed an emergency meeting of Metropolitan shareholders in a speech in which he included the following words:

'What is it we see in the world around us? At the opera, if we look at the lady occupants of the best boxes, who are glittering with the best diamonds, and ask who they are, we are told that they are the wife and daughter of Clodd, the great railway contractor. In the park, whose carriages, horses and equipages are the most fashionable? Why, those belonging to Plausible, the great railway engineer. And if we hear of some poor nobleman's estate being in the market, who buys it? Why, Vampire, the great railway lawyer.'[6]

This speech encapsulated popular perceptions of those who had enriched themselves through various kinds of railway business. Ironically it was made by a man of recognised ability who, while never seen as being guilty of sharp practice, was nevertheless as ruthless an expansionist businessman as any.

From 1870, it began to be clear that Britain's absolute industrial domination of the world so evident at the Great Exhibition of 1851 was drawing to a close. For much of this period, manufacturing industry was in the relative doldrums and substantial elements of agriculture were largely depressed. The impact on the major railway companies tended to push them towards improving their services rather than investing in major new lines. Around cities and bigger towns, some suburban lines were promoted by local landowners who wanted railways to provide a transport infrastructure for the residential commuter districts they were seeking to develop. A middle-class grouping was emerging which earned sufficient money to work in a city or large town but live some distance away in more salubrious surroundings. Landowners played a major role in promoting such lines and even in determining the number and type of houses and, based on that, the social character of a new residential development. Many such lines were promoted in the Home Counties from the 1880s and later. They were speculative ventures which sometimes thrust into deeply rural country and the gamble was that the coming of the railway would rapidly enhance the value of the land and the price of property. Now talk of 'peaceful amenity' and 'residential injury' gave way to lucrative deals in which previously recalcitrant landowners might allow long-established estates to be sold off for development. The entire estate might be dismembered and the 'grand house' demolished.

For about a century from the 1830s, the railways transported the materials of which houses were built and their internal furnishings and fittings; they carried the coal that heated homes and provided fuel for the factories and furnaces as well as the basis of the town gas used for cooking, heating and lighting; they conveyed the nation's food and drink; the raw materials of manufacturing industry and, as W.H. Auden was later to remind us, our letters and parcels. Some people may have scoffed at railways but it was difficult not to be a consumer of their services even for those who never went by train.

It was a heroic period of history. Terry Coleman (1965) put it well:

'The engineering of the railways was like nothing before. Only the cathedrals were so audacious in concept and so exalted in their architecture, but they were few and the building of one, in God's good time, could take a hundred years: the railways were many, and made in the contractor's good time, which was money…Only the canals of the eighteenth century can compare in any way with the railways that killed them. Only the cathedrals before them were so vast an idea: nothing before was so vast in scale.'

Coleman's comments were amplified by Eric Hobsbawm (1972):

'The iron road, pushing its huge smoke-plumed snakes at the speed of wind across countries and continents, whose embankments and cuttings, bridges and stations, formed a body of public building beside which the pyramids and the Roman aqueducts and even the Great Wall of China paled into provincialism, was the very symbol of man's triumph through technology.'

The railways went a long way to wiping out the effect of distance for the traveller. Railways reached into almost every part of the kingdom but by being largely focussed on London strengthened the hand of central authority and weakened provincial loyalties. Local building styles and materials were largely replaced by mass-produced standardised bricks and roofing materials. Local accents, dialects and clothing styles went into retreat. In conjunction with the telegraph and the newspaper, railways conveyed information and opinions as well as people and merchandise and minerals and did so at unprecedented speeds. They aided labour mobility, allowing workers to travel to where employment was available. Now large numbers of people were able to travel not only for business, professional or family reasons but for travel's educative and stimulating effects. Railways made commuting possible – wool magnates with their industrial and commercial premises in Leeds or Bradford might now reside at Morecambe. Their equivalents in the cotton industry in Manchester could live at Windermere, Llandudno, Southport or Lytham St Anne's. Railways reduced the duration and cost of land transport for goods which in turn enabled manufacturers to reduce their transport expenses and their prices.

Consumers benefitted from lower prices for coal and food, for example. Railways required coal, iron and engineering products on a vast scale both directly for itself and indirectly for the industries its existence encouraged or made possible. Railways demanded vast quantities of labour across a very wide range of skills. They required large amounts of financial investment and were big consumers of goods and services. They stimulated economic activity. The bigger railway companies and the men who dominated them accrued immense power. Cumulatively, this was a revolution.

A few isolated closures took place before the end of the nineteenth century. Some railway enterprises resulted from over-optimism or plain foolishness but few proved to be unviable as quickly as the passenger service inaugurated on 1 December 1892 by the East and West Junction Railway between Towcester and Ravenstone Wood Junction. It passed through sparsely populated country and the service ceased on 1 April 1893.

Despite the massive contribution of railways to the heyday of the British economic and social system in the nineteenth century, they were never without problems and never free from being the object of criticism. Rising real incomes for many in the second half of the century created pressure for more comfortable travel and improved onboard facilities. Such provision was expensive, but the companies faced official constraint so far as fare increases were concerned. They were also faced with a workforce increasingly organised in trade unions and unhappy with the long hours, rigid discipline and dangers of their work. The companies were generally very hostile to unions. They did everything they could to prevent the development of collective bargaining. Railway management believed that a military type discipline was required because of the dangers inherent to the operations of the industry and that allowing trade unions to exist was tantamount to encouraging mutiny. Unions were created to strengthen the bargaining position of their members but collective action by the workers in the industry was weakened by the existence of unions catering for different occupational groups. Hostility to union activity among their employees did not prevent railway companies from forming an organisation to strengthen their own collective interests and bargaining position. This was the Railway Companies Association founded in 1854. It campaigned against what was considered to be unnecessary government regulation and, later, against the idea of nationalisation and the spread of union membership.

It is not unfair to say that the railways overworked and underpaid much of their workforce, the members of which were regarded as 'servants' as evident in the name of the largest union, the Amalgamated Society of Railway Servants. By the last quarter of the nineteenth century, railway workers' wages lagged well behind other occupations. Railway employment was seen as a job for life barring any serious disciplinary offences but the latter could include involvement in union activity. The long hours that might be required of signalmen, sometimes a shift as long as thirty-six hours, might impair their judgement which of course could constitute a threat to safety. Official Ministry investigations into accidents often identified overwork as being to blame.

The Times, was not known for its sympathy to workers where industrial relations were concerned but it felt constrained to argue on 15 September 1871:

'We are not among those who would desire to stimulate or befriend trade combinations or strikes, but we confess that a great part of the excessive labour exacted from railway servants might have been avoided or mitigated if railway servants, like other skilled workmen, had known how to combine for the purpose of striking a bargain with their employers.'

Not only were overtime rates rarely paid but a 'servant' was expected to stay on duty until he or she was 'relieved' without receiving pay over and above the normal wage. A Select Committee of the House of Commons enquired and found abundant evidence of excessive hours being worked systematically. If that was not bad enough for their image with the public, the Select Committee then published evidence of railway workers being disciplined or dismissed for giving evidence which put their employers in an unfavourable light.

The unfavourable light in which many aspects of railway activity were viewed was not without justification. They had a virtual monopoly of inland transportation and acted accordingly. For non-passenger traffic, they cynically operated along the principle of charging 'what the traffic would bear', effectively meaning what they could get away with given their powerful position. The marked fall in prices called somewhat misleadingly the 'Great Depression', from the mid-1870s to the mid-1890s, hit many British industrialists. It was easy for them to apportion blame on the 'excessive' freight charges levied by the railway companies. One supreme irony was the decision of businessmen in Liverpool and Manchester to break the monopoly of the railways on freight haulage between the two great centres by building the Manchester Ship Canal. About 60 years earlier, their predecessors had welcomed the Liverpool & Manchester Railway which would break the monopoly and 'excessive' charges of the waterways. Now they built a new canal to break the railways' monopoly.

CHAPTER FOUR

Challenges facing the Landed Aristocracy in the Early Nineteenth Century

In 1820, the population of Britain was around fourteen million, three-quarters of them living in rural districts. By 1851, the majority of a much larger population of twenty-seven million lived in towns. In 1900, Britain was an overwhelmingly urban nation. This period was one of profound economic, political and social change.

At the beginning of the nineteenth century, British society was dominated by the landed class. At the top of a very hierarchical society were a few aristocratic grandees such as the Dukes of Newcastle, Bedford and Devonshire, who were in receipt of annual rent incomes of £30,000 or more plus various government emoluments. They were exceptionally rich. The rent income of the bulk of the landowning class, however, lesser aristocracy and the gentry, were far more modest from around £10,000 to a few hundred pounds a year but this meant that they were still definitely affluent. F.M.L. Thompson[1] estimated that the landed aristocracy and the landed gentry between them owned well over fifty per cent of England in the first half of the nineteenth century. He also estimated that the landed aristocracy consisted of no more than 400 individuals and the landed gentry of perhaps 3,300. They dominated landownership in most English counties. The exceptions were Cumberland and Westmorland with their hills, moors and much marginal land and the immediate home counties of Surrey, Middlesex and Essex where land prices were exceptionally high. He explained:

'For as long as the horse and the carriage were the symbols of social standing, and possession of stables and grooms the sign of a prosperous competence, the English landed aristocracy retained its prominent place. The power of horse and aristocrat was challenged by the railway, but both learned to recognise an ally as well as a rival to its influence. Both were vanquished by the horseless carriage of the twentieth century.'

Harold Perkin explains the role played by the landowning element at this time.

> 'The aristocracy and gentry were not only the richest class, individually at least, but they were in the strictest sense the ruling class. As the only group with both the leisure and the wealth for politics in a system run mainly by amateurs, they were the rulers of England at every level from the Cabinet to the parish. The King's Ministers were, with a few exceptions in the law offices of state, great landowners or their relations. The House of Lords was to all intents and purposes a House of landlords. Four fifths of the House of Commons comprised landowners and their relations, and the rest were chiefly their friends and dependants. In the counties the lord lieutenants and high sheriffs were drawn from the greatest landlords, while the effective county government for almost all purposes was in the bench of Justices of the Peace, drawn from the landed gentry. In the villages the squire's word, whether or not he was a J.P., was law, backed up by the threat of eviction or the withdrawal of his custom from the village traders. Three quarters of the population lived in the countryside, but even in the smaller towns the local landowners were almost as influential as in the villages, and it was only in the comparatively few great cities… that the men of the middle ranks, the greater merchants and lawyers, could control their own affairs and elect their own MP.'[2]

Feudalism as an economic and social system disappeared in England by the mid-seventeenth century and the aristocracy and gentry became the landowning class, able to do whatever they wanted with their landholdings in order to assure themselves a useful income. Some cultivated the land themselves or let the land to tenant farmers. Others let mineral rights or, in urban areas particularly, developed the land, particularly for building purposes. Some combined two or more of these enterprises. The more energetic added to their wealth through industrial and, sometimes, commercial activities. The landed interest had a common concern to improve the quality of its holdings, the value of land and its rental income. This could be done particularly by adopting the new scientific and technical applications which were becoming available. The landed interest had a progressive role to play in society by encouraging activities which not only benefitted themselves but were conducive of wider economic growth.

In the early days at least, the railways were viewed with alarm and distaste by many of the landed aristocracy. A few of these came from very old-established families, some tracing their lineage back to the days of William I. The result had been the creation of dynasties some of which had grown enormously in wealth and power over the centuries. Even with the massive changes brought about by the Industrial Revolution, they continued to revel in their social, economic and political privileges. This elite based on landownership had used its political power to ensure that British jurisprudence provided close protection for their property within a highly exclusive and seemingly immutable social system. Substantial numbers of relative parvenus had also entered the aristocratic and land-owning elites, often as a reward for services rendered to monarchs. Others had accumulated wealth from banking and commercial enterprises and they bought estates and made every attempt to emulate the lifestyle of the older-established landowning elite. Even many smaller landowners, the 'squirearchy', prided themselves on possessing sufficient income from rents so as to comport themselves as 'gentlemen', unburdened by the need to work in any normal sense of the word.

Ownership of a sequestered country estate epitomised superior social status. Many estates were large enough to ensure that the mansion was not visible from the gates or from any other outside point. Where sufficient money was available, the boundaries of many consisted largely of high walls, reinforcing the sense of privacy and isolation.

In the second half of the eighteenth century, many landowners had spent huge amounts of money on vanity projects which produced artificially 'picturesque' landscapes decorated with lakes and 'eye-catchers'. Often the existing mansion was rebuilt or a brand-new house built in the latest fashionable style. Men like Humphrey Repton and Lancelot 'Capability' Brown had bulging order books as many landowners spent with gay abandon, sometimes virtually bankrupting themselves in the process. One consequence was that many estates in the late eighteenth and in the nineteenth century were in dire financial straits. An estate which had been redeveloped in, say, the 1780s, would be coming into maturity perhaps three, four or more decades later. The owner of such an estate would naturally be hostile to anything such as a railway that threatened his seclusion and the integrity of the park.

Capitalist economic accumulation advanced from the eighteenth century and, particularly after the end of the French Revolutionary and Napoleonic Wars, it increasingly presented a challenge to older social, economic and political practices. Landowners had not always welcomed the intrusion of canals onto their land, but some had quickly learned that canals could provide opportunities for their own enrichment. The Duke of Bridgewater famously financed a canal to transport coal quickly, easily and lucratively from his mines at Worsley, to Manchester, close by. The railways, however, were initially viewed with greater disdain and, in many cases, serious concern. A reason for enjoying ownership of a landed estate was for the privacy and seclusion it offered. The progress of a horse-drawn barge along a canal through an estate was one thing but the railway was infinitely worse. It was noisy, produced smoke, smuts and cinders and carried passengers, common people, thereby destroying the treasured privacy. It might also disturb game and wildlife. Such was the concern about the 'iron horse' that the Act of 1829 authorising the Newcastle and Carlisle Railway even banned stationary steam engines from being erected where they could have been seen from the castles at Naworth and Corby owned by the Howard Family.

Lady Elizabeth Grosvenor, wife of the Second Marquess of Westminster, responded to a proposal for a new line in a manner probably not untypical of her ilk:

> '...we are in a state of approaching frenzy from receiving by last night's post a prospectus of a railway from London to Exeter by Salisbury cutting our Motcombe property right through and going within sight of the house, which, of course, if carried into effect would force us to give up the place. Such aggressions are, I believe, common in this enlightened age. Is it really not enough to drive one mad? It is really outrageous and (my husband) is writing to try and protect ourselves against it and to say that the line should go south of Shaftesbury.'[3]

A deviation was made taking the line about a mile north of the house.

However, anything which increased the value of land was of interest to the landowning class, some of whom lived well beyond their means. Railways were, at least initially, seen as a threat. It took a little time for many landowners to appreciate that railways could be the generators of economic growth from which they could benefit. If they protested loudly about loss of amenity from being forced to sell the land, railways could also be a cash cow.

Railways constituted a threat to a way of life and a social system which had evolved over time but was long-lived enough perhaps to be termed 'traditional'. The old ways of the landed interest were being challenged by radical changes including the modernisation of agriculture with the application of scientific and technologically based practices. These often followed enclosure for arable of what had previously been communal farming land. Many landowners proved open to innovation and adapted to, and prospered from, the challenges of the time. Uniquely in Europe, the law gave British landowners the right to ownership of any potential wealth under their land and many landowners exploited minerals like coal and iron ore, even if they were not themselves directly involved in their extraction and transport. For example, the Dukes of Northumberland, Norfolk and Devonshire derived huge wealth from the mining of coal on their land, the Dukes of Newcastle extracted lead from land in Derbyshire, Lord Ashburnham extracted iron in Sussex and the Duke of Bedford enjoyed royalties from copper extraction in Devon. Once they were enriching themselves by leasing mineral rights, it was likely that they would develop an interest in the form of transport needed to transport this new source of income. This frequently meant railways. It could be a good time for certain fortunate landowners who might combine their rental income with mineral royalties, selected business ventures and directorships and speculation in stocks and shares. If they had land in urban areas, particularly London, times could be very good indeed. An aristocratic family who not only had many rural landholdings but became involved in urban development were the Dukes of Devonshire. They did much to develop the towns of Barrow-in-Furness and Eastbourne. The Dukes of Norfolk developed Glossop. Sir Peter Hesketh-Fleetwood developed a new town near Blackpool as a port and modestly named it after himself as 'Fleetwood'. It was often the richest dynasties that became even richer by making the most of the many opportunities that presented themselves at this time.

Professor Perkin (1971) argues: 'The English landowner, almost literally, paved the way for what was to be the first Industrial Revolution in any country.'[4] He explains that through their contributions to the modernisation of agriculture, the landowners indirectly helped to feed the rapidly growing urban proletariat which provided the huge labour force essential for the operation of the primary industries. Before the age of the railway, some had invested in road improvements and the building of canals to provide the transport infrastructure needed for the early stages of industrialisation. Later, many landowners contributed to the financing of lines that the major railway companies did not wish to promote but which met local needs and boosted the economies of districts in which they had landholdings.

The landed interest also made an important contribution to the development of a modern industrial society through the practice of primogeniture. With the eldest son inheriting titles and the estate, younger sons were often given an education and a lump sum and effectively told to go away and earn a living. Many went into the professions and others into commerce or industry. They took with them the outlook of the landowning class into which they had been born. With this they then fertilised the rising bourgeoisie, which helps to explain why so many of the *nouveaux riches* bought estates and aspired to the lifestyle and values of the traditional landed interest. Many self-made men bought rural estates and set themselves up in the style of country landowners. For example, Sir Richard Arkwright, who made his fortune through cotton-spinning, built Willersley Castle near Cromford in Derbyshire. Josiah Wedgwood of pottery-manufacturing fame, built an elegant mansion at Barlaston in Staffordshire, while Matthew Boulton, who partnered James Watt in the pioneering days of applied steam power, bought an estate at Great Tew in Oxfordshire.

We will discuss many examples of landowners who used their influence to enrich themselves during the great era of railway building by extracting compensation and conditions which saddled railway companies with financial obligations that arguably made railway construction unnecessarily expensive in Britain. Many landowners were initially hostile to railways until they realised that by objecting to them on grounds which were frequently little more than simple self-interest, they could obtain generous compensation. Self-interest it may have been but their claims had substance because of their social standing. Railways, when completed and operating, generated economic activity from which they could benefit. They were in a 'win-win' situation. As early as 1863, a Select Committee concluded that soon after the opening of a railway, the rental value of land within five miles of a railway station would increase by about seven per cent.[5] It is not surprising that the initial antipathy to railways of many landowners gave way to a more favourable attitude based on this material self-interest.

When railways were being planned, their alignment frequently required them to cross land owned by these grandees, many of whom regarded them as dirty, noisy, disruptive, potentially harmful or even dangerous, as well as intrusive into the exclusive rural peace and quiet and privacy which they valued so highly. A railway passing through their estate would allow the common people travelling on them to view their estates from within. Owners argued that their quality of life was seriously damaged by trains full of gawping passengers making their disruptive way across land where previously the landowner had been master of all he surveyed. Additionally, railways interfered with the pursuits they valued highly as part of their social prerogative, such as fox-hunting.

This may sound like some sort of feudal atavism in an age of rapid change, but these people had clout. They could frequently make railway companies pay well over the market price for the land they needed. Few landowners were necessarily opposed to railways *per se*, but it was in their financial interest to claim a variety of residential and other 'injuries' which they would sustain as a result of the intrusion of railways onto their property. They did not necessarily need to take their objections as far as parliament. Often the mere mention of opposition was enough to bring the promoters to the negotiating table and a deal would be reached, buying off the influential landowner at an early stage rather than risking the legal costs that were likely to be involved if an unappeased landed grandee took his objections to the Parliamentary Select Committee. Such settlements may have been very generous, but they simply reflected the influence that many landowners were able to exert.

How much this added to the costs of railway construction is debateable. A land surveyor appearing before parliament claimed, perhaps ingenuously, to know of no cases where exorbitant sums had been given for land.[6] Be that as it may, the House of Lords consisted almost exclusively of landowners and the Commons contained large numbers of them and their relatives. As David Cannadine (1994) argues, 'The result was an overwhelmingly propertied and patrician polity.'

By the 1840s, the benefits likely to accrue from railway building were becoming increasingly obvious and we hear of landowners keenly involving themselves in railway promotion. The attitude of some, however, was inconsistent. As early as 1825, Earl Fitzwilliam had given guarded support to a Leeds and Hull railway scheme stating that he had no general antipathy towards railways but favoured those financed by local interest rather than distant speculators and that he also wanted to see railway development which produced a system rather than a mere mishmash of lines. In 1836, he supported a scheme for a line from Rotherham to Sheffield which would help the development of coalmining on land he owned in the vicinity. He was actively involved in 1844 in an ultimately abortive scheme for a line from London via Cambridge, Peterborough, Lincoln and Gainsborough to York and the north. On the other hand, he was opposed to the Great Northern Railway's projected line from London to York via Peterborough because it proposed missing such places as Stamford. He also opposed it because near Peterborough its proposed alignment passed across a small parcel of his land thereby, he argued, being likely to interfere with his fox-hunting. In 1845, this gentleman contacted George Hudson urging him to reach an accommodation with the truculent Earl of Harborough regarding the course of a line from Syston to Peterborough being planned in the neighbourhood of Stapleford Park. In 1846, he became a sizeable shareholder and director of the South Yorkshire Railway which helped his mining interests. In 1854, he sold the River Derwent Navigation to the Malton Railway for £40,000.

Earl Fitzwilliam was like many other landowners who were prepared to supply capital for specific local railway projects which they did not necessarily initiate but from which they might accrue financial gain. Another example was the Duke of Northumberland who gave financial support to the Border Counties Railway because of mineral interests he had in the bleak country which it traversed.

Railway companies usually valued having a prominent landowner or two as directors. Even better was to have one as a company chairman. In 1850, such figures included the Earls of Burlington, Carlisle, Yarborough, Lonsdale and Powys. The third Duke of Buckingham became Chairman of the London & North Western Railway in 1853, by which time it was the largest of Britain's railway companies.

Landowners may have had what seems today as inordinate influence, but that power was under challenge in a society changing at an unprecedented pace. The landed interest had received something of a setback as a result of the 1832 Reform Act.

This saw the enfranchisement of layers of the urban middle class intent on using their new voting power to ensure that parliament carried through measures in their interest rather than simply being a rubber stamp for legislation advancing the interests of the long-standing political elite. The 1832 Act did not end the ability of many aristocratic grandees to nominate favoured parliamentary candidates and to ensure that their own tenants voted as required, given that there was no secret ballot. The landed interest proved extremely durable in the face of the changing political situation. As Professor Perkin (1969) says:

> 'The landed class possessed a clear majority of the House of Commons until 1885...and of the House of Lords until long after the Parliament act of 1911 drastically reduced its powers.'

It was probably as well for landowners that not all were unyielding backwoodsmen. The strength of this group lay in not fighting but in adapting to the changes brought by an industrialising and urbanising society. In turn, while some newly enriched families purported to despise 'old wealth' as consisting of those 'who toil not neither do they spin', very frequently their aspiration was for themselves to gain admission to the upper echelons of the aristocracy. The social system was flexible enough to allow this to happen, at least on a controlled scale. Ambitious social climbers made their money in trade, acquired an estate, were favoured with a baronetcy, won election to parliament and finally expected to be rewarded with a peerage. Such people, playing a positive role in industrial and commercial development, were not, however, likely to be severe critics of an elitist social and political structure of which so many of them wanted to be a part.

The dependence of the aristocracy and gentry on income from land ownership meant that in the short term they could be subject to the vagaries that affected agriculture. Four major phases can be discerned in British agriculture during the nineteenth century. Agriculture boomed during the French Revolutionary and Napoleonic Wars to 1815, benefitting landowners. When prices and rents fell through the 1820s and 1830s, the landed interest used their domination of parliament to introduce the Corn Laws which, by artificially inflating the price of imported corn, greatly benefitted themselves, if no other section of society. From the mid-1840s to around 1870 there was a so-called 'Golden Age of

Agriculture' following which there was a generalised dip in the fortunes of the industry through to 1914. Historians have often dubbed this period the 'Great Depression' but care has to be taken with such a generalisation because it does not always take account of short-term fluctuations, of factors favouring certain parts of the industry rather than others and of regional differences, for example. The 1870s saw a period of poor harvests which hit cereal producers particularly hard while livestock and dairy farmers were scarcely affected. Wheat acreage fell and rents fell markedly especially in areas dominated by arable farming. In this period, British agriculture became part of a worldwide industry and this created vulnerability in parts of the industry which had previously seemed inviolable. Declining income acted as a disincentive to investment in agriculture and reduced the relative power and influence of the landed interest in the wider economy and society. During the last decades of the nineteenth century, the structure of agricultural society was severely shaken and the landowner's power much weakened. This was only the culmination of a process which had been taking place since the beginning of the century.

In their research and writing in the nineteenth century, Karl Marx and Friedrich Engels examined economic, social and political developments in Britain very closely because it was in Britain that capitalism had advanced furthest at that time. They were critical admirers of the energy displayed and the progress brought about by British capitalism in the middle of the nineteenth century, involving an energy and dynamism never again to be repeated. The battle for economic and political domination between the landed interest and the rising commercial and industrial class fascinated them and they analysed the significance of the passing of the Corn Laws in 1846:

'Up to 1846 the Tories passed as the guardians of the traditions of Old England…The fatal year, 1846, with its repeal of the Corn Laws and the shout of distress which this repeal forced from the Tories, proved that they were enthusiasts for nothing but the rent of land, and at the same time disclosed the secret of their attachment to the political and religious institutions of old England. These institutions are the very best institutions, with the help of which the large landed property – the landed interest, has hitherto ruled England, and even now seeks to maintain its rule. The year 1846 brought to light in its nakedness the substantial class interest which forms the real basis of the Tory Party.'[7]

They continued:

> 'The repeal of the Corn Laws in 1846 merely recognised an already accomplished fact, a change long since enacted in the elements of British civil society, viz., the subordination of the landed interest to the moneyed interest, of property to commerce, of agriculture to manufacturing industry, of the county to the city…The repeal of the Corn Laws brought down the price of food, which in turn brought down the rent of land, and with sinking rent broke down the real strength upon which the political power of the Tories reposed.'[8]

It certainly helped somewhat to relieve the pressure on the landed aristocracy and also the gentry, perhaps to a lesser extent, that that there existed a degree of social mobility which allowed them to absorb elements of the *nouveaux riches* especially women of marriageable age bringing with them generous dowries. Many landowners became involved in industrial and commercial activity. The notion of a purblind backwards-looking landed class totally unable to move with the times does not hold true although there were inevitably some exceptions. Even up to the First World War there were members of the aristocracy and gentry who looked down on plutocrats of the City, top lawyers and successful industrialists on the basis not that they had more money but that they themselves were gentlemen, enjoying substantial unearned income and able, if they chose, to spend their time in an unending round of exclusive social and leisure pursuits.

The power and prestige enjoyed by large numbers of landowners inevitably provoked criticism in certain quarters. A major strand in the great campaign leading up to the Reform Act of 1832 was an attack on aristocratic privilege. The prolonged agitation for the repeal of the Corn Laws contained a strong element of anger that landowners, a tiny minority of society, used their political power to inflate the price of bread. Some wanted punitive taxes on those who obtained much of their income from rent, regarding it as unearned income.

Men of humble social origins who had become extremely wealthy through industrial enterprise could hope to move into higher society through acquiring large country mansions and estates. There they abandoned the severe utilitarian principles that they had brought to their affairs as they climbed the greasy pole to business success and material wealth and, if possible, threw themselves into huntin' and shootin' and fishin'. These activities were pursued not so much with the larder in mind but as the kind of recreation expected of those who owned land. In the past, hunting had been the privilege of royalty and the aristocracy but now it was seen as the means by which at least some upward socially aspiring self-made magnates who purchased country estates could hope at the same time to buy themselves social status and acceptability.

In a century which saw high levels of open political conflict, especially from 1815 to 1850 and again in the 1880s and 1890s, the landed class showed that they were survivors even if they had to accept a curtailment of the overt power and influence they had exerted at the start. They were flexible enough not only to accept new blood but also to arrive at some kind of accommodation with the newly enfranchised middle class or bourgeoisie. Many of the latter, while revelling in their new political power, aspired to the social status and sense of entitlement of the landed elite. This being so, they often became defenders rather than critics of what was still a highly stratified society. The flexibility demonstrated by the landed interest proved to be an effective survival tactic without which they might have been heading for oblivion. However, the foundations of a British society dominated by the landed classes collapsed by the end of the century. Landownership ceased, with some exceptions, to be the basis of great wealth and became more a status symbol.

CHAPTER FIVE

How Railway schemes were promoted

From the seventeenth century, the landed class had used their control of parliament and the legislative process to create an imposing legal framework with which to support and protect their sources of power and wealth, chiefly that involving ownership of land. For the construction of turnpikes and canals, a complicated set of agreed legal procedures was in place concerning compulsory purchase. These procedures included a method of appeal which could be utilised by any landowner whose land was likely to be affected in this way and allowed for appeal to a Parliamentary Select Committee. This system was then put in place for the various railway schemes that materialised in the first decades of the nineteenth century. Procedures were systematised in 1845 with the Land Clauses Consolidation Act and the Railway Clauses Consolidation Act.

Every individual railway intended to serve the public required sanction through a Private Act of Parliament. This gave a legal basis for the powers of compulsory purchase which companies almost always needed to exercise. It also authorised them to issue shares and construct the line in the manner specified in the terms of the Act.

The process of obtaining parliamentary approval started with a Promoters' Petition outlining the benefits that it was claimed would be brought by the railway. The necessary officers of the company such as a banker, solicitor, company secretary and engineer would be appointed, ideally men perceived as being of professional probity. They were likely to be drawn from the area the company intended to serve. Also needed were company directors who ideally would be movers and shakers with the ability to provide a persuasive case if and when a bill was deposited for the purpose of obtaining parliamentary approval. This was a convoluted process which might face systematic and formidable opposition. It was always handy to have a titled aristocrat or two on the board as well as a sprinkling of MPs.

It was not unknown for people to be listed as 'supporters' whose support had never been given nor even canvassed. It was not a criminal offence in the nineteenth century to publish known falsehoods in a prospectus, but this was a source of understandable annoyance as the *Railway Chronicle* (27 September 1845) bemoaned:

'Not a day passes that the papers do not contain letters from parties denying all connections with embryo railway schemes to which their names have been attached…without their consent or cognizance.'

The use of such names, with or without permission, was an early example of 'celebrity endorsement'. The implication was that such supporters were prepared to vouch for the *bona fides* of the project. The *Railway World* (18 October 1845) pointed out that some individuals were paid for their endorsement.

Herapath's Railway Journal grumpily told the world on 9 January 1847:

'Names in the speculating period were the great and almost sole criteria of worth. They were considered as guarantors of soundness and value. The public took it for granted that the Honourable Mr So-and-So would not become the manager of a bubble scheme nor support a project intrinsically worthless…'

It was now time to set up a Provisional Committee, the function of which was to obtain the funding needed to conduct formal surveys, identify possible alignments and do the necessary legal work. Using these surveys, a preliminary estimate would be made of the costs of construction. Gaining entry to private land in order to conduct these surveys could be problematical, there being no legal right for the surveyors to do so. A survey would be made of the traffic currently passing along the projected route, this obviously being business which the railway company would be seeking to capture. A notice of intention would be published in local newspapers, listing the parishes through which the projected line would pass, identifying the owners of land that would be affected and giving notice of that land for which compulsory purchase powers would be sought. The landowner would be asked to provide an estimate of the value of his property that would be affected. Sometimes the railway company and the landowner would agree a figure at this early stage to save possible trouble and expense later.

The information gained would be used as supporting evidence of need and further potential when the case for the line was put to parliament. The legal work involved establishing ownership of the land along the identified alignment and ascertaining the various owners' attitudes to the proposed railway. Meticulous attention to detail was required at this stage in order to provide as watertight a case as possible before the scrutiny of the Select Committee and because of the virtual inevitability of opposition in parliament. Having satisfied themselves on these issues, the promoters would issue a prospectus with a view to attracting potential investors. Prospectuses were frequently pitched in hyperbolic terms regarding the supposed benefits that would occur if the line was built.

With or without hyperbole, a number of elements had to be contained in the prospectus. These were the proposed title of the undertaking; the membership of its Provisional Committee; the names of its chief advisors and officers; the amount of capital it was intended to raise and the number of shares into which this capital would be divided; a statement intended to justify the project by identifying the proposed route; the nature and level of the traffic likely to be generated and therefore of the possible financial prospects, and a form of application for shares. Maps of the projected line might be included.

An example can be taken from the prospectus of the Sheffield, Ashton-under-Lyne & Manchester Railway. This prospectus was published in 1836 for a line which would join Manchester and Sheffield via Ashton, Glossop, Woodhead and Penistone. It is typical of its sort:

'It is needless to expatiate upon the Advantages to be derived from a railway communication through districts so populous, so rich, and so important in a manufacturing point of view, as those upon the projected line; and from uniting Sheffield with the Port of Liverpool, where a very large proportion of the Manufactures of the former are shipped, promoting and expediting as it will intercourse between Manchester and Sheffield, and thereby increasing the general trade and business of those places, and of the several towns and villages between and thus connected with them. The present mode of conveyance for goods to and from Sheffield and Manchester is by wagon, and the time occupied in the transit is about forty hours; there is not the most remote probability of any competition by water, and consequently the exclusive carriage of merchandise and minerals between the two termini which can be taken by the railway at two thirds of the present cost and in one tenth the time, may be calculated upon as a prolific and unfailing source of revenue. The intermediate districts including Glossop, Hyde, Mottram, Newton, Dukinfield, Ashton under Lyne and Staleybridge [sic] will be, by this railway, so united to Manchester, as to derive all the advantages for conducting the trade of that extensive and important place and at the same time retain those peculiar to their several localities. In addition to these important benefits, inexhaustible supplies of coal, of the best quality, and of paviours, slate, ashlar and other stone, abounding upon the line and for which there is immense and increasing demand will be opened to the manufacturers and inhabitants, at a comparatively trifling cost. Indeed from the locality of the minerals it may be conclusively observed that their distribution to the consumers will be effected almost entirely by descending lines and consequently with additional facility and economy…'[1]

The prospectus would invite the public to apply for shares. Applicants would be told the number of shares to which they would be entitled and asked to pay a deposit to the railway company's banker. The subscriber would then be able to exchange the banker's receipt for a scrip certificate which he held until the company gained its Act of Incorporation. Once parliamentary authorisation was obtained the investor could be called upon to pay instalments up to the full nominal value of his shares.

A far more detailed survey, on a prescriptive scale, of the proposed route would be now be undertaken accompanied by copious information concerning in particular the geology of the terrain and any natural obstacles which would need to be overcome. Bridges and tunnels had to be described with their dimensions and clearances. The impact of the proposed alignment on all public and private rights of way had to be shown. Proposed junctions with other railways, existing or authorised, had to be explained in detail. A Book of Reference had to be produced identifying and listing all those who owned, occupied or leased land required by the railway. It had to be made clear whether they agreed or disagreed with the proposal or were simply neutral.

Landowners would not necessarily grant access to the surveying parties. The latter might go ahead openly anyway or resort to various methods of subterfuge to obtain the information they needed for the parliamentary scrutiny. Confrontations between landowners and surveyors might consist of verbal bluster but sometimes confrontations escalated. At Bicester, for example, the Riot Act had to be read after several injuries had been sustained. In Scotland, there was almost a re-enactment of old-time clan warfare between the surveyors of two rival schemes. The Scottish Grand Junction Railway led by the Marquis of Breadalbane clashed with the Caledonian Northern whose provisional Chairman was the Duke of Montrose. Neither scheme came to anything. On a number of occasions, members of surveying parties who had been involved in fights found themselves up before the local magistrates. When this happened, they could expect little clemency. The magistrates were frequently landowners themselves!

The information gained was intended to provide a much more precise estimate of the cost of construction, the result having to be endorsed by the engineers. This complex operation needed to be completed to a timetable determined by parliament and in a specified manner. If it failed to meet these rigorous demands, the process could and usually was unilaterally terminated. All this information had to be deposited not only with parliament but with the clerks of the peace of all the counties affected. Notices were required to be placed in all relevant local newspapers indicating where the public could have access to the documentation. Clearly, much time and money needed to be expended before a bill was submitted to parliament. Many bills that were submitted failed to meet the required criteria. They were 'thrown out on Standing Orders'. Standing Orders were intended to provide concerned landowners with comprehensive information about the railway company's proposals, the better for them to marshal effective opposition when the bill appeared before the relevant Select Committee.

The company would bring together the Plans, Schedules and Books of Reference that were required by parliamentary procedure and a parliamentary agent would be assigned with the purpose of ensuring that protocol was strictly adhered to. Ideally, he would also act as something of a mentor assisting the passage of the bill through sticky moments but his relationship with the company was not always a marriage made in Heaven.

The legal requirements surrounding the submission of plans for railway projects to parliament were very stringent and included deadlines for the deposit of the necessary documentation with the Board of Trade. Here we see the jostling and general mayhem that occurred as anxious railway promoters sought to deposit their plans at the very last minute. (Authors' collection)

Railway promoters had to fight their way to the Board of Trade entrance in order to register their schemes before the deadline expired.

A bill would usually be introduced in the Commons, ideally by a director of the company who was also an MP. It was a requirement that the public had already been informed of the proposal and that plans and sections to a scale of three inches to the mile were submitted. Collating this information and gathering it into presentable form could be a daunting task where a lengthy line was being promoted or where the line was intended to pass through a densely populated urban area. Detailed estimates of the cost of construction were required along with a list of subscribers. We will now call it the 'Bill' and its travails had only just started. It went before a Select Committee on Standing Orders for another check to ensure that all procedures had been adhered to. All but minor failings were likely to lead to its rejection and the Bill's opponents might try to throw a spanner in the works at this stage.

The Bill was then given a formal first reading, a second reading which could involve a debate and it then went before a Committee on Bills. All the relevant documentation had to be made available again and acceptable proof submitted that half the designated capital had been subscribed. The committee then scrutinised the proposals. Michael Robbins put matters very succinctly:

> 'In Britain railways generally came into being to meet a need, not to create a demand. It had to be shown that there were people and things wanting transport between the places concerned before the public would promise to subscribe money and parliament would give authority to build... the promoters...had to argue on the basis of the demand that could be demonstrated as existing.'[2]

The promoters would employ legal counsel in their attempt to show that their line would be fulfilling a very real need while those who objected would also usually have marshalled their counter-arguments and have them presented by counsel. As the railway network spread, it was often rival railway companies who most fiercely contested these proposals. Claims of non-compliance with Standing Orders were a common means whereby one railway company attacked the petition of a rival. Witnesses could be examined at this stage. Objectors would be avidly looking for any flaws in the promoter's case. It was a game with little quarter expected or given and no mercy was extended to the company that had observed protocol scrupulously but was shown to have made claims that could not be supported. The Bill would then fall.

Assuming that these hurdles were overcome, more challenges would follow. Much informal negotiation would be carried on behind the scenes with the respective counsel of promoters and opponents attempting to broker compromises or finally terminate the other side's chances. Compromise might be reached by agreement to make deviations, submission to the demands of an awkward landowner such as that the line should be in a covered

With the proceedings having all the gravity of a court of law, many witnesses must have found that an appearance before a parliamentary committee which was considering a railway bill to have been an intimidating experience. (Authors' collection)

way as it passed through his grounds or, most often, by what was basically a monetary bribe. If the Bill staggered through all these possible pitfalls and the committee pronounced its satisfaction, it then went back to the House where amendments might be proposed. Assuming there were no amendments, the Bill received its third reading and went to the Lords. Basically the same procedures were followed there which of course gave the Bill's opponents yet another chance to engineer its downfall. The parliamentary process had started in November and if it jumped successfully through all the hoops, the Bill might become law the following July or August. The promoters now had an Act specifying the legal powers they could employ. It had been a long and arduous process which was not for the faint-hearted. It is worth mentioning that once a railway scheme had obtained parliamentary sanction, it required the passing of a further Act to permit the scheme to be abandoned.

There might still be some outstanding relative minutiae to be considered before or in the early stages of construction and where agreement could not be reached between a company and one or more landowners, a system of arbitration was put in place when a jury of twelve men of 'substance' would be convened to adjudicate and arrive at costs where compensation needed to be paid. The railway companies complained that these juries favoured the landowners with the result that they were left with large amounts to find by way of compensation.

Inevitably, perhaps, the system outlined above was modified in the light of experience. An important reform in 1844 prohibited MPs from sitting on Committees adjudicating on bills with which they had an interest. Dyos and Aldcroft (1969) point out that during the height of the 'Railway Mania', such was the pressure of the weight of railway schemes coming up for consideration that the Committee on Standing Orders was simply swamped and only the most cursory attention was sometimes paid to ensuring that bills met the statutory requirements in their early stages.

There are debates about the extent to which these expensive legal processes made Britain's railways excessively expensive to plan, promote and construct. The services of a top counsel came with a hefty price tag while solicitors also required generous remuneration. The eminent barristers employed in these proceedings were highly skilled in the lucrative but dishonourable trade of humiliating and discrediting witnesses, many of whom would find the surroundings and the proceedings very intimidating. Although these wily and arrogant legal counsel may have scored points off even some of the great engineers of the time, the fame of people like the Stephensons lives on while the 'legal eagles' are deservedly forgotten. A rather incompetent barrister, speaking in a Select Committee in 1846, on being taken to task for various mistakes and oversights, is reported by Grinling (1966) as saying, 'What are the public interests to me? I neither care nor hope to know anything about this line when my labours are at an end.' The services of engineers and surveyors also did not come cheaply. The voluminous documentation that was required in these proceedings made money for printers and lithographers.

For any railway promotion to meet with success, an elaborate legal community consisting of clerks, agents, solicitors and barristers had to be employed. There was no practical way of obtaining the required Private Act without taking on and generously remunerating all the components of this legal paraphernalia. It must be remembered that in the process of petitioning for a railway scheme, the promoters, at least in the early years, were political outsiders pitted against the entrenched privileges, wealth and influence of important landowners who saw them as bourgeois upstarts. While railway promoters learned to be pragmatic about what was essentially bribery to gain the assent of landowners, they strongly resented it, knowing that they were paying landowners more than the market value of the land while the lawyers pocketed the seemingly excessive expenses that their services commanded.

The role of the legal profession came in for especial criticism for the costs they added to the process of railway promotion. If railway companies wanted to employ first-class barristers, they had to pay the going rate. Some counsel took several briefs at once and it was indignantly reported by the *Railway Gazette* of 20 May 1848 that they might earn as much as £1,200 a day.

As R.W. Kostal explains:

'Railway companies were hopelessly entangled in legal conflicts, and thoroughly infiltrated, exploited and beset by lawyers. While one little army of legal men had been enlisted to help promote, finance and operate railway lines, another had been mobilised either to defeat them, or to squeeze them for money. Still other lawyers took advantage of moments of public enthusiasm for railways to set up a parallel "industry" of fraudulent corporate "bubbles". This opportunism caused irrevocable damage to the credibility and prestige of legitimate railway enterprise.[3] ... The ranks of lawyers, more than any other occupational group, contained men with the blend of technical skill, business savvy, commercial contacts and raw avarice needed to promote bubble railway companies at a profit. Their most valuable attribute as promoters was the ability to attract capital while possessing little of it themselves. Lawyers understood the thinking, mores and vulnerabilities of the monied classes.'[4]

Bubble promoters set up sham companies that could obtain large amounts of money in subscription deposits and scrip speculation with not the slightest intention of building operational railway lines. At the height of the 'Railway Mania' it was as simple as taking candy from a child. As Kostal put it, 'Sham directors held lavish entertainment at the sham offices of sham companies.'[5]

The services of lawyers were a necessary evil – only they could provide documentation having the required appearance of legality and probity.

In the fall-out from the 'Railway Mania' the legal profession received a blast of opprobrium, not least from the railway press, for example, the *Railway Gazette* of 20 May 1848 fulminated:

'Railway bubbles have spread ruin over the whole of society. Millions of pounds of sterling have been taken from the pockets of the duped and unprotected, hundreds of families have been ruined for life... [they] have been hopelessly beggared, and by whom? – by a gang of lawyers.'[6]

The same journal (14 July 1849) asked somewhat rhetorically:

'What can be more monstrous than the spectacle the railway world now presents? Thousands of families beggared, tens of thousands about to be beggared – that scores of lawyers and engineers may roll in wealth!'[7]

Bradshaw's Railway Gazette cast doubt on their professional capability:

'What can a mere sucking barrister know about the practical details of railway matters? What can be more ludicrous...than to hear some of these overpaid wordmongers squabbling with, examining and cross-examining men such as Brunel, Stephenson or Locke?'[8]

With so many vested interests taking up time and therefore money, the parliamentary costs of many railway undertakings were greatly inflated. This was recognised at the time. George Burke was a senior partner in Burke and Venables who did much railway work. He told the Lords' Select Committee on Railways in 1846 that the expense of getting some railway Bills through parliament was excessive because of the vast number of niggling and minute objections that were raised by the supporters of rival schemes attempting to wreck their opponents' plans. On being quizzed as to whether he knew what was the largest number of objections made by an objector to any one Bill, with disarming frankness he replied, 'I was guilty myself of taking 400 once and discussing them for twenty-three days upon minute matters.'[9] Five rival schemes were put forward for a railway from London to Brighton. £180,000 of shareholders' money was spent on bitter parliamentary wrangles concerning their respective merits. The chairman of the one successful scheme to emerge from the verbal fracas told a Select Committee in 1839 that much trouble and expense could have been avoided had there been an 'impartial board' arbitrating on the matter at an early date. Probably the most profligate waste of money was the £433,000 spent by the Great Northern Railway and its allies on gaining parliamentary approval for its route from London to the North in 1845-6.

By 1855, it is estimated that railway promoters had spent around £20 million preparing, presenting and opposing railway petitions. *The Times* (9 September 1855) estimated that a further £5 million may have been spent by companies whose petitions failed. Much of this expenditure went in legal costs. *Herapath's* (10 September 1853) pointed out that the Shrewsbury & Hereford Railway spent £250,000 on parliamentary expenses alone, this being money that had to be spent before any construction work took place.

From the earliest times, railway companies were engaged in constant struggle with dissatisfied investors and creditors, rival companies, disgruntled business and private customers, employees wanting better wages and conditions and, of course, landowners. Many such disputes were settled through negotiations conducted by lawyers. If they went to court, lawyers again played a critical role. The railway promoters and railway companies did not want lawyers but could not do without them.

Returning to the legislation itself, a railway company's Act formed the basis of that company's existence because from it was derived all its powers. It also conferred on it various regulations, restrictions and requirements, some of which could be onerous and expensive. The initial Act of a company, the Act of Incorporation, consisted mainly of standardised provisions only differing in wording over the years. Specific Acts incorporated certain named persons and others into a company of proprietors under a specific title which constituted the company's legal name, even though a variant of it might appear on its seal or in its publicity, for example. The company's own Act conferred on it the legal power to construct a railway and other works and to raise a certain amount of capital through shares and loans for that and other purposes. Arrangements would be made to appoint a receiver and the initial directors would be named. Certain periods were specified for the acquisition of land and completion of construction while maximum rates and fares would be set out. Sometimes there might be terms empowering the company to enter into arrangements with another company which would manage and work the line and to lease or sell it to that particular company, or others, under certain specified conditions.

The Acts giving legal incorporation to a railway company, apart from the standard clauses they would be expected to include, might contain conditions unique to that particular railway. So it was that Acts might require companies to erect buildings in keeping with their historic surroundings as at York, Bristol and Windsor, for example. Sometimes the requirements were very specific. The North British Railway was required to build a signal box at a specified point where the line passed through Princes Street Gardens in Edinburgh. It also had to build it to stipulated dimensions, to have an internal stairway and only to burn smokeless fuel in its stove. The GWR when seeking legal authorisation for an extension to Shrewsbury Station was required to underpin the walls of the adjacent prison. Various highway authorities would insist on every major and many minor level crossings being provided with gates, a staff member on duty while trains were operating and accommodation for the crossing keeper. This could impose a considerable financial burden on the company concerned especially where the terrain involved was fairly flat and numerous level crossings were required, an example being the line from Peterborough to Northampton.

One of the oddest clauses was that written into the Act authorising the Ulverstone (sic) and Lancaster Railway. This required the company to pay £20 annually to 'the travellers' guide' who conducted people across the estuary of the River Leven in recognition of the loss of business he would experience with the opening of the railway.

CHAPTER SIX

How the Landed Aristocracy reacted to the coming of the Railways

In *Middlemarch* (1871) George Eliot describes the impact made by the arrival of surveyors for the London & Birmingham Railway in rural Warwickshire. The local landowners to a man deplored the railways and were determined that, if they were forced to sell their land, they would extract the highest possible price for it. The farm labourers were keen on a physical showdown with the surveyors but wiser counsels argued that such action was futile because the railways would come despite their efforts. As R.W. Kostal has said, 'the railway movement brought about the most dramatic infringement of private property rights in England since the Civil War.'[1]

The possession of an estate symbolised the social superiority of the landowning class in the eighteenth and nineteenth centuries. Preferably having a high wall around its perimeter, the estate allowed them to live in prestigious seclusion. If the estate had natural scenic features so much the better but the employment of a landscape gardener could enhance such features or even create an idyllic but entirely artificial scene if funds were available. The size and appearance of the estate was intended to gratify the owner as he gazed from the windows of his mansion. It is perhaps understandable that such people did not want noisy, dirty steam trains intruding into their sequestered domains:

> 'Landowners feared the disfigurement of their estates, the reduction of their rentals and the breaking up of their farms: they opposed the progress of dirty, noisy and allegedly dangerous locomotives…the trespassing of insolent surveyors and the invasion of rural areas by rough, immoral construction gangs. They claimed railways would ruin drainage schemes and country sports. Many, who drew revenue from turnpike trusts and canals, feared the new competition.'[2]

As railway surveyors went about their work, they generally sought to identify the flattest route possible. While fairly level terrain might be provided by river valleys in their lower reaches, the course of such valleys could be tortuous. A balance had to be established. The gentle gradients likely to be found in these valleys combined with the flat terrain might minimise the need for and expense of tunnels, cuttings and embankments. However, a circuitous alignment closely following the course of the river might require the frequent crossing and re-crossing of the river. The other pertinent problem was the question of ownership of the land through which the most suitable alignment was proposed and the attitude of the owner to intrusion from the railway. What extra expenses might be involved if one or more landowners were adamant in their opposition?

The railway companies had little option but to take landowners seriously. Some, but by no means all, were immensely wealthy and had the power and connections that went with such wealth. Even those who were less wealthy often had the same sense of entitlement and arrogance that went with their social origins and status. Few landowners welcomed the early railways with open arms. They deplored the idea that parliament could equip railway companies with legal powers of compulsory purchase of treasured land on their estates. That was outrageous enough, but railways would inevitably also bring disruption with them. It became obvious that the coming of railways could not be entirely prevented and the more pragmatic landowners then turned their attention to obtaining the most favourable compensation, monetary and otherwise, for the inconvenience and nuisance they claimed railways were bringing into to their lives. They generally had the advantage that the railways wanted their land quickly and with the minimum of fuss. Landowners therefore frequently obtained highly favourable financial terms after the necessary negotiations. Sometimes they were bought off before serious negotiations began.

'Many wealthy and politically influential landowners steadfastly resisted railway projects up to and beyond the mania of 1844-5. Others, while lacking any principled basis of objection to railway development, chose to mobilise their formidable political and legal resources to maximise profit from land sales.'[3]

Railway promoters knew that much of the opposition of landowners was about vanity and a feeling of pique rather than genuine loss of amenity. They also knew that financial compensation allowed such feelings to be assuaged. They learned that making an accommodation with powerful landowners at an early stage was likely to save money in the later, parliamentary stages of the promotion. In 1831, the L&B was engaged in negotiation with landowners along its projected route and it placed an announcement in a newspaper stating that:

'The utmost endeavours will be made to avoid all molestation to noblemen and gentlemen's seats near which the proposed line is intended to pass. The railway company has given directions to the surveyors to spare no expense for this purpose. It is always ready and happy to communicate with all parties who wish an alteration in the direction of the railway.'[4]

It was all, of course, grossly inequitable. Where disputes occurred, smaller landowners who could not hire the expertise required for litigation saw their interests largely being swept aside. The blatant inequality of how the law dealt with landowners of differing degrees of wealth even aroused the ire of the Duke of Wellington. In the tradition of Tory paternalism, he argued:

'...small proprietors who could not well come before Parliament to defend their interests, were placed in the hardest situation possible in the case of interference with their property on the part of railway companies.'[5]

The Liverpool & Manchester Railway

By the early 1820s, business people in Liverpool and Manchester felt that economic growth in both towns was being held back by what would now be called an 'inadequate transport infrastructure'. Three canals and various turnpikes were in existence, but they did not have the capacity to cope with existing traffic let alone with potentially expanding levels of demand. An approach to the canal companies suggesting that they provide better services was rebuffed in no uncertain terms. A railway seemed the obvious solution but the size of a project involving joining the two towns was daunting, given the lack of experience in railway construction at this time.

The initiative originally came mainly from the Liverpool end. William James, a well-known land agent and proponent of railways, joined forces with Joseph Sandars, a leading Liverpool merchant. James concentrated on identifying the best alignment while Sandars was given the job of drumming up financial support. James, whose energy and enthusiasm possibly exceeded his ability, claimed that he could build a line and have it ready for traffic in eighteen months.

Work on making initial surveys started in 1822 and soon encountered ferocious opposition. The canal proprietors had been sitting on a lucrative near-monopoly of transport between the two towns for many years and were not going to see their milch-cow put out to grass if they could prevent it. The turnpike trusts and stage coach proprietors also objected strongly although finding it hard to make common cause with the canal owners. Influential landowners to the east of Liverpool initially offered what seemed like total obstruction. The Earls of Derby and Sefton were leaders in the hate campaign against the dirty, noisy, pyrotechnic iron horse. The illegitimate son of Lord Sefton was an MP and in 1825 he wrote to a friend referring to:

> '...this infernal nuisance, the locomotive monster, carrying eighty tons of goods, navigated by a tail of smoke and sulphur, coming through every man's grounds between Liverpool and Manchester.'[6]

Surveying parties found themselves under attack from gangs of stone-throwing locals and rustics armed with pitchforks and other ad hoc weapons. Fights broke out and the surveyors found that their attackers delighted in trying to seize and carry away their theodolites which took on the role of trophies of war. The surveyors were eventually forced to employ a well-known local boxing champion of ferocious appearance to guard their theodolites. A canal proprietor of fiery temperament called Bradshaw also decided to harass the surveying parties under George Stephenson, forcing them to work under cover of darkness, by having his men fire off guns randomly across his land. Bradshaw did not just believe in physical resistance but circulated leaflets warning about the damaging effects that trains would have on farm livestock, crops, trees and thatched roofs. Truly the notion of 'not in my backyard' has a long and chequered history.

The original agreed alignment saw the line pointing north from Liverpool before turning east, skirting the northern edge of Lord Derby's Knowsley Park, passing through St Helens and traversing Chat Moss towards Manchester. This is interesting because it is clear that even at this early date care was being taken to avoid confrontations with powerful but unfriendly landowners. When James had encountered problems and delays and asked to be taken off the job, George Stephenson was employed because of his experience with the early days of the Stockton & Darlington Railway and his negotiations with awkward landowners. Stephenson did not think much of highfalutin' titled landowners and being a hands-on man, probably enjoyed a few midnight excursions trespassing on their land while carrying out surveys.

In 1825, a bill was presented to parliament. It failed, largely through the surprising inability of Stephenson to give satisfactory answers to the questions put to him by opposing counsel. He appeared both ill-informed and incompetent but in fairness he had been poorly briefed by his subordinates. He was replaced by Sir George and John Rennie, assisted by Charles Vignoles. Their recommendations were incorporated into a bill for which a much more convincing case was made and this became law in May 1826, despite vigorous opposition from the Earls of Derby and Sefton. The agreed route was on a very different alignment, more direct but involving greater engineering works and costing considerably more.

There had also been opposition, albeit unavailing, at the Manchester end. The Atherton Estate had been laid out as a desirable residential area and people there had claimed that the proposed railway would cause them a loss of amenity. This is precisely what did happen, the area deteriorating when the terminus at Liverpool Road was extended in 1836.

All eyes had been on the parliamentary debate around the Liverpool & Manchester (L&M). This was not a short line carrying coal to the nearest navigable water but a project on an altogether grander scale involving major engineering works and joining the commercial centre of the burgeoning cotton textile industry with a booming port engaged in trade with the Americas and the West Indies. All those who opposed railways – canal, turnpike and coaching interests and many landowners – knew that much depended on parliament's decision. If the L&M was to get the go-ahead, it would be likely to encourage other schemes, some of which were already being talked about. If it failed, it might snuff out these and discourage other schemes.

The opposition of the inland waterways and various road interests was materially based and understandable since railways posed a serious threat to their businesses. With landowners, the opposition was of a much more prejudiced nature. The steam locomotive was singled out as a remorseless, intrusive juggernaut, violating the countryside and its inhabitants, human and otherwise. The concept of compulsory purchase by railway companies seeking to make profits for their shareholders received the full force of the landowners' hostile rhetoric. Not known for giving priority to the interests of wider society, landowners argued that compulsory purchase was only acceptable where there was clearly substantial public necessity. Even in the earliest days of railways, few landowners went so far as to be irreconcilably opposed to railways. They learned quickly that a show of early opposition to a railway project usually meant that generous compensation terms could be extracted for the damage they claimed that a railway would impose on their way of life.

Those watching the progress of the L&M's bill in 1826 and wishing it well would have noted that witnesses appearing before a Parliamentary Select Committee for a railway company needed to be far better briefed and make a far tighter submission than that with which Stephenson was equipped when he appeared before the committee in 1825. Of course, high quality presentation of a bill in parliament was no guarantee of success but poor presentation would almost certainly bring about its swift downfall. Some submissions were thrown out peremptorily for not even observing the requirements of Standing Orders. It will also have been noted that a co-operative rather than a confrontational attitude towards landowners, even involving negotiated realignments before a bill went to parliament, was likely to ease the passage of that bill. Many landowners realised that the louder the objection they raised to a railway scheme, the greater the possible amount of compensation they would receive. It was not as simple as that but there were plenty of landowners willing to try it on and many of them did so successfully over the coming decades.

An early railway scheme was the Newcastle & Carlisle (N&C). The company duly deposited the items required for all submissions to parliament in time for the 1826 session, only for the Bill to be withdrawn in the face of a storm of protest from affected landowners, the most vociferous of these being the Greenwich Hospital Estates who had employed the well-known railway engineer, Joseph Locke, to survey an alternative to the route being proposed by the N&C. The company then admitted that its survey had been undertaken with undue haste and that it had carried out insufficient consultation with landowners. Lesson learned. A far more thorough survey followed involving greater consultation and agreement with landowners and a new bill was presented to parliament in 1829. This time only one major objection was raised, this being from a landowner who argued that the line near his estate was an eyesore and would be also be liable to flooding. His concerns evaporated when he was offered £3,000 for the seven acres of his land which the company wished to acquire. This was in effect an 'out-of-court' settlement. Railway promoters were learning empirically that making such agreements was likely to prove cheaper than confrontation employing expensive legal counsel before a Select Committee. It was impossible to predict how such a committee might assess the value of the 'nuisance' claimed by a protestor and there was always the possibility that a bill might be rejected completely after a protracted and expensive hearing in committee. In the event of defeat, a delay of at least one year would follow before a revised bill could be presented to parliament again.

There were many people who, in the 1820s, had either been hostile to the idea of railways in their entirety or sceptical of their effectiveness as a means of transport. The immediate success of the L&M after its opening in 1830, which was on a scale unforeseen even by its most optimistic promoters, provoked a more favourable perception of the potential of railways. A consistent and rabid opponent of everything to do with railways had been the *Quarterly Review*. It now unbent to the extent of advocating a nationwide network of railways. The L&M project was of immense importance in the history of Britain's railways. Its business impact, however, was largely local to the places it served and to their hinterland, even if its success quickly provided evidence of the potential of railways to reduce radically the cost of inland goods and merchandise transportation, plus the unexpected potential of passenger travel. The next logical step was for a scheme to build a longer line which joined a major provincial industrial centre to London. Enter the London & Birmingham Railway.

The London & Birmingham Railway

The energetic, enterprising commercial and industrial bourgeoisie of Birmingham observed with great interest the early and very evident success of the Liverpool & Manchester Railway. In the 1820s, there had been discussions about the desirability of a railway between London and the capital of the Midlands. The businessmen of Birmingham and district were concerned that the existing transport infrastructure was unable, efficiently and economically, to handle the growing output of the myriad of factories, foundries and workshops in their area. Even the canals, which had done much to assist the area's growth, were becoming congested. Without very expensive upgrading it was difficult to see how their capacity could be increased. Little could be done to speed up inland water transport. Without better transport it was thought that Birmingham was losing potential markets to Continental competition.

With the glowing example of the Liverpool & Manchester to draw on, late in 1830 meetings began to take place leading to the convening of a committee for the promotion of a line to London. This was obviously going to be a project far greater than any previous seriously mooted scheme, presenting a host of challenges but with the example of the L&M to make it ambitious but not unfeasible. The Rainhill Trials of 1829 had demonstrated the haulage potential of steam locomotives. What was envisaged was Britain's first long-distance main line. Finance was readily available, especially at the Birmingham end. It was decided to engage George and Robert Stephenson to conduct surveys as to the best possible route. They were the men of the moment. The company had a simple name – the London & Birmingham (L&B).

The promoters' concern was simply with what they thought would be the potentially lucrative traffic between the two cities. Any intermediate places through which the railway might pass were a minor consideration. Several possible alignments were identified by the Stephensons but the main issue seemed to come down to whether the line should run via Coventry or Oxford. George Stephenson came down strongly in favour of routing the line through Coventry and he presented a report to that effect to the directors on 23 September 1831. His aim was to provide the most level alignment possible even if it was not the most direct and also that alignment which was likely to involve the minimum of expensive civil engineering works. He also wanted a route which avoided wherever possible the estates of influential and potentially hostile landowners. He considered this to be essential, drawing lessons from the obstructive tactics he had experienced from powerful landowners in the area immediately east of Liverpool.

This is not an account of the promotion or construction of the London & Birmingham Railway but rather a consideration of the

George Stephenson was eulogised by Samuel Smiles as a prime example of the 'self-help' ethos. Of humble origins and lacking formal education, he nevertheless played a major role in the early development of Britain's railways. In later life, he moved to Tapton Hall near Chesterfield and this statue is at Chesterfield station. (A. Brooke)

interaction between a major early railway project and the great landowners of the time. It provides an object lesson in just how important it was in the early 1830s for railway promoters to pay due attention and frequently defer to the power and influence that major landlords could exert often before proposals for lines began to manifest themselves in public announcements, bills presented to parliament and surveying parties out in the field.

Stephenson initially preferred a route traversing the Chiltern Hills, an unavoidable barrier, and passing through Aylesbury and Uxbridge on its approach to London. No sooner was this possible alignment proposed than it generated fierce opposition from landowners whose estates would be affected. This blow was somewhat lessened when he was approached by the Countess of Bridgewater who suggested an alignment close to the Grand Junction Canal where it passed through her estate near Tring in Hertfordshire. Stephenson needed no second bidding. He made a deviation to avoid her estate and was able to take advantage of the Tring Gap in the Chilterns. In the Weedon area the alignment was altered to take account of the opposition of J. Thornton of Brockhall.

Nearing London, it was clear that the proposed alignment was arousing the hostility of the Earl of Essex at Cassiobury Park, the Earl of Clarendon at Grove Park, Lord Brownlow of Ashridge, Eton College who owned land at Weedon and the Kensal Green Cemetery Company as well as various lesser landowners. Stephenson, pragmatically, then surveyed an alternative route which avoided their various demesnes but this still meant that the L&B had to pay out £73,000 'compensation'. This may have been a good way of pre-empting opposition but it involved expensive extra engineering works.

This initial Bill was presented to parliament in 1832. The major landowners who opposed the railway had done their lobbying with the result that the House of Lords rejected it out of hand before it got as far as a Select Committee. The Lords stated that, in their opinion, the L&B had not presented an effective case for the railway to justify causing so much potential disruption to the landowners whose estates straddled the proposed route and whose opposition had already been made clear.[7]

Historical events can only be explained and understood by reference to the context in which they occur. The circumstances of the time help to explain why the first Bill of the L&B was dismissed in such a peremptory fashion. The years 1831 and 1832 saw the culmination of over a decade of political turmoil which some believed presaged a revolution. A class struggle was taking place in which the rising middle class, especially those with industrial, manufacturing and commercial interests, was demanding a political voice more proportional to its growing economic power. They wanted political reform, most specifically a widening of the franchise. More circumspect elements among the existing ruling elite were prepared to make some concessions as a way of heading off demands for more radical reform. Those leading the agitation for reform were supported by substantial numbers of middle-class people, backed up with mass working-class support in many large towns and cities. The many contemporary grievances that were felt by ordinary people found a focus in the demand for political reform. It was this involvement of working-class people that most worried the members of the traditional political elite. They had an extreme fear of the 'unwashed masses'. For the more entrenched elements among the landed interest, the traditional ruling elite, the 1832 Reform Act represented everything they loathed, an outrageous sustained attack on the political hegemony which they regarded as their inalienable right. They saw railways, especially the L&B, as the creature of the urban bourgeoisie and the railways epitomised the hateful assault that was unfolding on what they saw as a stable and hierarchical system whereby God had ordered and endorsed the kind of society which ensured that the rich man remained in his castle and the poor man stayed at his gate.

The L&B was being promoted by a body of urban bourgeoisie whose interests were perceived as diametrically opposed to those of rural landed society. The latter saw this scheme, considerably more substantial than any previous railway project, as opening the floodgates for increasing numbers of such schemes. It was the misfortune of the L&B's first parliamentary submission that it coincided with the huge furore around political reform. The Lords constituted the political powerhouse of the landowning class and they vetoed the L&B bill in a Canute-like attempt to hold back the waves of change. In doing so they were symbolically asserting their long-standing power and privilege. Often they hid their narrow class interest, their political power and the desire to protect their rural serenity and sporting activities behind assertions that the emissions from locomotives and the noise they made would, for example, set fire to crops and thatched roofs and scare precious livestock causing cows to abort and hens to stop laying eggs. Concerns were expressed about how railways threatened the livelihoods of those involved with the turnpike trusts, hotels and inns, those who made and maintained horse-drawn conveyances and also the employees of canal companies. Objections were raised about how the driving of railways through the landscape would carve up land into parcels too awkwardly shaped or small to be of continued use for agricultural purposes. This particular issue had not caused major problems during the major canal-building era but it was put forwards as one reason for opposing railways. Railways, it was claimed, would interfere with the natural drainage of the areas through which they passed and so it went on... .

It was the misfortune of this major scheme to fall foul of a transient conjuncture of events. The landed aristocracy and gentry perceived this line as being promoted by people furthering their urban interests and with the route along which it passed being almost entirely through rural and agricultural land, its purpose was seen as conflicting with the interests of country society.

To many in the twenty-first century, fox-hunting appears to be either repugnant or simply ridiculous. Historians, however, have to step out of the mores of their own time and attempt to probe the mindset of the people of the period they are studying. Therefore the words of F.M.L. Thompson are particularly appropriate. He described fox-hunting as:

'A sport eminently suited to the mounted and leisured aristocracy and gentry…It engaged the passion also of a cross-section of the whole rural community…In the nineteenth century, moreover, it was an increasingly organised activity, with a growing body of conventions and etiquette, which gave the hunting community a mystique and cohesion of its own. An expensive activity, the major part of the expense was frequently carried by a member of the aristocracy, whose enthusiasm for the chase was in this way the means of cementing his leadership of all branches of county society. The hunting interest…was perhaps the most real and fundamentally influential element in county society.'[8]

Britain, in the 1830s, was a deeply inequitable society in which wealth and power was concentrated in the hands of a tiny minority of the population. Although elements among the urban bourgeoisie were accruing considerable wealth at this time, 'old money' in terms of the landed aristocracy and gentry, at least until the Great Reform Act, still exerted a political influence totally disproportionate to their numbers and, in some cases, to their actual wealth as well.

'Old money', however, was feeling increasingly under threat and at this particular time the L&B was seen as the conduit for this threat.

Railways, backed up by statutory powers of compulsory purchase, jeopardised property rights and property was seen as sacrosanct. Maybe elevating property to the position of a fetish was only a cover for self-interest but such a deeply entrenched social and political elite easily assumed that its own interests were the same of those of wider society despite the majority of the population having little or no property.

The failure to secure the passage of their Bill caused the promoters and supporters of the L&B to convene, analyse the situation and draw up alternative tactics. Lord Wharncliffe, who had chaired the Select Committee which had dismissed the L&B's bill, told them to avoid confrontation with landowners enraged about parliament being prepared to violate the sanctity of private property with compulsory purchase powers. It was necessary to recognise this resentment. They still had the power to make life very difficult for railway promoters and it made sense to find ways of propitiating rather than confronting them over the issue of obtaining legal powers to cross their land. A simple expedient was to buy off the opposition of affected landowners before railway bills came up for consideration by parliamentary select committees. Lord Wharncliffe was widely respected and his suggestions were listened to and absorbed. The L&B promoters adopted a much more conciliatory, some might call it realistic, others servile, attitude to the landed interest, whenever possible being prepared to propitiate them with often overly generous offers for their land. Again, whenever possible, they would do this before the relevant bills went before parliamentary scrutiny. At the time, some openly called this bribery.

The promoters of the L&B decided to draw up another bill. They started by identifying the landowners they thought most likely to be troublesome and negotiated deals with some of them before the Bill went to Westminster. Their potential opposition was therefore bought off before it was allowed to become the subject of acrimonious and sometimes long-drawn out and expensive exchanges in the hothouse atmosphere of a Select Committee. Clearly, as this approach came to be employed by growing numbers of railway companies, landowners found that they had a potent bargaining tool in their hands. Materially, if not ethically, they cannot be blamed for negotiating what effectively were 'out of court' settlements, much to their advantage. They, like the railway companies, must have known that a Select Committee might put a very different and less favourable value on the land under dispute. Whatever the moral aspect of these negotiations, Harold Pollins (1978) has shown than the cost of purchasing the land for the L&B was between ten and sixteen per cent of the total cost of the project.

It was not long before criticism was being expressed to the effect that landowners were extorting vast sums of money from railway companies in respect of the land the latter required. One vehement critic with professional knowledge was Robert Stephenson who, in a speech to the Institute of Civil Engineers in 1856, lambasted the landowners for their 'extraordinary demands for compensation'. He gave an estimate that overall twenty-five per cent of railway construction costs were taken up by the purchase of land. He was a grounded man, not given to hyperbole and he offered no concrete evidence to support his claim. A consistently hostile critic of the alleged rapacity of the landed aristocracy was John Francis (1851) who accused them of 'immorality'. He argued that the landowners affected by the L&B scheme and many subsequent landowners were grossly over-compensated for the land they sold in order to allow a passage for a railway. He was an early historian of the railways who clearly had an axe to grind. He did much to foster the perception that the landowning fat cats fleeced the railway promoters for compensation so generous that the cost of constructing the L&B and subsequent railways was artificially inflated. The perception that they used their influence to work the system to their advantage became embedded and enduring. Defenders of the landowners pointed out that railways were speculative ventures aimed at making profits for their shareholders. While the railway companies would obviously try to obtain land as cheaply as possible, it was only natural that landowners should try to get the best possible price when compulsory purchase was being threatened. The interface between railway companies and landowners was much more than simply an issue about money. Two very different sets of interests and values were in conflict and it was a struggle for which of the old or the new force was to be dominant in society. The L&B symbolised what substantial sections of the landed interest saw as the dark forces being unleashed and it paid the price in 1832. It proved to be a pyrrhic victory for its opponents. The railway ultimately proved to be unstoppable.

The Eastern Counties Railway and Lord Petre

One of the best-known, even notorious, cases of what appears to be arrogant aristocratic bravura concerns the confrontation between Lord Petre and the Eastern Counties Railway (ECR). The Company wished to build a line passing through the grounds of Thorndon and Ingatestone Halls near Brentwood in Essex. Both houses belonged to Lord Petre who proposed an alternative alignment which, while still crossing his land, would be further from the two houses. He then made it clear that he would object in parliament to the ECR's original alignment unless they gave him the extraordinary sum of £120,000, made up of £20,000 for the strip of land eight miles long to be consumed by the path of the railway and £100,000 'compensation'. There were additional conditions including some preventing the building of stations at various specified locations.

The ECR, always a cash-strapped company, formally agreed to pay in full, the largest single payment made to a landowner, much to the chagrin of the shareholders when they found out. The Bill passed in 1836 but then the company refused to ratify the agreement and sought to put the case before a jury to adjudicate on the basis that agreement had not been reached over the cost of the compulsory purchase of Lord Petre's land. The ECR and Lord Petre now went head-to-head. When Petre won an injunction to prevent the company from calling a jury and also from entering his land, the ECR appealed the case and lost. This was time-consuming and had taken up most of the two years that were legally allowed under the 1836 Act for the purchase of land. When the ECR attempted to promote a second Bill to obtain powers for more time, Lord Petre succeeded in blocking this move. He was triumphant. The company had run out of money and was forced to make an arrangement with him whereby he agreed to accept the £20,000 as a down payment with the other £100,000 to be paid over five years. As if that was not enough, Lord Petre was able to impose further conditions on the company. On this basis, the Bill was passed in 1838. All the fight had gone out of the ECR. Its nose was further rubbed in the dirt when, three years later, it wanted to make a deviation and had to stump up a further £3,750 for additional 'severance' for a station at Ingatestone which Lord Petre had previously adamantly refused to allow and £600 for the land on which it was to be built. To add insult to injury, the station was to have some extraneous Tudor-style architectural features at Petre's behest.

In 1836, the ECR had engaged a team of surveyors to make an independent assessment of Lord Petre's claims. When the team reported, it was highly critical of his case. Contrary to what he said, the railway was not visible from Thorndon Hall, because it was in a cutting a mile away. His claim that the railway crossed an approach road to his estate was also false – the location was not on his property. The surveyors put a price of £3,600 on the land to be taken up by the railway and £16,400 compensation.

The amount that Lord Petre demanded of the ECR was entirely unreasonable and, as we have seen, some of the claims he made for compensation were spurious. He seems to have been particularly stubborn and high-handed but he did not want the railway and did not see why it should be foisted on him using the odious legal process of compulsory purchase. His grandfather had spent a fortune on the Thorndon Estate and Lord Petre saw no reason why he should not be allowed to enjoy it to the full. As far as he was concerned, it was his entitlement. What is not known and is unlikely ever to be revealed, is quite how he was able to manipulate the due processes in a manner so completely to his advantage.

The Blisworth and Peterborough Branch

Experience should be an effective teacher. Railway promoters in the late 1820s and early 1830s had certainly learned the hard way that it was better to propitiate than provoke landowners. In 1843, a line from Blisworth to Peterborough was authorised. 'The alignment of this railway encapsulated the experience of the 1830s in its shameless application of the criteria of initial avoidance and negotiation.'[9] This line was intended to give the London & Birmingham Railway access to the Fens which were poorly served by railways but whose rich agricultural land offered potentially lucrative traffic.

A route was identified which as far as possible utilised the natural conduit and gentle gradients of the valley of the River Nene. The bugbear was that the valley was occupied by what seemed an inordinate number of country estates and parks. The projected line entered the Nene Valley itself just south of Northampton and the original intention was to pass along the south bank of the Nene just penetrating the northern edge of the estate of Delapre Abbey. The owner, Colonel Bouverie, politely suggested that the railway should be realigned away from Delapre along the northern bank of the Nene. The only feasible new alignment was not a convenient one and it was estimated that the cost of this deviation would add a figure of £50,000 to £80,000 to the cost of construction. This was a setback, so the promoters talked to Bouverie again and an agreement was reached whereby the line would pass along the southern side of the Nene close to but not actually intruding on the Delapre Estate.

As the line went north-eastwards, a deviation from the original was made at Little Houghton. This took the line away from the Nene and was done to placate Lord Aboyne. Further north, at Thrapston, an alignment was chosen which would minimise disruption to other landowners.

Robert Stephenson, employed as the company's engineer, was no great admirer of Britain's landed aristocracy and this opinion can only have been confirmed at Lilford, a short distance north of Thrapston. Lilford Hall was located on the eastern side of the Nene but the owner had built ornamental gardens on land he owned on the other side of the river. Appearing before the Select Committee, Stephenson said: '...on examining the valley originally, I found the situation of the house was such that it would be inapplicable to keep the line in the valley, therefore a deviation was made.'[10] In deference to the integrity of the Lilford Estate, a considerable deviation was made, away from the Nene and to the east of Lilford Hall. This deviation added an estimated £25,000 to the costs of constructing the line. If that was not enough, the deviation intruded on land owned by Lord Montagu at Barnwell. The house involved, Barnwell Castle, was unoccupied at the time and Stephenson therefore envisaged less disruption to Lord Montagu's estate with consequent smaller amounts of compensation. However, much to Stephenson's chagrin, his assistant then ventured his opinion that the two settlements, Barnwell St Andrew and Barnwell All Saints were so beautiful that a deviation slightly to the west should be made to minimise the railway's impact. This deviation was made.

By now, Stephenson must have been wishing a plague on all the titled and landed aristocracy and the squirearchy, but he was not done with such people yet. Another deviation was made to the west of the River Nene and away from the village of Elton and Elton Hall. This was at the behest of Lord Caryfort. That his patience had almost totally been eroded is suggested when, shortly before reaching Peterborough, Earl Fitzwilliam, owner of the Milton Estate, made several suggestions to the company. These included one for a considerable deviation so as not to disturb a fox covert. With one exception, the Earl's suggestions were rejected.

Possibly no other single railway project of similar length had its eventual alignment so much shaped by the need to appease influential landowners. Penetration of estates was kept to the absolute minimum. A fine balance had to be reached between the possible cost of compensation if a landowner challenged the Bill in Select Committee and the cost of appeasing a possibly obstructive landowner by making a realignment of the originally projected route. The influence of the major landowners was sufficient to ensure that their interests were well looked after.

The Syston & Peterborough Railway and the Earl of Harborough

The Syston & Peterborough Railway (S&P) was a component of the Midland Railway which was formed out of various amalgamations in 1844. It was an extremely circuitous cross-country route from Leicester to Peterborough via Melton Mowbray, Oakham and Stamford. Even with the relatively small towns mentioned, this was a deeply rural area and the line passed through noted fox-hunting country in which the landed interest still had major influence. As such, its early history contributes considerably to an understanding of the complex relationship between railway promoters and engineers on the one hand and landed grandees on the other. The proposal for the S&P was agreed in October 1844. When first planned, the line would have taken a far more direct alignment in a south-easterly direction from Syston, north of Leicester, via Twyford and Manton then onwards to Stamford and Peterborough. The engineers were George and Robert Stephenson and for the sake of directness they planned an alignment through undulating countryside requiring a tunnel at Owston which was likely to have presented some geological difficulties. Liddell, an assistant engineer for the S&P, when appearing before the committee adjudicating on the project, averred that this proposed route had been abandoned on engineering grounds. Also there had been a strong lobby against it from local landowners and anyway it was perceived as desirable that any line between Syston and Peterborough should serve Melton Mowbray.

The committee must have been somewhat bemused later when George Hudson in his evidence stated that he had discarded the direct route after listening to local landowners with hunting interests who urged him to take the more circuitous route because it served Melton Mowbray and eliminated the need for the lengthy and difficult tunnel. Perhaps Hudson was being economical with the truth but, if not, this was a rare example of landowners kindly and altruistically suggesting an alternative alignment that would be of more benefit to a railway company in terms of the traffic it might generate. In his evidence, Robert Stephenson argued that his sole concern was to identify the best possible alignment and he would not have allowed himself to be influenced by the fox-hunting community who, he said, had never actually approached him in the first place. Both Stephensons made clear their preference for the direct route. Did discussions take place with the landowners, the existence and nature of which Hudson chose to omit from his evidence before the committee? The line, of course, went via Melton Mowbray and was to bring the railway into direct conflict with the Earl of Harborough at Stapleford Park as we shall see.

The line was promoted by George Hudson as a tactical counter to what he saw as a critical threat to his growing empire of railway interests. Not least he was concerned to safeguard his routes from York to London. They were particularly threatened by the far more direct route proposed by the London & York Railway via Grantham and Newark. In an attempt to reduce the possible impact of this line, he promoted lines to penetrate areas of the East Midlands through which it was likely to pass. He extruded a long cross-country line from Nottingham to Lincoln. He also built the S&P which was intended to join up at Peterborough with a line from Ely which was part of the Eastern Counties Railway of which he was chairman.

Once the choice of routing the S&P through Melton Mowbray had been made, the die was cast for perhaps the most notorious example of hostility by a landowner towards a railway company and its engineers and surveyors. The location was Stapleford Park through part of which it was proposed that the S&P should pass en route from Melton to Oakham. The line was projected to follow the valley of the River Eye in a roughly easterly direction before turning to the south-east and then for some distance keep close to the alignment of the Oakham Canal. The canal skirted the northern and eastern boundaries of Stapleford Park. The Earl of Harborough was a cantankerous individual known to harbour an extreme aversion towards the idea of railways in the vicinity of his estate and he was a major shareholder in the canal. He had gone on record telling a public meeting in Oakham that he was prepared to oppose the railway by all means possible and if he did not succeed, he would go and reside in Switzerland. He had made it clear that he would not permit railway surveyors to enter his property. Hudson had already decided that buying up the impecunious canal might provide him with an almost ready-made course for the railway near the Stapleford estate. The purchase of the canal went through in April 1845. The proposed alignment, however, still involved a small incursion into the estate in its north-east corner between the hall and the canal, not far from the hamlet of Saxby. Surveying the route at this point could not but involve entering the park and it was this which led to the well-known 'Battle of Saxby'.

Despite the fact that the earl had erected notices along the boundary of his land threatening dire consequences for trespassers, on 13 November, a team of surveyors and their assistants arrived on the scene intent on doing their job which involved entering the park itself. They used the canal towpath to approach the point of entry to the park believing that they were entitled to do so as it was a public right of way. It was indeed their entitlement but that cut no ice when they were intercepted by a party of the earl's men armed with pitchforks and other rustic weaponry. They were taken prisoner, they and their equipment were bundled into a wagon and all were hauled off to the residence of the nearest magistrate although their trespass was not actually a crime. The magistrate was out and so late returning that tempers had cooled somewhat and the two parties had dispersed. The earl's men decided to hang on to their opponents' theodolite, this instrument symbolising the black arts the surveyors practised.

Another attempt to conduct the survey a couple of days later led to a skirmish at Saxby Bridge. This time, the earl's forces had swelled to about forty and they were intent on preventing the surveyors using the towpath let alone entering the park. They brought up some wagons with which they blocked the towpath. An escalation had obviously been anticipated by the railway people who had scoured the drinking dens of Melton, Oakham and Stamford in search of sturdy bruisers happy to earn some money, drink some free beer and have a good scrap. Equipped with makeshift weapons, they arrived at Saxby Bridge looking every bit like an invading army. In an attempt to prevent a full-blooded fracas, the earl's steward and solicitor and legal representatives of the railway company were engaged in urgent discussions. It was evident that both sides were unsure that a peaceful settlement of the dispute was possible. The earl's men had also been reinforced and had brought up the estate's fire engine to pump water out of the canal and drench their adversaries if necessary.

A small force of rural policemen now turned up, making it clear that they intended to prevent a breach of the peace and arrest the first person who committed an assault. Saxby could never before have witnessed such excitement. A large crowd of spectators had arrived on the scene, some strongly supportive of the earl's men but others just hoping for some red-blooded entertainment. Bearing in mind what the police demanded, both sides laid down their weapons and for a while resorted instead to verbal taunts and to pushing and shoving. It was inevitable that a scrimmage would eventually occur but when it did, it was relatively good-natured, doubtless disappointing the watching crowd. Some degree of order was restored and it was agreed that both sides would withdraw their forces and that a couple of men from each party would be summonsed on charges of assault. Meanwhile the dispute would be brought before the courts for their decision.

This was really only a tactical delay, both parties knowing that further confrontation was inevitable. The S&P people launched another recruitment drive, casting their net as far away as Peterborough. The earl's people reinforced their barriers on the towpath but were aware that the surveyors might try a bluff and gain entrance to the park somewhere other than via the towpath. The circumference of the park was extensive and this meant that their forces were thinly spread. They had a secret weapon, however. The earl had a yacht on the lake in the park. It had been his whim to equip it with a number of small cannons. Normally these would never have seen a shot fired in anger. Now they were commandeered as part of the park defence force. They looked good but they were actually toys. While a token force from the railway tried to shift the barricades, several parties of surveyors backed up by a hundred or more 'bodyguards' entered the park some distance away and proceeded to attempt as rapid a survey as possible before more of their opponents arrived. When they did, it turned nasty. Reinforcements for both sides arrived and this was no mere posturing as injuries were sustained on both sides. The earl was ill but rose from his sick bed to rally his troops. What they lacked in numbers they made up for with valour and they inflicted a defeat on the invaders.

Numbers of those employed by the railway appeared at Leicester Assizes in 1845 in what became something of a test case counterpoising the power of landownership against that of the railway promoters. The legal ruling was that the earl's people had been justified in using force against the railway surveyors who were trespassing on private land. However, some of his men were found guilty of damaging the surveyors' equipment and some of assault.

It should have been the end of physical fisticuffs and their replacement by legal cut-and-thrust as the Bill for the Syston & Peterborough went before parliament for its approval in 1845. The earl objected to the railway in committee explaining how he had spent the last fifteen years on expensive improvements and extensions to the park and he considered it an utter disgrace that his efforts should be spoiled by the intrusion of a railway. If it was absolutely necessary to build a railway, then it should be built to the south-west of the park. Although this would provide a more direct route between Melton and Oakham, he acknowledged that it would involve more expense because the line would not be able to follow the easy route close to the River Eye. Despite the disturbance involved, he was prepared to sell some parcels of land to the company for this south-westerly route. George Stephenson dismissed this suggested alignment arguing that it would be more expensive and actually more damaging to the earl's land because deep cuttings and even a tunnel would be required.

Three alternatives were before the Select Committee. The most contentious was the line passing briefly through the park not far from the hall. Second was the 'direct' line running touching the south-west extremity of the park; the third involved filling in the canal and routing the line along its course near the park. Hudson's attempt to reopen earlier failed discussions with the earl was unsuccessful and then Earl Fitzwilliam, who had a large estate not far away near Peterborough thought to pour oil on troubled waters by proposing yet another alignment, this time north of the canal. This fared no better. The Earl of Harborough was not for turning.

Hudson, often very forthright in his dealings with people, showed great forbearance regarding the earl. Addressing the committee he said:

'I am quite ready on behalf of this Company to deviate this line if it becomes a matter of expense, rather than interfere with Lord Harborough – we would rather increase the expense than cause annoyance to his Lordship.'[11]

The committee decreed that the direct alignment to the south-west, involving a tunnel, should be used and they added a rider prohibiting access to any part of the earl's estate without his express written consent. The company then deposited a petition for a line to the south-west of the hall involving a tunnel under the Cuckoo Hill Plantation. This was unacceptable to the earl, who demanded a line completely outside the park. By this time, patience in all quarters must have been wearing thin. The surveyors were experiencing severe harassment not only from the earl's men but from the earl himself. He assaulted one of the surveyors and drove a carriage rapidly back and forth along a public road, the survey party having to throw themselves out of the way. One of the surveyors' conveyances was 'captured' and he ordered that its wheels should be sawn off. His men obstructed the surveyors by standing between the theodolites they were using, holding up rolls of cloth. Having agreed to align the route further to the west, the company, trying to make up for lost time, then cut corners and after skimping on the survey was severely embarrassed when the tunnel it was constructing collapsed and many of the earl's precious trees were destroyed.

The company was nothing if not persistent and it returned to parliament asking for the legal right to build a line using part of the course of the old canal but avoiding any intrusion into the park. They waited for the expected hostile response from the earl but none came, perhaps because he had been bought off with the sum of £25,000. The S&P including this alignment finally gained parliamentary approval on 30 June 1845. Construction went ahead and the line was built with an inconveniently sharp curve past the north-east corner of Stapleford Park. Known as 'Lord Harborough's Curve', this was realigned in 1892 after negotiations with a more conciliatory landowner. The old course was then abandoned. It was 1 May 1848 before trains were able to run the whole distance between Leicester and Peterborough.

This case has understandably gained considerable notoriety and highlights the problems that could be caused by a landowner who was persistently hostile and, in this case, prepared to use violence. Even the farcical collapse of the tunnel was largely caused by the surveyors having one eye on the job and the other on the lookout for more hostile activity by the earl's men. It should, however, not be taken in any way as typical. Events like those involved in the 'Battle of Saxby' capture the popular imagination but they give a very false impression. Many landowners objected to the intrusion of railways into their estates but most fought their corner in ways that did not make the news.

Stamford and the Marquis of Exeter

Stamford is a beautiful stone-built town on the River Welland about twelve miles north-west of Peterborough. It dates back to Roman times and was an important borough during the period of Danish rule. Its medieval prosperity was based on the wool and cloth trade but after that trade declined, Stamford eventually enjoyed further prosperity as a staging point on the Great North Road. It went into the doldrums when left off the main line from London to the north and for a time it became something of a backwater. It is at least partly due to this that we owe its continuing wealth of ancient buildings.

The town's relations with railways in the 1840s and 1850s are something of a *cause célèbre*. O.S. Nock, the well-known railway writer, was unequivocal on the issue:

> 'Several of the larger provincial towns made themselves notorious by refusing railways. Of this particular brand of short-sightedness there is no more striking example than Stamford. In 1840 it was a great and prosperous market town in south Lincolnshire; it lay on the Great North Road, and its importance completely overshadowed not only Grantham, but Peterborough as well. The Great Northern Railway was planned to go through it; for it was certainly the most important place between London and Doncaster. But the opposition of the Marquis [sic] of Exeter was so determined, and so staunchly backed by the townsfolk, that in the end Stamford was bypassed altogether.'[12]

Unequivocal Nock may have been, but he was mistaken. It was not nearly as simple as he suggests. The 2nd Marquess of Exeter, Brownlow Cecil, had many of the characteristics of his fellow landed aristocrats. He lived just outside Stamford in Burghley House, one of the country's grandest stately homes. His family were leading landowners and exerted enormous influence locally, not least political influence. He was determined to maintain his political hegemony at all costs. He would have been aware that he was living through rapidly changing times. The Reform Act of 1832 had been passed in the teeth of opposition from people like the marquess and it had enfranchised a section of the middle classes, a growing bourgeoisie with commercial and manufacturing interests and increasing material and intellectual influence. The marquess and his sort inevitably looked askance at this development. Just how hidebound a reactionary the marquess was can be seen by his staunch support for the barbaric local practice of bull-running for which Stamford was well-known. It has to be said that the innkeepers and shopkeepers of the town also supported it – it attracted huge crowds and was the busiest day of their year.

He was an old-fashioned aristocrat, but his power was on the wane by the 1840s and he has been wrongly reviled as the man who employed authoritarian and undemocratic methods of preventing what was later called the East Coast Main Line from coming through Stamford.

This extraordinarily grandiose mansion constitutes a sixteenth century vanity project. A smaller house had existed on the site before William Cecil, Elizabeth 1's right-hand man, began to enlarge and remodel the building in the middle of the sixteenth century. Close to Stamford, the mansion and its owners continued to exercise an almost feudal level of influence in the town.

Stamford was both a 'pocket borough' and a 'rotten borough'. It was the former because the marquess was normally able to nominate the only parliamentary candidates who had a chance of being elected and in the absence of a secret ballot he could be virtually sure that any voters who were tenants of his would support his candidates for fear of eviction if they did not. In 1809 and 1830, for example, when rival candidates were put forward, those tenants who voted for them were indeed evicted peremptorily. Stamford was 'rotten' because it had few voters but returned two MPs at a time when many rapidly growing industrial towns such as Birmingham and Manchester had no parliamentary representatives.

Such autocratic behaviour made the marquess extremely unpopular with many of the townspeople, not least because some of those who had been evicted were forced to move into already overcrowded slum housing elsewhere in the town. Opinions were hardening locally. In 1830, a candidate stood who was as much anti-Burghley House as he was a Whig and he gained one of the seats. The Whigs and the *Stamford News* laid into the Cecils for their self-interested domination of local politics. The Cecils even chose the clergy of the town's several parish churches. Supporters of the candidates approved of by the marquess were not above bribing voters but this was not an uncommon practice in contemporary politics and indeed it was also indulged in by the supporters of the Whigs. It was rumoured that the Marquess of Exeter spent the enormous sum of £14,000 trying to influence the result of the 1832 election. Later in that year, much of St Martin's, which was that part of Stamford south of the River Welland, was added to the borough of Stamford for electoral purposes. This was so much to the advantage of the marquess that the successful Whig candidate in 1832 threw in the towel, convinced that he could never win again. Changes to the eligibility to vote also worked to the advantage of the marquess, meaning that he had a larger proportion of a smaller electorate precisely at a time when the town's population was growing. Those who lived in Cecil-owned houses or worked for them had little option but to vote for Cecil candidates. The only way to break the stranglehold of the marquess was to build more houses to be occupied by people who were not dependent on the Cecils. There were open fields north of the town but the marquess used every means possible to oppose their enclosure and development for housing.

Stamford had stagnated during the Napoleonic Wars. Although its position astride the busy Great North Road generated income for hotels, inns, coach, wagon and carriage-makers and other businesses and provided many jobs, there was a feeling that the town was not growing relative to other comparable places. There were many townsfolk who considered that the power exerted by the Cecils was an obstacle to the economic rejuvenation of Stamford. Like many similar towns, Stamford had a brewing and malting industry but it was felt that the development of this and possible other industries required more effective links with the growing inland navigation and canal system. Even the River Welland which had been navigable for small vessels was silting up. As early as 1809, a scheme had been proposed for a canal to Oakham. There it would link up with the canal to Melton Mowbray which had opened in 1803. From Melton, the River Wreake was navigable to Leicester where there was access to a much wider network of canals and waterways. This had the support of much of Stamford's business community but the marquess was hostile to a development which might reduce his influence over the town. The proposed canal was an issue in an acrimonious parliamentary election. An antagonism was emerging, epitomising at a local level the wider struggle between the old social and political order and an emerging middle class energetically seeking to generate business and make money and perceiving the old order as an obstacle to that process. The canal was never built. The marquess was blamed for that. He was blamed for preventing the outward expansion of the town. He was blamed for discouraging modest industrial expansion. Stamford was becoming a politically divided town with the omnipotence of the marquess under growing challenge. He knew it and did not like it. He was cast in the role of *bête noire* and it was not long before he was being blamed for using his influence to prevent a direct main line from London to York from serving the town. This, it was reckoned, would have put Stamford very firmly on the 'railway map' and ensured commercial expansion and growing prosperity in the second half of the nineteenth century. Instead of which, Stamford had the worst of both worlds because it missed out on a major trunk railway which robbed the Great North Road of much of its traffic, seriously damaging Stamford's position as a coaching town and causing relative economic stagnation.

Stamford's first railway access was an arm's length one whereby a coach was laid on to Wansford to connect with trains on the cross-country line from Blisworth to Peterborough opened by the London & Birmingham Railway in 1845. In 1848, what was now the Midland Railway's Leicester to Peterborough line was opened throughout. It had been a long time coming but the fact that it passed through Stamford at all scotches the myth that the marquess was opposed to all railways.

The original planned alignment of this line (the S&P) took a route approaching Stamford through the Meadows, briefly along the north bank of the River Welland, crossing the Great North Road on the flat, close to the northern end of the town bridge and then in a slightly north-easterly direction out of Stamford. The townspeople wanted this line but the marquess declared his opposition to the alignment because he argued that it would cause congestion. This attitude did not endear the marquess to the citizenry because he owned the bridge and had refused to make it wider. As the *Stamford Mercury* acerbically put it:

'The sudden tenderness of the Marquess of Exeter for the people of Stamford is one of the finest pieces of humbug that the future historian of the Borough will have to record. It has been for ages a crying nuisance...The engineer and directors of the railway have pledged themselves to build a new safe and commodious bridge instead of this pet breakneck of the Marquess...'[13]

The bridge was already the source of everyday congestion and annoyance because it carried the Great North Road and was the main entry to the town from the south. It was too narrow for two vehicles to pass.

The Bill for this alignment went to parliament where it emerged that an engineer had been engaged by the marquess to survey a route for a line passing just to the north of the Broad Street area of the town. It would have been on land partly occupied by slum housing, brothels and disreputable beer houses on land belonging to the marquess. This again is evidence that he was not innately opposed to railways. The proposed station would actually have been conveniently placed for the town centre and there was some support for this alignment among the townspeople. Neither of these lines was proceeded with. Instead the marquess sold land on the south side of the Welland to the Midland Railway. The line obtained legal authorisation in 1845 and the decision was taken to proceed immediately with the construction of the sections from

Syston to Melton Mowbray and Stamford to Peterborough. Serious difficulties were, of course, still being experienced around Saxby on the Melton to Oakham and Stamford section. Until the business with the Earl of Harborough was resolved, it was decided to build a temporary station at the eastern end of Water Street. Passenger trains began to run from Stamford to Peterborough on 2 October 1846. Huge cheering crowds turned out to watch the inaugural departure despite monsoon conditions.

In May 1846, the western extension from the temporary Water Street terminus was authorised and a site for the new permanent station was chosen behind the town's famous old coaching inn, The George. A shallow tunnel was to be built under the street known as St Martin and extending a short distance to the east. St Martins was the exit of the Great North Road going south from the town. The tunnel would obviate the need for the railway to cross that road on the flat. Even this tunnel was the cause of controversy because it passed through land belonging to the marquess. It was said that he managed to extort £40,000 from the railway who initially offered him £30,000. The new station had a very attractive main building of local stone built in a loosely Gothic-Tudor style seemingly intended to complement the venerable appearance of much of the town. This station opened on 23 June 1848.

There had been several schemes put forward, from as early as the 1820s, for main lines from London to York by a variety of different routes. Some of these were a long way to the east of Stamford. However, any line that was to run roughly parallel with the Great North Road could be expected to pass through Stamford because it was arguably the most significant town between London and York.

In April 1844, a major project was announced in *The Times*. This was for a railway from London to York, through Hitchin, Biggleswade, Huntingdon, Stamford, Grantham, Newark, Gainsborough and Doncaster. It was the prelude to titanic battles in parliament. This proposal was the embryo out of which a major section of what eventually became the East Coast Main Line was to grow and, if it was to receive parliamentary assent and go on to be completed, it would pose a deadly threat to George Hudson's growing railway empire. What followed was a no-holds-barred battle within parliament supported by ruthless manoeuvrings elsewhere. In August, an alternative alignment was proposed through Peterborough but avoiding Stamford, much to the dismay of its citizens. This was the period of the 'Railway Mania'. There were no fewer than 246 railway bills scheduled to be considered in the parliamentary session of 1845. With such a volume of work and the delaying tactics of Hudson's party, this London & York Bill was simply timed out for that session.

The company which was then called the London & York combined with the Direct Northern in 1846 to become the Great Northern Railway (GNR). It decided to put forward a realignment of its route from London to York, this time via Peterborough. To the deep concern of the townspeople of Stamford, this line was planned to pass about four miles east of the town. A branch from this line to Stamford was proposed. This was seen as a final blow to Stamford's aspirations to play a prosperous role in the railway age similar to that it had enjoyed in the coaching age. Although the GNR's engineers had made it clear that the decision on the final alignment had been taken purely on engineering grounds, such was the fraught nature of local politics in Stamford that the marquess was widely blamed for this decision. While he had indeed made a statement that he did not want this line to cross his land at any point, Edmund Denison, who became the dynamic front man for the GNR had declared unequivocally in 1844 that the main objective of the line was to shorten the distance between London and York as far as possible. He declared that the route planned from Peterborough directly to Grantham and onwards was the best and most direct available. This line received parliamentary approval on 26 June 1846 as the Great Northern Railway Act.

The marquess was one of three major local landowners who saw their interests as being affected by what was being described as the 'Towns Route' of the GNR. The others were the Earl of Lindsey of Uffington Hall and Sir John Trollope of Casewick Hall. The latter was to find the route as finally aligned literally passing along the eastern edge of his park. Lord Lindsey, a stone's throw to the south-west at Uffington Park, complained loud and long about how destructive the GNR's line would be to the amenity of his land in the area. He raised a tirade of objections before the Commons Committee and was supported by the marquess who, likewise, if not in this case quite so vehemently, made points about how his rural privacy and serenity would be damaged by the GNR.

Denison was the hugely energetic man behind the Great Northern Railway's plan to build a direct line from Peterborough through Grantham, Newark and Retford to Doncaster. The decision was taken for sound engineering and business reasons and the fact that it bypassed Stamford had little to do with any supposed opposition from the Marquess of Exeter. (Authors' collection)

The Second Marquess of Exeter was certainly a reactionary member of the landowning elite and unwilling to accept the economic, social and political changes which were taking place with increasing speed. Ironically, the day that the GNR Bill became law, the Corn Laws were repealed. It was easy to see the Corn Laws as an example of outdated aristocratic misrule and abuse of power. The marquess was opposed to repeal. In this context the autocratic behaviour of the 2nd Marquess could be construed as the act of a man desperately wanting to hold on to his family's political power. He was prepared to back a minor cross-country line which was unlikely to have a significant effect on Stamford's industries and its balance of class forces. While he was not responsible for the Great Northern missing the town, had Stamford been directly on its line, the town might well have become much more industrialised and his hold over local politics could have come under sustained challenge. The notoriety he gained as a backwoodsman made it easy for him to be cast as the villain whose intransigence condemned Stamford to economic stagnation relative to its close neighbour, Peterborough.

Stamford eventually had to be content with its railway provision consisting of an intermediate station on the meandering cross-country line of the Midland Railway from Leicester to Peterborough, a rather curious connection via Luffenham, Seaton and Market Harborough to Rugby operated by the London & North Western Railway (LNWR) and two short and somewhat inconsequential branch lines. Stamford's loss at the time was certainly Peterborough's gain. It went on to be a major railway junction with vast marshalling yards, several engine sheds and other installations providing thousands of jobs and totally changing its character as it did so. Today's citizens and the many visitors to Stamford are glad that, for whatever reason, the main line missed the town.

The 'inconsequential' branches were lines from a new station at the eastern end of Water Street. The frontage of this station was built in a style designed loosely to complement the architectural glories of Burghley House. These lines were paid for by the marquess. The first to open, on 1 November 1856, ran to Essendine where connections could be made with the fairly limited number of trains that served the station on the GNR's main line. This allowed people from Stamford to travel to London without going to Peterborough and changing stations there. The second line, probably pointless from the very beginning, was opened on 8 August 1867 initially to Wansford Bridge and then extended to Wansford where passengers could avail themselves of LNWR trains to Peterborough, Market Harborough and Rugby. It was evidence of the superfluous nature of this line that it closed to passengers as early as 1929 and to goods in 1931. It has often been said that the marquess, full of remorse for having kept Stamford off the main line to the north, built these lines to make amends to the people of the town. As we have seen, the marquess was not responsible for the decision to route the main line to the east of Stamford. Also, from what we know of him, it is hard to picture the man as one given to bouts of remorse. Possibly he saw his influence in the town continuing to leach away and built these lines as a gesture which might earn a certain amount of much-needed goodwill.

The case of Stamford has continued to attract controversy over the years, including in the railway enthusiasts' press, and it is interesting to note that the then marquess felt it necessary to put the record straight from his point of view when he wrote a letter to the Editor of the *Railway Magazine* in March 1966 in which he said:

'…the decision to build the Great Northern through Peterborough rather than Stamford was taken on engineering grounds and not because of the opposition of my ancestor.'

The imposing façade of the Water Street station in Stamford, later called Stamford East. This was the terminus of the branch lines to Essendine and Wansford that were sponsored by the Marquess of Exeter. It was designed with a nod to the architectural glories of Burghley House, the palatial residence of the marquess nearby. The arms of his family, the Cecils, are carved on the façade. The building is now a private residence. (Authors' collection)

CHAPTER SEVEN

Other opposition from landowners

'Gentlemen, I detest railroads; nothing is more distasteful to me than to hear the echo of our hills reverberating with the noise of hissing railroad engines, running through the heart of our hunting country, and destroying that noble sport to which I have been accustomed from my childhood. [This was an MP speaking in 1840].[1]

'[They] cut up our most beautiful valleys, traverse, divert, and straighten our finest streams; they swamp our meadows and render them difficult of drainage; they make high embankments over parks and pleasure grounds and impede the most beautiful views; our suburbs are unhealthy for they have interfered with the ventilation of the streets and occupied our best fields with overground stations…'[2]

This quotation encapsulates in somewhat florid form many of the reasons why some people, most evidently but not exclusively landowners, objected to the building of the railways.

'Everyone wanted a railway, but not on their doorstep. Rarely a precise art in the hands of hastily trained assistants, surveying often produced inaccurate information when done furtively at night or while the landowner's attention was distracted elsewhere. Once the route had been decided, it might have to be modified to avoid opposition, a tunnel, embankment or bridge even being built to preserve a short cut to hounds, or peace for the pheasants'.[3]

The university authorities at Oxford owned much of the land around the city and were not particularly well inclined towards railways. They saw them as disruptive of the tranquillity necessary in the world of academe and they also did not like the idea that the hallowed stone buildings of the university might be soiled by the pollutants that steam locomotives produced. Christ Church College, a major landowner among the colleges, made it quite clear that the proposal of 1837 to build a station near Magdalen Bridge was a non-starter. A later proposal to build a station near Folly Bridge was thwarted, not by the university people, but by two influential landowners. In 1842, agreement was finally reached for a station on the western fringe of Oxford, some distance from any of the university's buildings. The university was able to stipulate that it had the right for its proctors to be on the station premises to check on the comings and goings of undergraduates. As with their counterparts at Cambridge, they had a jaundiced view of the proclivities of their students. They clearly thought that many were hell-bent on heading for the fleshpots of the Metropolis, to race meetings or other debauched activities.

One unusual objector to the railway at Oxford was the warden of Wadham College. He objected, not wearing his donnish hat, but as the chairman of the Oxford Canal Company which saw its business being threatened by the opening of the railway. His protestations were in vain. Public trains operated by the GWR began to run to Oxford on 12 June 1844.

In 1865 another threat to the character of Oxford appeared when the GWR announced its desire to erect a carriage-building and repair works at Oxford on unused land which the corporation was happy to lease to them. The opening up of railway links to Oxford had destroyed the coaching trade and also reduced traffic on the river. A railway works would provide a boost for the local economy and for employment. The university authorities did not favour the scheme, hardly surprising given the proximity of the proposed site to Worcester College and the city centre. Many alumni of the university, aesthetes, people who did not like railways or the GWR in particular set up a sustained protest. *The Times* and *Punch* joined in. The GWR backed away from what could have been a very tough fight and decided instead to concentrate rolling-stock building and repair at Swindon.

Kennington, just south of Oxford, witnessed one of the most extraordinary examples of opposition to new railways. A local landowner called Towle built himself a temporary makeshift house of wood and cardboard directly on the alignment of the proposed line from Didcot. His intention as the landowner was to receive the maximum compensation paid to householders who had the misfortune to find their dwellings standing directly in the path of a proposed railway and therefore earmarked for demolition. He got compensation but not as much as he had wanted.

Strathpeffer is a tiny town about four miles west of Dingwall. It is on the River Peffery and possesses mineral springs, some sulphurous, others chalybeate, containing strong traces of iron salts. By the late eighteenth century, it had become a select spa town, gradually developing the hotels and other amenities required by its well-to-do visitors. It would have expected to be served by a station on the Dingwall and Skye Railway to Kyle of Lochalsh and indeed was on the initial proposed alignment. In the event, Sir William MacKenzie of Coul, a prominent local landowner, laid down stringent conditions for disguising the presence of the railway where it passed through his estate. If these conditions were not met, he made it clear that he would use every effort to oppose the bill in parliament. Among the conditions he demanded was an unnecessary tunnel. The company was not prepared to do this and instead made a steeply graded deviation to the north of the town, passing through Achterneed. This line was authorised in 1865 and opened as far as Strome Ferry in 1870. The same landowner was able to have written into the line's Act a requirement to prevent 'excessive' whistling by locomotives where the road and the line ran close to each other between Achterneed and Dingwall. This was because he thought that such whistling would scare his horses. In 1885, Strathpeffer became the terminus of a short Highland Railway branch from Dingwall.

The building of the West Highland Railway to Fort William was as heroic a project as any in British railway history. It was a line which was going to be expensive to build and maintain while being unlikely to generate sufficient income to cover its expenses. However, it was believed that in breaking down the remoteness of the Highlands, it would help to reduce the area's economic and social problems and it therefore had government support. The original intention was to extend beyond Fort William to terminate at Roshven but this extension was not proceeded with because local landowners felt the line would have a harmful effect on the deer forests which they claimed made a substantial contribution to the local economy. The bill for the line to Fort William from Glasgow was passed in 1889. It had to run the gauntlet of opposition from local landowners some of whose estates consisted largely of bleak, empty moor and mountain. By the time the line opened on 7 August 1894, such opposition had largely evaporated as even the most hidebound lairds could recognise that the railway was likely to have a beneficial effect on the area's economy. With a more favourable attitude towards railways, it was not long before an extension to Mallaig on the west coast was being proposed. This passed with little opposition in 1894. The line went on to help the local fishing industry and improve access to the various islands by ferries plying from Mallaig. The extreme remoteness and inaccessibility of the area had been broken down.

These three examples picked at random give a flavour of the diverse nature of the opposition thrown up by influential landowners to railway projects. In this chapter we will examine many other cases of opposition all of which shed some light on the nature of social, economic and political forces in their localities at the time when railway schemes were being proposed and implemented. The examples are grouped in loose geographical regions. The authors do not attempt to provide a comprehensive coverage across Britain but to shed light on examples of cases where the intervention of local landowners may have had a major bearing on the alignment of a railway or where they may have been able to impose conditions on the railway companies with respect to infrastructure such as tunnels and covered ways. The interactions between railway promoters, affected landowners and local people were extraordinarily varied.

In the examples mentioned below, by no means all the landowners were opposed to railways *per se* but many of them wielded sufficient local power and often influence in parliament to ensure that they could receive concessions from companies wishing to promote lines through districts where they had landholdings. These may have taken the form of financial bribes to encourage the landowners to withdraw opposition before bills went to parliament thereby allowing the promoters to avoid further legal expenses. Sometimes the promoters had to meet legal conditions to placate landowners, such as those requiring inconvenient and expensive deviations or whims of the landowners in relation to covered ways or tunnels or perhaps ornate tunnel entrances, all likely to have been unnecessary from the strictly engineering point of view

By no means were all major landowners opposed to railways even in some of the grandest locations. In 1845, for example, the sixth Duke of Devonshire responded in a friendly fashion to a plan of the Manchester, Buxton, Matlock and Midland Junction Railway to build a line across the park attached to Chatsworth House. Like some other companies with grandiose names and grandiose intentions, this scheme never saw the light of day. Perhaps the Duke had known that it never would.

Mr Cookson was a landowner who commissioned a print which was circulated to MPs expressing his objection to the proposed alignment of the railway across his estate, The Hermitage, County Durham. He was claiming residential injury because of the proposed line. We do not know how accurate this representation is but the mansion is just about visible above the proposed embankment. (Authors' collection)

For landed aristocrats, their estate symbolised their superior social position. The possession of a large estate, perhaps with a high wall around its perimeter, allowed them to live in quiet, privileged seclusion. In the eighteenth century, many great landowners had spent vast sums of money remodelling their estates incorporating the latest fashionable practices. It was possible to buy what was virtually a bespoke landscape. These estates were often called 'pleasure grounds' because the ownership of them was intended to bestow pleasure on the owner as he gazed across the demesne. By the railway age, the sometimes drastic remodelling which had taken place earlier was softening and the great stands of trees were maturing. No wonder they resented the considerable investment made by their forebears being spoiled or even destroyed by the penetration of railways into their estates. Trains would be noisy, dirty and intrusive and the railway embankments, cuttings, bridges and tunnels could not but have a harmful impact on the idyllic features and prospects which had been so carefully constructed by the landscape gardeners.

Eastern Counties

Eye is a small, ancient town in Suffolk about ten miles north-east of Stowmarket. A proposal to link Eye by rail to the Ipswich to Norwich line of the Eastern Union Railway at Mellis failed because of opposition from local landowners, the most prominent being Lord Henniker. This arbitrary action had annoyed the local people who were convinced that the railway would provide a real fillip for the town's languishing economy. For this reason, a three-mile branch line to Mellis was promoted locally. It opened on 2 April 1867. The local landowners who had prevented the original proposal had relented by this time, especially when they saw how Diss, which was regarded as something of a local rival, had benefitted economically from being served by a major railway route. While the Bill for the line was going through parliament, businesses in Eye were complaining that the high cost of transport resulting from its lack of a direct railway connection was pushing the town further into the economic doldrums. Curiously, in the debate in parliament on the Eye to Mellis branch, the local turnpike trust supported the promoters of the railway on the grounds that the line would take much of the trust's goods traffic which would then allow the trust to spend less on road repairs! The old saying to the effect that those whom the Gods wish to destroy they first drive mad, comes to mind here.

March is an old market town located in the fenland known as the Isle of Ely. Flat terrain is what the railways prefer for their sidings and marshalling yards and they do not come much flatter than the fenland surrounding this town. March became a major railway junction equipped with what some people said were the largest railway marshalling yards in Britain. They dealt primarily with extraordinary quantities of coal traffic. This arrived at March from the South Yorkshire, Derbyshire and Nottinghamshire coalfields, most of it via the Great Northern & Great Eastern Joint Line with lesser quantities along the Great Northern Railway's East Coast Main Line via Peterborough where it turned east towards March over the metals of the Great Eastern Railway. At March, the coal trains were sorted and mostly despatched to London to feed its insatiable appetite for coal for industrial and domestic purposes. The railways in the nineteenth century were very labour-intensive and offered wages which, if not overly generous, were usually better than those of agricultural labourers. This explains the vehement opposition of farmers in the March district to the development of the marshalling yards and the associated locomotive stabling and servicing facilities. They accused the railways of luring the country workers away with the prospect of better-paid jobs. This, they argued, put unfair pressure on them to increase the wages they paid their workers.

The cross-country line from Kings Lynn to Dereham was promoted in 1844 largely by people with business interests in the two respective towns. With a railway, agricultural produce from the Norfolk hinterland could be more easily conveyed to the harbour at Lynn while coal and fertilisers, for example, could be conveyed from the harbour to the various communities along the projected line. The parliamentary passage of the Bill for the line was not all plain sailing, however. Samuel Tyson of Narborough Hall and various other local landowners opposed the Bill in parliament arguing that the claims put forward by the promoters for the levels of potential traffic were gross overestimates and that the line would not really serve any useful purpose. What therefore would be the point of a line that would disrupt their estates and the lives of the various communities along the route for no real gain? Some of these objections were being made by men who were shareholders in the Nar Navigation Company along which small vessels travelled from Lynn into the heart of the Norfolk countryside. The Navigation was very shallow, however and this severely limited the size of the vessels that could be used. These objections were set aside and the Bill received parliamentary approval on 21 July 1845, opening throughout on 11 September 1848.

The Midlands

The Grand Junction Railway was an early project to link the north-west with Birmingham. This was a long-distance line which opened in 1837 but not before it had encountered considerable opposition. It is ironic that a major opponent was James Watt, son of the better-known James Watt who was a pioneer in utilising the expansive power of steam. Watt Senior had grown rich and had left money to his son who made extensive investments in canals. This made him an implacable opponent of the Grand Junction. The company wisely decided to make deviations at the Birmingham end of the line designed to reduce the impact of any objections he might raise.

The then Duke of Buckingham threw his considerable influence against an early proposal that the main line of the London &

Birmingham Railway should pass through the town of Buckingham. The consequence is that Buckingham remained a small town somewhat off the beaten track. It joined the railway network on 1 May 1850, when a branch line was opened connecting Bletchley to Banbury via Buckingham and Brackley This line, or at least the section of it from Verney Junction, was promoted by Sir Harry Verney of Claydon House. Also supportive of this line was the Marquis of Chandos. The line passed near his family's home at Stowe. This line which was part of the London & North Western Railway's operations never 'grew up'. The Marquis later became Duke of Buckingham and Chairman of the London & North Western Railway. Although the line through Buckingham was a railway backwater, the station at Buckingham displayed some architectural grandeur which may well have been out of deference to the duke.

The line from Bedford to Bletchley was opened on 17 November 1846 and was operated by the London & Birmingham. On this line, four stations serving wayside communities at Fenny Stratford, Woburn Sands, Ridgmont and Millbrook were built in a very quirky, half-timbered, *cottage-orné* style. The line passes through land owned by the Duke of Bedford whose seat is Woburn Abbey and these stations were built in this style to meet the wishes of the duke who had shares in the Bedford and Bletchley Company. Clearly he was not opposed to this railway but able to assert his wishes as regards these stations.

The Duke of Rutland, one of whose domiciles is Belvoir Castle in the lovely Vale of Belvoir in Leicestershire, was an extremely powerful figure who acted almost as a potentate in those parts of the country where he had landholdings. He had 33,000 acres around Belvoir. His initial response to proposals for railways in the area was distinctly frosty. When the duke said 'no', he meant 'no'. However, when he learned that this land contained large deposits of iron ore, he underwent a miraculous conversion. A man who by accident of birth was immensely rich was about to become much richer through no effort on his part.

There was a station down in the Vale at Bottesford, north of Belvoir Castle. This was on the east to west line from Grantham to Nottingham originally promoted by one of those small companies with a grandiose name – the Ambergate, Nottingham & Boston & Eastern Junction Railway. This line opened on 15 July 1850, although only from Grantham as far as Nottingham. The Ambergate

Company was subsequently subsumed into the Great Northern Railway (GNR). The district did not at this time appear to offer great potential traffic and it was 30 June 1879 before the Great Northern Railway opened a line from Newark to Melton Mowbray. This eventually extended in a generally southerly direction through remote, hilly country past Melton to Welham Junction near Market Harborough. Much of this and associated lines became known as the Great Northern and London & North Western Joint Railway (GN&LNW Joint) and it went on to carry heavy traffic, particularly coal from the Nottinghamshire and Derbyshire mining districts destined for London.

In the late 1860s, these extensive iron ore deposits were discovered in the Leicestershire Wolds and across the border into Lincolnshire. Initially the duke contacted the Great Northern Railway. He informed them that his objections to the railway had been removed when he realised that it would be beneficial to the district. The duke's well-known concerns about the beauty and serenity of the Vale being desecrated by steam trains had vanished in a trice. Now railways were being presented as something that would bring prosperity to the Vale. Certainly jobs would be created if the ore was quarried but whatever prosperity might follow for the local population was nothing to the added prosperity likely to come his way. He must have been rather surprised when the initial approach to the GNR met with a largely indifferent response. Rather grudgingly, the GNR said that a meeting could be arranged if necessary. The duke was unused to rebuffs but he received another when his approach to the Midland Railway (MR) also met with a lukewarm response. Eventually, both the Great Northern and the Midland Railway opened lines into this area and the ore was delivered to the main line companies through an extensive network of narrow and standard gauge mineral lines. Much of this ore passed along the GN&LNW Joint on its way to the distant ironworks and blast furnaces.

The wayside stations of the GN&LNW Joint served small villages and were simple but adequate for their purpose. One station, however, stood out from all the others. This was Redmile. Belvoir Castle on its hill dominated the Vale and emphasised the duke's semi-feudal influence in the district. Redmile Station was physical evidence of the extent to which the new order in the shape of the railways was prepared to defer to the old order in terms of the duke – and this was as late as the 1870s! Redmile was the station that the duke normally used for his own travel and which tended to be used by distinguished visitors with business at the castle or guests at the sumptuous social events that were staged up on the hill. The building on the up line platform had a generous seven-bay glazed canopy and a *porte cochère* to greet and shelter such travellers as they arrived at or left the Vale. The private waiting room on the same platform was dominated by an outsized fireplace topped by a hunting scene, for this, of course, was classic fox-hunting country. There was even a luxuriously appointed gentleman's private urinal. A pole displayed a flag when especially important guests were expected. The station closed in 1953 and was later demolished.

Further confirmation of the hold that fox-hunting and its adherents maintained in this district was the renaming in 1883 of a wayside station further south as 'John O'Gaunt'. This was the name of a local fox covert. The station's previous name was Burrow and Twyford, referring to two nearby villages. The new name was virtually meaningless to travellers unfamiliar with the district. The Act authorising the line had stipulated the height of certain fences so as to ensure the unimpeded progress of the chase.

When the GNR was promoting its line from Marefield Junction, on the GN&LNW Joint, to Leicester, it ran into strong opposition at Scraptoft. Objections raised by landowners with fox-hunting interests led to the rejection by parliament of the proposal for this section. There were howls of indignation from people in Leicester. Edmund Dennison, Chairman of the Great Northern Railway, addressed a meeting in Leicester at which he dismissed objections as simply being ridiculous.

He argued that the opposition to the alignment at Scraptoft was not just concerned with issues of severance and residential injury but because the Quorn Hunt saw the proposed railway as a threat to its activities. He added, somewhat bitterly, that while the objections of the fox-hunting lobby had cut little ice when the Bill was going through the Commons, it had met with a more sympathetic reception in the Lords, hence its rejection. A new realignment was proposed and a revised Bill was passed allowing the GNR to enter Leicester and run trains into the imposing but underused Belgrave Road Station.

Continuing the ducal theme, we move north to where there was a positive plethora of dukes in the district rightly known as the 'Dukeries'. In the nineteenth century, this area of North Nottinghamshire had few sizeable towns, the largest being

Worksop, extensive accessible coal reserves and an extraordinary concentration of large mansions in landscaped estates. As such, it typified the interface between the old and the new. Railway promoters eyed the district with greed, keen to build lines to tap the coal reserves and carry away the 'black gold'. Aristocratic grandees were speared on the horns of a dilemma. If their landholdings contained workable coal measures, they could expect a very generous boost to their income. However, if they exploited the coal and let in the railways, the treasured seclusion of their estates was seriously threatened. In the event, some of the landowners simply took a pragmatic view, eager to enjoy the increased income from their mineral rights. Some had estates elsewhere to which they could retreat if they wanted peace and quiet. The most extraordinary of the landowners with whom the railway companies in this area had dealings was undoubtedly the fifth Duke of Portland whose estate was Welbeck Abbey. Rejoicing in the name of William John Cavendish Scott Bentinck, he was not an enemy of railways as such and in fact he used them when he wanted to go up to London, which was quite frequently. His mode of travel was eccentric. His estate contained a number of lengthy underground tunnels. He would enter his horse-drawn carriage with the blinds firmly tied down and be driven along a tunnel over a mile long from his residence to the Worksop Road. The carriage would arrive at Worksop Station and be loaded onto a flat wagon attached to a train destined for London, the duke remaining in the carriage for the whole journey. At King's Cross his carriage would be unloaded and then he was driven to his London town house in Cavendish Square. At no time during the journey were the blinds raised and even when he reached his London residence, alighted from the coach and entered the building, great care was taken to hide him away from prying eyes.

There was much about the duke, his interaction with other people and his lifestyle which put him in the first league of great British eccentrics. He was not just an oddball, however, and he displayed an admirably protective attitude towards beauty spots on or close to his Welbeck Estate. He was particularly concerned to keep railways at some distance from Cresswell Crags, the impressive limestone rocks partly in Nottinghamshire and partly in Derbyshire. These contain caves where many artefacts relating to prehistoric man have been found. He was also anxious to preserve some very fine stands of trees close by. He believed that smoke from the locomotives would have a harmful effect on the ancient oaks. The duke refused entry to his land for surveyors from the Manchester, Sheffield & Lincolnshire Railway (MS&LR) and had his estate workers maintain an armed guard around the clock. The Mansfield to Worksop project with which they were involved was withdrawn but a Midland Railway project for a line between the same two towns went ahead in 1861 with the duke's blessing. The MS&LR won running powers over this line.

At Worksop, the MS&LR did its best to insinuate itself particularly with the Duke of Portland and the Duke of Newcastle, whose mansion at Clumber was just four miles away. The station was on a scale considerably grander than might have been expected for a town of Worksop's size. We can only hope that the dukes were favourably impressed by the company's efforts to flatter them.

One of the greatest losses during the period of severe retrenchment of the railway system from the 1960s to the 1980s was the line from Derby to Manchester Central. This line, at least between Ambergate and Chinley, passed through beautiful limestone scenery which constituted difficult terrain for railway builders. It opened for passengers on 4 June 1849 and was built by the Manchester, Buxton, Matlock and Midland Junction Railway (MBM&MJR), a company which was assimilated into the Midland Railway. The district contained some big landowners and the MBM&MJR made considerable efforts to propitiate them. 'Old money' was represented by the Duke of Rutland at Haddon Hall and the Duke of Devonshire at Chatsworth House. The original intention had been to use the Derwent Valley but the Duke of Devonshire ruled that he was not going to allow trains to besmirch his estate at Chatsworth. Instead, the more difficult valley of the River Wye had to be traversed as the line made its way northwards. There was ducal intervention even with this less suitable alignment. The Duke of Rutland made it clear when he grudgingly agreed to sell land to the railway that he did not want to be able to see it from his Haddon Hall estate. So the promoter, by now the Midland Railway, was forced to extend what would have been a very short tunnel into a covered way, over 1,000 yards long.

Out of deference to the dukes, the stations at Bakewell, Hassop, Rowsley and Matlock were unusually well-appointed. Bakewell and Hassop had roundels displaying the arms of the aristocratic families. Rowsley and Matlock had the distinction of being designed by Joseph Paxton, originally the Duke of Devonshire's gardener, who went on to fame and fortune with many ventures including a large role in designing the Crystal Palace in which the very successful Great Exhibition of 1851 was held in Hyde Park. Rowsley was the station used by the Duke of Devonshire and it boasted a 'Gentleman's Room First Class'. Hassop and Rowsley were considerably bigger stations than might have been expected given the size of the communities they served. It perhaps says something about 'old money' that these stations had a restrained and dignified style suggestive of the confidence of the old-established aristocratic dynasties in their nearby mansions. Cromford Station, close to Willersley Castle which belonged to the 'new rich' Arkwrights, on the other hand, is very different. When the railway was opened in 1849, somewhat far-fetched comparisons were being made about the scenery thereabouts resembling the Alps. This may be the reason behind the architecture of the building on the up platform and the station master's house close by. These had a unique character and appearance, generally supposed to represent French influence, and were almost certainly designed and built out of deference to the Arkwrights who exercised an influence around Cromford not dissimilar to that of the ducal figures we have talked about.

The Earl of Lichfield had his estate at Shugborough Hall in Staffordshire. He was paid a considerable five-figure sum by the Trent Valley Railway who wished to take its line across part of the estate. He was given this money on account of what he described as the 'ruination' that would be inflicted by the railway. He also managed to get the company to build him a cut-and-cover tunnel, unnecessary for engineering purposes, so that the vistas from the hall would not be spoiled by the sight of trains crossing the estate. If that was not enough, the company was 'persuaded' to adorn the western end of this tunnel with various bizarre ornamental motifs including a Norman arch, turrets, mock battlements and machicolation. This artifice fitted in well with a clutch of eighteenth-century follies scattered around the estate which included a Chinese House, a Doric Temple, a Triumphal Arch, a Lantern of Demosthenes and a Temple of the Winds. The tunnel mouth must have felt quite at home in the middle of this lot. The line through the estate is now part of the West Coast Main Line.

Not far away at Trentham, the Duke of Sutherland managed to get the North Staffordshire Railway to build a wayside station in an Italianate style. This was designed by none other than Sir Charles Barry who had much to do with work on the new Houses

Shugborough Tunnel on the West Coast Main Line just south-east of Stafford showing the castellated entrance which was required by the Anson Family as part of the deal for allowing the railway to pass through their estate. (Authors' collection)

of Parliament built to replace those that had burned down in 1834. This station had a suite of private rooms specially furnished and decorated for the duke and his retinue when, twice yearly, he left Trentham to travel to his estate at Dunrobin in the north of Scotland.

Bourne is a small town in Lincolnshire, north of Peterborough. Although it had what, by the standards of the time, were reasonable communications by road and water, by 1850 it was isolated from the railway system and the local citizens feared for its future economic viability unless it could be joined to the railway map. The first line to be mooted was a short link to the Great Northern Railway's station which had opened in 1852 as part of the route from London and Peterborough to Doncaster and York. The original plan was to allow through running from Bourne to Stamford by approaching Essendine from the north-east. This plan was thwarted by the awkwardness of the vicar of neighbouring Carlby, through whose land the branch from Bourne was proposed to pass. He objected to the initial alignment because a plantation of yews of which he was very fond would be partly destroyed by the path of the railway. Nothing deterred him from his opposition and so a deviation was carried out which meant that trains from Bourne approached Essendine from the south-east and through running to and from Stamford would have required a reversal. The Bourne to Essendine line opened in May 1860. Bourne eventually went on to be the centre of a small network of lines converging on the town from all four points of the compass.

North East of England

It was with the initial proposals for the Stockton & Darlington Railway (S&D) that the process emerged whereby self-interested people with power and influence raised objections, sometimes of an extremely flimsy nature, to railway schemes in order to obtain generous financial compensation for the intrusion on their land and the nuisance they claimed that this caused. Lord Eldon was an early and vehement objector to the S&D on the grounds that the railway would threaten the income he obtained from wayleave payments from pit-owners who needed to transport their coal across his land. He also regarded the legal instrument of compulsory purchase as an unwarranted intrusion on his seigneurial rights. Another objector was the Earl of Darlington, soon to be Duke of Cleveland, who was concerned that the railway would spoil or even destroy the simple pleasures he derived from fox-hunting. The initial bill for the S&D failed and this forced the company to draft another bill involving a proposed route which would not interfere with the robust rustic pursuits enjoyed by the earl. It was this which caused Christian Wolmar (2007) to comment that the Industrial Revolution may well have been in full swing, but society still had its feudal elements who were able to have a lasting impact on the development of the railways.

George Stephenson was the engineer of the Newcastle & Berwick Railway which submitted a bill for parliamentary sanction on 1 March 1839. The scheme quickly ran into strong opposition from the former Whig Prime Minister, Earl Grey, whose estate was at Howick Hall, north of Alnmouth. The original alignment took the railway half-a-mile east of Howick Hall. This involved the railway crossing the 'Long Walk' which was the earl's private carriageway down to the coast. The earl complained bitterly about this and about the intrusion of the railway onto his 'pleasure grounds'. These sounded like horse trots or game coverts but turned out to be areas of arable land worked by the earl's tenants. Stephenson was not a man to be overawed by the earl and he was particularly nettled when the earl told him that the best route for the railway would be to the west of Howick Park. This would have involved a more expensive alignment. Grey then came up with an extraordinary proposal for the 'Northumberland Railway' which was to be a line powered on the atmospheric principle, then unproven and controversial. He gained some support among MPs and proposed to engage Isambard Kingdom Brunel but his plan met with much ridicule. This madcap scheme went as far as parliament, where it was rejected. The Newcastle & Berwick was one of the many irons in George Hudson's fire. He was in his pomp at this time. His intention was for it to make an end-on junction with the Berwick & Edinburgh Railway at Berwick thus completing a link, albeit a tortuous one, from London to Edinburgh by means of lines he controlled. Since this particular project was of crucial importance to him, he was prepared to alter the route and subsequently the Newcastle & Berwick gained the Royal Assent on 31 July 1845.

A little further south, the citizens of Alnwick wanted the main line to pass through their town, fearing economic stagnation if it was left isolated. The Duke of Northumberland whose Percy family dominated the town argued, probably correctly, that to take the main line through Alnwick itself would involve many engineering difficulties. He therefore refused to support the proposed alignment through Alnwick. Neither did they initially support the idea of a branch from the main line near Alnmouth and suggested that the road between the town and the main line station should be improved. The Newcastle & Berwick, however, made the branch to Alnwick, from the main line about three miles away, and it opened on 18 August 1850.

A very vocal opponent of schemes to build a railway to Scarborough was George Knowles who, in 1840, published a pamphlet in which he said:

'Scarborough has no wish for a greater influx of vagrants and those who have no money to spend. Scarborough is rising daily in the estimation of the public as a fashionable watering place, on account of its natural beauty and tranquillity, and in a few years' time, the novelty of not having a railroad will be its greatest recommendation.'[4]

Another opponent of proposals to serve Scarborough with railways was Earl Fitzwilliam who on 16 March 1844 presented a petition to the House of Lords signed by numerous citizens of Scarborough objecting to the proposed line from York. Despite this opposition, parliamentary approval was gained on 4 July 1844 and the line opened on 7 July 1845 to the accompaniment of considerable jollification in the town. Soon it was on its way to becoming a popular seaside resort.

In 1844, George Hudson was planning a line from York to Bridlington. This would have passed near Boynton and close to the estate of the influential Sir George Strickland. In high dudgeon he wrote to Hudson that the railway line:

> '...would be totally destructive of that place which had been the residence of my ancestors and family for five hundred years. I should, therefore, feel it to be my duty to my family and to myself to make every exertion in my power, and to spend all the money I could afford, in opposition to a plan so injurious to myself and, I believe, uncalled for by the general public.'[5]

This neatly captures the sense of outrage against the railways felt by a member of the gentry with an extended pedigree and the way that it was perfectly natural for such people to conflate their interests with those of the wider public.

Lord Hotham was adamantly opposed to a proposal to extend the York to Market Weighton line of the York & North Midland Railway beyond the latter town as far as Beverley. It took an extraordinary seventeen years for the railway company, by then the North Eastern Railway, to negotiate a deal with Hotham and even then it only got the go-ahead after agreeing to build a station at Kipling Cotes largely to serve his estate. It also had to agree not to run trains on Sundays. The extension to Beverley opened in May 1865.

The Duke of Cleveland played a crafty role in relation to the proposed Northern Counties Railway. He was actually opposed to this project but he publicly gave his assent after having obtained a sum of £35,000 over and above the actual value of the land he sold to the company. He did this in the full knowledge that such a figure, while benefitting himself enormously, would probably bankrupt the company before construction work even started. It did exactly this and one consequence was a delay of ten years before a railway reached Barnard Castle, County Durham.

North West England

As early as 1824, proposals had been made for a railway from Birmingham to the Merseyside area. These proposals came to nothing but on 6 May 1833, the Grand Junction Railway received parliamentary authorisation. The promoters of this line were scrupulous in avoiding most of the major towns along the proposed route. This was because previous proposals had foundered on sustained opposition from landowners along the original alignments and from canal operators. To avoid a repetition of this, the line kept away from canals and those towns where land for stations and other installations might prove expensive. Instead, the company, where possible, bought land which was marginal and therefore probably cheap and less likely to provoke stout opposition and demands for compensation. This helps to explain how Crewe developed later into the hub of the mighty London & North Western Railway. Before the mid-1830s, there was no such place as 'Crewe'. The Grand Junction Railway bought cheap land in the south of Cheshire with a small, scattered settlement known as Monks Coppenhall. The Grand Junction opened a station in 1837 and purchased additional land on which to build workshops, planning to transfer these from Edge Hill in Liverpool where additional space was limited. Another factor for the location of Crewe was that one projected alignment would have taken the line near to Sandbach where the Marquis of Stafford made clear his opposition. The rest is history, as they say. The railway promoters could not wholly avoid the local landed interest. Lord Crewe of Crewe Hall insisted that the North Staffordshire Railway planted an extremely long line of poplars on the north side of the Kidsgrove to Crewe line so that they would eventually obscure the sight of the trains.

The terrain between Bolton and Blackburn is hilly moorland. Both towns had emerged in the first part of the nineteenth century as major cotton manufacturing centres but the existing roads of the area made transportation slow, difficult and expensive. This was seen as holding back the development of the cotton industry. A railway line between the two towns could connect at Bolton with the line to Manchester opened on 29 May 1838. This would give much-needed easy access to 'Cottonopolis' – Manchester, the commercial centre of the cotton industry. A Provisional Committee was set up consisting largely of local businessmen who believed their interests could be advanced by the building of this railway. Directors were elected, one of whom was James Kay. He was a wealthy cotton spinner who, with his directorship, was clearly well-disposed to the railway. He had bought an estate at Turton, about four miles north of Bolton, adding a mock half-timbered wing to the existing residence known as Turton Tower. His purchase of an estate showed that he had made something of a transformation from a horny-handed industrial boss to, if not quite, a member of the landed gentry. He proceeded to act like one. He insisted that no station was to be built within 300 yards of his residence. He also demanded and got a turreted and castellated bridge carrying an access road to the estate across the railway. It was rumoured locally that he would climb up to the tower and spend a little time watching trains. This was 'trainspotting' in style! The line was built by the ponderously named Bolton, Blackburn, Clitheroe & West Yorkshire Railway and it opened on 12 June 1848. It later became part of the Lancashire & Yorkshire Railway.

A short distance north of Blackburn on the line built by the Lancashire & Yorkshire Railway from that town to Hellifield, a covered way was built near Gisburn so that the owner of Gisburn Park, Lord Ribblesdale, did not have his life blighted by having to gaze at trains as they passed through his estate. The terms of agreement reached between the company and Lord Ribblesdale also required the portals of the covered way to be adorned with a castellated parapet and with turrets. The line from Blackburn to Hellifield opened throughout on 1 June 1880.

A covered way was also required by the Earl of Wilton where the Manchester to Bury via Prestwich line of the Lancashire & Yorkshire Railway passed through his estate at Heaton Park in Manchester's 'Northern Heights'. The intention had been to take the line through a cutting but when the earl threatened legal action unless a stretch of line was placed in a covered way, the L&Y acquiesced. The company faced a bill £8,000 more than if a cutting had been used but they had been advised that if they had challenged this figure in the courts and lost, they might end up having to pay £20,000. The earl had no particular objection to railways but he did not want to see their smoke. The ground above the covered way was then landscaped in order to look natural. The line opened on 1 December 1879.

Silloth, in the extreme north-west of what is now the county of Cumbria, was the product of industrialists in Carlisle wanting a seaport of their own. In 1852, the Carlisle and Silloth Bay Dock & Railway Company was established to build a railway to, and a dock at, a location which consisted of little more than a few isolated farms and some humble rustic dwellings. Carlisle was a developing industrial centre and local businessmen were very much in favour of a deep water port which, with the railway, could provide facilities for cheap transport that could not be matched by the existing Carlisle Canal. At this time, Carlisle had cotton and biscuit-making industries in particular and they saw these associated developments as likely to give the economy of Carlisle a welcome boost. In the city itself, supporters of the Conservatives generally belittled the proposed dock and railway as a crazy scheme whereas those of a Liberal persuasion were mostly enthusiastic supporters. Powerful opposition to the Silloth scheme was raised by Lord Lonsdale, a major landowner with investments in the docks at Whitehaven down the coast. While self-interest was a major consideration, he did have a point when emphasising the extremely difficult navigational conditions in Silloth Bay. The subsequent development of Silloth owed everything to the coming of the railway and the circumventing of objections.

On occasions, even minor landowners were able to have their own conditions imposed on railway companies through the parliamentary process. For example, the owners of the Dallam Tower Estate were accommodated in the Act of 1867 authorising the Arnside to Hincaster Branch of the Furness Railway. To satisfy their wish to minimise obstruction to the view from their estate, the company was forced to build part of the line on arches, adding unwelcome and, from the engineering point of view, needless expense to the project.

In 1868, a short branch line was opened from New Mills to the small textile manufacturing town of Hayfield in Derbyshire. In 1869, ownership of this line was vested jointly in the Manchester, Sheffield & Lincolnshire Railway and the Midland Railway. Hayfield is in delightful surroundings on the edge of the Peak District. This line had been opposed by various local landowners largely on the grounds that it would transport the 'unwashed masses' of Manchester to the area, bent on drinking and other depravities. Their presence would pollute the area's rustic delights, causing crime and other antisocial behaviour and disturbing their rural serenity. Ironically, these predictions were to become at least partly true many decades later. At weekends and on Sundays in particular, large numbers of mainly working-class people used the trains to travel from Manchester to Hayfield. They were not rowdy, loutish or even unwashed. They descended on Hayfield to go rambling in the clean, healthy surroundings of the Peak District, making the

ιy from the tyranny of
surroundings. A major
f the choicest locations
vated land guarded by
ined to prevent public
unproductive, rough,
as for rearing grouse
ιought it was wrong
ιassed and frequently
ironic that landowners
line to Hayfield being
uncouth Mancunians
cendants had watched
trains and took to the
ιersuade what by then
ι withdraw its Sunday
ntains Act reached the
this private members'
who both argued that
ιng land. If passed, it
have the right to enjoy
heard before!

ct to railways crossing
s opposed to railways
railways were fine so

ι landowner who was
already involved with railways in an official capacity to demand that a company of which he was chairman should build its line so that it was not visible from his country residence. This was Lord Kinnaird, who chaired the Dundee & Perth Railway. His mansion was Rossie Priory, near Inchture. When the line opened in May 1847, the station called Inchture was well over a mile and a half from the village it purported to serve and this meant that his requirement of not being able to see the railway was met. These were the days when people were much tougher and thought nothing of walking distances on an everyday basis which most of their descendents today would

Freepost Plus RTKE-RGRJ-KTTX
Pen & Sword Books Ltd
47 Church Street
BARNSLEY
S70 2AS

go weak at the knees even contemplating. The villagers, however, felt somewhat slighted and pressurised the directors of the Dundee & Perth to build a branch to the village itself. They must have had some clout, because a light tramway opened to traffic on 1 February 1848. It was operated by a horse-drawn tramcar which was known locally as the 'Inchture Bus'. It seems to have ceased operating early in 1917, probably a victim of wartime conditions.

The Great North of Scotland Railway (GNSR) opened its Deeside Branch as far as Banchory on 7 September 1853. A private halt was built at Crathes for the Burnetts of Leys family, owners since the fourteenth century of nearby Crathes Castle, a masterpiece of the Scottish baronial style. The private halt was replaced in 1863 by a public station. Not many trains were timetabled to call at Crathes but the Burnetts were granted the seigneurial right to stop any train to suit their personal convenience. The extension beyond Banchory towards Aboyne took an alignment away from the Dee Valley into hilly and more difficult terrain around Torphins and Lumphanan. The public explanation given for what seems to be a pointless deviation was that this route was cheaper. The consensus seems to have been that the hostility of a landowner at Kincardine O'Neil, close to the River Dee, was the real reason for the alignment ultimately followed.

It is interesting to note that Queen Victoria made clear her opposition to a railway being built anywhere closer to Balmoral than Ballater. An extension to Braemar had been seriously considered albeit with doubts about its financial viability but with the queen registering her disapproval, there was little incentive to proceed with the extension. Her subjects may have contributed through their taxes to the cost of the building and maintenance of Balmoral but the queen did not want its tranquillity spoiled by visitors who might use a railway to access the area.

In 1865, the GNSR opened a line from Aberdeen and Dyce throughout to Fraserburgh. Various titled landowners were in a position to impose certain terms on the GNSR. Lord Saltoun insisted that the company built a station for his private use on land he owned at Philorth. When the later Fraserburgh to St Combs light railway was built in 1903, he insisted that the station at Inverallochy be named 'Cairnbulg' because it was close to the mansion of that name that he owned. Admittedly he had donated the land on which the station was situated. Other landowners were able to use their influence to dictate the alignment of the line from Dyce which meant that the GNSR was unable to serve a number of small settlements along the route.

Forfar was the meeting place of a network of lines built and operated by the Caledonian Railway. East of Forfar on the lines that went to Montrose and Arbroath was Guthrie. Here the line passed through land owned by a Mr Guthrie. He was a somewhat prickly character. He did not want to see or hear trains. After prolonged and not always cordial negotiations, during which various deviations and even a tunnel or covered way had been discussed, he partially relented and permitted the railway to follow its initially proposed alignment. To this day the 'Guthrie Arch' or 'Guthrie Gate' stands as a memorial to the influence landowners could exert. It is a castellated gateway built in a Tudor style giving access to the castle from the south with the railway, long since closed, running across the top of this 'folly'.

The Earl of Seafield of Cullen House objected to the proposal of the Great North of Scotland Railway to build a line along the Moray coast through Cullen. He argued most vehemently that such a railway would damage the quality of his life. This opposition may have had something to do with the earl's connections with the Highland Railway with which the GNSR had relations that were distinctly frosty. Whatever the truth, the earl had influence. To the chagrin of the GNSR, it was forced to make an expensive deviation away from its preferred alignment so as to avoid crossing the earl's estate. Heavy earthworks and substantial viaducts were the price the GNSR had to pay for propitiating the earl.

In the nineteenth century, Helensburgh was developing as a highly desirable residential location for people who made their money in Glasgow but could afford to commute to and from this town, well away from Glasgow's grime. The town gained its railway connection in the form of the Glasgow, Dumbarton and Helensburgh Railway in 1858. Helensburgh was also a popular resort for Glaswegians who took steamers down the Clyde, 'Doon the Watter' as they said in those parts. In the town, the pier and the railway station were some distance apart and the railway company which in 1865 became the North British, wanted to make a connecting line from pier to railway station. People in the town may not have been landowners on a ducal scale but, united against this development, they had enough collective strength to ensure that it never happened. The North British was forced to accept the inevitable and it decided to build a new station and pier at

Craigendoran, about a mile east of the town. Helensburgh retained its exclusive character.

Waverley Station in Edinburgh has an admirably central site albeit a low one because it is located where the Nor' Loch, a kind of open sewer, once stood. Its convenience is somewhat qualified by the fact that pedestrians have to climb out of it and the Waverley Steps up to Princes Street are widely regarded as the windiest place in Edinburgh. There were many citizens of Edinburgh who were extremely unhappy about the western approach to Waverley being built through Princes Street Gardens. One of the loudest critics was Lord Cockburn, an early conservationist who, in 1849, published a pamphlet titled *The Best Ways of Ruining the Beauties of Edinburgh*. The impact of this diatribe may have been reduced by the fact that it was published three years after the Edinburgh & Glasgow Railway had made its way through the gardens.

A train threading Princes Street Gardens as it heads eastwards towards Waverley Station. This was a sensitive location and there were protests about the intrusion of the railway before the line opened in 1842. There were further protests when the number of tracks was increased later. Most people would probably agree today that the railway is an object of interest at this point and many generations have enjoyed using the bridges across the tracks as a grandstand from which to watch the constant comings and goings at the west end of the Waverley Station. (Authors' collection)

In the first half of the nineteenth century, about twenty-five per cent of Scotland was owned by just twelve people. Fifty per cent of Scotland was owned by around seventy. The advantage of this extraordinary situation was that railway promoters generally had to negotiate with far fewer landowners than elsewhere in Britain. Some of these landowners were formidable, however. The Duke of Athol, for example, used his power to prevent the passage of the Perth & Dunkeld Railway Bill in 1837. The Duke of Buccleuch put up determined resistance to schemes to link Edinburgh and Glasgow with Carlisle. The Fifth Duke of Buccleuch in 1837 successfully opposed the projected Carlisle to Glasgow line that would have passed near his seat at Drumlanrig Castle. Another proposal was made in 1846 and this time it was successful but the price was a tunnel at Drumlanrig which would screen the railway from the castle. The same duke's opposition considerably delayed the building of a line from Carlisle to Edinburgh via Hawick. He was not wholly opposed to railways, however, supporting the Edinburgh & Dalkeith Railway which provided a rail link to his collieries in the district.

Southern England

The line between Horsham and Guildford was originally envisaged as being part of a major route from the Midlands to the south coast. It was promoted by the Horsham & Guildford Direct Railway along an alignment which was beautiful but deeply rural, offering little prospect of significant intermediate traffic. Other developments intervened and the line lost its possibility of becoming an important through line. It was therefore relegated to the role of a country branch line and was operated by the London, Brighton & South Coast Railway (LBSCR). There were a number of stations along the route, serving small communities, none of them much smaller than that served by the station named 'Baynards'. This was built at the request of the Reverend Thurlow of nearby Baynards House who sold land cheaply to the company in return for them building him a station. It was not a private station but that mattered little given the paucity of local residents. Not only did he in effect have his own station but he was granted the right to have a flat wagon carrying his coach attached to any train travelling along this route.

In 1857, the LBSCR obtained parliamentary sanction for what came to be known as the Mid-Sussex Line. The company enjoyed the blessing of the highly influential Duke of Norfolk of Arundel

Castle but ran up against a Colonel Wyndham who was insistent that he did not want a railway close to his house at Billingshurst. Consequently, the station was rather inconveniently situated for the town centre.

The LBSCR built a line from Midhurst to Chichester which opened on 11 July 1881. It was single track and ran through very scenic but sparsely populated countryside. The three intermediate stations, Lavant, Singleton and Cocking were built on an extraordinarily lavish scale given the limited population of the communities they purported to serve. The explanation probably lies with the presence nearby of Goodwood House, the home of the Dukes of Richmond since 1720. Providing such generous stations was a way of saying to rich landowners that the railway valued their presence and custom. Large country houses of this sort generated considerable traffic for the railways. They needed coal, foodstuffs, horses, fertilisers and a whole range of other supplies while the estates in turn generated business for the railway, despatching agricultural produce. They also brought prestigious passengers. Balls, shooting parties and other events were part of the annual social round and before the 1920s, the bulk of guests and others taking part would use the railway. This particular line lost its regular passenger services as early as 1935, little everyday passenger traffic ever having been generated. Some freight and aggregates traffic lingered on for decades.

On 9 July 1855, the LBSCR opened a branch line, seven miles long, from Three Bridges on its London to Brighton main line, to the old country town of East Grinstead. The promotion and building of this line had not been without controversy. A Mr Wilson had raised vehement objections to the alignment of this route between Rowfant and Grange Road. Wilson appears to have been an inveterate hater of railways and his objection in this case was that the railway would ruin his estate. He peremptorily demanded a diversion of the proposed alignment to the north of his land, this requiring the building of a short tunnel. The House of Commons committee considering the Bill rejected these objections but Wilson brushed aside this rebuff and decided to take the case to arbitration, a process that could be expensive. The company was irked because it saw Wilson's move as likely to cause itself further additional and unnecessary expense. A settlement was brokered but even then Wilson was not satisfied and he demanded the figure of £5,000 for about five acres of his land. The Board of Trade valued this land at £1,400 and Wilson did not get his £5,000.

Sir Charles Pepys, later Lord Cottenham, owned land around Kingston-on-Thames and refused to allow the proposed railway from London to Southampton to cross this land. The burghers of the town seem to have concurred with this opposition. Vested interests such as local barge owners, brewers and maltsters, coach proprietors and innkeepers felt threatened by the prospect of a railway. They were soon to regret the decision which resulted in this ancient town, the second largest in Surrey at the time, being somewhat out on a limb as far as railways were concerned. Brunel had at an early stage planned to take the line of the London to Bristol Railway through Kingston but did not proceed with this project, the line eventually passing a few miles to the north through Ealing and Southall. The intransigence of one man, in this case Pepys, was to the detriment of Kingston but served to benefit Wimbledon. At the time, this was a far less significant settlement than Kingston with a population of barely 2,000 when trains began in May 1838. At first, population growth was slow but in the late Victorian decades it was rapid and the population reached 41,000 by 1901 by which time it had become a favoured residential district. This was despite the fact that the London & South Western Railway, successor to the London & Southampton, did not provide the people of Wimbledon with a particularly good service. Their interest was largely in the longer-distance traffic. This probably explains why people in Wimbledon were pleased to welcome the District Railway which opened up a line from central London via Putney in 1889.

Opposition from Lord Cottenham and the town elders of Kingston caused the London & Southampton Railway to realign its route to pass through a corner of Cottenham's estate near what is now Raynes Park and to avoid Kingston altogether. The company (later the London & South Western Railway) had received the Royal Assent for its line on 25 July 1834 and services began to operate in May 1838. A station with the name 'Kingston' was opened, very much on the southern periphery of the town. Two years later, this station was replaced by one on the present site by which time substantial speculative housing development was taking place in the vicinity. House-building was booming as people who could afford to do so took advantage of the possibility of working in the City of London while living in what were still largely rural surroundings. Coaches from the centre of Kingston plied frequently to and from this station. The area around the station came to be known first as 'New Kingston' then as 'New Town' and later still as the rather odd 'Kingston-upon-Railway'. In 1843, the name 'Surbiton' was first suggested but it was twenty years before this was officially adopted. It was symptomatic of how a railway could aid urbanisation that land values of £50 an acre when the railway opened increased to £1,000 per acre twenty years later. The population of Surbiton increased from under 200 in 1837 to more than 9,400 by 1881. It is obvious that railways would be welcomed by those whose land could be so much increased in value by its presence. Those people who had initially objected to the railway coming to Kingston-on-Thames, the local business community mainly, soon realised that the main line railway, the up-and-coming form of transport, had passed the town by and there was a very real chance of economic stagnation. Trade on the Thames fell because river transport was uncompetitive compared with the railway. Even retail businesses were suffering as those people who could afford to do so would take the train up to the West End for shopping purposes. It was 1863 before the London & South Western Railway opened a line from London but even then, the station was located at Hampton Wick, close to Kingston town centre but on the opposite bank of the Thames. Kingston itself was never served by any line that became part of the London Underground system. Instead it had to be content to be served by the Southern Railway suburban network. The example of Kingston demonstrates the impact of initial opposition both from an influential local landowner and the business community of an old-established town of some importance and how that opposition shaped subsequent local patterns of urban development and transport in that particular area.

Brentford is a few miles north of Kingston. In 1855, the Great Western and Brentford Railway was incorporated to build a broad gauge line of three miles seventy-seven chains from the GWR main line at Southall to Brentford where there were docks on the River Thames. There was opposition from the London & South Western Railway and the Grand Junction Canal Company. Initially, there was also opposition from the Duke of Northumberland whose mansion of Syon House was near the projected line. However, he withdrew his objections, a public statement being made to this effect:

'His Grace the Duke of Northumberland, although not desirous of having a railway so close to Syon, has, with his accustomed liberality, sacrificed his private feelings to the advantage of the neighbourhood and allowed the line to pass without opposition.'[6]

Other formidable authorities had to be approached for approval before the dock at Brentford could be built. They included the Lord High Admiral and other Lords of the Admiralty, HM Commissioners of Woods, Forests and Land Revenues, the Corporation of the City of London and the Conservators of the River Thames. These bodies could insist on the implementation of any conditions they required and no railway company could ignore their strictures with impunity.

Eton College was a sizeable landowner and a powerful and determined opponent of railways. The Great Western Railway (GWR) was keen to serve the town of Windsor, perhaps hoping to gain prestigious royal patronage for its services. The idea of a railway link to the town was first mooted in 1833 and many of the townspeople of Windsor and Eton were enthusiastic about the prospect. The Provost of Eton took the opposite stance and declared that such a railway would serve no useful purpose. The GWR countered by declaring that it was preposterous that progress, as exemplified by a railway, should be hindered by a school. Since Eton College dated back to the fifteenth century and had been attended by large numbers of boys who had gone on to be part of the economic and social elite, this was tantamount to an attack on 'Old Wealth' by 'New Wealth'.

Despite the considerable power they exercised around Windsor and Eton, the college authorities realised that they could probably not prevent a line being built through Slough so they decided to try to ensure that no station was opened nearer than three miles away. Since this included Slough itself, the GWR resorted to the subterfuge of renting part of a public house in Slough to use as a booking office on the grounds that this was not actually providing the services of a proper railway station! The college authorities took the view that this constituted an infringement of the GWR's legal authorisation. The GWR responded by making much of the inconvenience that was being caused to the people of Windsor and Eton by the college's intransigence over the issue.

On 1 June 1838, the college appealed to the court for an injunction to prevent trains stopping at Slough but then displayed the utmost hypocrisy by almost immediately ordering a number of special trains to take its boys to view the Coronation of Queen Victoria. The court then refused to grant the injunction and, somewhat bloodied, the college withdrew its opposition to a station at Slough. The hatchet was buried temporarily when the

GWR agreed in 1840 to providing special trains for the boys at the beginning and end of their terms.

It did seem as if the college authorities had it in for the GWR because they raised no particular objections when the Staines & South Western, a subsidiary of the London & Southampton and later the London & South Western Railway, proposed to build a line to Eton. It was a silly situation and eventually some kind of common sense prevailed when the GWR obtained approval for a line to Windsor from Slough with various clauses requiring the company to ensure that its trains were not used by Eton schoolboys to travel up to London on half-holidays intent on dissipated activity in the dives of Soho. The Eton College authorities seem to have had a very pessimistic view of human nature because they also argued that 'rough elements' from London would descend on Eton, blighting the locality once the GWR line was in operation. The line from Slough was opened on 8 October 1849.

The route taken by the GWR into and out of Paddington was only decided on when other possible alignments had been considered and rejected. Thought had been given to sharing Euston Station with the London & Birmingham Railway and also to sites in the Pimlico area. The approaches to these would have passed through Brompton. One objector to such proposals described Brompton as 'the most famous of any place in the neighbourhood of London for the salubrity of its air'. Were the railway to be built, he claimed, Brompton would be ruined because 'streams of fire would proceed from the locomotive engines'.

Much of central London west of the City of London was built on land owned by the Portman, Howard de Walden, Grosvenor and Bedford Estates. The families that owned these were immensely rich and influential. They were able further to enrich themselves with some limited judicious selling of land to the railway promoters and powerful enough to ensure that they were not forced to sell land which they did not want to get rid of. The Duke of Bedford was very hostile to railways encroaching on his land and he was among a number of landowners who secured the rejection of the first bill submitted by the London & Birmingham Railway for a station at Euston Square. Eventually, the station was built but only after the London & Birmingham had been forced to pay a figure of £600,000 or more as against the £250,000 it had originally set aside for this purpose. It was the determination of the Duke of Bedford to preserve the exclusive character of Bloomsbury that partly accounts for railways from the north not penetrating central London any further south than Euston Road.

Landowners were able to impose some unusual conditions on the Metropolitan District Railway which was seeking parliamentary approval in 1862 for its first line from Farringdon to Westminster. Where Temple Station was to be built, particular care had to be taken to satisfy a number of demands of the Duke of Norfolk and the Strand Estate. No alteration to the Tallow Chandlers' Hall was to be made without specific authority from that livery company and where the line ran through the Inner and Middle Temple not only was the line to be covered in but locomotives were only permitted to sound their whistles in emergencies. Under no circumstances were they allowed to let off steam!

Short branch lines still connect the main line from Paddington to Reading and points west with Marlow from Maidenhead and Henley-on-Thames from Twyford. The line to Henley from Twyford opened on 1 June 1857. Marlow joined the railway network in 1873. It was later proposed to continue the line from Henley eastwards along the Thames to Marlow. In 1898, a Bill was presented to parliament for a line between Henley and Marlow and it gained some support because it was thought it would attract high-class residential development to the district and boost local tourism. Dissenting voices were raised, however, not least from the Leander Rowing Club. It vehemently denounced what it called the 'desecration' of the beautiful Thames Valley by this 'unnecessary railway'. It is clear that the Rowing Club was not just a bunch of people who liked messing about in boats, because it had a membership with clout. Many lived in the district and did not want their 'amenity' spoiled by the trippers and other common people who might be encouraged to visit this stretch of the Thames if the odious line was built. This obstructive attitude was lambasted in *Herapath's Railway Journal* as: '...special pleading in the interests of those who do not want their boat-houses disturbed...' The line between Henley and Marlow was never built.

Marylebone is the long-distance main line railway terminus in London that never 'grew up'. It was at the end of the London extension of what had previously been the Manchester, Sheffield & Lincolnshire Railway, the name pinpointing the area of its main activity which was shifting vast quantities of coal. In the early 1890s it boldly, and some say foolishly, decided to extrude a long, superbly built line from Sheffield, through Nottingham,

Loughborough, Leicester and Rugby, to London. It obtained its parliamentary sanction in 1893 and in 1897 changed its name to the 'Great Central Railway'. This line could not avoid disruption as it approached Marylebone through areas already densely built-up. Although many of those whose homes were to be demolished were working class and therefore deemed unlikely to launch an effective protest, the line was projected to pass through St John's Wood where there were many wealthy and influential residents. Even more to be feared was the Marylebone Cricket Club (MCC) at Lord's. Cricket was the game of the Establishment. The MCC was utterly opposed to any disturbance to its hallowed turf. Even at this late date, this was the clash of old-established and powerful tradition with brash commercialism in the form of the GCR. Around the issue of Lord's, 'All the old aristocratic antipathy towards the railway was revived'.[7] In this district, the Great Central minimised the disturbance it created by a cut-and-cover alignment and it avoided running under that part of Lord's on which matches actually took place. Some damage to the Lord's turf was unavoidable but the company quickly replaced it with turf recovered from a cricket ground at Neasden. A master stroke involved the Great Central propitiating the MCC by knocking down a school close to Lord's, relocating it to Bushey in Hertfordshire and presenting the site of the school to the MCC as additional land for the 'home of cricket'. The inviolability of Lord's was considered to be of far greater importance than the fact that in making the immediate approach to Marylebone, the homes of about 25,000 working-class people were to be demolished. Some were re-housed but large numbers of others were simply displaced.

The Charing Cross Railway Company was set up in 1859. Nominally independent, it was the product of the South Eastern Railway's (SER) desire to have a terminus in, or as close as possible to, London's West End. Such a station, actually located on land on the north bank of the Thames, would be a fitting terminus for its services, some of which included connections by ferry to the Continent. The line was to run from a junction with the SER just south-east of London Bridge and then via Waterloo and across the Thames to Charing Cross. The proposal met with ferocious opposition from the Governors of St Thomas's Hospital. The alignment crossed a corner of the grounds of the hospital but without requiring any demolition and involving the taking up of only one-sixth of an acre of its land. However, the governors were a powerful lot and the Act authorising the line contained a very unusual clause to the effect that the company, if required to do so, should buy the entire hospital and its grounds. Despite the small amount of land actually required, the governors demanded that the whole complex should be bought for which they required the sum of £750,000. This was an excessive figure and one that the SER was not prepared to pay. Much acrimonious haggling failed to resolve the issue and an independent arbitrator was called in who adjusted the purchase figure to £296,000 which the company promptly paid. A legacy of bitterness remained, however, and the hospital authorities refused to vacate the premises when required to do so on 21 January 1862. Workmen for the company then forced entry to the grounds and took possession. This caused the governors to obtain an injunction against the SER who in turn appealed. Matters were clearly descending to farcical levels but eventually a compromise was reached which allowed access for the company to that part of the grounds that they needed while the governors had to promise to vacate the building and remove all the patients in July. This time common sense prevailed and before long, a new St Thomas's began to be built on the south side of the Thames facing the Houses of Parliament and the SER went ahead building its line to Charing Cross.

When lines were being promoted in the south-eastern approach to London around Beckenham, the Cator Family, who owned considerable amounts of land in that area, had enough influence to insist on unusual clauses being inserted in the Act authorising the first line to pass through their land. This was in 1854 and it included penal clauses for any breach of undertakings that there should be no Sunday goods traffic at any station in a specified area of Beckenham, no Sunday reduced fares and a maximum of seven Sunday trains, none of which were to run during the time of divine service.

Teddy Hatfield of Kent was offered £6,000 by the South Eastern Railway for twelve acres, part of a parcel of 212 acres of land which he had bought a few years earlier for £6,000. He had asked £18,023 and loftily rejected the company's offer. Affronted, he took his case to be adjudicated on by a jury. To his chagrin, they valued the land at £5,265 and he then had no option but to accept the revised figure. Hatfield may have had his comeuppance but most landowners obtained a better price through a private negotiation with the promoting company than they would have received had the land been sold on the open market.

As late as the mid-1870s there were some landowners who simply refused to move with the times. A bill for a line from Westerham to Sevenoaks in Kent was going through the relevant Select Committee. An acrimonious confrontation took place between one particular landowning objector and the barrister for the promoters. The landowner was a Mr Tonge who clearly had not the slightest concern for the interests of the people of the district. He told the committee that he resided within three miles of a 'first class express station' and within one mile of a 'slow station' and that was as much as anyone could expect. The proposed railway, he said, would sever his estate in two and no amount of money would be sufficient compensation for damage to the estate he loved so much. When asked whether what he described as the 'inconvenience' of having trains passing a 1,000 yards from his house was more important than the welfare of the local populace, he stated that his priority was to protect the estate for his children. When the barrister asked him whether being able to see trains passing 1,000 yards from his house constituted a valid objection to the proposed line, Tonge replied that it was indeed 'a great objection'.[8]

The District and Circle Lines which became part of London's Underground system were built on the cut-and-cover principle, one of the reasons being to allow the fumes to escape from the steam locomotives that were used for many years until the trains were electrified. Leinster Gardens is just north of Bayswater and nos. 23 and 24 were demolished when the railway was being built. However this was a prestigious residential district and the inhabitants had enough clout to insist that the railway companies maintained the appearance and value of the street by restoring a façade to nos. 23 and 24 that was in keeping with the rest of the street. The two were nothing more than wooden facades fitted with dummy windows and doors without locks, bells and knockers. The pseudo-stuccoed fronts and their very inconspicuousness led to people living in the streets for years without realising that they were sharing their neighbourhood with a very effective *trompe l'oeil*.

The Isle of Wight is a world on its own. Many island landowners were opposed to the idea of railways on the Isle and their persistent opposition helps to explain the relatively late arrival of railways. The first salvos in the engagement came in 1846 when a prospectus was published for what would have been Wight's first line. A quintet of large local landowners rallied against this proposal. They included the Earl of Yarborough and Lords Ashburton and

Worsley, Sir William Oglander and Sir Richard Simeon. They wrote a letter to the editor of the *Hampshire Telegraph*, pointing out that those objecting to the proposal possessed 76,000 acres while the supporters of the line possessed only about 8,000 acres. They loftily dismissed the views of these smaller landowners and the bulk of the Isle's population who owned no land as being unimportant:

'Our answer is that we don't want your plan. It is not a question of which direction your lines may take; we say, and we have declared publicly that we don't require and we won't have any railways on this island.'[9]

These gentlemen succeeded in ensuring a Wight without railways for the best part of two decades. Inevitably, proposals for railways resurfaced in the early 1860s. This time, the most notable objectors among the landowners were the Earl of Yarborough of Appledurcombe House and Sir Richard Simeon of Swainston. Their antipathy to railways was seconded by the editor of the *Isle of Wight Mercury*. In 1860, he wrote an article countering proposals for the building of lines in which he ascended to lyrical prose with words such as these:

'The winds roar through the island-dells and storm across the island hills that stir the white crests of the Solent or agitate into anger the broad waters of the Channel; they bear no loud whistle, no whirr of ceaseless wheels to scare Naiad from her haunts or the Oread from her groves.'

Clearly the man was wasted on a provincial newspaper but this verbiage fell on stony ground. The first line ran between Cowes and Newport and opened for passenger traffic in 1862, following which there was a frenzied 'catch-up' which resulted in the island being considerably over-provided with railways. It is significant than when railways came to the island, it was as the result of various commercial pressures including some from the very people living there whose views the big landowners had so cursorily dismissed back in the 1840s. The world was changing.

It is interesting to note that the Earls of Yarborough displayed a marked antipathy to railways adjacent to or passing through their land on the Isle of Wight while being actively involved in encouraging railway and associated dock developments in South Humberside.

South Yorkshire

In the early 1840s, plans were afoot to promote a more direct line from London to York than the existing mishmash of routes in which George Hudson had a stake. The leading proponent of this scheme was the wealthy and energetic MP, Edmund Dennison, later to become the sworn enemy of Hudson as this line, when eventually built, administered a body blow to the vitals of Hudson's railway empire.

When preliminary surveying was taking place in the Bawtry area, south of Doncaster, local fox-hunting grandees made a physical attack on men of the surveying party. They were outraged that common upstarts working for a railway company should interfere with their simple pleasures. They had sufficient influence to force, in 1845, a deviation of the proposed route to the east of Bawtry. This added to the cost of construction because it took the line across flood plains, involved a diversion of the River Idle and the building of several bridges and viaducts that could otherwise have been avoided.

Ironically, in the 1970s there were plans to straighten a curve on the East Coast Main Line near Bawtry to raise line speeds particularly for High-Speed Trains. This would have involved building a new viaduct at Bawtry just to the east of the existing one. This never happened because of opposition from a local landowner, or so it was rumoured!

The Leeds & Selby Railway was an early venture, formed in 1829. Its promoters saw it as part of a railway route that would eventually link Liverpool on the west coast with Hull on the east. In parliament, it was vigorously opposed by the Aire & Calder Navigation, whose monopoly it seriously threatened. One of the canal company's major shareholders, Fountayne Wilson, predicted the ruination of the towns along the route of the canal and, clearly given to employing colourful language, said, that people in those towns: 'might sit down and weep like the daughters of Babylon'. The eastward extension of the Leeds & Selby was the Hull & Selby Railway and it encountered the opposition of Robert Raikes whose estate at Welton lay athwart the proposed alignment. He had recently rebuilt his mansion and employed Humphrey Repton to landscape the park. He declared that it would be a total nuisance, an eyesore and would destroy the 'picturesque privacy' that he enjoyed and his view over the Humber. His adamant opposition forced the company into making some deviations from its original planned alignment.

West Country

The Cornwall Railway experienced a permanent struggle against economic and geographical factors. A bill for a line to Falmouth failed in the House of Lords in 1835. A revised bill failed in 1845 but a further bill was proposed for 1846 with Isambard Kingdom Brunel as chief surveyor and engineer and this became law on 3 August 1846. A line was to be built between Plymouth and Falmouth and there were some associated branch lines. It was difficult terrain for a railway and Brunel was greatly constrained by the need for economy.

Brunel did much of the negotiation with landowners himself, having already gained considerable experience in the necessary skills through previous schemes with which he had been involved. Although a man who was not by nature very patient, he had plenty of charm and was usually able to agree terms with landowners that were mutually beneficial. His ability to work with them was remarkable, given the contempt he felt for them as a class. He had some radical leanings and considered the power they were able to wield as unjustifiable. In Lord Vivian, who had an estate at Glynn near Lostwithiel, he came up against a doughty opponent who also happened to be as financially straitened as the Cornwall Railway. The proposed alignment passed close to his house through the middle of a stand of fine trees. At this point the gradient would be 1 in 70 and trains would be labouring hard. Lord Vivian's point was that these locomotives would be expelling sparks and red-hot cinders in copious quantities threatening to cause fires. He and his father had overspent on the landscaping of their estate and they needed to be adequately compensated for the inconvenience to which they were being subjected. Lord Vivian took an instant dislike to Brunel, an attitude which only hardened the more the pair had to deal with each other. He described Brunel, among other things, as 'shifty', not an adjective generally associated with the man. A classic contest followed with Brunel as the avatar of the encroaching new order and Lord Vivian engaged in the role of championing the old. To and fro went the antagonists, Brunel needing to minimise his company's expenditure and Lord Vivian desperately intent on obtaining the largest possible cash injection in order to revive the fortunes of his estate. Eventually agreement was reached, the company agreeing to a deviation and Lord Vivian was compensated to a total of £29,000. As Professor Simmons has said: 'This struggle deserves remembrance for its cut and thrust; it was a direct, personal clash of landowner and engineer'.[10]

Lord Vivian's name is also associated with opposition to railways serving the town of Bodmin. Although the town gained a railway very early with the Bodmin & Wadebridge in 1834, this remained an isolated section of line until 1887 when a connection was opened to the Great Western Railway main line at Bodmin Road. The delay owed much to Lord Vivian's influence and was greatly resented by the townsfolk who were convinced that the town was stagnating because of its isolation from the national network. They may well have been correct in this assumption because Truro, with its station on the main line, grew in importance relative to Bodmin. It became a cathedral city and eventually took over the role of county town.

The Dartmouth & Torbay Railway was authorised in 1857. Although it incorporated Dartmouth in its title, it famously never reached the town. The line terminated at Kingswear, where a railway-operated ferry crossed the Dart. The ferry terminated at Dartmouth at a 'station' which, while not unique on Britain's railways, was distinctly quirky. It looked just like a railway station with the usual offices and facilities. What it lacked was platforms, rails and trains and its passengers arrived and departed by the ferry instead. The station might never have happened. In 1860, an attempt had been made to obtain authorisation for a deviation to Dittisham Ferry with the intention that a bridge would be built later to cross to the west side of the Dart. This scheme was thwarted by a local landowner who absolutely refused to allow the projected railway to cross his land. Perhaps we should be grateful. A bridge would have altered the appearance of the Dart Valley considerably at this point and would have made access to the town itself much easier, while impacting unfavourably on its historic character.

Ponsandane Signal Box was located just to the east of Penzance between that station and Marazion. A box of intermediate size, it had a decapitated look. It possessed a flat roof, very unusual on Great Western signal boxes. The reason for its odd appearance was that the local Bolitho family of Chyandour House demanded this flat roof so as cause the least obstruction to their view of the sea.

An interesting variation on normal types of opposition to railways can be seen in the desire of the London & South Western Railway to reach Plymouth. It had already thrust into North Devon but in 1883, a western extension in the form of the Plymouth, Devonport & South Western Railway (PD&SWJR) obtained parliamentary approval to approach Plymouth on a line independent of the existing Great Western route from Launceston and Lydford. This line was backed by the London & South Western but parliamentary sanction had only been obtained in the teeth of ferocious opposition from the Great Western. The latter company's lines in the area were, at this time, still broad gauge and a powerful factor favouring a second approach to Plymouth from the east was that both the Army and the Royal Navy wanted a through standard gauge connection to and from Plymouth and Devonport and their various installations and facilities elsewhere. For them the broad gauge, although its days were clearly numbered, was nothing but a nuisance and worse, it had possible negative implications for national security.

Abbotsbury was, and remains, a small village in Dorset some distance in a north-westerly direction from Weymouth. A plan to connect Abbotsbury to the Great Western Railway's line from Dorchester to Weymouth was first raised in 1872 but it evoked an extremely hostile response from the Earl of Ilchester. Small quantities of iron ore had been mined in the district for centuries but when coal was also discovered in the early 1870s, a number of local businessmen became very interested. The extraction of the iron ore was on a small scale but the earl, who owned most of the land in the neighbourhood, feared that coal-mining and the building of a railway could presage the start of intense industrialisation in this particularly scenic part of Dorset. His opposition to such developments made him very unpopular with those local business people who rated the development of trade above local environmental issues. It was soon realised that the coal reserves were very limited and that any industrialisation would be on such a limited scale as not to destroy the rustic delights of the area. Even more, it was realised that a railway might actually enhance its amenities. The earl then did a complete volte face and became a director of the Abbotsbury Railway Company. The Great Western backed the Abbotsbury Branch and it opened on 19 April 1886.

What was described as 'a body of Wiltshire Landowners' used the *Hampshire Advertiser* newspaper to drum up opposition to the proposed Southampton & Salisbury Junction Railway. They were particularly irritated by the company's claim in its prospectus that it enjoyed considerable local support and that the land it needed to acquire was of little value. They said, 'We trust, with the help of our Hampshire neighbours, that, by setting our shoulders to the wheel, we shall cast off the smoking engine from that "valueless land" which is nevertheless of "high price".'[11]

Near Chedworth, south-east of Cheltenham, the impoverished Midland & South Western Junction Railway was very unwillingly forced to make a detour from its originally proposed course in order to avoid the remains of a large Romano-British villa, the earliest parts of which date from the second century AD. This was at the behest of Lord Eldon, a powerful local landowner.

Swindon Railway Works of the Great Western Railway opened in 1842. A stentorian hooter announced the beginning and the end of shifts and it could be heard several miles away. This led the Fifth Viscount Bolingbroke, whose estate was just about in earshot, to complain bitterly that the hooter frightened his pheasants and even distressed some that were sitting on their eggs. The hooter continued to perform its duties.

West Yorkshire

A very early railway scheme was that first mooted in July 1829 for a line from Leeds to Selby. The promoters presented a bill to parliament, where it was opposed by various local landowners whose leading figure was the Dowager Marchioness of Hertford. They argued that it met no need, Existing waterways, it was claimed, satisfied the requirements of the two towns and the intermediate district. They also claimed that the superiority of railways over waterways as a medium of transport was not yet proven, at the time an arguably fair claim. Lusty opposition also came, understandably, from the Aire & Calder Navigation Company. It enjoyed a virtual monopoly of conveyance to and from Selby and Leeds and had every intention of retaining that monopoly. The Bill, giving legal sanction to the Leeds & Selby Railway, was passed on 29 May 1830. The announcement of the Bill's success was met in Selby with the ringing of bells. Presumably there were people in that town who anticipated an upturn of business when the monopoly of the Navigation Company was broken.

Various schemes had been put forward from the 1840s for lines from Leeds to the Wharfedale town of Ilkley and onwards to Skipton. These schemes eventually saw the light of day as a line promoted by the Midland Railway (MR) via the Aire Valley from Leeds to Apperley Junction and then through Guiseley, Ilkley and Bolton Abbey to Skipton. The other line belonged to the North Eastern Railway (NER) and ran from Leeds via Headingley and Arthington to Otley. There it became the Otley & Ilkley, a joint Midland and North Eastern operation to Ilkley, having a junction with the Midland line from Apperley Junction near Burley-in-Wharfedale. The later extension from Ilkley to Skipton was owned by the MR but the NER was to have running powers over this route. In the middle of the nineteenth century, this was still beautiful country with pockets of small-scale industrial activity mostly concerned with wool and cotton textiles, corn mills and paper manufacturing. Skipton and Otley were ancient settlements as, indeed, was Ilkley. The former were small towns while the latter was no more than a village. The Midland's line from Apperley Junction opened in 1865, the same year as the Otley & Ilkley Joint. These places are now on the fringe of the massive Leeds-Bradford conurbation but there is still much to be savoured in the lush green valley of the River Wharfe and the more rugged delights of the moors thereabouts. At that time, both companies expected their presence to generate industrial and residential growth in the district and both also envisaged the lines operating through traffic as part of their strategy of spreading their respective railway 'empires'.

The promotion of these lines had to run the gauntlet of opposition from a backwoodsman of the old school, Francis Hawkesworth Fawkes of Farnley Hall near Otley. The Fawkes family had been major landowners in the area since the seventeenth century, expecting their writ to be observed to the letter by the 'lesser' people of the district. Fawkes was a perfectly formed representative of the old landed gentry. He was not actually opposed to railways as such but he expected that his wishes with regards to their alignment on and around his land would be fully met. During earlier failed proposals in 1846 for a line through Wharfedale, his wishes had been respected and complied with. In the 1860s, however, he was going to find in the NER a railway promoter who had no intention of being browbeaten by someone it regarded as a throwback to ancient times. The scene was set for a classic confrontation between the old landed gentry and the upcoming *nouveaux riche*.

The Bills authorising the lines we have mentioned were passed on 11 July 1861. They were therefore law and Fawkes, who obviously would have had an opportunity to oppose them in a Select Committee, had chosen not to do so. This then made it all the more surprising when, in August 1861, Fawkes issued a pamphlet entitled *An Address to the Landowners of Wharfedale* in which he gave the substance of correspondence which had passed between him and the NER during June and July 1861. First, in a letter dated 24 June, he had raised concerns about local reports that the MR and

NER had entered into an agreement that neither company would proceed to build an extension from Ilkley to Skipton via Addingham and Draughton without the other's permission. He asked the NER whether such an agreement had been made and then launched into a tirade, saying that, if it was true, it would be disastrous for the agriculture of the Dale and would also harm the interests of local residents and visitors. He did not enlarge on why it would have these effects. The NER calmly replied that no such agreement existed but they had absolutely no objection to the MR going ahead with a line from Ilkley to Skipton if they chose to do so.

On 1 July 1861, Fawkes wrote to the NER in high dudgeon that his concern was specifically about a line from Ilkley via Addingham and Draughton to Skipton and not any other possible alignment between the towns. He then went on to add that the proposed station at Ilkley was planned in such a way that it would be physically impossible to extend it to Skipton. Again he specifically mentioned Draughton as an intermediate point that should be served by this line. He demanded an instant response to his latest letter. The NER was tiring of the constant testy demands that Fawkes was making and decided that the chairman should write a private letter to Fawkes rather than an official communication from the board. This transformed a grumpy old man into an incandescent old man who made it clear in his letter of 15 July that he regarded it as the height of impudence that the company refused to provide him with an official response. Now the NER had had enough and on 19 July a letter from the company secretary informed Fawkes that no further correspondence on the matter would be entered into. These letters were published in the pamphlet mentioned above which concluded with further rants. This in turn was answered in an open letter to Fawkes published by a small local businessman who clearly, unlike many others in the locality, did not stand in awe of Fawkes and his pedigree. His name was Jeremiah Garnett and he had 'trifling manufacturing interests' of the sort that Fawkes had disparagingly dismissed in his pamphlet. He questioned the assertion frequently made by Fawkes that he always had the interests of the people of Wharfedale at heart. It was mentioned earlier that Fawkes had raised no objections when the Bill for the Otley & Ilkley Joint was going through the parliamentary process, yet here he was complaining querulously after the Bill had been passed. Had Fawkes and other local landowners, he asked sarcastically, been 'Absorbed with the cares of property, or drowned in the varied pleasures of field sports, and the amusements of an unruffled life'? He accused them of putting their narrow interests before those of the local communities. The latter would benefit from the reduction in the price of coal and lime, for example, which would be brought about by the creation of railways through Wharfedale.

Clearly, this affair was a classic example of the old order of landed gentry, used to almost absolute power in their fiefdom and mistaking what they wanted for what they believed was best for their tenants and other local people. They found themselves confronted by a new order, a *nouveau riche* local businessman in Jeremiah Garnett and the hard-nosed directors and officers of the NER who regarded Fawkes as little more than an irritating anachronism. They represented the values of rising, dynamic and progressive capitalism at this time. The railway was both a symbol of this clash of two different worlds and cultures and a major contributor to that confrontation.

The railways near or in Wharfedale seem to have generated more than their share of intervention from members of the landed interest. The MR proceeded with its line from Ilkley westwards towards Skipton. In doing so, it passed near the famous beauty spot of Bolton Abbey where the Duke of Devonshire had one of his numerous estates. He made it clear that the price of his not opposing the railway was the condition that where it passed through his land, any cuttings and embankments were to be turfed over to minimise their visual impact. The company was then to be responsible for maintaining them in a satisfactory state. The duke's trees were to be protected and any that the company thought were interfering with signalling could not be cut down without permission. The location of any housing for railway workers had to be agreed with him first.

William Rookes Crompton Stansfield owned the Esholt Hall Estate including Belmont Wood through which the MR's line from Apperley Junction to Guiseley was projected. The conditions for parliamentary approval for the line contained his demand for a covered way, unnecessary from an engineering point of view. Also, possibly unique, was the requirement in the Act that where the line passed through his estate the track was to be laid directly on longitudinal sleepers to minimize the sound of passing trains.

Meltham was served by a short branch off the Lancashire & Yorkshire's Huddersfield to Penistone line. It was authorised by parliament in June 1861. It gained this authorisation despite vociferous opposition from one of the proprietors of the

Huddersfield brewing company, Bentley & Shaw. His house was close to the projected alignment. The local population was very much in favour of the line and he had become so unpopular locally that there was a boycott on the brewery's products which continued until at least the time that the line opened. This was not until 1869, because engineering problems were encountered during the line's construction and the brewer had kept making life difficult for the company and its engineers.

At Huddersfield itself, the Ramsden Trustees, who owned much of the land on which the growing industrial town was built, used their strong local influence to secure a price of £40,500 for land for which the Huddersfield & Manchester Railway had initially offered them just £10,000. This money was spent in acquiring even more land which they shrewdly knew would increase in value once the railway was built. This money made more money and one result was the architecturally distinctive quarter centred on the railway station, the façade of which is one of the most handsome in Britain. It has to be said that the station is far less impressive at platform level.

Railways and Landowners – some general points

One group of landowners not previously mentioned were government agencies. They did not necessarily make themselves any more amenable to railway promoters than obdurate private landowners. The Commissioners for Woods and Forests were well-established controllers of much Crown property and were not going to be pushed about by any upstart railway companies. They were able, for example, to force the Southampton & Dorchester Railway to take an irksomely circuitous route missing the town of Lyndhurst in the New Forest, a line authorised in 1847. The commissioners demanded a station on the edge of the New Forest going by the name of Beaulieu Road. Reluctantly, the London & South Western Railway built the station only to report gloomily a year later that receipts barely exceeded staff wages.

The Admiralty was interested in any railway proposals at locations where the land met the sea and the movements of shipping might be involved. This applied where there were proposals to build bridges or viaducts across water navigable by seagoing vessels or where a line was proposed to run below or close to high water level. Famous structures such as the Saltash, Forth and Tay Bridges, for example, were designed to satisfy Admiralty requirements and involving the companies concerned in extra expense in order to do so. Where the South Devon Railway ran close to the sea at Dawlish, the Admiralty required an alignment somewhat further inland than the engineer, Brunel, would have wished. There were several locations at which the Admiralty forced the Chester & Holyhead Railway into modifying structures and alignments. An example was the Britannia Bridge over the Menai Straits. An initial scheme for a bridge was rejected by the Admiralty, who insisted on headroom of 100 feet. This had to be taken into account when Robert Stephenson built the superb Britannia tubular bridge in 1850. Even the War Office was prepared to impose requirements on railway companies. At Dover, for example, it insisted on a deviation away from coastal defence positions and at Portsmouth only a branch line was allowed to serve the dockyard until the Harbour Station was opened in 1876, by which time the authorities had decided that the fortifications were obsolete. Steam locomotives would have presented a hazard where timber sailing vessels and the flammable materials that they required were concentrated.

Some caution should be exercised in making generalisations about the attitudes of landowners. Clearly, in the early days particularly, there were some who seem to have resented the accelerating forces of change, to which the railways themselves were making a major contribution. Others, who perhaps had no innate hostility to railways, found it expedient to put up a show of opposition. This they hoped would either convince the promoters at an early stage to compensate them generously or elicit favourable consideration if and when the promoters managed to get their bill before a Select Committee for examination and adjudication. Others, perhaps initially hostile or cautious, may have modified their views on learning that they had valuable minerals under their land, railways being capable of providing the best form of transport necessary for the minerals' exploitation and their consequent enrichment.

Other landowners, as we have seen elsewhere, were favourably inclined towards railways right from the very start. It would not be unfair to state that the major criterion influencing many landowners' attitudes to railways was material self-interest. Another was the ability to demonstrate that, even in a changing world, they still had the power to make railway companies dance to their tune. This was a kind of vanity.

The harsh realities of power and influence meant that it usually made sense for railway promoters to treat titled and other large landowners with respect or even with a degree of sycophancy. Some were wooed carefully and persuaded to invest in railway schemes, become shareholders or become involved in the business of provisional committees in the early stages of promotion. Many of the most prestigious were elected to boards of directors of railway companies where their names would be valuable for public relations purposes. Support from large landowners, or at least their consent not to oppose, was essential for the success of a Bill. There was little sense of equity where dealings between landowners and railway promoters were concerned. It was not an iron law, but generally the bigger, wealthier landowners were able to cut deals that were more favourable than those obtained by the smaller fry. In the case of the latter, railway promoters did not always offer to buy them off, knowing that they would not have the financial resources to oppose a bill in parliament. That was just the way of the wicked world.

It should be remembered that compensation was not just paid to landowners for supposed damage to the amenities of their 'pleasure grounds' but also for damage to other land they owned, much of which might be let out to tenant farmers. A railway could break up the cohesiveness of farmland which might only recently have been brought together by the process of parliamentary enclosure. The consequence of a railway passing through such land could be the creation of fragmentary parcels of little use for agricultural purposes and therefore likely to be less valuable. Landowners often demanded that railway companies provided occupation level crossings, over or under bridges where their property was severed by the intrusion of a railway. Some acts had clauses requiring the railway company to provide rabbit-proof fencing or to plant embankments with trees or shrubs of specified varieties and to keep these maintained and cut to a particular height.

George Stephenson, although a man of huge ability and extraordinary achievements, remained a 'rough diamond' to his dying day which meant that some people of snobbish tendencies always looked down on him. His son, Robert, was also highly talented but, unlike his father, he received formal education and displayed far more in the way of the social graces. What he had to say was therefore probably taken seriously by a wider range of people. He was elected as president of the prestigious Institution of Civil Engineers in 1856. In his inaugural speech, which was read for him in his absence, some very cogent points were made about railway developments up to that time. He estimated that the legislative sanctions which railways had had to observe at the behest of parliament had cost them around fourteen million pounds, a figure he thought was excessive. He observed that railway companies had been forced to pay landowners to obtain the land they required for their purposes, yet the estates frequently went up in value after they had been traversed by the railway. He was particularly embittered about the use of the word 'severance'. Landowners had claimed and received compensation on the basis of severance and yet nobody, including the legal authorities, was able to define exactly what severance meant. How could loss by severance be proven if severance could not be defined? In the pursuit of equity, Stephenson wanted a parliamentary tribunal created to deal with and adjudicate on issues around compensation, the membership of which consisted of MPs with legal, commercial and engineering experience rather than the 'gentleman amateurs' whose natural tendency was to favour the claims of the landed interest.

There were many who were critical of the attitude of landowners towards the railways. Among these were Samuel Smiles who declared, 'Landowners regarded railways as a golden mine'. *Herapath's Railway Journal* in 1873 commented, 'Some demands from landowners have been astounding and exorbitant'. Writers such as J. Francis (1851) and F.S. Williams in *Our Iron Roads* (1852) lambasted the attitude of landowners to the railways and the way in which they often managed to force changes of alignment which were of no benefit except to themselves and also generally insist on conditions which added much to the costs of building the railways. This was the view that prevailed for decades but it has been partially revised in more recent times. More recently, researchers like J.R. Hepple have shown that while some landowners certainly abused their influence for their own ends behind a show of hostility to railways, others openly welcomed them and used their influence to encourage their development. Once it was clear that railways could stimulate economic activity, cussed class-ridden opposition to railways largely gave way to a more open-minded but still self-interested attitude. By the 1850s, at least, it was clear that railways were here to stay and it would simply be foolish not to take advantage of the economic possibilities they offered.

Returning to vanity, it amused landowners to impose conditions on the railway companies which crossed or otherwise impinged on the estates. Mention has been made elsewhere of examples of tunnels which were unnecessary from the engineering point of view but could be considered as vanity projects. Marley Tunnel on the South Devon Railway near Brent was built to please Sir Walter Carew. Kemble Tunnel on the Swindon to Gloucester line of the GWR was built to hide trains from the sight of a local landowner, Robert Gordon. The poor old Eastern Counties Railway had to build three tunnels where its line passed through Lord Braybrooke's estate not far from Saffron Walden. Additionally, the station at Audley End had to be provided with a *porte cochère* on the up platform, so that his lordship and any distinguished guests could step straight from their carriages into the station building. Such a facility was conspicuously missing from other stations on the line. Cane Hill Tunnel on the London, Brighton & South Coast Railway was required by the London County Council to hide sight of the line from their asylum and vice versa. Primrose Hill Tunnel, north of Euston, had no strict engineering function because a cutting would have sufficed but it was built to propitiate Eton College who owned the land.

The attitude of landowners to railways changed from one of early wariness or hostility to an understanding that they could bring concrete advantages. Ironically, there were landowners who, previously having vehemently opposed stations, now demanded them as part of the deals they brokered with railway companies, often before bills went to parliament. Sometimes conditions were agreed on which seem to have had very little to do with the actual operation of the railway concerned. Thus, an agreement made by the Eastern Union Railway and the curiously named Sir William Fowke Fowke Middleton of Shrubland Hall in Suffolk, while specifying stations at Needham Market and Claydon, laid down that none were to be built on his land. Rather eccentrically, the agreement also decreed that no bridges around his estate were to be built of iron and that any gatekeepers in the employ of the EUR who Sir William considered guilty of misconduct were to be sacked. At Box Hill & Westhumble in Surrey the station has a most peculiar turret in a loosely French style. This was erected in response to the requirements of Thomas Grissell who owned nearby Norbury Park. Ironically, he was a landowner of 'new wealth' who owed his fortune to railway contracting.

A number of private stations were opened for the convenience of a local landowner. A few were even for the exclusive use of a specified landowner or gave them the right to stop any passenger train as they required. Examples of exclusive stations were West Moor Flag Station between Hereford and Hay-on-Wye on the Midland Railway for the local landowner G.H. Davenport and Watchingwell on the Freshwater, Yarmouth & Newport Railway in the Isle of Wight. This was for Sir Barrington Simon. Others allowed public use. The terms and conditions were either negotiated before a relevant railway bill was presented to parliament or were incorporated in the subsequent Act. Among stations where a local magnate had the right to demand taking up and setting down were Dearham on the Maryport & Carlisle and Crathes on the Deeside Line of the Great North of Scotland Railway. The sumptuous facilities provided for the Duke of Rutland at Redmile on the GN&LNW line in Leicestershire has been mentioned elsewhere while the Earl of Kintore had private facilities at Inverurie, again on the Great North of Scotland Railway. Black Dog Halt on the GWR's Chippenham to Calne Branch in Wiltshire was built in 1874 as a private station for the Marquis of Lansdowne of nearby Bowood House. Despite its private status, until 1939 it actually had its own station master! Black Dog only appeared in advertised timetables in September 1952. Where a whole station was not provided for a local magnate, part might be given over to private use. An example was Berkhamsted for Earl Brownlow.

Numerous landowners had the right to stop trains at specified stations, where halts would not normally be made. They usually did this either by giving notice to the staff at the station when it came to being picked up or informing the guard on the train when wishing to be set down. It was not even unknown for the landowner to turn up shortly before the train was due to pass through. He would then demand that the signals be set against it to enable him to board it when it came to a halt at the platform. Such arrangements must have absolutely exasperated the operating authorities. In 1893, the North Eastern Railway was bedevilled by no fewer than twenty-six such local agreements.

One place where such a right was frequently exercised was Tallington, a wayside station on the Great Northern main line north of Peterborough. It was close to Uffington House, seat of the Earls of Lindsey. One earl was particularly fond of demanding that the 'Flying Scotsman', the company's 'flagship' train, on its northbound journey should stop at Tallington, specifically to serve his needs as and when demanded. He was only required by law to give half-an-hour's notice and he further had the effrontery to demand the exclusive use of a first-class compartment, even if the train was full, which it often was. This provision was, theoretically, in perpetuity, and it remained in place until 1959, even if no longer exercised with any regularity. Tallington Station was closed in that year. The British Railways Act of 1963 terminated all remaining rights of this sort. The Duke of Beaufort of Badminton House owned land some of which was traversed by the cut-off route opened by the GWR in 1901 to make a direct route to South Wales from London. The duke was generously compensated for the inconvenience he suffered as a result of this intrusion and was granted the added bonus of being allowed to stop any train he chose at Badminton, an ill-used station which served little else than the 'Big House'.

In general, rural land values were enhanced by railways, at least in those areas that were close enough to be served by a station and, or, a goods facility. They provided faster, cheaper access to markets and allowed coal, fertiliser and other supplies to be brought in more cheaply. Landowners were not slow to appreciate the fact that land near stations usually rose substantially in price, sometimes by as much as twenty-five per cent. It was not unknown for initial hostility to railways *per se* to undergo a radical reversal when a landowner learned how others' rent rolls had been boosted after a railway began to serve their district. This provided no obstacle to some landowners who, aware that the value of their land was likely to rise as a consequence of a local railway being opened, still made substantial claims for compensation either before or while a bill was in parliament. They did so in the full knowledge that they were in a win-win situation and their attitude was one of unalloyed greed. Not only could they use their influence to extort generous compensation but, other things being equal, they would be further enriched as the newly opened railway began to exert a beneficial effect on the local farming industry and land values and rent rolls went up. The irony therefore was that railway promoters, whose lines usually conferred financial benefits on local landowners, paid those landowners handsomely for the privilege of further enriching them!

A phrase which turned up with great regularity when compensation for landowners was being mentioned was 'residential injury'. This was a catch-all expression which on occasion was interpreted as something as simple and seemingly innocuous as the occasional sound of a locomotive whistle. A claim for compensation based on the injury caused by a locomotive whistle may sound feeble but railway companies often found it wise to buy such opposition out at an early stage because it might prove cheaper to do so in the long run. Cash was usually the best way to propitiate opposition but shares in the company were sometimes offered additionally or instead.

The situation in towns and cities was less clear-cut. The value of land in central business districts tended to rise rapidly in the middle of the nineteenth century and particularly so close to railway stations. However, the railways could create urban blight in the district outside and around the town's centre which was often given over to a mix of industrial activity, often producing pollutants, with low quality housing for the poor. This kind of area, on 'the wrong side of the tracks', could be made worse as viaducts carved a swathe through densely occupied land, destroying what communal integrity they might have possessed and creating very tangible physical barriers. Other similar districts might be broken up and at least partly replaced by large areas given over to railway warehouses, yards, sidings and engine sheds, for example. The added deterioration inflicted by the railway on such marginal areas frequently saw their value fall. It was another matter on the fringe of the built-up area where the presence of railways might make land ripe for development, particularly for building of a better-quality residential character and consequently with an enhancing impact on its value. The early promoters of long-distance lines were not usually interested in short-distance passenger travel and the development of commuter suburbs on a large scale was a later feature. This did not stop some landowners, when a new railway project was announced, claiming that they were about to start residential development and raising their demand for compensation, given that the value of the land was about to be enhanced. Some even engaged in minimal preparatory work on a site so as to give some verisimilitude to their claim. Places which were in realistic commutable distance such as Redhill, Weybridge and Caterham saw marked rises in land values after the 1850s.

In Britain's bigger cities, the issues around landownership were every bit as pertinent as they were around smaller towns and in the countryside. Some fashionable residential areas such as Belgravia in London, Kelvinside in Glasgow or Edgbaston in Birmingham had a few owners with whom railway promoters would need to negotiate. They tended to avoid such districts as far as possible, partly because these landowners were usually very influential but even more because of the inflated price of land involved. The desire to keep such districts exclusive meant that leases or sales were often governed by restrictive covenants preventing non-residential building or residences of cheaper character. More often, the railways made their approaches to a city and built their yards and warehouses on land which was much cheaper. Such land may have been in the hands of a limited number of owners who, however, were prepared to break up their estates to allow mixed industrial and residential use. Such districts included Camden Town and Somers Town in London, Saltley in Birmingham and Tradeston in Glasgow.

A curious twist on landowners' attitudes to railways concerned the proposed Oswestry, Ellesmere and Whitchurch Railway in 1863. Sir John Hamer owned land at Bettisfield which would have been affected by the building of the line. He strongly urged the promoters to avoid despoiling a particular wood and what he described as some 'beautiful fields'. His wishes were observed and a deviation was made modifying the original route. When the Bill was being processed, Hamer appeared before the relevant Select Committee and made some unexpected points about the impact he thought the railway would have on the landscape:.

> 'I may be peculiar but I do not object to a railway; I look upon a railway as a fine work of art – I look upon a locomotive engine as a fine work of art and I look upon a puff of steam as such a feature in the landscape that if I were a landscape painter I should paint it in the horizon – therefore I do not object to a railway upon the common, hackneyed objection'.[12]

The opposition of landowners to railways was not a thoroughly principled one. Experience taught them that the coming of railways often significantly increased the value of their land. Being human, it was only to be expected that many cast aside initial hostility or instinctive reservations. Increasingly, as the nineteenth century went on, cash-rich landowners invested in railways and then frequently found themselves invited to take a seat on the board of directors. Railways may have been a major factor in encouraging a sense of 'in with the new and out with the old' but more progressive elements of the landed aristocracy provided a continuity amidst the turmoil of change that constituted the nineteenth century.

Britain in 1900 may have been a major urbanised and industrial society and economy very different from the Britain of 1800. The landed aristocracy did not simply collapse under the pressure of these changes but it showed that it was a pragmatic survivor, maintaining a formidable presence in the corridors of power. As R.W. Kostal (1994) explained:

> '...both the English gentry and the English railways had secured what they had each wanted most. Landowners had got both rich monetary compensation and the world's most advanced transportation system. Railway capitalists had obtained the material foundation of vast operational enterprises.'

The Venal Vicar

Even men of the cloth were not averse to exercising self-interest where railway projects were concerned as this passage concerning the proposed London and Birmingham Railway shows:

> 'A reverend gentleman complained that his privacy had been ruined, that his daughters' bedroom windows were exposed to the unhallowed gaze of the men working on the railway, and that he must remove his family to a watering- place, to enable him to do which he must engage a curate. All this was considered in the compensation demanded, and paid; yet no curate has been engaged, no lodgings at a watering-place taken. The unhappy family have still dwelt in their desecrated abode, and borne with Christian-like resignation all the miseries heaped upon them. The gilding of the pill, it seems, has rendered it palatable, and we have no doubt that if his daughters' rooms have a back window as well as a front one, he would be exceedingly glad if a railroad was carried across at the same price.'[13]

CHAPTER EIGHT

The need to regulate the Railways

Turnpikes and the navigation and canal companies owned and maintained their infrastructure while other companies operated the services, paying a toll for access and use of the facilities. It was believed that this encouraged competition among those providing haulage services on the canals and helped to keep charges down. Initially, a similar arrangement was envisaged for the railways. In practice, there were constant complaints about canal hauliers who charged excessive rates because they had a virtual monopoly. It was felt necessary to prevent railways developing similar monopolistic tendencies and so from the earliest days it was clear that railway operation would require some degree of government intervention. The appearance of practical steam locomotives emphasised this notion. These machines were faster and heavier than any previous form of traction. On the grounds of safety alone, it was felt that some government regulation was required. The arrival of the railways at a time of rapid industrialisation, urbanisation and other radical change challenged existing economic, social and political practices, many of them long-standing and deep-rooted.

The Liverpool & Manchester Railway was a success right from the start. This success, however, alarmed sections of the business world and many politicians. The Private Act of Parliament under which each railway company received its legal authorisation laid out clearly the maximum rates it could charge for various types of traffic. The evident general superiority of railways over other forms of land transport meant that parliament could be seen as supporting private businesses able to charge monopoly prices. This conflicted with the contemporary political economy in which notions of *laissez-faire* were uppermost. Competition was considered vital to maximise economic growth. What, if anything, could governments do in an era of *laissez-faire* to prevent railways abusing their potentially monopolistic position? Concerns around this issue meant that there were misgivings in business and political circles about railway development in general as well as predictable opposition from landowners, turnpike and canal companies and others to specific proposals. Should the railways be left alone to make profits by whatever means if, in doing so, they were clearly operating against the general interests of the public? Should the state be involved in regulation? If so, under what conditions and to what extent should intervention take place? Arguments about the relationship between the state and the railways have continued ever since. The question certainly would not go away in the nineteenth century. Select Committees inquiring into various aspects of railway management were set up either by the Lords or the Commons in every year between 1835 and 1840 and then in 1843, 1844, 1846, 1849, 1853, 1863, 1864, 1872, 1881-2 and 1893, while two Royal Commissions reported in 1846 and 1867. Many of these proceedings resulted in new legislation, the outcome of which was an attempt to circumscribe the powers and freedom of action of the railway companies. By 1914, over 200 general statutes had been passed pertaining to railways.

Something of a precedent had already been established with the turnpikes and canals. Around 30,000 miles of turnpikes had been built. Each of these was authorised by its own specific Act of Parliament which required the turnpike trustees to meet certain terms and conditions. While some turnpikes were managed in exemplary fashion, it was evident early in the nineteenth century that the supervision and direction of many were extremely lax and that tolls were sometimes simply being pocketed by the trustees rather than spent on maintenance. Canals also required parliamentary authorisation. Their superiority for certain types of traffic over the roads had caused many canal companies to levy excessive charges, something which had provoked anger and led to calls for government intervention. Docks and harbours and the suppliers of utilities such as water and gas were also subject to legislation stipulating conditions which, at least in theory, they had to meet. Clearly there were precedents for state involvement.

Railways were beginning to make an impact nationally in the early 1830s. It became increasingly evident that no previous peacetime economic and industrial development was to have such widespread repercussions. The safety implications were clearly enormous. There were innumerable accidents in the early days and it was difficult to dispute the need for compulsory national safety standards and that government was the only agency through which these could reasonably be implemented. Governments were also concerned to safeguard the interests of two sections of the public who would be affected by railways: the owners of land scheduled to be purchased for railway development and the possibly gullible small investors who might be manipulated by unscrupulous businessmen.

Railways were like other great innovatory forces in that they destroyed as well as created capital. Railways destroyed jobs and ways of life as well as helping to create new ones. Governments recognised that turnpike trusts and canal companies could suffer loss at the hands of railway competition and so they were allowed *locus standi* to oppose any railway bill. Those whose property was affected by proposed railways were also granted this. In practice, the most common source of opposition to proposed railway bills came from other railway companies.

Unlike most major railway networks on the European Continent, Britain's railways were built without any thought-out, long-term plan. In France, for example, government and railways entered a partnership whereby the government planned the network and had representation on the boards of the railway companies. They were then able to insist on the implementation of measures relating to such things as rates and safety. In Britain, the prevailing liberal political economy encouraged free enterprise and competition. Enlightened self-interest in promoting and operating railways would ensure that the public interest was met through the workings of that supposedly benevolent but invisible force known as 'The Market'. But what would happen if railways were allowed to proliferate without any form of control? A railway represented a huge financial commitment and was intended to produce a profit for those who had sunk money into it. Might their investment not be threatened if railways were operated entirely without some measure of control? As early as the 1830s, there were suggestions that governments would identify useful routes and invite people to invest in them. The profits would be disbursed to the investors for a fixed period after which the state would take over and buy the lines.

A proposal in 1836 for an official periodic scrutiny of canal and railway companies was rejected by parliament. The aged and crabby Duke of Wellington believed that parliament was wilfully neglecting a sufficiently rigorous scrutiny of all railway proposals coming before it. He considered it desirable to insert in all these Bills some clause to enable the government to revise the enactments contained in them at some future period. He failed to obtain much support for this viewpoint. The MP who said, '...it is by the government not meddling with capital that this country has been able to obtain superiority over every other country', was neatly encapsulating the received wisdom of the time.[1]

From the start, the directors of railway companies bitterly resented any official intervention in their affairs. With hindsight, we can see that some level of regulation was inevitable to ensure that the railways operated in the interests of the public rather than simply existing to produce profits for their shareholders. They gained a monopoly of high speed inland transportation but also, very importantly, they were to carry a large amount of mail and be used to carry troops to potential flashpoints during the Chartist years from the mid-1830s to the late 1840s. By then, they were contributing greatly to the economic life of the country. Governments had little option but to implement some degree of control even in an age of *laissez-faire*. Interestingly, a railway engineer of the stature of the rough-hewn George Stephenson early on accepted the need for regulation on such matters as speed limits, signalling and braking systems and was moved in 1841 to write on the matter to the president of the Board of Trade suggesting that the Board should establish a committee of railway engineers to supervise such matters.[2]

One outcome of an uneasy mix of *laissez-faire* with a minimum of government interference was the creation of a network of railways rather than anything resembling a system. With a plethora of different railway companies, it quickly became obvious that a host of potential problems could arise if a goods consignment needed to be sent from, say, Truro in Cornwall to Whitehaven in Cumberland. Between the different railway companies there was a byzantine variety of different goods rates, passenger fares structures (sound familiar?) and other tariffs. Some companies refused to handle the rolling stock of other companies, a problem exacerbated by the existence of two main gauges. Something needed to be done. It was typical of the times that when a system was put in place, it operated on a voluntary rather than a statutory basis.

In the early days of Britain's railways, a passenger undertaking a journey involving the use of trains operated by two or more companies had to buy a fresh ticket when wanting to use the train of a second or subsequent railway company. Passengers found this irksome. Despite the greater speed of the railway, some of them yearned for the good old days of stagecoach travel where a passenger needed to buy only one ticket for any journey no matter how many coach operators this might involve. A solution was found with the Railway Clearing House (RCH) which came into being on 2 January 1842 and was given official recognition and encouragement but no statutory powers. It was intended not only to provide the necessary everyday accountancy service but to facilitate co-operation between companies and the settlement of accounts for complicated journeys involving more than one company, like the consignment sent from Truro to Whitehaven, for example. Initially, only nine companies subscribed to avail themselves of its services but by 1870, over ninety-four per cent of the railway network made use of its services. Membership of the RCH required that the companies involved used what became the gold standard – the Edmondson card ticket. Before the grouping and later nationalisation, the RCH had not managed to eliminate all petty inter-company disputes but it did manage to create a uniform system for classifying goods. It closed in March 1963.

The many and varied concerns being expressed about the dangers of allowing railways to grow and spread untrammelled led, uneasily, to a recognition that some element of intervention was required with respect to that nebulous concept, the 'public interest'. In 1839, parliament recognised that:

> 'The safety of the public also required that upon every railway there should be one system of management under one superintending authority. On this account it is necessary that the company should possess a complete control over their line of road although they should thereby acquire an entire monopoly.'[3]

A succession of parliamentary acts was passed throughout the rest of the nineteenth century, marking a compromise between the desire to encourage virtually unbridled business enterprise and the need to ensure that the railways operated within parameters involving national standards with regard to safety, for example.

The Regulation of Railways Acts in 1840 and 1842 set up a Railway Department at the Board of Trade. Of the 1840 Act the *Railway Times* (13 June 1840) said:

> 'We have always declared…that from the moment when railways became the general, and in some sense compulsory, mode of conveyance, the public would not rest satisfied without a government superintendence of the exercise of powers granted

to the companies by their respective Acts, and that it was for the interest of the proprietors themselves that such superintendence should exist.'

The Railway Department had powers to demand the submission by companies of data concerning rates, fares and accidents in particular. It also established a Railway Inspectorate with powers to examine and report on new lines and to investigate accidents but without any clearly defined legal basis. In 1842, the inspectors were empowered to delay the opening of a new line and to identify conditions to be met before public services could commence. These inspectors were officers of the Royal Engineers. It was felt that such men combined sound engineering knowledge with the integrity needed to operate impartially in what might be controversial circumstances. The introduction of an Inspectorate did not go unchallenged. A number of professional railway engineers, of whom Brunel was the most prominent, looked askance at the inspectors appointed by the Board of Trade. They called into question whether such men had sufficient experience and knowledge to assess the actions of professional railwaymen and issue instructions on how things must be improved. Brunel, indeed, made clear his aversion to any railway regulation. Addressing a Select Committee on Railways on 22 March 1841, he said:

'I do not conceive, myself, that it is of advantage to the public, in the management of the railway system, that any power should be given to the Board of Trade, or any central body, to issue regulations for the management of the concern.'[4]

In 1844, a Select Committee was set up under the chairmanship of William Gladstone, the energetic President of the Board of Trade. It made recommendations which, if enacted, would have considerably increased state intervention in railway affairs at a time when the freedom of private enterprise was sacrosanct. This committee strongly criticised the parliamentary committees for the manner in which they examined each bill individually and in isolation from other schemes and without any sense that each sanctioned railway scheme should be considered against the requirement for a national system serving the needs of the country as a whole, cutting out unnecessary duplication. Attempts to implement such an approach never met with much success because of vested interests. Gladstone also wanted the option of the nationalisation of the railways in the future. Although this aim was enshrined in the Railway Regulation Act of 1844, it was of course never enacted in his lifetime and Gladstone found himself constantly frustrated by the obstructive efforts of the powerful and well-organised railway interest lobby.

He may have lost the battle, but he fought a good fight. On the second reading of the Railway Bill, a fellow MP described him as making 'a slashing speech, hitting out at right and left'. He pulled no punches as he described the influence of his opponents as 'insidious'. The Railway Regulation Act of 1844 represented an emasculated version of what Gladstone had wanted but for all that it was a very significant piece of legislation. Clause II of the Act declared:

> 'That the Companies may be required to provide upon such new Lines of Railway as a minimum of third class accommodation, one Train at least each way on every week-day, by which there shall be the ordinary obligation to convey such passengers as may present themselves at any of the ordinary stations, in carriages provided with seats and protected from the weather, at a speed of not less than 12 miles per hour including stoppages, and at fares not exceeding a penny per mile...'

The result of this was, of course, the much derided 'Parliamentary Train', often run at the most inconvenient times for the kind of passengers most railway companies clearly did not want. It was gently lampooned in *The Mikado* by W.S. Gilbert: 'He shall only suffer to ride on the buffer in Parliamentary trains'. These trains may have been spartan but they represented a great advance on travelling 'outside' on a stage coach which meant clinging on for grim death and being subjected to every kind of weather the capricious British climate could throw at such passengers. Incidentally, the existence of the 'Parly' annoyed the Sabbatarians because the Act meant that on those lines that already operated services on Sundays, the running of at least one train now had legal endorsement.

In return for putting on the 'Parly', railway companies were relieved of the passenger tax on all third-class journeys in such trains. In 1883, the Cheap Trains Act repealed the passenger duty on all penny-a-mile fares while simultaneously requiring the companies to introduce workman's fares as and when required by the Board of Trade. This was part of an attempt to tackle the inner-city overcrowded housing problems by encouraging working people to migrate to the suburbs.

The 1844 Act was important for being an attempt to get the state involved in supervising aspects of the everyday running of the railways. This idea was anathema for many politicians and it is evidence of the continuing influence of *laissez-faire* that, for the rest of the nineteenth century, when issues arose which required legislation, they were dealt with on an individual and ad hoc basis. However it is significant that this Act was passed in the same year as a major Factory Act restricting workers' hours of employment, the repeal of the Corn Laws and the Bank Charter Act which allowed banks only to issue Bank of England notes. These were challenges to the dominant tide of economic liberalism and an indication of the gradual emergence of a new form of political economy. Governments also became involved in the provision of welfare and education from the middle of the nineteenth century. The setting up of the Railway Department at the Board of Trade in 1840 had not been an isolated incident. Rather, it was part of a general trend towards the intervention of government in more and more branches of national life. Governments of the nineteenth century could not entirely shrink from regulating fares and rates, from positive action around safety measures, the potentially damaging tendency to monopoly and other issues involving an interface between the railways and the public. The increasing role of the state can be seen where the private acts authorising individual railways laid out mandatory and specific requirements relating to such matters as the adequate fencing of lines, regulations about level crossings and in some cases speed limits.

Attempts to create a government body to supervise the railways saw the appointment of five 'independent' Commissioners of Railways in 1844, chaired by Lord Dalhousie. Rather mockingly they were soon nicknamed the 'Five Kings'. They took over those duties with respect to railways which had previously been exercised by the Board of Trade. It was intended that, under government direction, the commissioners should report on projected railway schemes, recommending a veto of those thought unsuitable. They would also try to bring about a sense of system with regard to new railway schemes rather than the existing haphazard approach which encouraged competition but which was leading to unnecessary duplication. Another group of Railway

Commissioners took over in 1846. Neither body was ever given effective power. In the economic uncertainties of the late 1840s, it was not surprising that their enemies in the *laissez-faire* camp succeeded in having the latter abolished in 1851. Responsibility for the railways then reverted to the Board of Trade once more. It was a pot-mess. As early as 1854, Edward Cardwell, then President of the Board of Trade, condemned the situation whereby the railways had grown up in a haphazard fashion rather than through any system of well-devised legislation.

Fares have always been a contentious issue and these extracts show that early on in the history of the railways there was a perception that many companies were exploiting their monopoly position to levy excessive fares:

'When the various leading Railway Companies were first formed, the public hailed their formation because they were led to believe that the principal object which their originators had in view was the accommodation and benefit of the community...The proprietors assured the public, times without number, that they would, by reduction of fares, give them the benefit of whatever success should attend their enterprise.

'In this, the public have been grossly deceived. The Railway Proprietors, instead of reducing their fares, have kept them up at the rates which had been fixed on... The leading lines have proved more successful than the most sanguine had ventured to anticipate. But the benefit is exclusively enjoyed by the shareholders. The public have derived no advantage from the success of these undertakings. Instead of lowering the fares, as the country had been led to expect, the Railway Directors have proposed dividing the unexpectedly large revenue derived from their respective lines among the shareholders...These are stubborn facts...They disclose a state of matters constituting a monopoly of the very worst kind. The Directors of the leading Railway Companies, having secured a monopoly of conveyance, act towards the public as they think proper. They make their own terms because they know the public have no remedy...The public are grossly and grievously wronged in this matter. And they have a right to look to the legislature for redress. The railway companies have broken faith with the public, it is the duty of Parliament to interfere, and see that the public are righted...'[5]

In 1846, the Gauge Regulation Act decreed that the standard gauge should be the norm for future railway construction. It was an unsatisfactory measure in that it allowed the Great Western Railway to continue operating the broad gauge. The Act recognised that it was in the public interest to have just one gauge for the national network but it was not prepared to act decisively and require the extension of the standard gauge throughout. It therefore condemned the broad gauge to a process of slow attrition and decline, not eventually completed until 1892. Admittedly, a more interventionist approach was taken when, for example, in 1854, the GWR, having absorbed two local companies who used standard gauge track, was precluded from replacing it with broad gauge without the permission of the Board of Trade.

As early as the mid-1830s, the tendency to monopoly in railway management was becoming apparent. From the 1840s, a process of consolidation took place involving mergers, take-overs and the creation of large and powerful conglomerates such as the Midland, London & North Western, Lancashire & Yorkshire and North Eastern Railway Companies. Governments were not keen to intervene in this process despite the fact that it followed the classic pattern of capitalism which is towards monopoly or, at least oligopoly, rather than competition. When the North Eastern Railway was authorised in 1854, it gained an almost complete monopoly of railway operations in the territory over which its lines extended. Attitudes began to change over time. A proposal to merge the Midland with the Glasgow & South Western Railway was refused by parliament in 1867 and again in 1871 and 1874 and a similar proposal to merge the London & North Western with the Lancashire & Yorkshire in 1871-2 did not go ahead on the grounds that a large part of the Midlands, of Lancashire and West Yorkshire, the Lake District and parts of Wales would be almost monopolised by the gigantic company that would be created. By this time, the influence of the 'Railway Interest' in parliament was on the wane and many MPs now looked askance at proposals to create such huge companies. In 1872, a Parliamentary Committee was established to examine issues raised by railway amalgamations. In 1871, twenty-eight companies controlled about eighty per cent of Britain's total track mileage. 'Monopoly' remained a dirty word in both parliamentary and popular perceptions. For example, the substantial towns of Hull, Southampton and Plymouth complained over decades about what they saw as the unhealthy lack of competition of the railways serving their districts. The concept of competition may have been sacrosanct but unrestricted competition and government concern to let market forces dictate could and did lead to large amounts of capital being invested in what was over-provision even at that time. The chickens came home to roost in the twentieth century once railways were being challenged for much of their traffic by road transport. Over-provision was exemplified by three fully equipped main lines operating between Liverpool and Manchester in addition to two other lesser routes.

Concerns about possible conflicts of interest between the railway companies and the public were reflected in an editorial in *The Economist* (24 December 1864), which argued that 'railways do not thoroughly compete with each other' but instead attempt 'to combine and settle their charges against the public'. For this reason, it argued that they ought to be brought more closely under the 'superintendence and correction of the state'. A Royal Commission on Railways convened between 1865 and 1867 but the hold of *laissez-faire* remained unchallenged.

Decline of competition and its effects on the economy and railway users rumbled on only to surface shortly before the First World War. A representative from the Board of Trade told a parliamentary committee in 1911 that whereas in 1872 sixteen companies with 9,522 miles of track controlled eighty-five per cent of the total mileage, now only thirteen companies with a combined mileage of 14,022, owned eighty-eight per cent of the total. The spirit of unbridled competition was condemned in the committee's report as having been wasteful and now outdated and it made clear its belief that amalgamation was what was needed.

A long-running source of criticism aimed at the railways was that they discriminated unfairly between one type of customer and another over freight charges. In the early days, when the railways had been seeking to consolidate their superiority over other forms of transport, there had been few complaints about excessive or discriminating charges. Once the railways had established a monopoly in the conveyance of many kinds of consignment, however, complaints came thick and fast that the railways were exploiting their monopolistic position and charging as much as they could get away with. Not only were the companies the recipients of complaints to this effect but parliament was as well for allowing the continuation of these discriminatory practices which acted against the popular interest. A spokesman for the North Eastern Railway told a Royal Commission in 1867:

> 'The charges are not regulated by a mileage charge, nor solely according to distance. Within the limits of the company's legal powers they are determined by the consideration, in the special circumstances of each case, of what will fairly remunerate the company for their current and capital expenditure, and what the traffic is able to bear.'[6]

Although parliament in giving legal authority to a railway company stipulated upper limits for its freight charges, it made no efforts to prevent discrimination in charges below the maximum it laid down. The Railway Clauses Consolidation Act was passed in 1845, intended to prevent undue discrimination between customers who were being provided with similar services but the wording was so vague as to render the Act inoperative. The Railway and Canal Traffic Act of 1854 known as 'Cardwell's Act' looked to have tied up the loose ends but proved no more effective in laying down and enforcing measures which prevented 'undue preference'. A perpetual complaint was that railway companies discriminated against individual traders by charging differential prices for what the users saw as the same service and also of unfairly charging reduced rates for imported agricultural goods which disadvantaged domestic farmers. The attempt to control the railways was not helped by the fact that they were under no obligation to publish their charges, thereby making it difficult for customers to establish whether they were the victim of discriminatory rates.

In 1873, the Railway and Canal Traffic Act required the railway companies to publish their freight charges. It also created a new body, the Railway Commission, to hear and rule on complaints about undue preference. A witness appearing before the 1867 Commission said that there was a widespread perception that railway companies discriminated between traders and that this was a cause of widespread resentment. He did not, however, furnish the Commission with any concrete evidence. Once again, legislation did not bring about the decisive changes hoped for by many of those who had little option but to use the freight services provided by the railways. The bull was finally grasped by the horns with the Railway & Canal Traffic Act of 1888 and derivative legislation in the early 1890s, which fixed a mandatory new national scale of charges.

Although there was more transparency, the legislation now made it very difficult for the railway companies to raise their charges. In the period approaching the First World War, their costs increased while their income was effectively 'pegged' and this was a cause of a very acrimonious period in industrial relations, including the first national railway strike in 1911.

The lack of effective safety precautions on the early railways made travel hazardous. It is perhaps surprising that there were not more accidents in the 1830s and 1840s given what now seem to be very casual attitudes around safety. In the 1850s and 1860s accidents increased, probably because many lines were running faster and more frequent trains and as railway layouts became more complex there were increased possibilities of conflicting movements. In 1840, the Regulation of Railways Act required companies to submit to the Board not only their traffic returns but also details of all accidents involving personal injuries. Even such limited measures to regulate railway activity were of course highly controversial, given the economic and political wisdom of the time. Some MPs argued that interference with the railway companies' activities would act as a disincentive for them to take responsibility for their own actions. The disinclination on the part of governments to interfere with the operation of the railways was *laissez-faire* taken to its ultimate and was indirectly the cause of much avoidable injury and death.

The Board of Trade was obviously concerned and constantly recommended the adoption of such safety measures as continuous brakes, means of allowing passengers to alert the train crew while the train was in motion, the block signalling system and the interlocking of points and signals. There was much criticism of the railway companies, given the general perception that they kept profits up and costs down by delaying or avoiding such systems unless they became mandatory. The North Eastern Railway seems to have been singled out as particularly at fault in such matters.

The Regulation of Railways Act of 1868 required all railway companies operating public services to adopt an efficient means of communication between passengers and what is now called the 'onboard team'. The early systems used were not always very effective and there had been a number of assaults and even murders, one or two very well publicised, which might have been avoided had the victims concerned been able to attract attention or use some means of bringing the train to a halt. The problem was that whatever kind of safety system was installed, it seemed to exercise a magical allure to which some passengers simply had to succumb. This was the reason for the introduction of the penalty fine of £5 for misuse of the communication system.

In 1870, the public was shocked to learn that there were sixty-five fatalities to the public in railway accidents that year, an increase of nearly fifty per cent over 1869. This unsurprisingly increased public demands for radical improvements in safety measures, yet the railway companies continued to drag their feet. This despite the revelation that of 281 railway accidents in 1870 and 1871, it was considered that no less than 113 could have been avoided with interlocking.

The Regulation of the Railways Act 1871 made it compulsory for railway companies to notify the Board of Trade of all accidents involving loss of life or injury to railway employees and members of the public. It also gave the Board the power to investigate any major accident, produce a report on its findings and make recommendations in an attempt to prevent a repetition. Unfortunately, this provision did not at that time have statutory backing. Progress on improving safety measures was steady but still slow until the Armagh Accident of 12 June 1889. Seventy-eight people including twenty-two children were killed and 260 seriously injured. It unfortunately required a catastrophe on this scale to bring about decisive action. Inspectors ruled that the accident could have been avoided if the company concerned had employed continuous brakes and block signalling. Another Regulation of Railways Act was rushed through making it compulsory for railway companies to employ the block system, interlocking signalling and continuous brakes on passenger trains.

Another source of criticism of the railways was their treatment of employees who were killed or injured at work. It was far more dangerous to work on Britain's railways than to travel on them in the nineteenth century. In the period 1841-75 about 6,200 people were killed working on the railways and about 1,300 travelling on them.[7] The companies did not accept corporate responsibility for such incidents and therefore only provided any compensation at their discretion. From 1872 to 1875, almost 3,000 railway employees were killed on duty compared with 155 passengers.[8] The generally accepted view of railway directors and management and of politicians was that such accidents were almost always the fault of their employees' negligence or misconduct. The *Edinburgh Review* commented. '…no accident occurs of which it may not be said, that proper precautions…would not have prevented it'.[9]

A Royal Commission examined safety on the railways and considered a petition signed by 10,000 railway workers. This submitted the opinion that of the 765 railway workers killed on duty in 1875 and the 3,618 who were injured, a substantial proportion were the victims of causes which the railway company had the power to prevent. Working hours were excessive it was claimed, manning levels often inadequate, working places badly lit or otherwise hazardous and insufficient money was spent on by the employers in preventing incidents. They believed that if the principle of employers' liability to pay compensation for death or injury was accepted, the casualty rate would be substantially reduced.[10] Employers' liability gradually spread through the railway industry. Whereas in 1875 one in every 334 employees in the railway service was killed at work, in 1899 the corresponding figure was one in every 1,006.[11] It seems that the introduction of employers' liability made the railway companies more careful of their workers' safety.

In 1896, the Light Railways Act was passed to encourage the promotion of rural branch lines of a basic nature by greatly simplifying the complications and therefore the expense of obtaining the normal Act of Parliament. Official government policy was to stimulate the rural economy, agriculture having been in the doldrums for a couple of decades. The improved transport facilities that railways could provide were seen as a means of achieving that necessary boost. The government committed a substantial sum to subsidise projects that took advantage of these new rules. A subsidy of up to fifty per cent of the construction costs of an approved line would be available in the form of a grant or a loan. A grant of twenty-five per cent could be made towards the cost of construction as long as the local authority also contributed. Further finance could be made available if the Board of Agriculture or the Board of Trade was convinced that a particular project would prove beneficial. About sixty railways took advantage of the Light Railways Act but the Act perhaps did not generate the hoped-for response.

In 1867, a Royal Commission had decided that nationalisation was unnecessary and governments lost interest but the issue did not go away. The growth of socialist ideas from the 1870s put the subject on the agenda of the emerging Labour movement. One writer in 1887 complained about the money that was wasted under private ownership and he specifically mentioned 'excessive and ridiculous compensation paid for land' and 'money wasted on legal expenses'.[12] These points were made before and have continued to be repeated since. Two interest groups were formed to promote the issue – the Railway Nationalisation League in 1895 and the Railway Nationalisation Society (RNS) in 1908. Nationalisation of the railways and indeed other major industries was part of the socialist agenda which had much support at that time. The unions in the railway industry and the Labour Party, created in embryonic form in 1900, supported the idea of railway nationalisation. Large numbers of railway workers resented the militaristic discipline to which they were subjected, were unhappy about pay and conditions and, with inside knowledge, were concerned about shortcomings in some aspects of safety. Those advocating nationalisation were also able to exploit a widespread resentment by parts of the business community at railway activity, not least around the issue of their rates and charges, which were seen as excessive and too complex.

In 1913, the RNS put forward a cogent case for nationalisation. It argued that lack of government control had led to expensive and wasteful duplication of resources. State regulation did not go far enough and the railway companies had learned ways of evading some of the stipulations that were in place. Private ownership was not in the public interest and very radically it was suggested that a Railway Council be set up with members representing the various sections of the community to oversee the effective management and operation of the nationalised railway system. It was believed that such a system would effect useful economies and provide the users with better value for money.

It has to be asked whether it made sense for the railways of Britain to be operated by over 120 individual private companies involving a massive duplication of services, facilities and bureaucracies. This is something which, of course, the modern British privatised railway system replicates with different organisations operating services, providing maintenance, leasing rolling stock and so on. This is all evidence of how the lessons of the past have been ignored in the privatisation dogma of the late twentieth century.

At least some of the problems encountered by the railways after the First World War, and increasingly after the Second, were rooted in the dangerous legacy of nineteenth-century dogma regarding *laissez-faire* and virtually unregulated competition. Britain, basically, had too many railways and so adapting to changing circumstances, particularly the rise of road transport, was a particularly painful process.

It should not be forgotten that the liberal economic practices associated with *laissez-faire* and which informed the attitudes of successive nineteenth-century governments to the railways, were not restricted to that sphere. They were applied widely to industrial, commercial and social contexts. They underpinned the ruthless exploitation in the workplace of millions of men, women and children, an equally ruthless despoliation of natural resources and the creation of massive concentrations of filth and toxicity on a scale never seen before. Parliament was intent on providing the optimal legal conditions for the development of capitalist enterprise and competition. Reforms that improved working conditions, that tackled environmental blight, developed a public health system, created an educational system for the masses and eventually led to the franchise, at least for the male population, conflicted with the concept of *laissez-faire*. The reforms that were introduced were less for altruistic motives on the part of the rich and powerful than because of a realisation that overworked employees were inefficient workers, that a level of minimum education was necessary for an efficient industrial workforce, that epidemic disease was as likely to kill the rich as the poor and that workers were developing an awareness that through collective action they had bargaining power with the employers. They wanted what they considered to be a fairer share of the wealth their labour created. Reforms were necessary to ameliorate the tensions inevitable in an urban industrial society with wide differences in wealth, power and prospects.

The kind of Big Business with which we are familiar today had its origin with the railways of the nineteenth century. Modern business is characterised by gigantic joint-stock companies having multi-million pound capitalisation, much of which is in the form of shares held individually by small investors or indirectly again by such people through the policies they hold with corporate investors. Before the railways came, most business enterprises were owned by individuals, families or partnerships and were limited in size by the amount of capital that they could make available. A few types of business, including canals, turnpike trusts and docks which needed relatively large amounts of capital, were predecessors of the modern joint-stock type of business concern and these kinds of organisation only gained formal legal sanction in 1825. However until the Companies Acts of 1856-62, the shareholders, no matter what the level of their financial commitment to the enterprise, were fully liable for its debts. Clearly this acted as something of a deterrent for the person looking for a safe if moderate return on an investment which, although small, might represent their life savings. The Companies Acts gave legal sanction to the modern limited liability company. The railways, each the result of its own unique Act of Parliament, were set up from the start as joint-stock companies with limited liability. This was necessitated by the sheer size of their operations. In 1858, the average authorised capital of Britain's eighty-nine largest railways was £3.6 million and that of the London & North Western which was the largest company was £43.8 million. With the growth of the joint-stock railway companies and trading in their shares came the possibility of irresponsible speculation in shares, enough to foment a financial crisis on a national scale in the 'Railway Mania'.

> 'Being first in the field, the railway companies were open to all the temptations of an unregulated competition in avarice and speculation; but they were also the whipping boys of public indignation and the guinea pigs for the first experiments in parliamentary control and the development of modern company law.'

In the nineteenth century, the railways never quite managed to get rid of the popular perception that there was something shady about their financial dealings. It remained awkwardly unresolved whether they were simply private businesses run to make money for their investors or a service essential to the life of the nation and which therefore required some degree of public control exercised through government and the law.

CHAPTER NINE

The Railway Interest

Inevitably, railway companies, large and small, tried to enlist the interest and active support of MPs, particularly those representing the districts which the companies served or intended to serve.

A distinctive group of MPs associated with the railways emerged and became known as the 'Railway Interest'. This was a loose term applied to a varying number of MPs who held directorships or senior administrative posts in railway companies in the nineteenth century or had other close connections with railways through civil engineering or architecture, for example. They acted as an interest group generally defending and developing the cause of the railways although they did not necessarily always speak with one voice because some might be associated with companies that were deadly rivals. They might cross swords when, for example, bills were going through the parliamentary process involving a conflict of interest between companies. Despite such differences, it was only to be expected that these members would make common cause in attempting to prevent or minimise government regulation of the railways that would have the effect of costing railway companies money and possibly damaging the value of their shares.

These members sat on the board of one or more railway companies and were therefore expected to use their influence to advance the interests of those particular companies in which they frequently had substantial shareholdings. As the railways spread, so did the number of MPs with fingers in the railway pie. In 1866, the 'Railway Interest' was made up of 161 Members of the Commons and 49 of the Lords. Many other MPs had family or business ties with the railway members. In 1846 the *Annual Register* identified 157 Members as having significant railway interests while in 1848 *Bradshaw's Shareholders' Guide* identified 90 MPs who it suggested were Railway Members. Some leading companies had four or more MPs on their boards. The Eastern Counties Railway, for example, had four MPs on its board, the London & North Western and Lancaster & Carlisle had five and the South Wales Railway six. *Bradshaw's Railway Manual, Shareholders' Guide, and Official Directory* appeared annually from

1847-1922 and listed the members of the 'Railway Interest' but their numbers and influence had largely petered out well before the First World War.

Several men who became greatly enriched through their railway activities saw the advantage they could gain by becoming MPs themselves. In 1845, George Hudson became the Member for Sunderland. A number of leading engineers and contractors sat in parliament. Robert Stephenson was an MP for twelve years. Joseph Locke represented Honiton from 1847 to 1860 and Samuel Morton Peto was MP successively for Norwich, Finsbury and Bristol. Sir William Tite, who was a noted architect, doing much railway work, represented Bath from 1855 to 1873. Sir Daniel Gooch, of Great Western Railway fame, represented a seat in Wiltshire for twenty years.

It is hardly surprising that questions were asked about the integrity of MPs whose financial interests were so closely tied to the railways. When issues concerning regulation surfaced in parliament, they were consistent in opposing any government intervention in railway affairs. They argued that the railways should be self-regulating and that where matters such as safety were concerned, they could be trusted and left alone to introduce improvements designed to benefit the public as and when the need for them was proven. These 'Railway MPs' belonged to both main parties but when necessary could operate as a cohesive group because voting divisions were not generally whipped along party lines until the end of the century.

The magazine *Punch* was a consistent and hostile critic of these 'Railway Members', arguing that they were a highly partisan group able to exert undue influence on behalf of the railways while, of course, furthering their own interests. *Punch* in its early days was highly radical and given to reflecting on and voicing a wide range of issues of public concern, not least the seemingly inexorable advance in the size of the railway network and the power that the major railway companies were able to exert. Any perusal of early editions of *Punch* makes it clear the editorial policy was generally critical of railways, those who promoted them or who acted as directors. This antipathy to directors led *Punch* to aver on one occasion, perhaps not entirely in jest, that the planet would benefit if one railway director was hanged every day.

There was an informal group of MPs who were hostile to railways. Many had financial interests which might clash with those of the railway companies. They might have investments in canals and therefore resent the challenge presented by railways. Many such MPs were landowners. They may well have been supporters of the Corn Laws whereas their opponents were likely to support the Anti-Corn Law League and be in favour of Free Trade. The Railway Interest drew parallels between landowners' self-interested determination to keep the price of bread artificially high by preventing corn imports and their manipulation of political power to extract the highest possible price for land wanted for railway projects. Of course, Railway Interest MPs rendered themselves vulnerable when making such criticisms. After all, their ostensible purpose as MPs was to represent the interests of their constituents. Even if they did that, most were busy using the railway connection to further their own interests. Until the early 1870s, the railways had the funds, the administrative machine, the technical and legal expertise and the political influence to fight off any systematic attempt by governments to regulate their activities.

The Railway Interest discerned a distinct threat in 1844 when Gladstone at the Board of Trade was intent on drawing up a bill which would include proposals for the nationalisation of the railways at some time in the future. Not only railway MPs but railway journalists were incensed by this proposal. 'If it is suffered to pass, farewell to all private enterprise in this country. Such an invasion of private rights and vested interests never was...before contemplated,' thundered Herapath. A strong deputation met ministers and senior MPs and lobbied anyone who would listen. Meetings took place in smoke-filled back rooms and the railway lobby managed to secure considerable modifications favourable to the railway companies and particularly around the terms of possible future nationalisation, all to the chagrin of Gladstone.

Railways were always on the receiving end of criticism. They spread their tentacles across the kingdom and became an accepted part of the fabric of everyday life for substantial parts of the population. By the 1870s, a number of issues involving the railways were the subject of parliamentary debate and constant public controversy. These included: the frequency of accidents involving passengers; the strong tendency to mergers; what were regarded as excessive fares; likewise with freight rates; employers' liability as applied to railways; the handling of disciplinary issues by the railways and the hours of work that they required and the dangerous nature of much railway work.

The argument of Railway Interest MPs was that the Acts of Parliament by which railway schemes gained legal standing had taken account of all formal objections and thrashed out conditions for each scheme which ensured that all aspects of the public interest had been taken into consideration. It was therefore wrong for parliament to pass general legislation with respect to railways that overrode the terms and agreements written into each specific Act of Parliament.

The Railway Interest created a body, 'The Railway Companies Association', to represent the general interests of railway companies and their shareholders. However there was no one voice for the interest and instead a number of companies who pursued their own agenda rather than concerning themselves with what might have been best for the industry as a whole. However, despite conflicts among members of the Railway Interest, they were able to present a united front and successfully see off nationalisation threats in 1844, 1867 and in the 1870s. In broader terms, however, they were unable to prevent increasing government intervention in the railways and indeed only the mining industry was subject to greater state regulation by 1914.

Nineteenth-century MPs had considerable freedom of action and although they might call themselves Whigs or Tories, Liberals or Radicals, their political behaviour was markedly independent. A leading Liberal Party member of the Railway Interest had no trouble in joining with a Conservative counterpart to fight a proposal seen as being harmful to the railways. This was not the age of the modern career politician whose progress depends on toeing the party line. From the 1870s, party discipline began increasingly to assert itself, partly because of extensions to the franchise, and the influence of a lobby group like the Railway Interest went into decline.

CHAPTER TEN

Other types of opposition
to the Railways

The various railways built before the 1830s were small-scale schemes. As the beneficial impact that railways could make became increasingly evident, so support for them grew but then so did opposition, especially where vested interests might be affected.

A repeated source of resentment was the right of compulsory purchase conferred on railway companies by Parliamentary Act. This was seen as an infringement of freedom and of private property, an issue which may not have cut much ice with the majority of the population who, with no political rights, were not free in any meaningful sense of the word and had little or no property to speak of. For the propertied minority however, many of whom were landowners with social and political influence, this was a very serious concern. They argued that the land they were forced to sell for the purposes of railway development was often obtained by the companies at prices well below its real value although we have seen that this was by no means necessarily so. There was a host of other reasons that could be found to object to railways.

The author of an article on the Lambourn Valley Railway offers some contemporary but unattributed comments from a source clearly very hostile to the coming of the railways: Referring to the 'Railway Mania' our disgruntled commentator argues:

'The commercial code of 1845 was, as far as railways were concerned, framed upon anything but moral principles. The lust for gain blinded the eyes of men, who, before that period, could see clearly enough the difference between right and wrong, between trading and gambling, and between legitimate and illegitimate speculation. Men who would have scorned to do a dishonest act towards any other real tangible living man, did not scruple to do acts towards that great abstraction, the public, which no morality could justify...The country at large pays a great deal more for the railways besides the price of a ticket when one happens to want it. It cuts off the means of communication from hundreds of neighbourhoods when coach runs are stopped!'[1]

Similarly jaundiced views were expressed in the diary of a Middlesex parson about the impact of the railway in the then rural location of Southall Green, to the west of London in the 1830s:

'A remarkable change for the worse took place about this time in the hitherto retired neighbourhood of Southall Green. The railway spread dissatisfaction and immorality among the poor, the place being inundated with worthless and over paid navigators [navvies]; the very appearance of the country was altered, some families left, and the rusticity of the village gave place to a London-out-of-town character. Moss-grown cottages retired before new ones with bright red tiles, picturesque hedgerows were succeeded by prim iron railings, and the village inn, once a pretty cottage with a swinging sign, is transmogrified to the *Railway Tavern* with an intimation gaudily set forth that "London porter" and other luxuries hitherto unknown to the aboriginals were to be procured within.'[2]

The Royal Commission on Metropolitan Railway Termini

The centre of London is surrounded by an irregularly spaced ring of main line terminus stations. A map will quickly reveal that these stations are placed around the periphery of inner central London and none could be described unequivocally as being 'central'. It could have been very different.

At the height of the frenzied activity known as the 'Railway Mania' in 1846, no fewer than nineteen proposals were put forward for lines that would penetrate the centre of London. However, many grandee landowners including some of the most influential in Britain had estates in London and were opposed to any lines crossing their land on the surface or on elevated structures such as viaducts. Additionally, many smaller landowners, a wide variety of businesses and numerous corporate bodies, some of them ancient and august such as the Corporation of London, were also hostile to these proposals. It was clear that any and indeed all of these lines would cause huge disruption to land which was already intensively built on. Proposals were being voiced for one or perhaps two great terminal stations into which all of London's railway passenger traffic could be concentrated. It was feared that such a development would lead to the almost complete destruction of central London. Concerns over this issue led to the establishment of the Royal Commission on Metropolitan Railway Termini, which reported in 1846. It heard evidence from interested parties and made recommendations that were not legally binding but which established a guiding principle. The railway companies, the confidence of which must have been peaking at this time, lobbied hard for access to the centre of the capital and had probably felt that they would be able to overcome any opposition. They found that they had underestimated the power of the vested interests ranged against them though, as we shall see, over time some companies had at least partial success in penetrating the inner districts of the Metropolis.

A central 'exclusion' zone was identified from Park Lane in the west, along the line of what became the Marylebone and Euston Roads and south to cross the Thames and include part of Southwark and Lambeth. It was strongly recommended that no surface railways should be allowed to penetrate this area and that new termini should be kept to the periphery. Although it was accepted that keeping railways at a distance meant that Londoners and others might have to travel further to reach peripheral termini, the commission concluded that any such inconvenience was outweighed by avoidance of the massive disruption that would be caused by the building of lines, stations and associated yards and other installations in the central area. In the same year, 1846, Charles Pearson, a 'mover and shaker' and Solicitor to the City of London, proposed the construction of what would have been a gigantic central station, possibly in the Farringdon area, into which most, if not all, of the main line companies would run their services. The existing stations were already generating large amounts of road traffic and associated congestion. The chaos that would have been caused by the building and operation of this central station does not bear thinking about. Interestingly though, a single great station is a feature of many large Continental cities.

The conclusions of the commission came to be extensively observed in the breach and it could be said that the railway promoters had the last laugh. The then Ludgate Hill Station and Charing Cross, Victoria and Cannon Street Stations were all built on the northern side of the Thames within the designated zone. Liverpool Street and Broad Street Stations just penetrated it. Waterloo and London Bridge were major stations on the South

Bank and within the zone. Additionally, a number of sub-surface lines on the cut-and-cover principle were built starting with the Metropolitan Railway from Paddington to Farringdon in 1863. The building of these lines, although very disruptive at the time, was much less so than what would have been experienced had main line termini been built in more central locations.

These lines were built to tackle London's chronic road congestion:

'London in the 1850s was booming but in danger of sclerosis. It was a victim of its own success. Increasing prosperity, more residents, more visitors, more business – the road system was already reaching saturation and beyond. It was clear that main line railways were not going to be allowed in Central London and some radical solution to road traffic gridlock was urgently required. No link between the various major termini could possibly be built at surface level or on viaducts through central London.'[3]

The end of prospects that a grand central station would be built in London eventually provided one of the arguments in favour of building what turned out to be a complex system of sub-surface and deep-level tube underground railways of which London was the world pioneer.

The railway companies were frustrated by their inability to penetrate the centre of the city exactly in the way they wanted. In fact, in approaching London and identifying sites for their passenger and goods stations, they had to take into account myriad factors other than those simply to do with engineering. They had to face objections from various public authorities; the opposition of landowners; the limited availability of suitable land at acceptable prices; issues around buildings on land they required and, increasingly as the nineteenth century went on, the delicate question of whether they should have responsibility for those displaced by their activities.

The Metropolitan Board of Works did not object to railways as such, but it had the power to impose its will on railway companies, for example laying down onerous conditions on the District Railway where it wished to build a line along the Victoria Embankment. The Marquess of Westminster was unhappy about his Belgravia estate being penetrated by the railway into what became Victoria Station. He agreed to accept it with a hefty financial tag but had the power to require it to be designed in such a way as to minimise its environmental impact and nuisance value. The power of vested interests around inner London was a source of great frustration to companies wishing to maximise the business opportunities provided by London.

London's Underground

In London, the Underground is taken for granted. It is expected to be convenient, frequent, punctual, clean, cheap and hassle-free. Running the system is a hugely complex operation and most of the time it works remarkably well. When it isn't working, Central London becomes even more chaotic than normal; the Underground is part of its fabric.

The section of cut-and-cover or sub-surface line from Paddington to Farringdon was the world's first underground railway. It opened in 1863. This line was built to relieve road congestion. Gridlock is still there, only worse. It was probably inevitable that there would be opposition to the building of the pioneer and subsequent sub-surface lines. The construction of these lines caused considerable disruption of the sort only too familiar to a later generation of Londoners with Crossrail and other projects. There were objections to the building demolitions that were required. Official figures stated that just 307 people were displaced. Some contemporary estimates put the figure as high as 12,000. From the start, there were concerns about the smuts and smoke that would be produced by the steam locomotives pulling the trains. People living close to the line complained that their garden shrubs would be killed by the sulphurous fumes emitted by the steam locomotives. Stations like Baker Street which were entirely subterranean were permeated by a poisonous and almost impenetrable fug which caused travellers to cough, splutter, expectorate and complain bitterly. This murk was a godsend for pickpockets. The carriages were lighted by oil lamps which emitted a foul smell and dripped on passengers. Early underground travel was not for the faint-hearted.

The Times was highly sceptical about the likely success of the proposed underground line:

'A subterranean railway under London was awfully suggestive of dark, noisome tunnels, buried many fathoms deep beyond the reach of light or life; passages inhabited by rats, soaked with sewer drippings, and poisoned by the escape of gas mains. It seemed an insult to common sense to suppose that people who could travel as cheaply to the city on the outside of a Paddington 'bus would ever prefer as a merely quicker medium, to be driven amid palpable darkness through the foul subsoil of London...'[4]

In spite of apocalyptic predictions that the building of underground railways would arouse the wrath of the Devil, who would then wreak his revenge in ways too horrible to contemplate, and equally dire warnings to the effect that tunnels and retaining walls would collapse, crushing those brazen and stupid enough to travel on it, the line from Paddington to Farringdon was an almost total success. The choking atmosphere was eventually overcome with electrification. This was not before another disgruntled traveller had put pen to paper and written to *The Times*:

'I was almost suffocated and was obliged to be assisted from the train to an intermediate station. On reaching the open air I requested to be taken to a chemist close at hand. Without a moment's hesitation he said "Oh, I see, Metropolitan Railway", and at once poured out a wine glass of what I conclude he designated Metropolitan Mixture. I was induced to ask him whether he often has such cases, to which he rejoined, "Why, bless you, Sir, we often have twenty cases a day."'[5]

The 'Bayswater Tremor'

The Central London Railway (CLR), predecessor of today's Central Line and commonly known as the 'Twopenny Tube' for its initial flat fare, originally ran from Cornhill, soon renamed 'Bank', to Shepherd's Bush. The official opening was on 27 June, 1900. It was an early deep-level tube line and was well used from the start. No sooner had it started operating, however, than complaints began to be made about the vibrations that trains were causing in buildings they passed under on their subterranean journeys. The most vociferous complainants were well-heeled and well-connected inhabitants of affluent districts like Mayfair. Unlike the *hoi polloi* whose views could largely be ignored, the views of such people could not be so lightly dismissed.

A group of experts, commonly known as the 'Vibration Committee', was set up by the government to investigate the problem and to draw up a report with recommendations. It swiftly pointed the finger at the heavy and massively built electric locomotives that were in use and were creating vibrations as they moved ponderously along under the Metropolis. Blame was also extended to the uneven surface and lack of rigidity of the specific type of rails and track used on the CLR. In 1903, lighter electric multiple unit trains replaced the locomotives and the vibrations ceased.

The Improved Railway Communication Association

This particular episode involves support for a better railway service with pressure on a particular company to provide it. The citizens of Worthing thought that the London, Brighton & South Coast Railway (LBSCR) was giving them a poor deal. Although Worthing was located on the line running west along the coast from Brighton, the townspeople were irked by having to travel to Brighton and change there for London. This took time and the connections were often poor. They wanted direct trains to London but thought that the LBSCR was far more interested in concentrating on the lucrative and prestigious traffic to and from London and Brighton. The Association was formed in 1874 and attempted to put pressure on the company to improve the service but it would not be budged. The Association did not take this indifference lying down and promoted a bill for a west to north curve from the Worthing and Hove direction to the main line to London at Preston Park. This was intended to allow through running from the coast line to and from London. This prospect shocked the LBSCR sufficiently for them to offer to build the spur and operate the trains as long as the Association did not proceed with the Bill. The outcome was the line known as the Cliftonville Spur and it opened on 1 January 1879.

Issues around Crime

Jeffrey Richards and John M. MacKenzie pointed out one of the paradoxes of railways and their stations:

> 'The station became at one and the same time one of the principal forces in society for order, regulation, and discipline, and a new focus for violence, crime and immorality.'[6]

While the railways did spawn their own miscreants, clerks engaged in fraudulent book-keeping and employees who pilfered goods in transit, for example, their advent offered rich opportunities for the wider criminal fraternity. The close confines of a railway carriage compartment provided an ideal scenario for a robbery, assault or even a murder particularly before the means existed for a potential victim to summon help or stop the train. A number of murders which attracted considerable interest took place up to the late nineteenth century by which time communication cords were universal and all trains equipped with lighting, many having side corridors and connections to adjacent carriages as well.

In the *Derby Mercury* in July 1854, a correspondent signing himself an 'American Traveller' wrote:

> 'I am not a timid man, but I never enter an English railway carriage without having in my pocket a loaded revolver. How am I to know but that my travelling companion may be a madman escaped from confinement, or a runaway criminal? And what protection have I against their assault, if it should please them to attack me, but the weapon I carry?'[7]

This correspondent strongly advocated the adoption on Britain's railways of a communication cord of the kind already in use in the USA.

The criminal fraternity is nothing if not ingenious and opportunistic and it welcomed the railways as opening up a whole range of new possibilities. The activities of criminals caused one complainant to the *Railway Times* to advocate a return to what he described as 'the good old days of Dick Turpin' who he regarded as a 'brave and noble fellow compared with the cowardly brutes who were infesting railway carriages'.

Those whose business involved the transportation of gold and silver for example, welcomed the coming of the railways in the belief that the speed of trains made it unlikely that anyone would attempt to ambush a moving train in order to plunder its valuable cargo. However, while there is no record of a masked and mounted highwayman stopping a train and uttering the immortal words 'Stand and Deliver', there were many occasions on which criminals managed to steal bullion, money and other valuables while trains were in motion or immobile in stations, yards and sidings.

Crowded stations were a happy hunting ground for beggars, pickpockets, luggage thieves and prostitutes while card-sharpers frequently found gullible victims in trains that were on the move. Pimps and perverts were on the lookout at big city stations for vulnerable young people running away from home. Whenever

THE MODERN DICK TURPIN; OR, HIGHWAYMAN AND RAILWAYMAN.

Ghost of Turpin. "HO-HO, MR. DIRECTOR! DOING A BIT IN MY LINE, EH?"
Railway Director. "YOUR LINE? HA! HA! YOU WERE HANGED! WE ROB BY ACT OF PARLIAMENT!!!"

This Punch cartoon by John Tenniel depicts the ghost of Dick Turpin attempting to waylay a train. The implication is that Turpin robbed illegally but the railway director astride the locomotive's boiler is also a robber but he robs legally by parliamentary means.

crimes were committed on trains and around railway premises, indignant outcries would be heard blaming the railways. This was somewhat unfair because they might provide the means and opportunity for the commission of crime but they did not themselves cause criminal activity. The railways actually helped the fight against crime by adopting the electric telegraph not only for safety purposes but as a high-speed method of communication which was successfully used to apprehend many criminals.

Railways and 'Heritage'

Conservation is often thought of as a twentieth-century development, perhaps only really having an impact after the Second World War. It is nothing of the sort as the early days of the railways show.

Railway promoters engaged energetically in building projects were intolerant of obstacles. Many difficulties were placed in their way by landowners and we have seen how the railway companies fought, bribed, flattered or otherwise persuaded their opponents into acquiescence. Often the protests of landowners at supposed desecration by the railways represented little more than self-interest but even in the mid-nineteenth century, there were aesthetes, antiquarians and others who ranged themselves either against railways as a whole or against those projects which threatened places or buildings of beauty or historical merit. Sometimes the railways rode rough-shod over such objections. At other times they were prepared to change their plans or make concessions to hostile opinion. Here we give some examples of destruction threatened or carried out by the railways.

It should be noted that demolition of ancient buildings was not pioneered by the railways. Piecemeal urban improvement over centuries had seen projects to straighten streets or widen them by demolition. All but one of the City of London's old gateways had been pulled down by the early 1760s. Other towns had knocked down ancient gateways and the buildings on London Bridge were removed around 1830. Improvement to traffic flows in this locality had already involved much demolition but the coming of the railway threatened parts of St Saviour's Church (later Southwark Cathedral). Protests were launched and much of the building was saved. To this day the close proximity of the railway detracts from the visual impact of the building.[8]

The Great Western Railway in approaching Bath from the east sought to assuage local feelings by creating an ornamental cutting where the line passed through Sydney Gardens. On leaving Bath going westwards, the line was built on a low stone-built viaduct with Tudor motifs, again a gesture to the city's ancient charms.

The broad gauge Wilts, Somerset and Weymouth Railway was projected in the mid-1840s. Among its opponents was the Dorset Field Club, a local environmental group which did not want the line to pass close to Poundbury Camp, an Iron Age hill-fort. This group clearly had influence. The desecration of this ancient monument was avoided.

In 1844, the Brighton, Lewes & Hastings Railway was incorporated. Lewes is an ancient town of considerable importance because of its strategic position. It contained a large, complex castle and also had a massive priory of the Cluniac Order which very unwillingly surrendered to Thomas Cromwell, Henry VIII's minister, in 1537. With singular spitefulness, Cromwell had most of the buildings razed to the ground. Local citizens helped themselves to much of what was left as a quarry for building material. Later citizens must have had a higher regard for the remaining fragments. When it was proposed to build the line from Brighton, its alignment cut right through the site. The Sussex Archaeological Society was founded to prevent further destruction. Its efforts were brave but largely unsuccessful.

Around 1850, the London & North Western Railway (LNWR) wanted to build a branch line from Watford to St Albans. The initial intention was to align the branch around the southern side of the city to a terminus at St Michaels' on the western side. This aroused widespread protest because the railway was likely to have impinged on part of the site of the ancient Roman town of Verulamium. The thrust of the protest was around the lack of respect the railway company was showing for such a venerable and historic location. Somewhat abashed, the LNWR decided to terminate instead at the present site of St Albans Abbey Station, rather inconvenient for the city centre, because it is located at the bottom of the hill on which the city stands. The line opened on 5 May 1858.

At Newcastle-upon-Tyne, much of the town walls and parts of the castle were demolished to make space for the Central Station, this being opened on 29 August 1850. The destruction of the castle at Berwick-upon-Tweed provoked protest. Some of the masonry from the castle was recycled and used in the station building which, perhaps by way of atonement, was adorned with a number of crenellations and other features reminiscent of castles. Parts of castle works at Berkhamsted, Huntingdon and Northampton were destroyed. The city walls at York were breached for the purpose of building a passenger station. In a place of such historic significance, it is strange that this occurred with little local dissent despite the location covering the site of three Roman baths. On the approach to Manchester Central Station, the viaducts were adorned with castellations as a gesture to appease local antiquarian feeling concerned that the site of an ancient Roman fort had been disturbed by the building of this structure. Gilsland, known as Rosehill until 1869, was an intermediate station on the Newcastle and Carlisle railway and situated between Carlisle and Haltwhistle. Its construction involved the demolition of part of Hadrian's Wall.

Robert Stephenson, engineer of the Chester & Holyhead Railway, planned to bridge the River Conwy immediately east of the town of the same name and had to take into account the magnificent Edwardian castle and the ancient town walls. Earlier, Thomas Telford's road bridge at the same spot had been designed to harmonise, at least in theory, with the castle. Under pressure from the Commissioners of Woods & Forests, Stephenson was required to provide crenellations on the portals of his remarkable tubular bridge. Where the line penetrated the town wall, he erected a Gothic-style arch which has blended in so well that few people would think that it wasn't the genuine article.

Friction was continuous between the railway companies whose lines approached Edinburgh's Waverley Station from the west and influential local citizens who objected to the despoliation of Princes Street Gardens. This line was opened in 1846 and the station itself partly occupied the site of the Nor' Loch which had been a stinking midden into which the inhabitants of the Old Town threw all manner of waste. It seemingly mattered little that the loch had been drained, the ferocious stench extinguished and the site utilised for what became the city's main railway station. Now the well-loved gardens would be polluted by the sight, sound and smell of noxious steam locomotives. If this was not bad enough, traffic built up so much that the line through the gardens had to be quadrupled.

Where the Chester & Holyhead needed to cross the Conwy River, Stephenson showed his virtuosity by combining the innovative concept of a tubular bridge with the mock turrets, battlements and machicolation reminiscent of medieval fortified buildings. Here a Stanier 'Black 5' 4-6-0 emerges from the bridge with an eastbound express. (Authors' collection)

Robert Stephenson as Engineer for the Chester & Holyhead Railway exhibited great sensitivity where the route was aligned to pass close to the walls of Conwy Castle and actually to penetrate the ancient town walls. He built this 'gothic' arch where the wall was breached and today most people could not even 'see the join'. (D. Brandon)

The University of Glasgow can proudly trace its roots back to 1451. It was located at the eastern end of the city with an entrance on the High Street and not far from St Mungo's Cathedral. By the nineteenth century, the site was becoming too cramped, the buildings were crumbling and the area was becoming engulfed in the filth produced by Glasgow's prodigious industrial growth. In the 1860s, a decision was taken to move to a new site at Gilmorehill on the west side of the city. The historic buildings were either demolished or taken over and used by the City of Glasgow Union Railway Company who recalled the former use of the site by employing the name 'College' for its goods station. Some muted concerns were expressed at the time about the virtual obliteration of such a significant part of Glasgow's history. Ironically, in view of the heated criticism about the Midland Grand Hotel at St Pancras, there were many who disapproved of the appearance of the new buildings at Gilmorehill. They were built in a loosely Gothic style with a few Scottish baronial features. The architect in both cases was George Gilbert Scott.

A glory of old London was the view looking east up Ludgate Hill towards St Paul's Cathedral. The London, Chatham and Dover Railway built a bridge which obscured this view as shown by the French artist, Gustav Dore. The railway company incurred widespread resentment for what was regarded as a piece of environmental vandalism. (Authors' collection)

Built in the 1860s, a line of the London, Chatham & Dover Railway crossed a viaduct at the foot of Ludgate Hill and was widely lambasted at the time for ruining the view of St Paul's Cathedral from the west. This view had long been considered one of the finest pieces of streetscape in London. Grumbles about what was considered as vandalism continued until the viaduct was replaced by a tunnel in 1991.

The Didcot, Newbury & Southampton Railway (DN&SR) was incorporated in 1873 but it was the early 1890s before the line was opened throughout. In the 1880s, there had been objections to the proposed alignment near Newbury on the grounds of environmental damage to an area of great beauty. Readers may remember in the 1990s, the vehement protests about the proposed route of the Newbury bypass. Part of this used some of the formation of the abandoned DN&SR. Eco-warriors descended on the area, outraged that another scene of sylvan beauty was to be sacrificed for the perceived interests of the road lobby and that a colony of rare snails was likely to be displaced and condemned to disappear.

In 1878, a railway line was completed by the North Eastern Railway (NER) through Wensleydale from Northallerton to Hawes with an end-on junction with a short line of the Midland Railway from Hawes to what was then called Hawes Junction on the Settle and Carlisle Line. Once this line was complete, there was a revival of an earlier scheme for a possible line from Manchester to Northallerton. This would pass through Skipton and Upper Wharfedale and link up with the NER's Wensleydale line at Aysgarth. Trains would then proceed eastwards to Northallerton from where they could gain access to potentially lucrative traffic around the rivers Tees, Wear and Tyne. This scheme, surfacing in 1880, would have crossed the River Ure on a bridge close to the renowned beauty spot of Aysgarth Falls. This proposal provoked the wrath of what would now be called the 'environmental lobby'. Protestors against the excesses of the railways were learning as they went and improving their tactics. They now formed an interest or lobby group with the name of the Aysgarth Defence Association. This had sufficient money and the organisational skills to produce a booklet called *The Railway Viaduct at Aysgarth Force* which polemicized against the proposals and achieved wide circulation. Many meetings were held across the country and the Association gained the support of the influential art critic and aesthete John Ruskin. Another supporter was the then President of the Royal Academy, Sir Frederick Leighton, who announced that the public would not accept the defilement of a place of such natural beauty as Aysgarth Falls. The Aysgarth Defence Association was not to be underestimated because it hit on the master propaganda stroke of putting Turner's painting of the Falls on exhibition in London with the intention that the movers and shakers of the Metropolis should be made aware of the appalling environmental vandalism that was being proposed. In the event, the proposal remained just that, a proposal. It was mundane economic reality rather than environmental lobbying that meant that Aysgarth Falls fortunately emerged unscathed.

At Nottingham, the Great Northern Railway opened a connection in 1899 to serve the new Victoria Station and this ran from Weekday Cross to Trent Lane Junction. Although only a short piece of line, it incurred controversy because it involved destruction of some of the caves carved out of sandstone and known as Sneinton Hermitage. The local anger was understandable because these caves were reputed to have been in continuous use as human dwellings as far back as pre-Saxon times.

The Red Hall at Bourne in Lincolnshire is a handsome brick-built small mansion of the early seventeenth century which was appropriated to act as the station building by the Bourne & Essendine Railway which opened in 1860. About three decades later, the Red Hall was threatened with demolition with the building of the Midland and the Great Northern Joint Railway's line approaching the town from the west. A petition was drawn up locally with the endorsement of the Society for the Protection of Ancient Buildings and addressed to the two companies. It urged them to realign the route from Saxby so as to spare the historic building. It might have seemed a bit of fuss of purely local interest but national newspapers and influential periodicals such as the *Illustrated London News* took up the story. The happy outcome was that the building was saved in 1890-1 and converted into the stationmaster's house. It survives to this day, used by various local groups, although Bourne's railways are long gone.

One sensitive spot in a town with many affluent and influential residents was the Stray at Harrogate. This was originally common land but in 1770 was dedicated in perpetuity as open land free for access by all. The existence of this extensive open land so close to the town centre endeared it to the hearts of the local citizenry and when the North Eastern Railway proposed to cross it in the early 1860s, they were compelled to place it in an unobtrusive stone-lined cutting. Several attempts by the Great Eastern Railway to pierce Epping Forest were thwarted by those determined to preserve what was left of this ancient woodland for posterity. When much of it came to be controlled by the Corporation of the City of London, any more attempts were doomed to failure. That was one body that did not negotiate unless it wanted to.

The Great Central Railway was forced by a well-orchestrated campaign by local antiquarians and the Borough Council at Leicester to divert its projected route away from Roman remains and the ruins of the castle. They were also legally required to preserve a Roman mosaic pavement and allow public access to view it.

Throughout the nineteenth century, an embryonic preservationist movement emerged. Those involved were not necessarily anti-railway but were determined for a variety of reasons to oppose or force modifications to specific proposals advanced by the railway companies. A comprehensive survey would show many failures but also growing successes as lessons were learned about how to campaign effectively.

Railways and Towns

It should be remembered that although the railways have generally been seen as contributors to economic growth and towns for that reason wanted to be on the 'railway map', growth did not occur simply because a town joined the network. There were towns whose size and prosperity did not increase as a result of the arrival of a railway; there were a few that seemingly prospered without a railway and others that actually went into decline after gaining a railway connection. Railways, after all, might take people or business away from a town, perhaps to a rival elsewhere. The market at Wiveliscombe in Somerset, for example, went into headlong decline after the arrival of the railway enabled people to travel to the larger market in Taunton. Not all towns, therefore, welcomed railways with open arms. Population could rise and fall, irrespective of the presence or otherwise of a railway. Bath and Cambridge, for example, gained their first railway connections in the 1840s, yet in the years immediately following, the population of both fell. Only a detailed study of individual towns can establish the exact nature of the impact that the railway made and whether the welcome or the hostility they extended to the railway was justified. Here we examine a number of towns some of which objected to railways *per se,* perhaps changing their mind later and others which happily joined the railway system only then to become critical of some aspect of the way in which the railway served the locality.

The effective monopoly exercised by what became the London & North Western Railway at Coventry was a long-standing bone of contention with the local business community. Despite its place on the main line from London to Birmingham and being the junction for lines to Leamington and to Nuneaton, it was impossible to escape the impression that the London & North Western and its successor the London, Midland & Scottish Railway was not very interested in making the most of the traffic potential of what was a sizeable industrial city. Its poky little station was frankly an insult and was viewed as such locally until it was rebuilt in the early 1960s.

Northampton has often been held up as a place which missed out on being located on a main line because of the intransigent opposition of influential townspeople. It is claimed that this opposition was determined enough to force the Stephensons, father and son, to choose an alignment just over four miles west for the London & Birmingham Railway (L&B). Initially it would appear strange that this trunk line did not to serve Northampton which was already a substantial town offering considerable traffic potential. A myth was created, echoes of which persist to this day, concerning Northampton's supposed opposition but the real reason for the L&B missing Northampton lies in geological factors rather than local feeling. It was Robert Stephenson who did the detailed work on the L&B project and his decision to bypass Northampton, about four miles to the west, was taken on engineering grounds. Stephenson was aiming at a ruling gradient of 1 in 330. In going south from Rugby, a tunnel could not be avoided near Kilsby. This tunnel, although it unexpectedly proved very troublesome to build, could avoid the stiffer gradients that would have been encountered further east. Certainly there had been a number of Northamptonshire landowners who objected to the L&B and would have put up a show of objection to any line in the area, whatever its alignment, especially when they learned that there was a good chance of financial compensation if objections were raised. The Stephensons were consistent in their approach to trying to minimise likely engineering difficulties. A few years later, when George Stephenson was building the North Midland Railway, he took a route from Chesterfield through Rotherham and avoiding Sheffield in spite of its potential for good business, so as to avoid expensive engineering challenges on the southern approaches to Sheffield.

The townspeople feared for the general prosperity of Northampton and of its shoe-making industry in particular if Northampton was not served by a main line railway. They lobbied hard for a line from Leicester and the East Midlands to serve the town on its way to join up with the L&B. Various schemes were put forward but in the end they had to be content with a secondary line of the London & North Western Railway through the difficult upland country from Market Harborough. A loop line leaving what became the West Coast Main Line and running through the town before rejoining the main line at Roade was opened as late as 1881. There is no evidence that Northampton's economic development and especially that of the shoe industry was hampered by the lack of a main railway line.

Another town, which had confidently expected to be on a major trunk route but which instead had to put up with being the focus of a number of secondary routes, was Lincoln. Until the 1840s, there was every expectation that Lincoln would be astride a major trunk route from London to York and the North-East. Indeed, several schemes were put forward for such a route passing through the city but none came to fruition and the Great Northern Railway passed through Newark, about fifteen miles west. En route from London and Peterborough, this line served Grantham, Newark and Retford on its way northwards and these towns were expected to provide better traffic potential than rural Lincolnshire, even though difficult terrain was encountered between Peterborough and Grantham. It has often been said that a key player in preventing a trunk route to the north coming through Lincoln was one of its MPs, Colonel Charles de Laet Waldo Sibthorp. He was a landowner on a moderate scale but had no particular influence in the House to oppose the Great Northern Railway or any other railway. The Great Northern Railway's decision to choose the route to the west was largely the responsibility of the Great Northern's energetic Deputy Chairman, Edmund Dennison. His major concern was for the most direct route to the north.

Thetford was a curious case of an ancient but relatively small town that took great exception to being told that it would get a railway connection but only on the end of a branch line. The Norwich & Brandon Railway was authorised in 1844 and it included a branch to Thetford. This was not good enough for the townsfolk who feared that if left off a major railway, they would lose business to Norwich. Strings must have been pulled because the railway company decided to reconsider its decision. A deviation from the original route was made and Thetford secured its place on what eventually became a significant secondary main line.

Uxbridge in Middlesex was a major staging point on the busy road from London to Oxford and much of the town's prosperity depended on catering for road travellers, their coaches, carriages

A DANGEROUS CHARACTER.

Policeman Sibthorp. "COME, IT'S HIGH TIME YOU WERE TAKEN TO THE HOUSE; YOU'VE DONE QUITE MISCHIEF ENOUGH."

Colonel Charles de Laet Waldo Sibthorp was Lincoln's famous eccentric MP in the nineteenth century. His quirks were many but he was perhaps best known for his splenetic hatred of railways. He was the caricaturist's dream and in this *Punch* cartoon he is shown dressed as a railway policeman but equipped with this trademark monocle, marching off a woebegone and handcuffed steam locomotive to the House of Commons.

This is an example of a notice placed in a local newspaper to try to rally opposition to a proposed railway scheme at Ipswich.

TO OPPONENTS
OF THE
Ipswich, Norwich, and Yarmouth projected Railway.

IT is the intention of several influential Land-owners to oppose the above Railway, and they are desirous of being joined by other persons who may find themselves aggrieved by this project, a Meeting will therefore be held on Tuesday next, the 20th instant, at the King's Head Inn, at Bungay, at One o'clock precisely, at which meeting all persons interested in opposing the above Line of Railway are invited to attend either by themselves or their Agents.

Signed,
CALVERLEY RICHARD BEWICKE.
Barsham House, Suffolk,
14th Jan., 1846.

For any intermediate information which may be required, apply to Messrs. Margitson and Hartcup, Solicitors, Bungay.

and wagons and the needs of horses. It put up strong opposition to early proposals that might have placed it on a major railway route. It is claimed that it was this vehement opposition which deterred the Great Western Railway from routing its line to the west through the town which was already one of significant size and importance. In the event, the Great Western Railway passed through West Drayton, two miles south, instead. It did not take the burghers of the town long to realise that their hostility was misplaced and, almost in panic, they promoted the Great Western & Uxbridge Railway in 1846. Although the project was absorbed by the GWR in 1847, it was as late as 8 September 1856 that the line opened fully. Eventually,

Uxbridge came to be served by lines from three directions but all of a relatively minor nature. The town expanded greatly in the nineteenth and twentieth centuries but it might have been much bigger had it been eager to welcome railways back in the 1830s. It is actually far more likely that what caused the GWR main line to avoid Uxbridge was not so much opposition from people in the town as engineering factors and the desire to keep the route out of Paddington as straight and flat as possible.

Some seaside resorts were hostile to early proposals for them to be linked to the developing railway system because they wanted to remain 'select' They thought that railways would lay on cheap trains bringing hordes of urban working people behaving in an uncouth and probably drunken fashion. They would lower the tone and scare away their better-off, established patrons. Weston-Super-Mare was an example of this attitude. The residents of the small, scattered settlements that were later consolidated to form the nucleus of Bournemouth were also not keen on railways. They wanted to keep what was a very attractive part of the coast exclusive. It was considered that day-trippers would bring their vulgar appearance and their vulgar habits with them. They would destroy the serene pleasures that made the area so attractive to the well-heeled visitors who already enjoyed its charms. Sidmouth in Devon was a small seaside watering place priding itself on being select and many of its citizens did not want a railway which would bring trippers and other social riff-raff. A branch from the Salisbury to Exeter main line of the London & South Western Railway opened in 1874 but the station was located at an inconvenient spot nearly a mile from the sea front. It was hoped that this would deter the *hoi-polloi*. Sidmouth stayed small and select. Some places did indeed manage to remain select but it has to be said that railways contributed greatly to the making and expansion of the popular seaside resorts. By the latter half of the nineteenth century, the railways were carrying sizeable numbers of middle-class visitors to resorts for a week's holiday and larger numbers of urban working-class families on day trips.

Southampton was joined to London by the London & South Western Railway (LSWR) in 1840. This benefitted the business being conducted through the port and whetted the desire of the local commercial community to develop further business by opening up railway links particularly with the West Midlands. This, it was thought, would allow Southampton to gain useful business by handling manufactured goods made in that region and aimed at the export market. The LSWR was the only railway company serving Southampton and it showed little interest in assisting the town to develop such a link. It was not long before local traders were complaining about the monopoly exploited by the company and the indifference it displayed towards the business aspirations of Southampton's commercial community. The LSWR made itself more unpopular because in order to extend its lines westward from Southampton, it built a new station, first called Southampton West and renamed 'Central' in 1935. This was inconvenient for the centre of Southampton and local people were incensed because many trains from London proceeding west used this station rather than the more handily placed Southampton Terminus. It did not help that the new station was built in a quiet residential district whose inhabitants were soon complaining about noise and dirt pollution. The town's traders joined in, complaining that shops opening up towards this station were drawing business away from the centre. The LSWR was execrated in the town as a London-based and largely London-financed monopoly, seemingly insensitive to local needs. The major trunk route to and from the Midlands was never built.

Scarborough has an unusual place among British seaside resorts in that visitors came to take its supposedly therapeutic mineral waters a century or more before they were drawn to its attractions as a place to engage in the new, late eighteenth-century craze for sea-bathing. It was a long way from the towns, especially those in the West Riding of Yorkshire, which provided most of its clientele and this meant that its visitors tended to be well-heeled and many of them possessed their own carriages. It prospered in its dual role as a spa and seaside watering place and many local business people, residents and visitors wanted to maintain its social exclusivity. The first proposal to build a railway to Scarborough failed, in part because of robust opposition from a local coalition who opposed the railway. This group actually congratulated itself on saving Scarborough from an awful fate and they were sure that they would be thanked for achieving this. Inevitably, it was not long before railways came to Scarborough, the first being a line from York in 1845 and they brought with them working-class people intent on enjoying its charms. Although the nature of the place was to some extent changed with the coming of the railways, even to this day Scarborough has something of a dual character with its popular and its 'posh' ends. As usual when a line opened, a special inaugural train conveying dignitaries was put on and when it arrived at Scarborough, large, cheering crowds greeted it. A public holiday had been declared in the town, the bands were playing and the place was *en fête*. This suggests that the bulk of local people welcomed the coming of the railway, recognising that it was likely to bring business to the town, irrespective of the views of those who wanted to keep the town 'exclusive'. Of course, they may have been in such a jubilant mood simply because they were having a day off.

Swanage stands at the eastern extremity of the Isle of Purbeck. In the first half of the nineteenth century, most of its inhabitants enjoyed the sequestered nature of the place and did not want a railway. In fact, for many of them it was bad enough that a railway from Bournemouth to Dorchester ran through Wareham, the nearest inland town of any size. Early proposals to build a railway into the Isle of Purbeck, a misnomer because it is actually a peninsula, by the Southampton & Dorset Railway in 1847 and 1850 had come to nought. After the London & South Western Railway took over, another bill for a line to Swanage was defeated. However, the Isle was penetrated by railways of a sort because a network of small tramways was built to carry locally excavated ball clay to wharves on the periphery of Poole Harbour. By the 1870s, many local people were beginning to regret the lack of a railway, feeling that progress was passing their town by. Swanage was developing into a genteel watering place which stayed small and select precisely because, without a railway, it was not particularly easy to get to. That was the way that some townspeople wanted it to stay. Others felt its prosperity would be increased if a railway was built which could bring in more visitors and generate more money. In the event, Swanage was late in gaining its railway, the line to the town opening for passenger traffic on 20 May 1885. Swanage did gain more visitors but they largely remained the kind of people who did not want too much razzmatazz.

Ilfracombe was a small north Devon town, much off the beaten track and highly desirous by the mid-nineteenth century of having a railway. It was believed that this would inject some much-needed new economic life into the town. Both the London & South Western and the Great Western Railway had designs on Ilfracombe through subsidiary companies. A curious twist on responses to railways saw riots in the streets of Ilfracombe after the House of Lords rejected the Bill for the first proposed line to the town. Local people hanged or buried effigies of other local people they believed had been opposed to this particular Bill. Things got to the point where the Riot Act had to be read. A second proposal to parliament was also rejected soon afterwards. The town eventually gained its railway connection. This was in 1874 and involved the line approaching the station via precipitous gradients, the town itself being spectacularly but very inconveniently placed high above the town.

Lyme Regis in Dorset provides us with the rather odd case of a town which wanted its own railway and a railway company which initially displayed interest in the idea and then spent decades either prevaricating or ignoring the idea. Lyme Regis was a small seaside resort, necessarily 'select' because of its remoteness from the large centres of population and also because of the difficulty of access. By the middle of the nineteenth century, local people were concerned that, unless it could be connected to the railway network, the town would simply stagnate, losing potential visitors to other resorts which were served by railways. A railway might also revive the flagging fortunes of the town as a minor seaport. Initially the London & South Western Railway (LSWR) declared an interest in building a branch line to Lyme Regis but it became apparent that this was tactical politics, the object being to keep the Great Western Railway out of the area. Once that threat had been seen off, they seemed to lose interest. Self-help seemed to be the order of the day and a bill for a line to be built by the Lyme Regis Railway Company was passed in 1871 with the LSWR agreeing to operate the services. Much to the frustration of the townspeople, the LSWR again seemed to lose interest even though a ceremonial first sod-cutting ceremony took place in 1874. The parliamentary powers lapsed. In 1898, a petition with around 2,000 signatures was submitted to the LSWR who failed to respond. Finally, a well-connected local landowner managed to persuade the LSWR to support the construction of a line to the town from Axminster on its Salisbury to Exeter main line. Public services started on 24 August 1903. The earliest moves to build a line to Lyme Regis had been made back in 1845 so the town had had to put up with almost sixty years of waiting. As it was, the local company that ran the line quickly found itself in financial difficulties and the line was absorbed by the LSWR in 1907.

Oswestry in Shropshire was a market town which was not connected to a railway in the early 1840s. This may have been because the town was a focus of a number of roads and had hotels and the other services associated with stage coach travel. Their influence may have created sufficient opposition to persuade the

Shrewsbury to Chester Railway to avoid the town by passing just to the east through Gobowen. Oswestry later became the focal point and headquarters of the Cambrian Railway's system with its engineering works and a case could be made for including it in a list of minor railway towns. We can only speculate on how much more prominent a railway town it might have become if it had been located on the main line from Shrewsbury to Chester.

The Horncastle Railway Company received the Royal Assent on 10 July 1854. The line ran from the small town of Horncastle through the tiny and sedate watering place of Woodhall Spa to a junction with the Great Northern Railway's Lincoln to Boston line. This short and obscure line provided a microcosm of the history of many similar lines. There had been considerable opposition to the line on the grounds that it would have a damaging effect on the town's retailers. This proved to be correct as those townspeople who could afford to do so, used the trains to get to Lincoln in particular or Boston to take advantage of the greater range of goods in the shops. Local people were realistic enough to know that people from those towns would not come by train to shop in Horncastle. Why then, they asked, should they support the building of a railway that would benefit those towns rather than their own? The railway brought in cheap manufactured goods which, over time, undercut items made locally and led to the closure of a number of small firms and redundancies among their workforces. The railway competed directly with the Horncastle Canal which was forced to cut its tolls in 1855 and finally succumbed in 1889. The townspeople had the railway to thank for a reduction of four shillings per ton in the price of coal. Buses and road hauliers began to cream off traffic from the 1930s and with passenger traffic being uneconomic, closure was proposed in 1952. This aroused a storm of protest from such organisations as the local authorities, the Chamber of Commerce, the Agricultural Workers' Union and the Women's Institute. They succeeded in delaying the closure for a couple of years but passenger services were discontinued from 11 September 1954. Few members of these organisations used the passenger trains in their final years. Complete closure of the line took place on 5 April 1971.

The first railway line authorised to serve Sheffield was intended to join that town to Rotherham. The project ran into vehement opposition from a vicar in Rotherham who collected a large number of signatures on a petition against the proposed line. The main thrust of the objection was that the railway would encourage 'idle, drunken and dissolute' elements of Sheffield's population to travel to Rotherham. The protest was in vain and trains started running on 31 October 1838.

It was not that Leeds did not want a railway. It did not want a particular railway. The North Eastern Railway (NER) served the town with lines from York and Hull which terminated at an inconvenient site in the east of the city at Marsh Lane. A line from the Thirsk direction ran into the more conveniently located Central Station, shared with the London & North Western and Great Northern Railways. Also in the centre of Leeds was the Wellington Station of the Midland Railway. In 1863, the NER proposed to build a line on which its trains to and from York and Hull could run into yet another, albeit much more convenient city centre station, enabling them to close Marsh Lane to passengers. The problem was that in order to do so, it would have to build a viaduct crossing many major city streets such as Albion Street, Park Row, Kirkgate and Briggate. This would involve much demolition and subsequent large-scale disorientation of the commercial district through which it would pass. It would also pass undesirably close to the parish church of St Peter's. The NER's proposal provoked instant hostility and with so many local people of influence being opposed to it, the NER had little option but to withdraw its proposal and substitute a line, most of it on a viaduct, slightly to the south. This scheme involved the demolition of an area of notorious slums with no provision for their inhabitants to be re-housed but the 'movers and shakers' were happy with this scheme and it received parliamentary approval in 1865. It ran into the 'New' Station, adjacent to Wellington, which it shared with the London & North Western.

Railway Navvies

The navvies or navigators were the men who did the hard and most skilled physical work involved in draining the Fens, building the canals and then constructing the railways.

One of the earliest observers of the railway scene to comment on the activities of the navvies was John A. Francis in 1851.[9] He saw them largely in a positive light, applauding their derring-do and how they cut a dash and paying tribute to their strength and endurance although he conceded that they were rugged and uncouth, 'savages in the midst of civilisation'.

This view was more favourable towards the navvies than the general consensus. By 1846, the perception of the navvies and

To those who have Signed, and those who contemplate Signing, the Petition against the Syston & Peterboro' Lines CROSSING ON A LEVEL at the Bridge.

GENTLEMEN,

Spare your Humanity, since you will not extend it! The evil you sign against is most problematical —the good you would oppose most positive! You tell us our lives *would be* endangered *by* the Railway—we tell you our lives *are* in danger *without* it! You tell us that life may be lost by an accident—we tell you that *our* lives may be lost from starvation! We ask for work that we may *live*—we are told we are permitted to *live* in a *Workhouse!* A Railway is offered which will bring to *our* own desolate homes the comfort and blessing of cheap Coal—and *you* mock humanity by refusing this, affecting to regard our safety! Truly "the corruption of reason is worse than brutality itself!" Pray retire to your own cheerful firesides, eat, drink, and be merry—think for *yourselves,* if you please; but leave *us* alone! We ask not *your* aid—we seek not *your* advice—we detest and despise *your* opposition!

Signed, *on behalf of the Poor,*

HUMANITAS.

[Robert Bagley, Printer, Stamford.]

Level crossings were frequently a cause of local controversy as can be seen from this handbill relating to Peterborough. (Authors' collection)

their activities had become of sufficient concern that a Select Committee on Railway Labourers was convened at a time when it was estimated that 200,000 such men were at work. Of particular interest to the committee were the nature of their overnight accommodation, their unpredictable and often violent, drunken behaviour and their constant exposure to danger at work, some of the dangers brought on by the very recklessness of which Francis approved. A number of witnesses appeared before this committee. A civil engineer avowed that some were housed in worse conditions than the average pig could expect. A clergyman described navvies as 'spiritually destitute' and having what appeared to be wives but without the sanctity of marriage. One witness claimed that many were 'socialists', for some a more serious misdemeanour than unmarried co-habitation or violent drunkenness. The committee was sharply critical of the truck system of payment where part of the wages took the form of vouchers which could only be redeemed in the contractor's 'tommy shop' where the navvies were ripped off with expensive and inferior goods. Little notice was taken of the committee and its reports and recommendations.

Navvies building the South Wales Railway in the mid-1840s were blamed for the raiding of gardens and the purloining of domestic fruit and vegetables. At Chepstow on Sunday, their day off, they were the subject of complaints that numbers of them lounged around the High Street where they smoked, swore and skylarked at a time when 'decent' folk were making their way to worship. When, in 1847, the same railway company had financial problems and numbers of navvies were laid off, they were blamed, without concrete evidence, for a number of housebreakings.

The real issue which made the navvies such a source of controversy was that in rejecting all the contemporary standards of civilised society, the navvies were a concentrated focus for the perennial pent-up fears of the Victorian middle classes regarding the 'unwashed masses' and the possibility that they would get totally out of control. There can be little doubt that when the projects on which they were involved were prolonged, the presence of large numbers of navvies must have had a very disruptive impact, especially on small rural communities. At one point it is recorded that 4,000 men were employed in the building of Box Tunnel in Wiltshire. Such numbers cannot but have led to tensions locally. It is likely that crime rates went up in districts with a strong navvy presence but figures to that effect may be misleading given the rise in professional policing which is likely to have led to more arrests for offences such as drunkenness and affray.

Terry Coleman gives a vivid summation of the life of the navvies outside work:

'An anarchic elite of labourers who worked in constant danger, miles from civilisation, and lived according to their own laws. At Woodhead in 1845, where 1,100 men were camped in shanty huts, they even had their own marriage ceremony which consisted in the couple jumping over a broomstick, in the presence of a roomful of men assembled to drink upon the occasion, and the couple were put to bed at once, in the same room. They were heathens in a Christian country, they drank, had many women but few wives, broke open prisons, and were not received in good society...they were compared to an invading army. They came, made their earthworks and their depredations, and went, taking a few of the local women and leaving the ruin of a shanty town.'[10]

The depredations of the navvies engaged in the mid-1840s in building the Caledonian Railway's line from Carlisle to Glasgow became particularly notorious. Drinking and fighting apart, their particular speciality seems to have been cattle rustling. Having slaughtered the beasts they had feloniously obtained, they would sometimes engage in a monster booze-up and barbecue while the farmers, whose animals were the main item on the menu, were often forced to look on impotently for want of an effective law enforcement agency in the rural areas through which much of the line was built.

As late as the 1890s, misdemeanours by navvies were still able to make the news. When the line from Bourne in Lincolnshire to Saxby was being built, there was a rash of poaching and petty larceny, outbreaks of drunkenness and, more seriously, a bare-fist combat between two navvies that ended with the death of one of the contestants with the other being sent for trial on a charge of manslaughter. Of course it was not news when navvies simply got on with their work which was what they obviously did most of the time. When there was trouble, then those who wanted to could find in the navvies' behaviour a stick with which to beat the railways.

It is interesting to note how the navvies saw themselves vis-à-vis the public's perception of them. One, on being interviewed, said:

'You know Sir, us chaps are just like them Israelites as you read of in the Bible; we goes from place to place, we pitches our tents here and there, and then goes on just like they did...'[11]

Sabbatarianism

As the railways spread in the nineteenth century, so too did the influence of Sabbatarianism, especially in Scotland. There were particular reasons for this. From the eighteenth century, the English ruling class had set out to destroy the clan system, marginalise the Gaelic language and suppress the wearing of the tartan. Many of the longstanding clan chiefs were replaced by new English, often absentee, landowners. They tended to put much of their land over to pasture for sheep or create deer forests for the pursuit of game. Either way, far less labour was needed. The Highland Clearances were a brutal example of the strong imposing their dictates on the weak. Vast numbers of ordinary highlanders were forced to move to the industrial areas or to emigrate, particularly to North America. A huge legacy of resentment was created. Those who remained knew that open political struggle was impossible but found other collective ways of expressing their outrage at what had happened, the blame for which they put on the rich and powerful English. One outlet for expressing their discontent was in the stern radical evangelism of the Protestant Free Churches.

Religious fundamentalists regarded Exodus Chapter 20 verses 10-11 as an instruction that it was sinful to engage in any commercial enterprise which involved paid employment on Sundays. In 1781, the Lord's Day Observance Act had been passed which discouraged rather than prohibited commercial activities on Sundays. This was a real living issue which generated acrimonious debate. The coming of the railways exacerbated this debate. Should the system close down entirely on Sundays or might exemptions be made for railway operations that could be deemed as essential? Early on, the Glasgow, Paisley & Greenock and the Arbroath & Forfar Companies ran no trains on Sundays for fear of upsetting local religious feeling. The seriousness of this issue for some people was shown by the clergyman who lambasted the board of directors of the Caledonian Railway for running mail trains on Sundays telling them they were 'infidels, scoffers, men of unholy lives, the enemies of all righteousness, sinners against light, traitors to their country, robbers and murderers.'[12]

This quote, although hyperbolic, gives some idea of the emotions that were aroused over railway operations on Sundays in Scotland. It was not an issue that was going to go away because, in 1838, an Act was passed which gave the Postmaster General the power to require railways, for appropriate financial payment, to carry mails at such times as the Post Office required – including Sundays. Some companies, such as the Highland, operated only the legally required mail trains on Sundays and no other services.

The superbly scenic railway line from Dingwall to Kyle of Lochalsh thrust into wild and remote country. It was hoped that it would help stock-rearing by transporting local livestock to the south without the serious loss of condition which came through droving them overland. It was also thought that it could help the development of the fishing industry. The company concerned, the Dingwall & Skye, was an impecunious company and it decided in the first instance to make Strome Ferry the terminus rather than the Kyle. The line opened on 19 August 1870. The company allowed the 'Free Kirk' to hold their services in the waiting room at Strome Ferry. This may have made for a good piece of public relations but the Free Kirk was totally opposed both to any frivolous activity and to other than absolutely necessary employment on what they defined as 'The Sabbath'. Strome Ferry was to prove to be the location of the most concerted attack by Sabbatarians on a railway company for daring to conduct operations on the supposed 'day of rest'. The depth of feeling around Sabbatarianism and resentment against the treatment accorded the ordinary Highland people were responsible for the events at Strome Ferry in the summer of 1883.

The Dingwall & Skye had found a lucrative traffic in the bulk conveyance of locally caught fish by train to markets in the south. On Sunday mornings, a train had regularly been despatched with only a few low-key rumblings, but this was to change on 3 July 1883, when a large number of protestors tried to prevent the train being loaded. Scuffles broke out. The despatch of the train was delayed causing much of its cargo of fresh fish to be thrown away. Protests ended at midnight but a repetition was threatened for the next Sunday. This time, large numbers of police were on hand. Although the train and its cargo were duly despatched, the authorities were irked by what they saw as the lack of respect for the law and examples were made of those regarded as ringleaders. They were tried in Edinburgh, well away from local juries, and sentenced to short terms in prison.

The events at Strome Ferry were taken seriously by the authorities, not least because they were viewed as part of the ongoing protests in the Highlands against the process of eviction. Attention was drawn to the activities of the rapacious landowners and enough pressure created to establish a Royal Commission. It became obvious that if clearances continued to take place unabated, the Highlands could be turned virtually into a depopulated 'desert'. One solution was identified in the building of new railways which would open up access and allow for possible economic diversification and benefit the crofters and fishermen. It was agreed that any such lines were unlikely to be pay their way and that they would have to be underwritten with government funding. Cynics pointed out that such lines would also assist the Westminster government's control over these distant places. The line from Dingwall was extended to Kyle of Lochalsh in 1897. Lines to Fort William and Mallaig opened in 1894 and 1901 respectively. The line to Oban was completed in 1880 and Ballachulish joined the railway system in 1903. Other lines that had been considered back in the 1880s failed to materialise. Crofters, incidentally, gained legal security of tenure in 1886.

Peace may have broken out over the issue of Sunday employment after the Strome Ferry affair, but events came to a head again as late as 1929. The LM&SR proposed running Sunday passenger services over the line from Dingwall to Kyle of Lochalsh. Sunday excursions had been spreading in other parts of the Highlands and the Sabbatarian activists decided that decisive action was needed to prevent further violation of the sanctity of the Sabbath. The running of trains for pleasure on Sundays was simply unacceptable. It was claimed that those people who lived close to the line (there were not that many of them) did not want their Sunday peace to be disturbed by trainloads of pleasure-seekers passing their homes. The Free Church was in no mood to compromise. The Church fulminated that that the LMS was 'bringing the curse of God on themselves and upon the people of this land' by running these accursed trains. Sunday, they railed, was the day which God had given man for rest from labour and he would assuredly punish those who disregarded His Commandments.

The LMS chose to ignore these outbursts and ran an excursion train over the line for the first time on 14 July 1929. It carried 300 passengers who, hopefully, enjoyed the experience and the occasion went off without incident. Or did it? The death of the Kyle Stationmaster on the day this first excursion arrived was welcomed by some with undisguised glee as evidence of God's wrath at this cavalier disregard of his strictures. The man had actually been in poor health for some time. The stationmaster was described as having dropped dead as the excursion was leaving Kyle on its return journey. The 'Christian' periodical involved claimed to have extracted this piece of information from a daily newspaper. It was later forced to issue an apology for its triumphant tone in describing the poor man's death. In fact, he had not even been on duty that day, being on sick leave.

It is likely that many of the excursionists had been looking to use the ferry to reach Skye. No such luck! The ferry did not operate on Sundays. Significantly, the next time a Sunday excursion ran to Kyle of Lochalsh, the ferry to Kyleakin on Skye was operating. Money talked.

The first Tay Bridge famously collapsed on 28 December 1879, taking with it a train complete with locomotives, carriages and passengers, all plunging into the icy waters of the River Tay. The day was a Sunday. Immediately some people of religious convictions were commenting with vindictive relish about this being condign divine retribution for the sin of travelling on a Sunday. For example, the *Christian Herald*, in its edition of 7 January 1880, commented:

'This catastrophe may be regarded as a judgement of the Almighty on those who, in a land of Sabbath observance like Scotland, commit the outrage of violating the sanctity of the Lord's Day by unnecessary travelling…we can pray that this solemn judgement may be a salutary and not unheeded warning to all other Sabbath breakers.'[13]

In 1901, the new municipally owned electric tramway system opened in Ayr. It was instantly embroiled in a furore because of its decision to operate services on Sundays. The loudest protestors were those of a religious persuasion whose concern was that running trams on Sundays flouted God's writ. Others who objected less stridently were some simply wanting peaceful Sundays and others who thought that Ayr was too small and had insufficient demand to warrant Sunday tram services. Inevitably, protest also came from a temperance lobby. This argued that Sunday trams would encourage hardened drinkers to pose as bona fide travellers whereby they would be able to purchase and consume alcohol in the town's hotels. In the event, Sunday tram operation proved profitable enough for it to become established. The predicted alcohol-fuelled misbehaviour of Ayr's diehard topers did not occur. Sundays went on much as before but people could get round the town more easily and quickly.

It did not help the Sabbatarian argument when other people of a religious persuasion announced that they would happily use the trams to take them to Sunday worship. The Sabbatarian standpoint was riddled with contradictions. Did they refuse to use gas or electricity supplies on Sundays? Did they refuse to buy and read a Monday newspaper which was the product of labour on a Sunday? Would they refuse urgent medical attention on a Sunday?

Sabbatarianism was not an activity restricted to Scotland. As early as 1835, two shareholders in the Hull & Selby Railway tried, unsuccessfully, to persuade the directors not to run any trains on Sundays. Later, the company decided not to run any trains on Sundays catering for passengers in what we now call the 'leisure market', which may have been due to their influence.

In its edition of 4 June 1847, the *Lincolnshire Chronicle* fulminated about the activity of the East Lincolnshire Railway building its line from Louth to Grimsby:

'We regret it is our painful duty to report that on Sunday last workmen were employed on the line running through Fotherby. We look upon this as a gross violation of the Sabbath, as not only being disgraceful to the contractors of the works and operators of the line, but England as a nation and we sincerely hope, for the well-being of our country, that steps will promptly be taken to the extent of our existing law to prevent so painful a repetition.'[14]

This poster rants against the desecration of the Sabbath by the running of trains on Sundays. It did not take railway companies long to realise that there was business to be had in running special trains for pleasure-seekers on Sundays. These used stock that would otherwise be lying idle and the Newcastle and Carlisle Railway got in on the act early, in this case in 1841. (Authors' collection)

The influence of Sabbatarianism was patchy. The Great North of Scotland and the Somerset & Dorset, for example, were companies whose lines simply shut down on Sundays while the North Eastern chose not to operate trains on certain of its lines. The relative significance of the issue can be seen by the closure of about two-thirds of the railway system in Scotland on Sundays but only about one-fifth in England. Some companies did not operate trains at those times on Sundays when religious services took place. Shareholders of some railway companies made the personal decision not to take that part of their fees or dividends that they considered might have been generated by business operations on Sundays although we do not know how they identified the relevant appropriate amount.

The Barry Railway opened its line to Barry Island on 17 August 1894. Barry Island became the archetype of the day-trippers' resort. Large numbers of trains came down from the mining and industrial communities in the valleys, especially on summer Sundays. A cheap excursion to the seaside delights of Barry Island was too good an opportunity to miss for the thousands who crammed into the often austere accommodation that was provided for these trains. Some families made several trips in the season much to the chagrin of the preachers in the valley chapels who found they were addressing increasingly empty pews during the summer months. Come autumn, the pews would fill up again.

The origin of the Lord's Day Observation Society was in the Society for Promoting the Due Observance of the Lord's Day, founded in 1831. Its annual subscription was high and its membership was therefore mainly drawn from the well-off. In the social and political conflict that was such a feature of the nineteenth century, at least up to 1850, it seemed like just another group of privileged people setting out to deny the working classes their little enjoyments, in this case on the one day of the week on which most of them did not do paid work. One of the prominent members of the society was Sir Andrew Agnew, Independent MP for Wigtownshire, who unsuccessfully brought private members' bills against Sunday railway operations in 1833, 1834 and 1836.

The vast bulk of working people simply did not see observance of the Sabbath as an issue. For them it was a blissful respite from work and they had no desire to be told how to spend their Sundays by people they often regarded as well-heeled and sanctimonious busybodies threatening them with the wrath of

God. The influence of Sabbatarianism waned somewhat in the increasingly secular society of the later nineteenth century but, interestingly, there was a marked increase in lines that closed on Sundays in the years leading up to the First World War. This was less for religious reasons than the hard commercial reality that many Sunday trains were underused and unremunerative. By 1914, some companies had been pressurised by the unions into granting time-and-a-quarter for those employees working on Sundays and this obviously had an impact on the costs of Sunday operation.

A counter-movement to the Sabbatarians was the National Sunday League which was set up to campaign for the opening of places of 'rational recreation' such as museums and art galleries on Sundays. The Sabbatarians were basically fighting a losing battle because, as early as 1857, it was estimated that 42,000 people were leaving the main London stations on a summer Sunday bent on seeking pleasure which was not usually of the serious or cerebral kind. A legacy of Sabbatarianism remained, however. Even to the present time, many parts of the railway network operate reduced services on Sundays and some lines are not open at all.

The influence of Sabbatarianism led many people to see Sundays as singularly joyless days. The author Wilkie Collins in *The Moonstone* (1868) described the British Sunday as 'tyranny'.

Church and Railway
The Railway Signal was an evangelically inspired periodical aimed largely at railway workers. It opined:

> 'While the railways have done much to advance the material interests of men they have also afforded precious opportunities for advancing their spiritual and eternal interests.'[15]

We have seen how railway activities on Sundays incurred the wrath of the Sabbatarians but the development of a railway network assisted some prelates in their activities. As railways spread through South Lancashire, so the bishop of the new diocese of Manchester was far more able to visit the parishes under his jurisdiction. Taking a more liberal standpoint than the Sabbatarians, one Mancunian bishop argued that visiting an exhibition or enjoying an excursion by train was greatly preferable to dissipated and drunken behaviour on Sundays. Not all around the Anglican Church agreed. A Church of England tract of 1845 described railways as 'the masterpiece of Satan'.

A concern of all religious denominations in the Victorian era was the lack of bums on seats at services in places of worship. Many alternative activities, often of a profit-making nature, became available during the nineteenth century particularly in the urban areas whose communities frequently were highly cosmopolitan having arrived from wide-ranging places of origin. In an attempt to win their allegiance and also doubtless hoping to maintain some degree of spiritual control over them, the Church of England and some railway companies co-operated in the building of churches in places such as Swindon, Crewe and Wolverton which can be described as 'railway towns'. It is significant that some railway companies urged their employees to attend worship on a regular basis and made it clear that in doing so they might put themselves in a favourable light as regards promotion. Presumably non-attendance might have the opposite effect.

Mentioned elsewhere is the reputation, not entirely justified, of the navvies for drunken, riotous and generally godless behaviour. Various denominations felt they had a duty to minister to the navvies' spiritual welfare and they sent missionaries to the navvy encampments and even built mission halls. Organisations concerned with bringing some piety into the lives of the navvies and hopefully saving their souls included the Christian Excavators' Union and the Navvy Mission Society founded respectively in 1875 and 1877.

Drink was viewed as an insidious influence by such campaigners. Elizabeth Garnett of the Christian Excavators' Union was one of the most tireless workers attempting to rescue navvies from the depravities that blighted their lives. She focussed particularly on what she saw as the problems created by drink. From 1878 to 1893 she edited the *Quarterly Letter to Navvies* which combined spiritual harangues with inveighing against the demon drink and practical tips about things that would now come under the heading of Health and Safety. Tea was eagerly promoted as a wholesome alternative to alcohol as was hymn singing and one edition of the *Quarterly Letter* had a hymn with this uplifting chorus:

'Yes, I am an English navvy, but oh, not an English sot,
I have run my pick through alcohol in bottle, glass or pot.
And with the spade of abstinence and all the power I can,
I am spreading out a better road for every working man'.

Tipping Railway Employees

Tipping was a practice which was largely frowned on by railway travellers and by supervisory staff and managers alike. In most cases, companies would instantly dismiss any employee proved to have been touting for or receiving gratuities. Some, who were most critical of tipping deplored those who gave tips as encouraging railway 'servants' to break the terms and conditions of their employment which in turn suggested a contempt for the authority of the employers. It was argued that a tip was no more than a bribe to encourage an individual to undertake the duties for which he was employed. Few of those who vehemently criticised the practice turned their wrath on the employers for paying the low wages which encouraged touting. Rather sanctimoniously, it was claimed that tipping demoralised those doing the tipping.

Grumpy correspondents penned indignant letters to the newspapers. They fulminated about porters systematically ignoring passengers who required their services unless it was clear that a tip was going to be offered. There were even accusations of threats of violence from platform workers who were not offered tips. It was also alleged that staff might maliciously give misleading information if they thought that a tip was unlikely to be forthcoming. Such letters ignored the widespread bribing of guards and other railway employees by passengers, who, for example, wanted a compartment to themselves or were smoking in specifically non-smoking compartments.

Such complaints also ignored the tipping that had been an accepted part of coach travel and which made an already expensive mode of travel even more costly since virtually all those employed on the coaches themselves as well as in the hostelries along the route expected to be tipped and were routinely satisfied on that score.

Opposition from Politicians

The Duke of Wellington had a well-known aversion to railways. One of the reasons was his preoccupation with his own privacy, particularly when travelling. He thought that railways threatened that privacy. Nor did he like the idea of common people travelling around for pleasure and education. He declared that, '…third class facilities are a breach of contract, a premium to the lower orders to go wandering uselessly across the country.' This ludicrous pronouncement was made late in his life by which time the old warhorse was widely derided for his hostility to all change of a progressive sort. He also commented that railways were dangerous because they would allow subversive radicals to travel around spreading their seditious views. He did, however, believe that a railway was needed between Hastings and Ashford so that, if necessary, troops and military supplies could be moved quickly to any point close to what he considered to be a particularly vulnerable stretch of coastline if war was going to occur.

The word 'celebrity' is grossly overused in twenty-first-century Britain, but it would not be unfair to say that a man of the stature of the duke was a celebrity by the standards of the nineteenth century. However, before the railway age, his name may have been well-known but his appearance was not, despite his famously prominent nose. So it was that among the crowds that turned out to witness the public opening of the Liverpool & Manchester Railway, many were there at least partly to vent their spleen on him for his opposition to political reform. He was prime minister from 1828 to 1830 but even then, many of the protestors did not know how to distinguish him from the throng of the great and good who were also milling about on that occasion.

William Gladstone made much use of railways in the 1860s and 1870s during his political campaigns at election times and on what came to be called 'whistle-stop tours'. At the larger stations, he would descend from an ordinary service train, leap on to a luggage barrow and proceed to address the crowds. Large numbers would have turned up, not necessarily receptive to his political harangues but wanting some free entertainment. This they got, particularly on one occasion when the speech by a local dignitary welcoming him went on so long that his train left without him. The railway companies and his fellow passengers by no means welcomed Gladstone's peripatetic activity because, with a blithe disregard for the convenience of others, he expected the train times to be adjusted to suit him.

The railways helped to consolidate the domination of politicians based in London on the rest of the country. It gave them a sense of security knowing that there was a network of railways which would enable them to move troops to potential trouble spots quickly and efficiently. At the same time that railway promotion and building was at high levels in the 1830s and 1840s, there were a host of social grievances which provoked much direct political action which was seen as posing a threat to public order. Even politicians who thought that no good could come of the way that railways were providing a means for the common people to travel around, recognised their value in moving troops and police to places where trouble might occur. An edition of the *Illustrated London News* in August 1842 depicted troops marching into Euston Station before boarding trains of the London & Birmingham Railway to take them north to deal with incidents involving the Chartists and commented:

> 'The construction of the British railway network raised markedly the efficiency of the military force which was maintained on home service, by making the troops stationed in the southern part of England more readily available for the restoration of order in the manufacturing districts of the north.'[16]

As the Quartermaster General informed a parliamentary committee:

> '... you send a battalion of 1,000 men from London to Manchester in nine hours; that same battalion marching would take seventeen days; and they arrive at the end of nine hours just as fresh, or nearly so, as when they started...Without that conveyance, you could not have done one tenth part of the work that it was required of the troops to do, and necessarily to do, in the year 1842.'[17]

Railways Displacing People

Railway companies frequently thrust their way through densely built-up urban areas to reach their city stations by wherever possible acquiring cheap land on which stood poor-quality working-class housing and small industrial premises often occupied by businesses engaged in noxious, polluting trades. This was evident in London with the London & Greenwich Railway which opened in stages between 1836 and 1838 and, for example, the southern approach to New Street, Birmingham and, in Manchester, what came to be called London Road Station. In the case of Birmingham, New Street Station is specifically mentioned as taking over the site of numerous slums and brothels.[18] The Manchester South Junction Railway carved its way through a similar area on the south periphery of central Manchester on a viaduct well over a mile in length and crossing thirty streets. It imposed an indelible stamp on the topography of this part of Manchester. Such viaducts not only involved clearance of rundown properties but also effectively divided up and physically separated the districts through which they passed much in the manner of the later urban motorways.

The new municipal authorities that emerged in the nineteenth century were probably happy to see some of the worst local housing being razed to the ground by railway development. Neither these bodies nor the railway companies were likely overly to concern themselves with the fate of those who were displaced. Being tenants, these people had no legitimate outlet for their outrage at the way in which they were treated. Only later in the century did working men begin to get the vote in parliamentary and local elections. The inhabitants of these rookeries, however, were unlikely to be enfranchised while there was still a property qualification. Given that there were few votes to be had by paying attention to the wishes of those at the bottom end of the social ladder, the people of the city rookeries had no option but to be victims of circumstances over which they had no control.

The site of the future Carlisle Citadel Station contained notorious slums occupied, among others, by immigrants from Ireland who, according to the *Carlisle Journal*, put up a ferocious physical fight when the time came for them to be evicted from their squalid dwellings. They may have been squalid but those dwellings were their homes. Predictably, their efforts were unsuccessful. More usually, those displaced simply accepted the situation with sullen resignation.

In acquiring the land for their London passenger termini and goods depots, wherever possible cheap land was bought up and this often involved acquiring and clearing districts already containing industrial and residential property of low quality. Railways were not pioneers of this process because when St Katherine's Dock was built in 1827-8, over 11,000 people were displaced.

Attitudes were mixed. The impoverished inhabitants who usually made up the majority of those displaced were generally unceremoniously decanted into other slum property nearby which then became even more squalid and overcrowded. In carving a swathe through these crime and disease-ridden districts some desirable slum-clearance was carried out. At the same time the sheer environmental squalor of these rookeries, rarely previously penetrated by 'respectable' people, were often now exposed to the public eye. This caused certain more liberal elements of the middle classes to campaign for greater social justice in the relationship between slum-dwellers on the one hand and the landowners and railway companies on the other.

The approaches to and the site of St Pancras Station and other Midland Railway facilities in the area involved the acquisition of large amounts of land which contained some of London's very worst slum housing. From 1853, bills promoting railways that were being presented to parliament had to specify how many dwellings were to be demolished if the figure proposed was to be over thirty. In this case, it was several thousand dwellings and as many as 52,000 people were likely to be displaced. The records do not reveal the fate of these people but the likelihood is that the vast majority were simply dumped into other nearby substandard housing stock rendering it even more overcrowded. If there were protests from the inhabitants they have gone unrecorded but these people were virtually powerless. *Laissez-faire* was about letting so-called market forces rip. The inhabitants of Agar Town and Somers Town found themselves the victims of powerful economic forces over which they had absolutely no control.

Philanthropists led by Lord Shaftesbury campaigned for some restitution for working people displaced from their housing by railway developments. In 1853, the government required railway companies to produce 'Demolition Statements' indicating the number of working men likely to be evicted under any particular scheme. The companies found various ways of evading the law or

A contemporary representation of the building of St Pancras gives some idea of the monumental scale of the works and the disruption caused. (Authors' collection)

minimising their responsibilities and Demolition Statements came under criticism for their lack of candour.

When the site for London's Marylebone Station and its associated yards and sidings was being cleared late in the 1890s, much removal of existing property had to be carried out. This involved the demolition of some fashionable villas but also some of the most overcrowded and insanitary of London's many slum dwellings. 4,448 people of what were described as the 'labouring class' were evicted. For about 2,690 of these people, the Great Central Railway through the Wharncliffe Dwellings Company built six five-storey tenement blocks which may have looked somewhat barrack-like but were a huge improvement on their occupants' previous homes. Most of the other displaced working people simply had to fend for themselves and find accommodation where they could.

J.R. Kellett estimated a minimum of 120,000 people displaced by railway construction in the immediate environs of central London in the period 1840-1900.[19] Only a small percentage of these would have been re-housed at the expense of a railway company. Railways were accused of creating slums but the process of slum-making was too complex to be ascribed to railways alone.

It was true, however, that where inner-city districts were carved up and divided by railways, mostly on viaducts and less often in cuttings, the coming of the railway encouraged an accumulation of coal and timber yards, small industrial premises which were often producers of considerable pollution such as knackers' yards and tanneries, alongside housing for the poorest and most desperate. *The Times* summed the matter up succinctly:

> 'The poor are displaced but they are not removed. They are shovelled out of one side of the parish, only to render more overcrowded the stifling apartments in another part...But the dock and wharf labourer, the porter and the costermonger cannot remove. You may pull down their wretched homes: they must find others, and make their new dwellings more crowded and wretched than their old ones.'[20]

The *Illustrated London News* joined in by describing countless houses of: 'Precisely the same original bad quality as those which have been pulled down...'[21] In 1861, *Punch* described a 'Goths and Vandals Railway' forcing its way into London. Whereas much of the printed media had enthusiastically, almost uncritically, welcomed the railways twenty or thirty years earlier, the reality of the large-scale demolition in the inner city areas and the social cost involved meant that at least over this issue, much of the media was very critical of the railways.

In *Dombey and Son* in 1869, Charles Dickens in his inimitable fashion describes the view from the carriage window of the train approaching the city terminus:

> 'Everything around is blackened. There are dark pools of water, muddy lanes, and miserable habitations far below. There are jagged walls and filthy houses close at hand, and through the battered roofs and broken windows, wretched rooms are seen, where want and fever hide themselves in many wretched shapes, while smoke and crowded gables, and distorted chimneys, and deformity of brick and mortar pinning up deformity of mind and body, choke the murky distance. As Mr Dombey looks out of his carriage window, it is never in his thoughts that the monster who brought him there had let the light of day in on these things; not made or caused them. It was the journey's fitting end, and might have been the end of everything; it was so ruinous and dreary.'

At Nottingham, the building of Victoria Station and the line southwards to Weekday Cross and over the viaduct towards Arkwright Street involved 6,000 people losing their homes. A local newspaper commented that this provided a timely opportunity to clear some of Nottingham's most notorious slums. Twenty-four pubs, a church and a workhouse were among other buildings razed to the ground. It also mentioned that the railway companies involved were legally required to erect 300 new homes for some of the displaced. The clearance of the slums was desirable but since the rents of the replacement dwellings were going to be at least twice that of those being demolished, it was doubtful whether many of them would end up actually being occupied by those who had been displaced. There was much anger as the railways drove their way through central Nottingham but there was little that slum dwellers could do about it.

The Charing Cross Railway involved the demolition of the homes of around 4,500 people in the densely packed district between Waterloo Road and the Thames. No provision was made for them to be re-housed. However when Liverpool Street Station was enlarged in 1887, the Great Eastern Railway was required

Gustav Dore was a prolific French painter and book illustrator. He spent much time in England, clearly being fascinated by London's teeming social underbelly. In 1872, he published London, many illustrations in which depict the East End. Here we see the cramped and polluted approaches to London but as with so many of his works depicting London's poor, he manages to depict them with sympathy for the dignified manner in which they live out their hard lives. (Authors' collection)

to re-house 600 people for whom ten tenement blocks were erected in Spitalfields. Although the poorer working-class people whose dwellings were knocked down to make way for railway installations generally had a rough deal, it is perhaps significant that when the Southern Railway was formed at the grouping, it inherited 1,523 tenement dwellings from its component companies. The building of these had been part of the legal conditions specified for particular railway projects.

Even a short branch line like the Salford Docks Branch of the Lancashire & Yorkshire Railway, only one mile forty-four chains in length, involved the demolition of 177 houses. The railway

George Cruikshank was a prolific artist, illustrator, campaigner and observer of contemporary life. Here he depicts an approaching steam locomotive as a ruthless destructive force. He did not like railways but he was better known for his graphical propaganda against what he saw as the evils of drink. (Authors' collection)

company was required under the terms of the relevant Act to build just seventy-four dwellings as partial replacement.

As is well-known, the Cheap Trains Act of 1883 encouraged railway companies to offer fares at greatly discounted prices to 'workmen'. This was a somewhat belated attempt to tackle the appalling slum problems of London and also to compensate for the displacement of slum dwellers that had taken place when railway projects had been built on cheap inner-urban land. While the theory was that the cheap fares would allow those displaced to move to healthier locations on the periphery of London and commute to and from their employment, the continued existence of pestilential slums suggests that the problem of slum housing was not solved simply by providing concessionary fares. Additionally, the fares, though certainly cheap, were beyond the reach of many of the slum-dwellers and the Great Eastern Railway, known for its workmen's trains, catered far more for skilled workers, clerks and shop workers than it did for the lowest-paid, casually-employed population of the slums.

Punch **was** a serious critic of much to do with the railways before it mellowed somewhat and found in them an almost endless source of humour. This cartoon from 1845 depicts the apparently merciless onward progress of the railway.

Fares and Directors' Fees

A constant throughout the history of railways has been bellyaching about fare rises and, in tune with current controversies concerning the privatised railways, grumbles in the early days about the emoluments paid to directors and senior managers. Sometimes, complaints extended to what it was claimed were needlessly expensive ornate and palatial railway stations. It almost goes without saying that there were also many complaints about inhospitable stations with only the barest facilities where it was impossible to obtain shelter from the elements. An old chestnut was the waiting room where the fire had been allowed to go out on cold days while the porters' room had a roaring fire emitting the heat of a furnace.

The Liverpool & Manchester Railway had the serendipitous experience of realising that there was a sizeable but hitherto unconsidered market in passenger travel for what we would now call 'leisure purposes'. People with sufficient disposable income were soon taking advantage of the new facility and enjoying the enriching experience of a day trip to Manchester for the Liverpudlian or to Liverpool for the Mancunian. Such excursions were beyond the pocket of most working-class people and a demand rapidly emerged for cheaper fares that would allow more people access to what was seen as a desirable form of 'rational recreation' for the masses. *The Economist* joined the clamour for a systematic reduction in third class fares:

'Far be it from us to insinuate that it is the duty of a railway company to sacrifice its interests and profits for the purposes of inducing a great locomotion amongst the people... but railway companies have hitherto committed the common fault – that of looking chiefly for support to the higher and wealthy middle classes; whereas experience has proved that in every pursuit, even in literature, that the policy is most profitable which embraces the wants and patronage of the great masses of the working population, whose united incomes are infinitely greater than those of any other class.'[22]

The Economist continually returned to this theme over the next few years. Eventually it tired of failing to make an impression and, rather grumpily, concluded, 'The Government, if they owned the railways, might give the working classes their share in the benefits of quick locomotion, though they will never get it from others.'[23]

Issues around fares rumbled on throughout. There were objections to people who were better-off taking advantage of the cheap fares available on workmen's trains. In 1904, the deputy general manager of a railway reported indignantly after seeing a party of revellers in full evening dress using an early morning workmen's train to go into town. In the absence of requiring intending passengers to produce incontrovertible evidence of the fact that they were 'workmen', how could the system be policed? In practice, workmen's trains were open to just about anybody who was prepared to get up early in the morning and could tolerate the conditions in the austere rolling stock that was used. However, the good old British class system ensured that there were better-off passengers who, while ever on the lookout for a bargain, would not have been seen dead in a workmen's train.

Railway Freight Charges

Throughout the history of Britain's railways, customers have complained about the rates they charge for the carriage of minerals and merchandise. Before the coming of the railways, conveyance charges were largely based around the mileage involved. The canals to a degree, but far more the railways, moved into a pricing policy in which the value of the goods being carried was an important component. As railways took so much of the market in long-distance haulage, complaints were increasingly heard from traders about the lack of transparency regarding rates never mind what was considered to be excessive charging and the belief that certain types of business which the railways wanted were given undue preference when rates were being set by the railway companies. These complaints seem to have been most pointed where a company had a near or complete monopoly of a region as the North Eastern Railway (NER) did of the area from the north bank of the Humber up to the Scottish Border.

Colonel Sibthorp

'I have the greatest dislike against directors, guards, policemen, and everyone connected with railways. I think a stoker will go any lengths to attain his end; and I am of the opinion that every railway engine is more or less an engine of destruction, and that nothing will stop it once it has made up its boiler to go a certain distance.'[24]

Thus spoke Colonel Charles de Laet Waldo Sibthorp, an MP for Lincoln almost continuously from 1826 to 1855. The authors take great delight and pride in British eccentricity and Sibthorp is right up at the forefront so far as home-grown eccentrics are concerned. Fortunately for us, one aspect of his eccentricity was his notorious aversion to railways.

He considered all railways to be 'public frauds and private robberies'. He once said that he would prefer to meet a highwayman or see a burglar on his premises, than meet an engineer. He reckoned he would be safer with the highwayman or burglar, both of whom in his opinion were more respectable.

He was an absolute gift for *Punch* which delighted in portraying him as a latter-day Don Quixote tilting not at windmills but at steam locomotives upon the railway. They liked to call him 'our gallant Colonel' and revelled in depicting him with his bushy black whiskers, his eyeglass and his dapper but totally outdated tailcoat and other accoutrements. He was a little coxcomb of a man, opinionated, intolerant, prejudiced and hyperbolic and absolutely guaranteed to take a reactionary stance on any issue under discussion. He proudly boasted that he had never travelled by the railroad and that he hated the very word 'railroad' as much as he hated the Devil. According to him, railway schemes were 'dangerous, delusive, unsatisfactory and, above all, unknown to the constitution of the country!'

When Sibthorp got up to speak in the Commons, the bars emptied as MPs rushed to enjoy the free, hilarious entertainment he provided. What he said became more outrageous the longer he spoke. He took himself utterly seriously and totally lacked humour although it is significant that no one ever accused him of insincerity. He could not understand why his speeches were met with howls of laughter and he mistook the jeers of his fellow MPs for approbation. Apart from his role as an unwitting clown, Sibthorp had no particular influence in the House, largely because on most issues he found himself in a minority of one.

When Gladstone was pushing through his Regulation of Railways Act in 1844, Sibthorp's comment was that he wished Gladstone had brought in a bill to annihilate them altogether. A small landowner himself, he railed against the compulsory purchase powers of incorporated railway companies and claimed they would cause: 'the absolute annihilation of every estate in the country for the benefit of a few speculators'.[25]

Sibthorp predicted that when the public had seen through the 'nefarious' activities of the railways, sanity would be restored with turnpikes and horse-drawn conveyances would return to the fore once again.

No to the Nameplate!

A curious example of a kind of opposition to railways was voiced by the headmaster of Uppingham School in Rutland. In 1930 R.E.L. Maunsell produced what proved to be his very successful 'V' or 'Schools' Class 4-4-0 for the Southern Railway. All forty of them were named after public schools mostly, but not exclusively, in the territory served by that company.

Uppingham's headmaster was absolutely adamant that he did not want the name of his school besmirched by being attached to a steam locomotive. Some headmasters might have been flattered and pleased by what was essentially free publicity since these locomotives' nameplates had a small additional plate stating 'Schools Class'. 'Uppingham' nameplates were cast but the locomotive involved, no.923, spent most of its life displaying the name 'Bradfield', instead.

A similar attitude was evinced with regard to the very competent large mixed-traffic 'V2' Class 2-6-2s designed by Nigel Gresley for the London & North Eastern Railway. This class numbered 184 locomotives of which eight received names. There had been plans to bestow a name on at least one other member of the class. This name would have commemorated the Royal Grammar School, Newcastle. Apparently appropriate nameplates were cast but the headmaster loftily rejected the proposal that the school should be honoured in this way. Maybe he knew a thing or two about railways and had a sneaking suspicion that if a 'V2' was to carry the school's name, it might be allocated to the local engine sheds of Gateshead or Heaton, the former being particularly notorious for the grimy turnout of its locomotives even if they were in good mechanical condition. A bedraggled 'V2' clanking around Tyneside bearing the school's name might have been a poor advertisement for his academic establishment.

CHAPTER ELEVEN

Railways up and running and still generating criticism

This chapter deals less with opposition to railways *per se* than with aspects of railway operation which aroused criticism.

Early Attitudes to Railway Travel

'What can be so palpably absurd and ridiculous than the prospect held out of locomotives travelling twice as fast as stage-coaches? We would as soon expect the people of Woolwich to suffer themselves to be fired off in one of Congreve's rockets as to trust themselves to the mercy of such a machine going at such a rate… We trust that Parliament will, in all railways it may sanction, limit the speed to eight or ten miles per hour.'[1]

A well-known opponent of the coming of the railways was Thomas Creevey, MP, who was a friend of Lord Sefton, initially also hostile to railways, not least to the Liverpool & Manchester Railway (L&M) which he saw as potentially harming various interests including his estates in the neighbourhood of Liverpool. Anyway, Creevey presumably swallowed his qualms, at least temporarily, and took a trip on the L&M before it officially opened and he was impressed, although not favourably:

'…the quickest motion is to me frightful; it is really flying, and it is impossible to divest yourself of the notion of instant death to all upon the least accident happening…The smoke is very inconsiderable indeed, but sparks of fire are abroad in some quantity: one burnt Miss de Ros's cheek, another a hole in Lady Maria's silk pelisse and a third a hole in someone else's gown. Altogether I am extremely glad indeed to have seen this miracle, and to have travelled in it. Had I thought worse of it than I do I should have had the curiosity to try it; but having done so, I am quite satisfied with my first achievement being my last.'[2]

Class distinctions based on ability to pay were emphasised with the coming of the railways and could be seen in carefully demarcated waiting rooms, sometimes in refreshment rooms and most definitely in the travelling accommodation on offer to passengers. The board of directors of the Manchester & Leeds Railway in 1838 decided that they would operate three different levels of service. First class

First Class

Second Class

Third Class

England in 1842: Going to the Derby

The rigid class distinctions of nineteenth century British society were replicated in the services provided by the various railway companies. These formed a staple diet for the graphical satirists of the time as shown in the *Illustrated London News*. Here the artist depicts the differences in passenger accommodation and decorum.

would have compartments per carriage seating six with everything designed to offer the greatest comfort possible. Second class carriages would house twenty-four passengers with low divisions between compartments, windows only in the doors and no cushions on the seating. First and second class passengers enjoyed the luxury of roofs but not so those travelling third class. They had to make do with open, box-like wagons which did not even have spring buffers that might absorb some of the shock of any impact. There were many complaints about early rail travel but fewer about the accommodation offered to those with the means to travel first class.

First class may have been seen as preferable but a reverend gentleman from Rutland writing in *The Railway Times* still managed to find much to complain about during one of his early journeys:

'If money is no object you travel first, and you are showed [sic] into a carriage which has five inmates and a half already. There is a grim dowager and her companion, an anxious mamma, nurse, boy of six or seven, and horror of horrors, a squalling baby. Your grown fellow-travellers scowl at you as an intruder. The boy fidgets about, and treads on your toes, desiring to paw you with his bread-and-butter fingers. Most dreadful of all, the baby sets up a scream. You remind yourself that you have a journey of perhaps four score miles in this pleasant company.'

It was quickly appreciated that railways could offer unprecedented freedom of movement to those who could afford the fares. They usually also offered great savings in time and they quickly tapped into a market of travel for pleasure that few had previously thought existed. In spite of these advantages, there were many Jeremiahs who were determined to let those who insisted on travelling by this new-fangled contraption know that there was a price to pay for doing so. They made gloomy prognostications about the likelihood of death or injury resulting from railway travel and they revelled in describing the discomforts and inconveniences that were bound to be experienced even before the train left the station. Passengers, it was claimed, frequently became over-anxious about the prospect of travel and this gave them an unfortunate tendency to loose bowels, a condition for which early trains offered no succour. Pickpockets and luggage thieves performed their predations on crowded station platforms. The same crowded platforms caused passengers to come into close contact with people from the 'lower orders'. Railway

The Pleasures of the Rail-Road. Showing the Inconvenience of a Blow up.

Coach travel was hazardous but the speed and weight of railway trains made accidents in which they were involved potentially much more dangerous. Boiler explosions on early locomotives were by no means uncommon as is shown in this semi-serious, semi-humorous caricature. (Authors' collection)

servants were insufficiently obsequious and the men's urinals stank. Once aboard the train, passengers might have to put up with uncouth, smelly and dirty fellow travellers, some of whom passed the time uttering oaths, eating, drinking or even smoking; with uncomfortable seats; with overcrowded, cold, draughty and dark surroundings; and with noxious aromas emanating from consignments being carried in the guard's van such as fish. The lubrication for such items as axle boxes might consist of vegetable oil or animal fat, adding to the cocktail of uncongenial olfactory experiences. As if these hazards were not enough, there was the ever-present danger of death and destruction as a consequence of accidents on the line. These claims all had some degree of justification. We will deal with them in further sections below.

One journal advised travellers to sit on opposite sides of the carriage on their outward and return journeys thereby acquainting themselves with both lots of scenery and sights in preference to keeping the vision inboard: 'this would surely be pleasanter than a three or four hours' study of physiognomy at a stretch, for want of any better occupation'.

There are many people who solemnly declare that there is no respect for law and order in modern Britain and that large numbers of people are happy to abuse the system. However, on 3 July 1839, the first day of public passenger services on the Manchester & Leeds Railway, no fewer than 110 passengers were apprehended attempting to indulge in the luxury of first class railway travel while only possessing second or third class tickets.

We would like to be able to say that early railway travel was superior in every possible way to previous modes of getting about by road but this account of a journey in the early days of the Nottingham to Lincoln line shows that train travel could provide a challenge:

'We were jolted just as if we were crossing broad and deep ruts, and at seven miles from Lincoln we came to a dead stop. The engine was so worn out and unfit for work that the fire in the furnace had actually burnt its way through the iron, and there were hot cinders falling out as fast as they could, the water getting cold, and no longer any experience of steam. Happily there was a drain near at hand, and pick-axe and shovel were speedily put into requisition, and a large tile extracted, which, broken in half, served to stop up the aperture. The posts and rails which fenced off the railroad were taken and broken up for fuel, and we at length crawled into Lincoln.'[3]

The Lancashire & Yorkshire Railway was the butt of the *Bradford Observer's* irritation on many occasions in the middle of the nineteenth century on account of what the paper saw as the incompetence of its management and the unreliability of its passenger services. It was convinced that the company gave its goods trains priority over passenger services and suggested that notices should be erected on its stations to the effect that 'Passenger trains will run as circumstances and the goods trains permit'.

Letters to the Editor
Disgruntled people with an axe to grind have long made use of the Letters to the Editor section of newspapers as a medium for venting their spleen. The coming of the railways provoked this fraternity

into peevish outbursts aimed at almost every aspect of railway operation. The purpose of such letters, presumably, other than a moment's glory when the writer saw their name in print, was to bring perceived faults and shortcomings to the public's notice via the newspaper, perhaps in the hope that something might be done to address the grievances highlighted. Typical was the letter received in 1849 by the editor of a local paper at Bingley on the Midland Railway not far from Bradford. The station was described as 'wretched and disgraceful' and consisting of little more than a tiny office with a leaking roof, a small shed and a waiting room permeated by the stench from the adjacent urinal. What, the correspondent asked, was the editor going to do about it?

A rich seam was tapped. Among issues raised were: late trains; trains that went too fast and the inevitable concomitant, trains that proceeded with infuriating slowness; trains that were uncomfortable and, in cold weather, too few foot-warmers being available; people with second- or third-class tickets travelling in first-class accommodation; working people travelling in soiled clothes; passengers offended by being in close proximity with people they regarded as their social inferiors; overcrowded trains; dirty carriages and a particularly piquant one – objections to travelling in a compartment in which the fellow passengers consisted of police or prison officers accompanying one or more prisoners.

It was only to be expected that smoking on trains produced a fertile source of complaints. It was not unknown for passengers in smoking compartments who themselves smoked to complain about fellow-smokers who smoked 'offensively', noxious fumes given off by foul old briars or cigars often giving rise to such outbursts. A more frequent cause of friction, however, was those passengers who brazenly smoked in 'no-smoking' compartments. A British Anti-Tobacco Society was formed to encourage private prosecutions for such blackguards and to campaign for more non-smoking accommodation.

Scrutiny of the letters pages in many newspapers of the mid-nineteenth century unearths a rich seam of railway-related subjects on which irascible correspondents held forth. They provide insight into the social attitudes of that part of society who had the time and inclination to bombard newspaper editors with their grumpy misanthropic ranting. A well-known railway director described such people as 'Grumbledories' and Robert Louis Stevenson dismissed them as 'canting dilettantes'.

The smoke emitted by steam locomotives for long generated cantankerous outbursts from letter-writers. In 1839 and 1845, Acts required locomotives 'to consume their own smoke' but no one ever found a way of satisfactorily achieving this objective. A letter to *The Times* in 1864 fulminated to the effect that 'between Slough and Wycombe the country is poisoned and the passengers asphyxiated by the foulest, the blackest, and the most sulphurous pest of smoke'.

The twentieth and twenty-first centuries have proved equally fertile for the provision of issues about which to complain to newspapers. Some are the perennial complaints about fellow-travellers. The smoking habit continued to be a constant source of disgruntlement until smoking was banned but new technology has rolled on inexorably and the use or misuse of mobile phones and other electronic equipment seems destined to arouse every bit as much ire as smoking. Train speeds, punctuality and cleanliness, or otherwise, and catering have remained hardy perennials but more fleeting issues have included nationalisation, privatisation, unmanned level crossings, the pernicious phrase 'train station' and the 24-hour clock.

One particularly disgruntled correspondent bombarded the local paper in York about steam locomotives whistling incessantly at night in the early 1960s. We would expect him to have welcomed the replacement of steam but he quickly found a new cause for grumbling – this was the throbbing of the 18-cylinder Napier diesel engines of 'Deltic' locomotives, idling when they were stabled overnight.

Danger on the Line

A host of guides and manuals were published in the early years of the railways, providing advice for those who were thinking about the possibility of travelling or had actually taken the plunge and decided to take a train. Although these manuals were not necessarily written by people hostile to railways, they were frequently couched in terms which might have deterred all but the least faint-hearted. One such urged its readers:

'Get as far from the engine as possible. Should an explosion take place you may happily get off with the loss of an arm or a leg, whereas if you happen to be placed near the said piece of hot machinery and an unfortunate accident really occurs, you would probably be smashed to pieces.'

Any traveller might dispute whether 'happily' was the word they would apply to 'only' losing an arm or a leg.

The early railways were very dangerous places. Safer operating practices emerged as a result of learning by trial and error. It strikes us as absolutely hair-raising that early train regulation and control was under the 'Time Interval' system which involved each train being allowed a set time to travel along a section of line of a given length. When that time had elapsed, it was decreed safe to despatch another train along that section. An obvious flaw with this system was the possibility that the first train broke down, derailed, crashed or otherwise failed to complete its journey. With no effective form of communication between one regulating point and the next, the system was an accident just waiting to happen.

The Railway Traveller's Handy Book advised its readers about selecting the best part of the train in which to travel should there be an accident:

'The middle of the train is the safest, because in the event of being run into from behind, or meeting a train in front, the force of the concussion would, in either case, be considerably expended before the centre part is reached. The carriages nearest the engine are regarded as dangerous in case of an accident occurring to the engine itself, or in the event of its running off the line, when it usually manages to drag the next two or three coaches with it. The tail of the train is not liked, because it moves – in summer-time especially – in a perpetual cloud of dust, which is not calculated to improve the attire or benefit the lungs. The oscillation, jerking, and other eccentric movements of the train are also felt with greater force at the end than in any other portion; and it does sometimes happen that the last carriage or two, by the severance of the coupling-irons, become separated from their travelling companions, and are left standing stock-still on the line, while the forward portion of the train speeds on its way unconscious of, and therefore unheeding, the catastrophe.'

Railway accidents in the early days were met with indignant outcries. The reality was that railways in their pioneering days killed fewer people than were then being killed on the roads. There were innumerable accidents caused by road coaches being driven carelessly, going too fast, often when racing rival coaches or attempting to keep up with unrealistic timetables. It seemed odd that people accepted that such accidents would happen but looked askance at railway accidents, apparently on the grounds that they should not be allowed to happen on the more highly capitalised railways than with the coaching companies. The problem was that when a railway accident occurred, the speed and weight of the train in a collision or a derailment usually made for a spectacular incident, potentially killing or maiming larger numbers than those likely to be involved if a road accident.

Accidents occurred when badly maintained locomotives and rolling stock derailed, rails broke, bridges collapsed, embankments

The great Victorian cartoonist and illustrator Sir John Tenniel gives visual expression to Punch's concern about the poor safety record of the railway companies in the mid-nineteenth century. It puts the blame on the companies for putting the making of profit before passenger safety while blaming their own employees for negligence when things went wrong.

RAILWAY RESPONSIBILITY.

Mr. Punch. " NO, NO, MR. DIRECTOR, *THEY'RE* NOT SO MUCH TO BLAME. IT'S *YOUR* PRECIOUS FALSE ECONOMY, UNPUNCTUALITY, AND GENERAL WANT OF SYSTEM THAT DOES ALL THE MISCHIEF."

slipped, landslips blocked cuttings but it also has to be said that many injuries and fatalities were caused by people standing on the track not realising that unlike a horse-drawn vehicle, a train could not swerve to avoid an impact. Passengers sometimes panicked and leapt out of a train, if their hat had blown off for example. Some early passengers decided to try riding on the roof of a carriage, much like they might have done with a stage coach, only to have their brains bashed out by bridges. From earliest times, there were maliciously inclined individuals who threw missiles at trains or put obstacles on the line hoping to produce a derailment. Whether

THE PATENT SAFETY RAILWAY BUFFER (1857)

Punch is maintaining its constant pressure on the railway companies in this 1857 cartoon suggesting that railway directors might be rather more mindful of safety issues if they had to ride on the front buffer beam of locomotives hauling trains.

or not the blame for accidents could be ascribed to the railway, irresponsible journalists sensationalised them and helped to create a negative impression.

Even today, on those rare occasions when railway accidents occur, the media home in on them hungrily and 'explain' why they happened with a mixture of crass ignorance and exaggeration because they make for a good story. They do this with relish while ignoring the daily toll on Britain's roads.

Fellow Passengers

There always were passengers who had a jaundiced view of their fellow travellers. We sense this in a traveller in one of the early open wagons with hard benches and holes drilled in the floor to let rainwater out. Describing the 'teeming hundreds', he wrote of:

> '...rough sailors with tarry hands and bronzed faces, pretty servant maids, Jewish pedlars, Irish labourers, soldiers on furlough, housewives and farmwives, taciturn clerks and merry tipplers, excited children and worried mothers.'

Before the age of the railway, the rich could afford their own horse-drawn road conveyances. Travelling in these emphasised their wealth and superior social status. With the arrival of the railways, some insisted on still travelling in their own conveyances, albeit being mounted on flat trucks. Again this was a mark of prestige. The privacy that the rich enjoyed in this way was not available in stagecoaches or the carriages of their rail-borne successors. Both forms of transport involved people travelling in close proximity to others and exposed them to the habits and behaviour, acceptable or otherwise, of their fellow passengers. Railways helped to bring about a considerable increase in travel and the unhappy experiences that sometimes resulted provoked adverse comments and criticism aimed, often unfairly, at the railways. After all, it was difficult to know what other kind of accommodation they could provide which would eliminate the close personal encounters about which complaints were made.

Warnings abounded about the potential horrors awaiting the innocent traveller who was forced to travel for a considerable length of time in a compartment occupied by just one other passenger. Perhaps he (it was almost always a 'he'), might turn out to be an insufferable bore bent on recounting his entire life story in mind-numbingly minute detail. Others who could make the journey a misery were those who insisted on smoking foul-smelling pipes, over-friendly drunks who insisted that you were their best mate ever and other drunks who either slept and snored sonorously or became argumentative or aggressive; reprobates bent on robbery or those described with Victorian frankness as 'lunatics' whose behaviour was entirely unpredictable. None of the manuals advised their readers that the majority of journeys involving just two passengers in a compartment passed off uneventfully, as indeed did the majority of journeys in multi-occupied carriages.

The Railway Traveller's Handy Book commented with some asperity on the issue of conversation in railway carriages:

'Generally speaking, the occupants of a railway carriage perform the whole of the journey in silence; but if one passenger be more loquaciously inclined than the rest, he is soon silenced by abrupt or tart replies, or by a species of grunt expressive of dissent or dissatisfaction. Sometimes a conversation is got up, but it is of a spasmodic and ephemeral nature, lasts for about the first five minutes of the journey, and then relapses into solemn silence, never again to be broken. This is most unnatural and unreasonable. Why should half a dozen persons, each with minds to think, and tongues to express those thoughts, sit looking at each other as though they were afraid of employing the faculty of speech?'

Travelling in trains or being on railway premises certainly elicited some strange behaviour but it was probably unfair to blame the railways as such for these events. For example, two students appearing before magistrates were fined for making 'uncouth' noises and spitting on the hat and a book held by a doctor in the same compartment. These youths may well have acted in a similarly boorish manner wherever they had been – it was just that the railway carriage provided a convenient locale for their antisocial behaviour. Wimbledon magistrates had to deal with the case of a man accused of sitting naked and drunk in a ladies' waiting room, with his hat on the table and his shirt draped on a bench on the platform. Ultra-fastidious passengers made many complaints about being forced to read obscene messages scratched on carriage windows by lewd miscreants.

Complaints about smoking were constant throughout the nineteenth century, and later. Many companies prohibited smoking in trains for the dirt, pollution and damage it created but found it very hard to police their by-laws effectively. Smoke was one thing but many smokers also had the filthy and unhygienic habit of expectorating. The number of smokers increased considerably during the century and one enterprising manufacturer even marketed an ingenious 'railway pipe' which could apparently be instantly concealed when officialdom appeared. In 1868, the problem was given formal recognition when companies were required to provide designated compartments for smoking. It still proved difficult to enforce rules on smoking.

Another, rather more delicate, issue which generated disgruntled comments was that of passengers producing 'windy emanations' as they were sometimes coyly known. These are a natural bodily function but age, diet and general health may exacerbate the frequency and pungency of such phenomena. While few passengers were likely blatantly to give full rip, attempts at silent expulsion might still produce audible results and noxious aromas. A give-away that something was imminent might be indicated by the passenger who would suddenly move to the door, lower the window and point his posterior outboard. This was probably no more acceptable than a brave but failed attempt to be surreptitious. John Ruskin once found himself sharing a compartment on a train from Chester to Ruabon with what he described rather ungraciously as 'two cadaverous sexagenarian spinsters'. The windows were firmly shut and Ruskin had little option but to breathe 'the richest compound of the products of their own indigestion'.

Morality is a relative concept, perceptions of what is or is not moral varying through time. Some Victorian people blamed railways simply for undertaking their natural function, one of which was that of transporting people. According to such people, in doing this, railways placed them in moral jeopardy because they were travelling with people they did not know. Some such fellow passengers might have sinister intent while others were of inferior social standing. It was unthinkable for a middle-class traveller to engage in social intercourse with someone to whom they had not previously been introduced, particularly if the person was of the 'great unwashed'. The same school of thought reproached the railways on moral grounds for providing the means whereby people of evil intent could carry out criminal acts. Thus, a miscreant might use a train to travel to a destination which offered rich possibilities for criminal activity. This notion seems very odd today and even decades ago it would never have occurred to most people to blame the railways for doing business transporting withdrawn bank notes and thereby indirectly causing the Great Train Robbery!

Women travelling alone in a compartment were thought to be particularly vulnerable to the danger of robbery or sexual molestation. This perception led to the creation of women-only compartments. Much was made of the threat to lone women travellers by the case of 44-year-old Colonel Valentine Baker. He was an eminent socialite and commanding officer of a prestigious military unit who, in 1875, found himself in the dock charged with assault and 'attempting to ravish' a woman in a compartment of a train travelling from Petersfield to London. The case attracted much salacious interest, not least because of Baker's social standing. He was convicted of indecent assault but not of attempted rape. He was sent to prison for twelve months, required to pay a substantial fine and the affair ended his potentially brilliant career in the army. Men often tried to ensure that they did not share a compartment with a lone female traveller for fear of entrapment and claims being made against them for assault.

Many travellers tried to avoid compartments containing one or more children. It was also inevitable that passengers' dogs could be a source of friction among travellers in the close confines of a railway carriage.

Railway Refreshment Rooms and Catering

From the earliest days, railway refreshment rooms were the butt of pictorial, vocal and written criticism. They did indeed leave much to be desired and the criticism often became positively mordent. Catering has been an aspect of railway operations which has continued throughout to stimulate interest, often of a critical nature. Railway catering became an Aunt Sally and critics and comedians returned to the well-worn theme time and time again. Railway catering became notorious in terms of its presentation, price and quality.

Before on-board catering facilities were available, there was a conflict of interest between company staff trying to operate timetables effectively and various freelance hucksters using railway premises in an attempt to sell their wares to people on the platforms or passengers on trains. A rather irascible minute for discussion at a board meeting of the Liverpool & Manchester Railway contains opprobrious comments about the 'inconvenience and nuisance of the existing practice of hawking about Eccles Cakes and Ale and Spirit to railway passengers at almost every stopping place between Warrington Junction and Manchester'.

In the early years of the Great Western Railway (GWR), a contract was arranged with Messrs J. & C. Rigby that required all trains at Swindon to halt for at least ten minutes so that passengers could alight and buy refreshments. This practice became a rich source for contemporary humourists who revelled in the antics of hungry and thirsty travellers leaping out of their trains at Swindon, running pell-mell along the platform to the refreshment room and then jostling and elbowing to get served. Equally risible were their attempts to swallow such hot items as soup or tea before rushing back to their compartment within the very short allotted time. It was a case of Devil take the hindmost and those who were slow or not prepared to use their elbows to get served often perforce went without. Frequently, passengers managed to get served only to return to the platform and see their train steaming away. Others just managed to get their refreshments only then having no time to consume them as whistles indicated the train was about to depart. The received wisdom was that such abandoned comestibles were recycled and served to the next trainload of famished and thirsty passengers that arrived at Swindon. Complaints flooded in from those who found little that was funny in their experiences at Swindon. The adverse publicity damaged the Great Western's public relations but the company was tied to the terms of the contract. Trains stopped at Swindon not necessarily for operating purposes but simply to honour the terms of the contract. In 1895 they bought Rigby's out and some sanity was introduced into Swindon's catering arrangements but it cost the GWR a lot of money.

The kind of arrangement made at Swindon between the Great Western and the catering company existed elsewhere such as Wolverton, originally on the London & Birmingham Railway, and it seems that the association with these private companies gave railway catering in general a bad name. There were complaints about overpricing, rude staff, watery tea, stale buns and curling sandwiches. Wolverton was noted for its awful pork pies. Comparisons were made between the catering facilities on French railways and those in Britain, invariably to the detriment of the latter. When the writer and dedicated railway traveller W.M. Ackworth went to the refreshment room on Aberdeen Station in 1890, all he could find was 'a sandwich composed of equal parts of gristle, fat and sawdust'. It was Ackworth, however, who then had to praise the excellence of the salmon just caught in the River Tay which appeared on the breakfast menu at Perth refreshment rooms.

Accusations were made that tea and soup were dispensed from the same urn in some refreshment rooms. The mustard served at the Great Northern station at Peterborough was described as being like 'yellow water'. In his short story 'Mugby Junction', Charles Dickens describes the horrors of the Down Platform Refreshment Room at a thinly-veiled Rugby by saying sarcastically that its proudest boast was that it had never actually refreshed anyone. Dickens had intimate knowledge of railway catering because his speaking tours meant he had to make frequent use of refreshment rooms. He had recently used the facilities available at Peterborough in the witching hours of a long night in 1856 when he wrote:

'The lady in the refreshment room...gave me a cup of tea, as if I were a hyena and she my cruel keeper with a strong dislike to me. I...had a petrified bun of enormous antiquity in miserable meekness.'

At Peterborough, a present-day passenger leaving the station is confronted by the Great Northern Hotel, opened in 1852. The American novelist Nathaniel Hawthorne took a jaundiced view of its services when he stayed there in 1857 and wrote:

'We left Peterborough this afternoon and...were glad to get away from the hotel: for although outwardly pretentious, it is a wretched and uncomfortable place, with scanty table, poor attendance and enormous charges.'

Anthony Trollope in *He Knew he was Right* (1868) was even more scathing about railway refreshment rooms when he wrote:

'The real disgrace of England is the railway sandwich – that whited sepulchre, fair enough outside, but so meagre, poor and spiritless within, such a thing of shreds and pairings, with a dab of food, telling us that the poor bone whence it was scraped had been made utterly bare before it was sent into the kitchen for the soup pot.'

It is possible to record accolades extended with respect to the quality of the catering in the refreshment room at the Midland Railway's once very important junction at Normanton near Wakefield. There, all agreed that an excellent six-course meal was on offer. The down side was the impossibility of having it ordered, prepared, served and consumed in the twenty minutes allowed for the refreshment stop.

One emerging criticism of railway refreshment rooms in the latter part of the nineteenth century was that they attracted heavy drinkers acting antisocially. Under the guise of serving bona-fide travellers, refreshment rooms, at least at the big stations, enjoyed even more generous opening hours than other licensed premises. Hardened topers would buy a cheap single ticket to the nearest station down the line and thereby gain legal admission to the platform and the bibulous delights of its refreshment room.

Louth in Lincolnshire is an old market town boasting a medieval church with one of the most handsome spires in Britain. It is not a place easily associated with the depths of human depravity yet in 1879, the Holy Trinity Temperance Association felt it necessary to open temperance refreshment rooms at the station. This group of worthies was deeply concerned about the increase in female immorality it believed was being brought about by the railways. It was alleged that innocent young maidens were being apprehended as they left trains at Louth by predatory males who seduced them and led them into lives of unremitting debauchery. It is unclear what impact an alcohol-free refreshment room might have had in ridding Louth of this reprehensible practice.

Not everyone viewed refreshment rooms with disdain as this excerpt from Sir Cusack Roney's *Rambles of Railways* shows:

'...there was an attraction at those refreshment rooms that rose superior to all the hot soup, the hot coffee, the hot tea, the buns, the Banbury cakes, the pork pies, the brandy, whisky, gin and "rich compounds"...we refer to the charming young ladies in whom were concentrated all the beauty and grace that should be corporated [*sic*] in modern Hebes...sweet faces, worthy types of English beauty, all the more worthy because with them is combined the modest demeanour, emblem of purity, without which all is absent that adorns woman and renders her enchanting.'

Railway Humour

Although all human beings have the capacity for laughter, what is considered funny is largely determined by the culture and mores of a particular period and also individual temperament. The railways of Britain had an immeasurable social and cultural impact and were the recipients of humour, sometimes affectionate and gently mocking, at other times ironic and occasionally even savagely mordent. Spoken, written and graphical humour can provide valuable insights into perceptions of railways at different times. Of course, what might have been regarded as side-splittingly funny in 1850 would possibly not so much as raise a titter today.

Punch satirising the discrimination evident in the relationships between railway servants and the different classes of the travelling public.

Humourists must have welcomed the advent of the railways for bringing them fortuitously an almost endless source of inspiration. So much humour is around wry comments on human behaviour and the misunderstandings that can occur between people. Railway stations and the insides of railway carriages provide a fruitful locale for such scenarios. So did the arcane and impenetrable mysteries of railway timetables, the patent absurdity of some railway rules and regulations, the quaint nature of rustic branch lines and the quirky behaviour of many railway employees.

The misunderstandings that result from ambiguity provide a rich seam of humour. We give just one example. We have an old lady who is convinced that any train journey is fraught with grave danger. She takes a seat in a carriage as near the centre of the train as possible. The guard comes along examining tickets. 'How often does this railway kill a man?' she asks. 'Only once,' comes the laconic reply.

Some of the most classic cartoons with railways as a subject appeared in *Punch*. This periodical first appeared on I7 July 1841. It quickly established a reputation for radical campaigning against corruption and incompetence in the Establishment. It did not like avaricious, power-drunk railway promoters and it was highly critical of the financial shenanigans that were a feature of the 'Railway Mania'. *Punch* frequently attacked what it saw as the priority

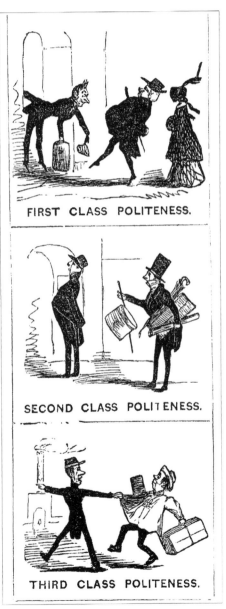

FIRST CLASS POLITENESS.

SECOND CLASS POLITENESS.

THIRD CLASS POLITENESS.

that railway directors gave to profits over such things as safety. This theme was to return to certain parts of the media with a vengeance after the railways were privatised and there was a rash of serious accidents in the bad old Railtrack days.

Punch, although often having a serious point to make, found in railways an inexhaustible fount of humour. A key element in British humour is the prevalence of issues surrounding social class and *Punch* exploited this to the full. A cameo was the occasion on which a ticket collector in addressing first-class passengers said, 'May I trouble you for your tickets?' With the second-class passengers his gambit is, 'Tickets, please.' When he reaches the third class he merely vouchsafes a blunt, 'Now then! Tickets.'

ROLAND DAVIES

"Notice how she jumped on that curve?"

Even with such unlikely scenarios as this, railways have continued to be a source of affectionate humour and therefore the providers of pleasure. (Authors' collection)

Cartoonists found a rich seam in the idiosyncrasies of Britain's rural branch lines. (Authors' collection)

"First ticket I've sold since the train stopped halting here."

[Punch

Complaints about Stations

'Tithebarn Street' was the name given to a section of a terminus station in the northern area of Liverpool's city centre which served various lines that eventually amalgamated to form part of the Lancashire & Yorkshire Railway. The station opened in May 1850 with the usual pomp and ceremony accompanied by paeans of praise for its sumptuous facilities. Quickly, however, complaints were heard about the difficult access from street level up an exposed flight of steps which were steep and frequently slippery. On reaching the circulating area at platform level, passengers were annoyed at having to steer through mountains of luggage. Those making the complaints pointed out that this luggage belonged to the substantial number of emigrants (often refugees) from Eastern Europe arriving at east coast ports who were making their way across England to embark at Liverpool on ships for North America. It was clear that there was little sympathy for the plight of these travellers. The fact that a few items of luggage probably contained all they had left in the world was a minor point compared to the clutter they created. Tithebarn Street was replaced by the capacious new Exchange Station in July 1886.

Railway enthusiasts are used to querulous members of the public and sensation-seeking journalists woefully ignorant on railway affairs taking issue with this or that aspect of railway operations, or, indeed, with the railways as a whole. However when leading members of their own fraternity join in the criticism, then it is obvious something is seriously wrong. Therefore the words of Charles Rous-Marten writing in *The Railway Magazine* for February 1899 are particularly significant. He wrote:

> 'Probably no railway station since iron roads were first invented has ever come in for such an avalanche of gorgeous [*sic*] and whole-hearted abuse as has fallen of late upon that of the London, Chatham and Dover Railway at Ludgate Hill Station...I have not a syllable to say in praise or defence of Ludgate Hill Station. Nor, for that matter, has, I believe, a single soul belonging to the owning company.'

Cambridge was one of those, fortunately rare, stations where at one time, the main passenger traffic was concentrated on one very long through platform, although in the case of Cambridge at least, there were bays at both ends. A scissors crossing allowed the main platform in effect to operate as two platforms by servicing two trains simultaneously. This was inconvenient from the operational point of view and unpopular with passengers so around 1850, an island platform was built on the up side, reached by a footbridge with steep stairs. The stairs in particular were the subject of continuous complaints and claims for injuries sustained and in 1863, the island platform was removed and improvements made to the main platform. Ironically, a new island platform has been built in recent years.

Preston found itself on the railway network at an early stage. The main station in the 1840s was in Fishergate and as traffic built up, the facilities at this station became increasingly inadequate and the object of rancorous comment by its users and the press. From 1846, this station was under joint ownership and it was clear that the relationship of the partners was not a marriage made in Heaven. A contemporary local historian described the station as:

> 'One of the most dismal, dilapidated, disgraceful-looking structures in Christendom. It was not only very ill-looking, but an exceptionally inconvenient, dangerous station. Passengers requiring to go across from one side to the other had to walk along the line…'

Clearly there was little general improvement and conditions were so bad that in 1865, Preston Corporation approached the then two joint owners, the London & North Western Railway and the Lancashire & Yorkshire Railway, in an attempt to persuade them either to build a new station or to make radical improvements to the existing one. The lack of response caused the *Lancaster Guardian* on 24 February 1866 to give vent to its wrath:

> 'They have white-washed, patched up and daubed the station in every possible way, and on Thursday they actually gave instructions – in regard to the old station which has been condemned by everybody for years – which is smashed in every way – which is almost roofless, and which is the dingiest old shed in railwaydom – for the dirty old iron pillars supporting it to be gilded at the centre… A wag once said that the height of folly was to paint a mud cart white: but the latest decorative display at Preston Station is tantamount to burnishing one.'

Preston Corporation did not merely lie back but was so irate that it made representations to the Board of Trade who sent Colonel Yolland, the Government Inspector of Railways, to Preston to investigate the complaints. Nothing had followed when, on 18 August 1866, part of the roof fell in, causing some injuries. Still no action was taken and in a letter to the editor of the *Preston*

Guardian on 8 September 1866 a correspondent calling himself 'Bothered Passenger' wrote angrily:

> 'Surely there never was such a station as Preston…At the west side there is really not a quarter of the room for the amount of traffic and number of passengers…If fate would some day take off the limb of a director or some noted official, the fiat for a new station would not long be delayed. Would it be sinful to wish that such a boon would be granted forthwith?'

A rebuilt and greatly improved station was brought into use in July 1880.

Railway companies were quick to seize the opportunity for income offered by letting advertising space. Vertical surfaces, including even the risers on station footbridges, soon came to be covered with exhortations to purchase Beecham's Pills or enjoy the life-enhancing experience offered by Iron Jelloids. Tin signs drew attention to the merits of an eclectic range of commodities such as Brasso, Bovril and Ketton Cement. Haters of the world of commerce and its brash and intrusive propaganda took exception to the sheer quantity of these signs while satirical journals like *Punch* mocked the stations so extensively covered by advertisements that strangers on trains were unable to identify the name of the station when the train pulled in. In 1893, a Society for Controlling the Abuse of Public Advertising was established with William Morris among its leading lights and it led the crusade for the regulation of intrusive advertising. Now, in the twenty-first century, much work remains to be done on this issue.

Tunnels

Many were the dire warnings about the hazards of tunnels and the need to avoid travelling through them. There were, however, many journeys on which tunnels could not be avoided.

One commentator described tunnels as 'holes of impurity'. The author of *The Railway Traveller's Handy Book* thought that tunnels, before the days of lighting on trains, were the most likely place for murderous assaults to take place and recommended that travellers should make themselves ready to beat off any assailant as soon as the train plunged into darkness.

We should not mock the fears expressed about tunnels by travellers on the early railways. Nothing like these tunnels, especially the longer ones, had been seen before. Trains without lighting in the carriages and travelling at speeds never previously approached, even if very moderate by today's standards, would suddenly plunge into a darkness which might be absolute if the tunnel was lengthy. Obvious questions would assail the minds of travellers, especially those of a timid disposition. What would happen if the tunnel roof collapsed? What would happen if there was a derailment or other accident? What if a miscreant should use the darkness to attempt robbery or to force himself on an innocent female traveller? These fears were not entirely irrational because there were indeed roof falls, derailments and collisions and robberies and sexual assaults did take place. What made these situations more threatening was the knowledge that in most cases, the carriage doors were locked.

Much was made of these potential hazards by those who opposed the coming of the railways or had an axe to grind perhaps against one particular railway. So it was with Dr Dionysius Lardner. He was an academic, a Professor of Natural Philosophy, but also a publicist keen to be in the limelight through making statements that provoked controversy. Much of his extensive published work was rational but he incurred ridicule for some prophecies which were rash at best. He was not an opponent of railways as such but he was no admirer of Isambard Kingdom Brunel and the Great Western Railway. When he made public pronouncements he did so in a manner such as to brook no possible argument. One of his best-known gaffes was that which he made when holding forth about the dangers likely to befall passengers on trains going down the falling gradient through Box Tunnel. He described the tunnel as a 'monstrous cavity' and predicted that if the brakes failed, a train would emerge at the western end travelling at 120mph and carrying a cargo of dead passengers since they would all have been asphyxiated. Brunel was having none of this nonsense and calmly responded by saying that the good doctor had forgotten to take friction and air resistance into account and that the speed on leaving the tunnel was likely to be 56mph. Charles Dickens summarily dismissed Lardner by calling him 'the prince of humbugs'.

There were many other scientists and members of the medical profession who were opposed to all railways or aspects of railways and who held forth on the hazards of tunnels frequently using pseudo-science to support their arguments. We should not be surprised to learn that other 'experts', medically or scientifically qualified or not, who countered these views by pointing to the positive health benefits to be extracted from railway tunnels. A particular favourite was to describe the rapid improvement in the health of asthmatic children who inhaled the sulphurous fumes produced by steam locomotives in the confined space of a tunnel. Gloomy prognostications were voiced about how the noise made by two trains passing in a tunnel would have a damaging effect on the nerves of passengers. Others revelled in relating how they travelled through tunnels time and again and had suffered no neural damage when their train passed another.

So the antagonists engaged in a lively and knockabout cut-and-thrust but tunnels were here to stay. There were passengers who could never entirely reconcile themselves to tunnels until carriage lighting became more-or-less universal. There were certainly a number of incidents where women passengers were attacked in the Stygian darkness of railway tunnels and in preparation for such a horrible possibility, some would put a hat pin in their mouths, sharp end outwards, with which to repel unwanted advances.

Railway companies did what they could to counter unfavourable perceptions of tunnels. The Liverpool & Manchester Railway very perceptively allowed the public to walk through its lengthy Crown Street Tunnel at Liverpool before trains began to run. Admittedly the tunnel was lit but the exercise was intended to show those who took advantage of the offer that nothing malevolent lurked in its inner recesses. Clearly some of the directors understood the need to allay a primeval fear among many people concerning holes in the ground.

Again to allay fears and give a sense of solidity and permanence, some railway companies adorned tunnel entrances with ornamentation reminiscent of medieval castles. These entrances might feature mock turrets, crenelations, loopholes and machicolation. Two examples are on the lines of the former Midland Railway at Red Hill where the main line crosses the Trent and at Clay Cross in Derbyshire. Other such structurally unnecessary features were, of course, sometimes built at the request of local landowners.

Health Hazards of Railway Travel

From the lofty heights of the twenty-first century, we may laugh at the fears expressed by early travellers concerning the hazards of railway travel. In the context of their times many of these fears were very real.

Signalling and safety systems had to be developed by trial and error because nothing faster and heavier than railway trains had ever moved on land before. Accidents of varying severity were common. Deaths occurred but injuries were more frequent. A physical injury was usually easy to identify but more nebulous were the conditions such as impaired memory, sleep disturbance, anxiety and hearing loss that it was claimed were brought about as a consequence of railway accidents or which were sometimes the negative effects of simply travelling by train. Then, as now, there were plenty of travellers happy to go to court in order to obtain compensation for injuries supposedly sustained through the agency of a railway. Once litigation was on the agenda, then it was inevitable that not only would members of the legal profession be involved but so would medical practitioners, locking horns 'proving' or 'disproving' cases for compensation.

In these circumstances, the services of supposed 'experts' are frequently called upon. An example was Sir John Eric Erickson, a Professor of Surgery who, in 1866, published a treatise titled *On Railway and other Injuries of the Nervous System*. He invented a term, 'Railway Spine', which he argued was responsible for many of the conditions that passengers claimed they had sustained as a consequence of travelling by train. It involved chronic inflammation of the spinal membranes. For the purposes of obtaining legal compensation via the courts, it was extremely convenient that 'Railway Spine' was endorsed by so eminent an authority as Erickson and that the symptoms could apparently develop some time after the accident even if the victim had suffered no obvious physical injury. The essential vagueness of the diagnosis of 'Railway Spine' was backed up by assertions from Erikson that the condition intensified over time and that recovery was unlikely. All this helped claimants for compensation but disadvantaged railway companies because courts were reluctant to call into question 'evidence' provided by an authority of the status of the good professor. This was a charter for malingerers and fraudsters and the railways were forced to employ their own 'experts' to try to blow false claims out of the water.

Even where there was no issue about compensation, hypochondriacs gratified themselves indulging in the various conditions they claimed were brought on by or exacerbated as a consequence of travelling by train. A major hazard involved 'chills'.

These were a conveniently vague category not unlike the later phrase 'nervous disorder'. Quite why railway travel should be so conducive of chills is hard to determine given that travel by coach also created considerable exposure to the elements.

Members of the medical profession ranged themselves either in opposition to or in defence of railway travel. Conflicting evidence and 'proof' were bandied to and fro. One senior medical officer for a French railway claimed that one-fifteenth of footplate workers suffered from various disorders of the brain and nervous system to lumbago and spinal trouble directly as a result of their employment. Different conclusions were drawn by a doctor working for the General Post Office, who averred that their employment had a positive effect on the health of those working as travelling sorters on mail trains. Apparently many confided in him that their health had improved greatly since they had been employed in this capacity. The same doctor happily revealed that GPO employees who worked on such trains who had previously been gawkily thin had now put on weight and were comfortably upholstered while those who had been distinctly overweight were revelling in having slimmed down considerably.

There is no limit to the extent of human self-obsession. Some people who suffered disturbed sleep and consequent tiredness blamed it on being over-anxious about missing a train in the morning. It was hardly the fault of the railways that such concerns were generated in some peoples' minds. There were doctors who claimed that rushing to catch a train was itself the cause of damaging levels of stress. It could be particularly harmful to rush for a train having just eaten a big meal. It was claimed that this could cause collapse or even death. If the poor traveller managed to survive the trauma involved in getting to the station and actually managed to catch the train, he might have to endure the hazards of being in a railway compartment that was too hot because no windows were open or, because all the windows were open, was too draughty.

As august a publication as *The Lancet* produced scholarly treatises which identified 'vibratory illness' as an undesirable concomitant of the motion involved in railway travel or discussed the unhealthy outcomes that could result from gazing out of the carriage window at the passing scene. Damage to the eyes was a likely outcome.

In 1862, *The Lancet* held forth about the fatigue created by train travel:

> 'The rapidity and variety of the impressions necessarily fatigue both the eye and the brain. The constantly varying distances at which the objects are placed involves an incessant shifting of the adaptive apparatus by which they are focussed on the retina and the mental effort by which the brain takes cognizance of them is scarcely productive of cerebral wear because it is unconscious...'

More fatigue is likely to be caused by the reader trying to make sense of this turgid prose than was ever going to result from 'vibratory illness' contracted in a railway carriage.

The practice of reading on a train caused controversy among the medical profession. Some experts claimed it did no harm while others thought it had a harmful effect if the reading material was on cheap paper and badly printed. Another prestigious publication, the *British Medical Journal*, claimed that first-class carriages were the most detrimental to the health because the thick textile fittings with which they were equipped absorbed large quantities of water and were therefore dangerously damp. It was frequently asserted that railways were potential carriers of epidemic disease.

Some members of the medical profession pandered to hypochondria by enlarging on the hazards provoked by travelling in a jolting train and doing little to reassure nervous travellers by telling them that passengers who appeared to have just dozed off were likely to be experiencing a stupor caused by 'concussion of the brain'. One 'expert' who may or may not have been a doctor argued that railway collisions were good for rheumatism. No empirical evidence was put forward to support this assertion.

On several occasions, *The Lancet* drew attention to the excessive working hours demanded of many railway workers and ascribed at least some of the dangers of railway travel to their over-exhaustion. These observations were taken up by *The Times* and other national newspapers drawing the attention of the wider public to the long hours and poor conditions of much railway employment and even calling for the right of railway workers to join a trade union.

Dr A.B. Granville wrote in *Spas of England*, published in 1841, that trains travelling at twenty or thirty miles per hour would 'affect delicate lungs and produce apoplexy...occasion catarrhs, and multiply agues'.

R.D. Blumfield was a journalist who, in 1887, gave a graphic description of a journey on the Metropolitan Railway from Baker Street to Moorgate. He did not enjoy the trip:

'I had my first experience of Hades today, and if the real thing is to be like that I shall never again do anything wrong. I got into the Underground Railway at Baker Street...the smoke and sulphur filled the tunnel, all the windows had to be closed. The atmosphere was a mixture of sulphur, coal dust and foul fumes from the gas lamps above, so that by the time we reached Moorgate Street I was near dead of asphyxiation and heat. I should think that these Underground railways should soon be discontinued, for they are a menace to health.'

Engine Sheds

Steam engine sheds or, in British Railways parlance, 'Motive Power Depots', were a constant source of complaint, most of all from those living nearby. Sheds of any size may have drawn train-spotters like flies to a jam pot but with their smoke, soot and other filth and their noise they made life a misery for their neighbours right around the clock with perhaps only a little relief on Sundays. The din and dust created, for example, when coal fell many feet into an empty steel tender from a mechanical coaling plant, was indescribable. Despite instructions to keep nuisance to a minimum, the very nature of their existence meant that sheds constituted a nuisance which would not be tolerated today. Those in urban locations tended to be situated where land was cheap which meant that their neighbours were often industrial premises and working-class housing. The denizens of such housing tended to have little influence. The noise and environmental pollution continued, unabated.

Brookwood Necropolis

The headlong expansion of London's population in the middle years of the nineteenth century threw up myriad social problems. Large numbers died of epidemic disease in the appallingly unhealthy conditions, one of the problems being the shortage of space for burials. Overcrowded burial grounds posed serious health problems.

The idea began to be mooted that space close to London but outside the continuously built-up area could be used for burials and that transport of coffins could be carried out quickly, safely and hygienically by railway. A site was found at Brookwood, near Woking in Surrey, consisting of no less than 2,000 acres. A main line railway already existed between London's Waterloo Station, passing Woking on its way to the south-west. A short branch could be built off this line bringing coffins and mourners directly into the proposed cemetery.

This would seem to be a very appropriate way of starting to tackle an urgent problem but no sooner was the idea suggested than it stirred up a hornets' nest of indignant objections. There were many people who still viewed railways with aversion and who were appalled at the idea that they would be used to transport the dead to their place of interment. The newspapers were bombarded by hot and bothered correspondents who declared that such a practice in a Christian country was absolutely intolerable and equivalent to defiling the dead. Few of these correspondents had any possible solution to the problem that water filtering through burial grounds was getting into water supplies with lethal effect and that some interments were placed so shallow in overcrowded conditions that it was not uncommon for dogs to dig down and make off with body parts from recently buried cadavers. These correspondents obviously had nothing positive to offer but they were joined in opposing what became the Brookwood Necropolis Railway by the Bishop of London. He had severe reservations concerning the affronted feelings of middle- and upper-class mourners who found themselves on a train with other mourners whose state in life only entitled them to travel third class. Such perceptions were not to be lightly dismissed at this time and after the London Necropolis and National Mausoleum Company was established in 1852, the facilities on offer were graded first, second and third class. Even in death, class distinctions were observed.

Less well-known was the Great Northern London Cemetery Company. The object underlying this company's operations was to provide a decent and dignified but cheap service for those people who found it an extreme challenge to pay for a funeral. The company built a station at Maiden Lane, Belle Isle, just north of King's Cross and trains ran to a large site just north of Colney Hatch (later New Southgate) where a special station was built. The service started around 1861 but it seems that money could not be made by serving the funerary needs of the less well-off and the operation closed down in 1873.

Herbert Spencer

Spencer is perhaps best described as a philosopher and sociologist but he was also interested in mathematics and science and so many other areas of human endeavour that he can justifiably be termed a polymath. He was one of the most influential thinkers of his time and he wrote extensively on evolution, it being he and not Charles Darwin who coined the phrase 'survival of the fittest'. From the point of view of economics and politics he was a libertarian whose views moved increasingly to the right as he grew older.

He had experience as a railway engineer as a young man and retained an interest in railways throughout his life. He was unhappy about the ethical practices of what we might now call 'corporate capitalism', represented in his time by the larger railway companies. He was particularly critical of the manner in which some directors used the companies in which they had a leading role to feather their own nests at the expense of the shareholders who were often kept in the dark about what was really happening. He also pointed out that some of these mavericks held multiple directorships in companies which, on occasion, could have conflicting interests. Spencer criticised the legal profession for contributing to the financial crisis around the 'Railway Mania' by their role in promoting intentionally fraudulent railway schemes.

He also had railway contractors in his sights. In the *Edinburgh Review* he wrote:

> 'They are as insatiate as millionaires in general and so long as they continue in business at all, are, in some sort, forced to provide new undertakings to keep their plant employed…lines are forced into being, which it is known from the beginning will not pay.'

The lines to which he refers became known as 'contractors' lines'. Promoters and contractors needed new projects on which to work but by the 1860s the most potentially lucrative ones had already been built. Regardless, fundamentally unsound projects were authorised funded by borrowing. The subsequent failure of the companies involved in such projects was a major reason for the crisis of 1866-7 in which a number of banks, most prominent of which was Overend & Gurney of Norwich, collapsed with effects felt throughout the economy.

In his later years, he was highly critical of the Great Central Railway's extension to London because it would disturb the tenor of life in select St John's Wood and he always had an objection to locomotive whistles which he believed were all too often sounded needlessly.

Railway Bookstalls

Given the impact of railways, it would be easy to suppose that early railway travellers, being so enthralled by the experience of train travel, would gaze with rapt fascination at the sights passing before their eyes. Not so. From the earliest days of railway travel, there was an assumption that passengers would find travelling by train a tedious and boring experience which required some kind of diversion in order to make it at least tolerable. One diversion from boredom is eating; another is immersion in printed matter. Soon vendors were peddling their wares on station platforms only largely to be replaced by fixed bookstalls. Possibly the first fixed shop selling printed material was one at Fenchurch Street Station in 1841. The name W.H. Smith & Sons appeared and soon became dominant on the more important stations, at least in England and Wales. Smith's were not the first railway bookstalls but the winning of a contract in 1848 to rent stalls on the busier stations of the London & North Western Railway was the starting point of a major nationwide business. In Scotland, John Menzies obtained a monopoly of railway station bookstall provision. Confusingly, W.H. Smith's eldest son was also called W.H. Smith and he did much to build the company up.

One theme of this book concerns attitudes to railways and their activities. As we have seen, criticism of railways came in many forms. Bookstalls on railway stations would seem to be a pretty unexceptionable development but no, their appearance provoked outrage when some people lambasted them for being little short of brothels! It was alleged that the presence of a bookstall attracted large numbers of beggars, thieves, ladies of the night and other undesirables. It was not made clear quite what drew these various subcultures to cluster around bookstalls but it might have been something to do with the fact that titivating and morally decadent printed matter was on display for all to see as well as, horror of horrors, 'French novels'! These vied for the travellers' hard-earned pennies with beer bottles, tacky cakes and all manner of luridly coloured sweetmeats. Soon, criticism of bookstalls and the goods they sold extended to the staff of these establishments. They found themselves being described as 'dissolute ne'er-do-wells'.

The nineteenth century was a period of slowly improving education and rising literacy. These created a marked and growing demand for a wide range of reading matter. Some travellers may have eagerly grabbed the opportunity to while away a train journey by losing themselves in escapist, sensationalist or even that kind of literature often described in those days as 'lewd'. Nowadays such material would be regarded as no more than titillating. The phrase 'railway literature' was used pejoratively by those who were, or pretended to be, above such things. The word 'yellowback' was also coined for this material from the predominant colour of the wrappers on the books of one particular publisher. Yellowback then became a term applied to cheap reprints, irrespective of the nature of their contents.

It is only fair to say that bookstalls sold a wider range of reading matter than their detractors chose to recognise. They sold cheap copies of poetry books and of the works of popular novelists such as Sir Walter Scott and they may actually have assisted the beneficial spread of reading habits. The publisher John Murray, anxious to counter the opprobrium aimed at early bookstalls, was to the fore in producing literature specifically for the bookstalls that met the approval of the Victorian chattering classes. These were described as providing 'sound and entertaining information and innocent amusement'. Now earnest travellers could journey by train while being edified by studying *Specimens of the Table-talk of Samuel Taylor Coleridge* or, if that palled, *Jesse's Gleanings in Natural History*. Matthew Arnold, the Victorian poet and cultural critic, noted healthy sales of popular scientific works from bookstalls and was gratified that some were bought by railway servants clearly bent on self-improvement. W.H. Smith even had small lending libraries in some of their bookstalls.

The end of the stamp duty on newspapers coincided with the spread of the railway network and these factors both greatly assisted the growth of the newspaper industry. W.H. Smith became the leading distributor of newspapers. Stamp duty was finally abolished in 1855 which, in conjunction with the spread of improved rates of literacy, greatly increased the potential market for newspapers and other printed material. Although a modern industrialised society needed increasing numbers of literate and numerate people, there was always a fear among some of the rich and powerful that reading might give the lower orders access to subversive material and encourage them to get above their station in life, no pun intended.

CHAPTER TWELVE

Attitudes to Railways in the Arts

Over two centuries, railways have provoked a large and diverse range of artistic and literary responses, condemnatory and celebratory. They have proved to be an infinitely rich and flexible medium for artistic and literary expression. Here we claim no comprehensive coverage but merely provide some examples of this expression.

The Lake District

William Wordsworth was the most celebrated of the Lakeland Romantic poets. He was born at Cockermouth on the edge of the Lake District. After a variety of experiences, not least in the French Revolution, Wordsworth returned to live in the Lake District in 1799 and embarked on a highly productive period of poetry writing and publishing. In 1833, he wrote a poem entitled *Steamboats, Viaducts and Railways* declaring that the benefits that could accrue from railways outweighed any damage they might do to the environment. As he grew older and wealthier, his youthful revolutionary idealism was replaced by a very conservative and elitist mindset. Evidence of this was his outspoken opposition to the proposal in 1844 to build a railway from Kendal to the shore of Windermere between Bowness and Ambleside. Kendal was fated to be just off the main line to Carlisle over Shap, part of the route which became known as the West Coast Main Line. The line to Windermere ensured that the Lake District did at least get some connection to the main railway network, despite and not because of the likes of Wordsworth.

The juxtaposition of mountains and lakes was meat and drink to the Romantic Poets and had already been drawing numbers of well-heeled visitors, attracted not only by the scenery but also the remoteness and peace and quiet it offered. Wordsworth wanted time to stand still in the Lakes. Industrialisation and the horrors with which it was associated such as railways could develop elsewhere but should not be allowed to blight the Lake District. Wordsworth had just been made Poet Laureate and was a man of some influence. He fired off letters to the newspapers and to leading politicians of the day. One of the recipients was Gladstone. Wordsworth informed him that the railway would destroy the area's beauty and peacefulness and, on the Lord's Day in particular, undermine its morals. The threat of the railway brought forth one of Wordsworth's most memorable lines: 'Is there no nook of English ground secure from rash assault?' His fulminations met with a mixed response. He had his supporters but he was also denounced for being a snob. He did not want common tourists and he looked down on them anyway because he did not consider them sensitive enough to appreciate the environmental delights the Lake District offered. The line from Oxenholme through Kendal to Windermere obtained parliamentary approval in 1845, Wordsworth having failed to rouse much support from local landowners. The continuation to Ambleside never happened, probably more on grounds of its huge potential expense than because of Wordsworth's disapproval. A few further lines penetrating the Lake District opened subsequently without much protest at their impact on the environment. They helped to open up access to this area of outstanding beauty by visitors whose spending power had to be measured against pressures on the environment they created by their presence. Wordsworth's attitude to the railways was an early example of what has come to be known as 'nimbyism'. It was especially so since his opposition to railways was selective. Some time past, he had inherited a sizeable sum of money and had asked a friend who knew about such things to recommend railway investments which would generate the best return. When Wordsworth described the power of the railways as: '…the Thirst of Gold, that rules o'er Britain like a baneful star', he was perhaps being somewhat disingenuous.

Protests broke out again in the Lake District in the mid-1870s. By this time, widespread admiration for the achievements associated with the Industrial Revolution was being tempered by criticism of the environmental blight and dehumanising conditions evident in the mining and manufacturing districts. Proposals were advanced for a line through the heart of the Lake District from Keswick to Windermere. By now there was an appreciation of how the sights and solitude of the Lakes acted as a necessary antidote to the worst of urban living for those who had the means to get away from the former to the latter. Now the heavyweights in the campaign to stop the railway were the poets Tennyson and Browning and the art critic and aesthete John Ruskin. The latter was every bit as much a snob, describing the more plebeian visitors to the Lake District as 'the stupid herds of modern tourists'. He continued:

> 'All your railway company can do for (the tourists) is only to open taverns and skittle grounds round Grasmere, which will soon, then, be nothing but a pool of drainage, with a beach of broken ginger beer bottles; and their minds will no more be improved by contemplating the scenery of such a lake than Blackpool'.

He thought such visitors would be too drunk to appreciate the beauty of Helvellyn and that it would be like casting pearls before swine to admit such people to the Lake District.

The scheme failed not because of such Olympian tirades but because sober assessment indicted that the line was unlikely to generate sufficient traffic to make it viable. Further proposals for mineral railways in environmentally sensitive parts of the Lakes combined with the commandeering of Thirlmere as a water supply for Mancunians, led to a hardening of the conviction that enough was enough. In 1883, the Lake District Defence Society was set up, with wide support of a less precious nature emphasising that the Lake District was a priceless resource which ideally should be open to anyone from whatever class who appreciated and wanted to make use of its charms. The society went on to fight off a number of other proposals for railways in the Lakes as well as to publish propaganda raising awareness of the need to preserve its beauty for future generations.

By the second half of the twentieth century the railways were seen as far less environmentally damaging than private cars *en masse*, juggernaut lorries and motorways. On some summer days the roads in parts of the Lakes were virtually in a state of gridlock but some lines had already been closed. As early as the mid-1970s, the only British Railways lines left were the long route from Carnforth to Barrow, Whitehaven, Workington and Carlisle along the southern and western periphery of the Lakes, the West Coast Main line along its eastern periphery and, ironically, the branch to Windermere from Oxenholme and Keswick. Insult was added to injury when the A66 to the Cumbrian Coast was upgraded and actually used the formation of the closed line from Keswick to Cockermouth and Workington along the shore of beautiful Bassenthwaite Lake. It is hardly surprising that this road scheme generated much opposition. The arguments used against it were not dissimilar to many of the arguments made against the railways back in the nineteenth century.

John Ruskin was particularly incensed by the building of the Midland Railway's main line to Manchester through the heart of Derbyshire's Peak District. This involved the building of a stone viaduct over Monsal Dale, a well-known beauty spot. Apparently, he contemplated suicide but instead contented himself by thundering:

> 'There was a rocky valley between Buxton and Bakewell…You enterprised a Railroad through the Valley, you blasted its rocks away, heaped thousands of tons of shale into its lovely streams. The Valley is gone, and the Gods with it; and now, every fool in Buxton can be at Bakewell in half an hour, and every fool in Bakewell at Buxton… you Fools everywhere.'

Ruskin and railways were simply irreconcilable. He even disliked the Furness Railway's dainty little steamer *Gondola* which plied its trade on Coniston Water. He was totally unable to concede that there might be any merit in their buildings and installations or any benefits accruing to them as a means of transport:

> 'There was never more flagrant or impertinent folly than the smallest portion of ornament in anything concerned with railways or near them…the whole system of railway travelling is addressed to people who, being in a hurry, are therefore, for the time being miserable'.

He thought being a passenger on a train was little different from being a parcel. He saw the railways as redolent of everything detestable about modern life, disrupting and even destroying the tenor of traditional life and culture to no useful purpose. He even saw them as immoral, the embodiment of everything that was worst about the capitalist spirit, not least the personal greed railways encouraged. He harked back to some imaginary past society in which spiritual rather than material values promulgated a greater sense of trust and community. Railways, for him, epitomised the deplorable triumph of liberal economics.

Henry James, on visiting the Isle of Wight in 1879, criticised the ugly embankments and tunnels which resulted from the building of what he described as 'the detestable little railway'. Another querulous traveller was Thomas Carlyle, the writer and social critic.

Having arrived at Liverpool after a journey of thirty-four miles completed in under an hour and a quarter, he wrote:

'I was dreadfully frightened before the train started: in the nervous state I was in, it seemed certain to me that I should faint, from the impossibility of getting the horrid thing stoppt[*sic*].'

On a more modern note, the eminent art historian and expert on architecture, Nikolaus Pevsner, described Knaresborough Viaduct on the line between York and Harrogate as 'one of the most notable railway crimes in England'. It is likely that most of today's visitors would think it a crime to remove the viaduct.

Railways did bring a sublime element into the landscape. Cuttings and embankments were raw and bare and brick or stone bridges and eye-catching viaducts and bridges imposed themselves arrogantly on the landscape but they usually soon mellowed and weathered. Cuttings and embankments quickly attracted vegetation while

This lithograph by A. Tait dated 1845 shows the monumental viaduct of the Manchester & Birmingham Railway towering over the valley of the River Mersey and the blighted streets of Stockport. Then, as now, this absolutely dominates the town centre and is perhaps the feature which first comes to mind when Stockport is mentioned. The artist manages to give the impression that the viaducts and the trains that go across it are somehow both literally and metaphorically far removed from the squalor below. (Authors' collection)

This viaduct, on the route of the Great Western Railway out of London Paddington, may be the location of Turner's painting Rain, Steam and Speed although some people claim the Maidenhead Bridge as its scenario. Rather oddly, the description appended to this picture said that the viaduct afforded an excellent view of Hanwell's Lunatic Asylum. (Authors)

viaducts and bridges softened and became assimilated especially if they were made of local stone. Since the vast majority of railways were fenced, the sides of railway lines often became in effect wildlife reserves long before the concept gained official recognition.

Charles Dickens and Others

Charles Dickens was a child during the age when every boy wanted to be a stage coach driver. Coaches and the experience of coach travel feature in much of his early writing and it is evident that he had considerable affection for the world and way of life they represented. He then clearly developed a somewhat reluctant fascination with railways. The London & Greenwich Railway was a pioneering line in London and he followed its construction with great interest. He quickly appreciated how the railways facilitated the busy countrywide programme of talks and readings which helped to get him so well known. Railways appear in much of his published work from the 1840s and it is clear that he is intensely aware that was living through an era of enormous change characterised by the growing ubiquity of the railway.

Dickens was a very frequent user of trains and had an extremely perceptive eye for what was around him. He wrote about railway refreshment rooms in his story *Mugby Junction*. 'Mugby' is, of course, Rugby. He gave a superb evocation of the sensations created by a presence on the platforms during the hours of darkness:

'A place replete with shadowy shapes, this Mugby Junction in the black hours of the four-and-twenty. Mysterious goods trains, covered with palls and gliding on like vast weird funerals, conveying themselves guiltily away from the presence of the few lighted lamps, as if their freight had come to a secret and unlawful end...An earthquake accompanied with thunder and lightning, going up express to London. Now, all quiet, all rusty, wind and rain in possession, lamps extinguished, Mugby Junction dead and indistinct, with its robe drawn over its head, like Caesar.'

As noted earlier, he made uncomplimentary comments about the refreshment room at Peterborough in which he was forced to spend some dismal time during the small hours of a day in 1856. The refreshment facility at Stafford also found itself on the receiving end of his sarcasm when he described the tea urns as '...honeycombed within in all directions, having supplied for years decomposed lead, copper and a few other deadly poisons'.

Although Dickens was physically unhurt in the Staplehurst accident of 9 June 1865 on the South Eastern Railway, he was traumatised by the experience and never fully recovered. By a macabre coincidence, he died five years to the day after the accident. It is known that after the accident, he no longer enjoyed travelling by train, was wracked with anxiety when he was forced to do so and that his literary output fell. In 1866, he published *The Signalman*, a short story about a very conscientious railway signalman plagued by premonitions of his own death on the section of line for which he was responsible and which included a tunnel where an accident had occurred. It was adapted by the BBC in 1976 as one of its *A Ghost Story for Christmas* series and Denholm Elliott gave a moving performance playing the signalman.

Dombey & Son (1847-8) contains vivid descriptions of railway building activity and its impact. He described how the arrival of the railway changed the face of the district involved and how in urban areas it cut through neighbourhoods and created an artificial barrier between districts which had previously been contiguous. Although he realised that this caused problems overall, he thought that the railways could be a force for good. Having described the sight of the great cutting being built from Camden Town to Euston Station, he concluded:

> 'In short, the yet unfinished and unopened railroad was in progress; and from the very core of all this dire disorder, trailed smoothly away, upon its mighty course of civilisation and improvement.'

The story's villain, James Carker, described by Dickens as having a smile 'like the snarl of a cat', meets a condign death under the wheels of an express train at a location often thought to be Paddock Wood on the South Eastern Railway in Kent. Dickens does not economise on gory detail:

> 'He heard a shout – another- felt the earth tremble- knew in a moment that the rush was come – uttered a shriek – looked round – was beaten down – caught up, and whirled away upon a jagged mill, that spun him round and round, and struck him limb from limb, and licked his stream of life up with its fiery heat, and cast his mutilated fragments in the air.'

Elements of humour are never far away in Dickens and he wrote a wry account of how the Christmas turkey he wanted delivered to his local station by train was burned to a cinder when the van it which it was being carried caught fire. He was clearly fascinated by railways and as a frequent user knew much about their everyday workings. He was also extremely critical about the cupidity of railway shareholders, the territorial aggression of many large railway companies and also of successive governments that allowed railway development to proceed in a random, wasteful way. For all that, he had shares in the Great Western Railway.

In 1846, Dickens started publishing the *Daily News*. This newspaper contained much material relating to railways and it is clear that it supported railways as symbols of economic growth and social progress. Those who opposed railways he regarded as opponents of all economic and social advancement.

John Clare, the Northamptonshire poet of humble origins, was clearly something of an early environmentalist. He kept a journal from 6 September 1824 to 11 September 1825 and on 4 June 1825 he made the following entry:

'Saw three fellows at the end of Royce Wood who I found were laying out the plan for an "Iron Railway" from Manchester to London it is to cross over Round Oak Spring by Royce Wood for Woodcroft Castle I little thought that fresh intrusions would interrupt my solitudes after the Enclosure they will despoil a boggy place that is famous for Orchises at Royce Wood end.'

Clare was deeply rooted in the simple pleasures offered by the countryside around his village of Helpston, near Peterborough. We sense some trepidation in what he writes concerning the impact of a possible railway on the flora and the tranquillity of the district. Nothing came of the project which was almost certainly the 'London Northern Railroad Company' which proposed a line from London to Manchester at this very early date.

R.S. Surtees is associated with stories about hunting but railways infiltrate his writing in various places. In the story *Mr Facey Romford's Hounds* we hear:

'London now being accessible to everybody – accessible either to the flying express, the moderate two pence a mile or the still more reasonable Parliamentary trains, according as time or money is most valuable to the traveller, people get sucked up to the capital almost incontinently, just as their forefathers talked of going to sessions or assizes.'

Elsewhere in the same story we are treated to an evocative description of events at a wayside station:

'At length, after a long pace-slackening glide, the train stopped before a sort of Swiss cottage, and a large black and white board in the centre announced "Fifield Station". The porters then began running along the line of carriages, exclaiming "Field! – Field! – Fifield Station! Change here for Shenstone, Comb and Danby! Change here for Shenstone, Comb and Danby!"'

The Sherlock Holmes stories of Arthur Conan Doyle remain perhaps the most enduring of the British detective genre. We sense that Conan Doyle had an enthusiasm for railways which was not always quite matched by his knowledge of their workings. Holmes and the faithful Dr Watson make much use of railways as they follow their investigations and the Great Western Railway is the most frequently mentioned of the lines that take the doughty duo on their missions in pursuit of justice. It is in *Silver Blaze* that Holmes makes the immortal revelation, 'Our rate at present is fifty-three and a half miles an hour'. Watson replies by stating that he had not been observing the quarter-mile posts. To this Holmes replies drily: 'Nor have I. But the telegraph posts upon this line are sixty yards apart, and the calculation is a simple one.' Writers of the crime and detective genres must have greatly thanked railways for providing them with such a useful resource to draw upon when weaving their plots.

In Benjamin Disraeli's novel published in 1845, *Sybil, or the Two Nations*, the fear harboured by many of the landed aristocracy towards the railways is summed up by the character Lord de Mowbray. He said, 'I fear (the railway) has a dangerous levelling tendency to equality…Equality is not our metier. If we nobles do not make a stand against the levelling spirit of the age, I am at a loss to know who will fight the battle. You may depend on it that these railroads are very dangerous things!' Another titled character is Lord Marney who, at one point, says, 'She must talk to young Huntingford; everything depends on his working with me against the Cut-and-Come Again branch line; they have refused me my compensation, and I am not going to have my estate cut up into ribbons without compensation.' This clearly alludes to aristocratic resistance to the railways. Elsewhere, Sybil is travelling with her companion Stephen and says, 'Think you not it would be a fairer lot to bide this night at some kind monastery, than to be hastening now to that least picturesque of all creations, a railway station?' Stephen, clearly pro-railway, replies, 'The railways will do as much for mankind as the monasteries did.'

Also in *Sybil*, when there is violent civil disorder among the poor of the town of Mowbray, a battalion of the Coldstream Guards is summoned by train and this is perhaps the first mention in literature of the new capability of moving troops quickly by train to potential trouble spots, something which considerably enhanced the power of central government over events in the provinces.

Elizabeth Gaskell wrote *Cousin Phillis* in 1864. The villain of the piece is a Mr Holdsworth, a railway contractor engaged on a building project in her neighbourhood. He is dashing and sophisticated and Phillis is rather swept off her feet, thinking that he might be able to take her away from her humdrum provincial life. A courtship develops and Holdsworth, who has to go to undertake a contract in Canada, promises to marry her on his return. Her patient wait is interrupted by a letter in which the blackguard tells her he has married a Canadian woman. Poor Phillis is heartbroken and the reader is left deploring the conduct of the egregious Holdsworth. Is Mrs Gaskell saying that this behaviour is what is to be expected of railway contractors?

William Makepeace Thackeray was a prolific contributor to *Punch*. He wrote an article called *Jeames's Diary*. It satirised a junior clerk who speculated successfully in railway shares during the 'Mania' and begins the process whereby he is transformed into C. Jeames de la Pluche, an affluent figure respected by bankers and able to hobnob in the best social circles.

G.K. Chesterton made clear his affection for the railway when he wrote:

'The only way of catching a train that I have ever discovered is to miss the train before. Do this, and you will find in a railway station much of the quietude and consolation of a cathedral. It has many of the characteristics of a great ecclesiastical building; it has vast arches, void spaces, coloured lights, and above all, it has recurrence of ritual. It is dedicated to the celebration of water and fire, the two prime elements of all human ceremonial.'

Anthony Trollope

Anthony Trollope was employed by the Post Office and his duties required him frequently to travel by train. He therefore had some knowledge of railway operating practice and it seems he was unimpressed by railway waiting rooms in particular and stations in general and on one occasion he was driven to say, 'Everything is hideous, dirty and disagreeable, and the mind wanders away, to wonder why station-masters do not more frequently commit suicide.'

Trollope is probably best-known for his *Chronicles of Barsetshire* novels. In *Dr Thorne* (1858), Trollope introduces his readers to one of his most memorable characters, Sir Roger Scatcherd. He has made a name for himself as an energetic although not over-scrupulous contractor for utilities and public works, culminating in a number of railway projects and his efforts have been rewarded with a baronetcy. Trollope does not paint a favourable picture of Scatcherd. Not only is he grasping and ruthless but he is also a habitual drunkard. It is thought that Trollope modelled Scatcherd on Sir Morton Peto, much given to flaunting his affluence, who enjoyed two decades of fame and fortune before being brought down with the collapse of the banking house of Overend and Gurney in 1866-7. It is clear that Trollope has an aversion to railway engineers and promoters. In *The Way we Live Now* (1875) he models his character Augustus Melmotte on George Hudson. Melmotte is totally unscrupulous and ruthless in pursuit of his interests. He becomes an MP to increase his influence. He bullies and blusters his way into controlling a large part of the railway network but he overreaches himself and is forced to flee abroad.

Trollope also makes a swipe at railway catering with: 'Dr Thorne was always in a fever of thirst when he got home from the railway, and always made complaint as to the tea at the Junction'. In *The Small House at Allington,* (1864) Trollope has a honeymoon couple travelling by train to Folkestone. The husband, a Mr Crosbie, is rather put out when the unlit train enters a tunnel and he sees an opportunity to hold his new wife's hand only to be rebuffed when she says, 'I do so hate tunnels'.

Trollope vividly conveys his fertile imagination and rich powers of observation where he describes the 'platform superintendent' at Paddington who arrives to sort out a brawl on what he clearly considers to be *his* platform:

'By the time some mighty railway authority had come upon the scene and made himself cognisant of the facts of the row – a stern official who seemed to carry the weight of many engines on his brow; one at the sight of whom smokers would drop their cigars, and porters close their fists against sixpences; a great man with an erect chin, a quick step, and a well-brushed hat with an elaborately upturned brim. This was the platform superintendent, dominant even over the policeman.'

In *Barchester Towers* (1857), the issue of Sunday travel becomes a bone of contention between Archdeacon Grantley and the overbearing Mrs Proudie, the bishop's wife. The reader can enjoy a detailed description of Willesden, posing as *Tenway Junction* in *The Belton Estate* (1866). Like some other Victorian novelists, Trollope used the railway as an agent of Nemesis for a character they wanted to dispose of, in this case he has Lopez commit suicide under an express train in *The Prime Minister* (1876).

Railways and Writing
'Romance brought up the nine-fifteen', wrote Rudyard Kipling in his poem *The King*. Built ostensibly for the prosaic purpose of making profit by charging to transport people, mail, manufactures, merchandise and minerals, the railways have inspired an extraordinary wealth of writing. Books for dedicated enthusiasts seemingly cover every conceivable aspect of this multifarious subject and yet more still come. The presses churn out a full supporting cast of magazines and periodicals. Novelists, poets and playwrights have drawn extensively on railways. What is shared by the writers? Could it be precisely that 'romance' to which Kipling alludes? We would suggest that adventure, excitement, mystery and nostalgia are elements that have brought many writers of imaginative literature to embrace railways in their works. Those elements may also be alluded to by the writers of non-fiction history. Trains have the power to stir emotions and that is perhaps the essence of their romance. Significantly, when the Great Western Railway celebrated its centenary in 1935, among the publicity material it produced was a film called *The Romance of a Railway*.

Others were excited by the speed of trains which surpassed anything previously possible with land transport. Often the progress of a train was likened to the flight of the swiftest birds. Such were the speed that trains could attain that references were made to 'sorcery' and 'magic'. Robert Louis Stevenson in *From a Railway Carriage* describes the speed as 'Faster than fairies, faster than witches'.

Edward Thomas, in *Adelstrop*, gave one of the best evocations of a small village station on a secondary main line, that between Oxford and Worcester. He captured the sense of serenity and timelessness at this station when an express train unexpectedly drew to a halt there on a hot summer's day. We do not know whether Thomas had an enthusiasm for railways but his purpose here was to contrast the tranquillity of this wayside station on the fringe of the Cotswolds with the murderous mayhem that was taking place on the Continent at that time, a sphere of action in which he was later killed.

In *Anticipations* (1902) H.G. Wells argued, 'There has never been any sustained attack on the idea that the steam railway was the most significant invention or innovation in the rise of industrial society'. Leon Trotsky said that revolution was the locomotive of history. Karl Marx, explained that the eradication of space by time which the railways achieved was a critical factor in the development of modern capitalist society. He identified an interdependent triumvirate of the railway, the electric telegraph and rail-borne fast mail services as crucial to that process. Not much romance in these comments it may be said but elsewhere H.G. Wells again, in *The War of the Worlds* (1898), wrote:

'From the railway station in the distance came the sound of shunting trains, ringing and rumbling, softened almost into melody by the distance. My wife pointed out to me the brightness of the red, green and yellow signal lights hanging in a framework against the sky. It seemed so safe and tranquil.'

Here are elements of romance. All three writers are paying unconscious testimony to the centrality of railways in modern culture. All are grateful for its invention.

Arnold Bennett, in *Whom God Hath Joined* (1906), describes the feelings of travellers on the platform at Knype-on-Trent, the main station of his *Five Towns*, while they await the London express:

'The worlds of pleasure and business meet on that platform to await the great train with its two engines. The spacious pavement… is alive with the spurious calm of those who are about to travel and to whom travelling is an everyday trifle…And yet beneath all this weary satiety there lurks in each demeanour a suppressed anticipatory eagerness, a consciousness of vast enterprise, that would not be unsuitable if the London train were a caravan setting out for Baghdad.'

Sir John Betjeman perceived romance in what most people would see as the mundane. He liked railways because in his day they were

Sir John Betjeman was a lover of railways and indeed of many things old and inefficient. He was a much more significant cultural influence than his slightly bumbling and eccentric manner might have suggested. He was a passionate defender of Victorian architecture at a time when it was generally held in low esteem. Although unable to prevent the demolition of the Euston Arch, he was instrumental in fighting threats to demolish St Pancras and the erstwhile hotel that formed its frontage to Euston Road. He is commemorated by this statue at the present-day St Pancras. (A. Brooke)

old-fashioned, often had considerable character and, importantly to him, were pretty inefficient. He probed with his perceptive eye into areas of human experience largely eschewed by other poets and communicated his affection and enthusiasm in gently mocking verse that was as quirky as the man himself. Railways figured in his autobiographical poem *Summoned by Bells* where he alludes to their influence on his life.

Betjeman was intrigued by 'Metroland'. The image of Metroland was largely associated with inter-war Britain and was used to promote passenger travel on the lines of the Metropolitan Railway which reached from Baker Street Station into outer parts of Middlesex, the Buckinghamshire Chilterns and the Vale of Aylesbury. This was part of London's countryside and the Metropolitan was engaged in two money-making processes which ultimately were contradictory. Unusually for a railway company, the Metropolitan, through a subsidiary, the Metropolitan Country Estates Ltd, owned much of the land around its tracks and built houses, often on greenfield sites, close to its stations. This project, which prospered, was unashamedly aimed at those reasonably affluent people who wanted to live in leafy, quiet surroundings but with a good train service enabling the breadwinner to commute to and from employment in Central London. The consequence was the appearance of suburbs of well-built houses, tending to be increasingly expensive and therefore more socially exclusive the further they were from Baker Street. A kind of suburbanised countryside replete with golf courses emerged, possessing a character that fascinated and amused Betjeman.

Something of what the developers intended can be found in advertising material for the Cedars Estate near Rickmansworth developed from about 1921:

'The estate will be laid out to provide village greens and open spaces with unusual stretches of wide and well-made roads. A portion of the beautiful woods will be left in their natural state.'

It was this conceit to which Betjeman gently alludes in the first lines of *Middlesex*:

'Gaily into Ruislip Gardens
Runs the red electric train,
With a thousand Ta's and Pardon's
Daintily alights Elaine;
Hurries down the concrete station
With a frown of concentration,
Out into the outskirt's edges
Where a few surviving hedges
Keep alive our lost Elysium – rural Middlesex again.'

Less subtle was the writing of George R. Sims. This gives a flavour of his work:

> '"Metroland", "Metroland",
> Leafy dell and woodland fair,
> Land of love and hope and peace;
> Land where all your troubles cease –
> "Metroland", "Metroland",
> Waft, oh waft me there:
> Hearts are lighter, eyes are brighter
> In "Metroland", "Metroland".'

The contradiction of Metroland was that as more and more development took place, the tendency was for the goose that laid the golden egg, if not to be killed, at least to become a less prolific layer. The Metropolitan encouraged leisure travel outwards from London for those able to get away from its noise, dirt and squalor. What better than to ramble the verdant countryside, sampling the pleasures of picturesque rustic taverns? But Metroland's countryside was shrinking and becoming less verdant. The simple inn was now a Brewer's Tudor roadhouse.

'Rain, Steam and Speed'

J.M.W. Turner is not only one of Britain's best-known landscape painters but he has also given us what is surely one of the most-discussed paintings incorporating a railway theme. A cottage industry has almost developed around interpretations of the purpose and meaning of the painting. Is the painting simply a record of what Turner saw when he thrust his head out of a carriage window on a Great Western Railway train in 1843? Perhaps we should be entirely happy with such a conclusion but art historians and others will not let it lie. They are convinced that Turner wants us to think about something deeper when we peruse this work. It can be viewed as a lament for a pastoral way of life being ruthlessly thrust aside by the inexorable advance of the iron horse and its steam power. Even the hare which he depicted running in front of the locomotive cannot outpace the oncoming and relentless fiery machine. Hamilton Ellis sees in the painting a man in his declining years having to face up to the train as a symbol of a radical new age and expressing both awe and intimidation at the sight. More recently, Robin Gilmour (1993) has described the painting as a celebration by a contemporary artist of a marvellous new force thrusting its way through a storm in such a way as to show that this machine is powerful enough to challenge elemental forces. Although these perceptions have contradictory elements, it is clear that there is a common understanding that the painting encapsulates tensions created by the inevitability of change and there being victims of that change.

The construction of railways brought an element of disorder into the countryside, dependent in some cases on the nature of the topography and geology of the area. Structures like bridges, viaducts and embankments, however, frequently blended quickly into the scene and we all have an image of an idyllic Great Western Railway branch line wending its way through lush countryside looking as if it is an organic part of the scene. No matter how felicitously the countryside may have physically absorbed the railway and its works, it is clear that the railway presented a challenge to an established social order. Even the most remote and rustic of branch lines employed sophisticated products of science and technology which were part the creation and partly agents of an unprecedented period of intense economic and social transformation. A fragile rural idyll is being destroyed before Turner's eyes. It was a transformation which was to see the end of the domination of isolated rural agricultural society by the local mansion, estate and its owner. Tensions involved in this change are captured in *Rain, Steam and Speed*.

The painting can be regarded as an example of the sublime in the art of the Romantic period. An element of the sublime is the terrible. Turner depicts a Thames Valley landscape of a sort that had changed relatively little in centuries through which the railway thrusts itself, violating the scene as it does so. The locomotive, not portrayed in detail, is a source of sublime terror. It is a machine of immense, actually unprecedented, pent-up power, yet the force of which it is capable is controlled by a mere mortal on its footplate. There is a sense of awe to be extracted from its headlong progress mixed with terror at the prospect of anything untoward happening. Turner is known to have had a life-long fascination with machines and there may be no coincidence in the fact that he has chosen to express his feelings by portraying a Great Western broad gauge express train. One of these at speed would have presented a truly magnificent spectacle, imparting both fear and admiration.

Is it any coincidence that Turner chose the Maidenhead Bridge over the Thames as the location for the statements he was making in *Rain, Steam and Speed?* The Great Western was of course engineered by Isambard Kingdom Brunel, a man who brought a quite extraordinary audacity into his works, almost as if he had to prove that he could do what lesser men said was impossible. So it was with the Maidenhead Bridge. This displayed the flattest brick arches ever erected which Brunel's detractors (and there were many) confidently predicted would collapse as soon as a train attempted to cross them. It seems that Turner did not know Brunel personally but it would have been impossible not to have known about the man and his works. The audacity of Brunel and his absolute belief that mankind could use science and technology to push back the boundaries of what was considered possible is likely to have appealed to Turner. It may have been with a mixture of admiration and concerns about the implications of the changes that were so manifestly happening to the country that Turner chose this location for his artistic purpose. Some critics believe that the painting depicts a train crossing Wharncliffe Viaduct near Hanwell.

In a Railway Carriage

When Abraham Solomon in all innocence gave his painting *First Class: The Meeting… and at First Meeting Loved* its public debut in 1854, he little expected the storm of moral outrage in which he would soon be enveloped. The interior of a first-class compartment is depicted and a young man whose face cannot be seen is clearly engaged in chatting up a rather demure-looking young lady while her companion, presumably her father, snores away in a corner seat. This was too much for ultra-fastidious middle-class Victorian morality. Who was this presumptuous young fellow taking advantage of the maiden's innocence in such an unscrupulous fashion? Was he even of the class of people entitled to travel first class? Why depict a scene of such depravity? To save his own reputation, Abrahams was forced to make changes and he produced an amended version for 1855. Now the kindly looking older man is happily engaged in close conversation with the younger man who, although his face is still not fully visible, is wearing the uniform of a junior naval officer and is therefore by definition a gentleman. This implies that he has no dishonourable intent towards the young lady while, importantly, he is also entitled to travel first class. The young lady herself is now seated in the corner, further away from the two men. As in the first version, she appears to be sewing but whereas in the first representation she is shown with her eyes averted, she is now allowed to look at him because he has her father's approval. She appears to like what she sees.

Critics have commented on the extensive use that artists made of railway carriages and compartments when commentating visually on the social and class demarcations that were such a feature of the Victorian period. Artists like Solomon made one kind of use of this scenario, the cartoonists of *Punch* made another, often more pungent and satirical use of the space the railway provided.

The Railway Station

The work of the Victorian figurative or genre painters is of great cultural interest because their paintings not only provide vivid depictions of contemporary life but give an insight to the attitudes, values and obsessions of the Victorians, most especially of the middle classes. William Powell Frith had already made an impact with his *Derby Day* (1858) but in 1862 he produced *The Railway Station* which has been described as 'the most important painting ever made of the mid-Victorian urban milieu'.

We do not know whether Frith liked railways, but he had an eye for a painting that would strike a chord with the public and make him money. He knew that the Victorians liked to see scenes from everyday life. Also, they recognised how advanced technology in the form of the railways allowed them to broaden their horizons through cheaper and easier means of travel than had been available before.

On the massive canvas that Frith painted we see crowds milling about on a departure platform at Paddington. Here was an unexceptional diurnal scene which provided the ideal scenario for an observation of character and class, a piece of human theatre. Here are a hundred and one human dramas. They include a mother kissing her small boy goodbye as he is off to his first boarding-school, a confused foreigner being intimidated for an extortionate fare by a bullying cab-driver and two police officers arresting a criminal hoping to make his getaway on the train. Many of the figures, including the detective and the miscreant, were identifiable as actual people. If nothing else, the painting shows the extent to which, just thirty years on from the opening of the line from Liverpool to Manchester, railways were etched deeply into the life of the nation. Reproductions of *The Railway Station* sold like hot cakes. No one else, however, ventured to create a similarly gigantic and complex painting. Railways had become an accepted part of everyday life, taken for granted perhaps. However, criticisms of them for their tendency towards monopoly, for their fares and charges policies and their slow adoption of improved safety measures meant that the public viewed them with less awe and affection and artists wishing to make money went elsewhere for their sources of inspiration.

J.C. Bourne

The response to Solomon's painting and Trollope's unfavourable portrayal of railway contractors and promoters indicated, at least to some eyes, a negative image of railways and what they brought with them. The lithographs produced by John Cooke Bourne in the 1830s and 1840s, on the other hand, provided a powerful boost for public perceptions of the railways or at least of two of them, the London & Birmingham and the Great Western Railway. They portray the building of the L&B and the completed works of the GWR's line from London to Bristol in minute, superbly drafted detail. The impression that comes across is of a positive, progressive, even heroic development, the product of human energy, ingenuity and developing scientific and technical expertise. Their production provided positive publicity and was encouraged by the railway companies concerned. Navvies had not had a good press but his views of the L&B showed them grafting away to great and beneficial effect. Bourne unwittingly left future generations with invaluable pictorial evidence of the early days of railway development during this heroic early phase of railway building.

The railways were criticised and opposed in many quarters for their intrusion into the countryside, not only into the private domain of landowners but also for their attack on the shape of the countryside through their various civil engineering structures and installations. Bourne's illustrations of the construction of the L&B make clear the hazardous nature of man's tampering with nature to create such a line and those of the completed GWR show that the effort was worth it and that the results could actually enhance the landscape.

John O'Connor was clearly carried away by the exuberance and sheer presence of his subject in *St Pancras Station, seen from Pentonville Road* (1884). His viewpoint is looking down the bustling but mundane Pentonville Road to where the station or at least its hotel frontage rears up, bathed in an ethereal golden mist. For O'Connor, the station is heroic, a reflection of the boundless energy that motivated the Victorians to many of their greatest achievements.

A Few Films

In 1936, Noel Coward published the one-act play *Still Life*. This formed the basis of the film *Brief Encounter*, of interest to us because much of the action takes place in and around a railway station. It records a short-lived and intense although doomed relationship between two frightfully respectable middle-aged, middle-class types. Celia Johnson and Trevor Howard play the lead roles with understated brilliance. The film touched many middle-class hearts, probably most of all women for whom early dreams of a life of romance have been replaced by comfortable but dull and predictable married routine. The consequence is a lack of fulfilment which only becomes evident when a chance meeting in the prosaic surroundings of a railway refreshment room stirs feelings which social convention dictates are best left dormant. The station used for filming was Carnforth, then a junction of some importance north of Lancaster and the director, David Lean, deliberately filmed the action during the hours of darkness to bring out the romance of night-time railway action, contrasting it with the budding romance in the distinctly unromantic refreshment room. This is not primarily a railway film but it was and remains very popular not only with those who enjoy love stories but with many railway aficionados. The station, changed considerably from when the film was made, has become something of a shrine. The moral of the film is that marriage triumphs over adultery.

Gun-runners were the villains in the popular 1931 film *The Ghost Train* where the action all takes place in the waiting room of a small station in the West Country. The film recognises the value of a railway station for bringing together an antediluvian collection of individuals stranded overnight and forced to interact with each other because they believe they will witness a haunting. It remains a suspenseful film. The remake in 1937 featured Arthur Askey who may have wowed cinema-goers then but whose antics now simply look ridiculous.

Developing the gun-runner theme was one of the best-loved British comedies of all time, *Oh, Mr Porter*, made in 1937 and starring Will Hay and his stalwart foils, Graham Moffat and Moore Marriott. The action takes place in and around a ramshackle branch line backwater called Buggleskelly, actually Cliddesden on the closed Alton to Basingstoke line. Buggleskelly is near the Irish border where sinister gun-runners are active, deterring the inquisitive by talk of a haunted mill nearby. There is plenty of railway action in this film which, with some licence, conveys well the deeply rural character of such branch lines. This is probably the best of the films featuring Will Hay.

The Railway Children in its 1970 version remains a firm favourite for its gorgeous Yorkshire scenery, the attraction of the steam trains for the children, its sense of an injustice being righted and its tear-jerking sentimentality. The story was written by Edith Nesbit in 1906. As with so many novels written at that time, it tends to patronise the working-class characters for being not very bright but amusing and well meaning.

Perhaps the most English of railway films for the way it places a rustic branch line in the most idyllic countryside is *The Titfield Thunderbolt* (1952). Here is Englishness galore, with a gloriously eccentric railway-mad vicar and his collection of oddball parishioners defying the bureaucrats in London who have decreed that their local branch railway has to close. They kick against the authorities, rescue an ancient locomotive from a museum and proceed to run the trains themselves. Attempting to thwart their every effort is the devious owner of the local bus service. The film was made when the future of many rural branch lines was being seriously called into question and it therefore placed topicality alongside comedy.

Of documentaries dealing with the everyday activities of railways, *Night Mail* (1936) has stood the test of time. The prosaic running of the overnight mail train from London to Glasgow calling only at Crewe is made into a romantic saga showing the role the railway played in linking people and distant communities. A glory of the film is W.H. Auden's highly atmospheric verse and a musical score by Benjamin Britten.

Thomas Hardy

Thomas Hardy was a devout Christian and a man not given to levity. He began an apprenticeship in architecture at the age of 16 and in 1862 moved to London where he was a junior in the busy practice of Arthur Blomfield. The Midland Railway was thrusting south from Kentish Town towards its planned terminus to be called 'St Pancras' in 1865-6. This involved carving a swathe through the festering slums of Agar Town and Somers Town and also through a part of the burial ground of the Old Church of St Pancras. The contractor involved in clearing the graveyard was almost criminally slapdash. A scandal blew up after the vicar of St Pancras stated that he had seen broken coffins and disinterred human remains scattered about, apparently at random. Questions were asked in parliament and work stopped until a better form of supervision was put in place. Hardy was put in overall charge of ensuring that the human remains were moved with dignity for reburial at another site. His brief was to visit the site unannounced and since the work went on around the clock, he was sometimes there in the hours of darkness. The site was well-lit but what he saw was not for the faint-hearted. Some coffins fell to pieces as they were moved, new coffins being provided for the remains but despite Hardy's efforts it was obvious that the remains became mixed up. On one occasion, Blomfield and Hardy visited the site together and saw a coffin fall apart before their very eyes. It contained a skeleton and two skulls!

The gruesome activity in the churchyard drew many spectators, some there simply to gawp at these macabre sights and others claiming to be there to protest against this desecration of the remains of those who had been interred in the 'sure and certain hope of a glorious resurrection'. There was a widespread feeling of revulsion against railways and the Midland in particular that private profit-making businesses could be granted parliamentary sanction to carry out activities conflicting so starkly with widespread views about the respect that should be accorded to the dead. When the Midland sought, in 1874, to acquire the rest of the burial ground, their plans were thwarted. In 1889, another attempt was made but the company was only able to acquire a very small part of the land it required. The Midland had aroused widespread opposition over the whole issue and lost not only goodwill, but because train movements into and out of St Pancras were made difficult by the restricted number of lines accessing the station.

Hardy was deeply affected by his experiences at Old St Pancras Churchyard and he penned his well-known poem *The Levelled Churchyard* giving some expression to his feelings about the lack of reverence accorded to the occupants of the burial place. In it he revealed a somewhat unexpectedly wry sense of humour. Here we give a flavour:

'O passenger, pray list and catch
our sighs and piteous groans,
Half stifled in this jumbled patch
of wretched memorial stones.

We late-lamented, resting here,
Are mixed to human jam,
and each to each exclaims in fear
"I know not which I am."

The wicked people have annexed
The verses of the good:
A roaring drunkard sports the text
Teetotal Tommy should!

Here's not a modest maiden elf
But dreads the final trumpet
Lest half of her should rise herself,
And half some sturdy strumpet.'

Hardy was not hostile to railways as such. In the short story *Faint Heart in a Railway Train*, he describes with enthusiasm the changing scene to be viewed from the carriage window. The train pulls into a station and he sees a lovely woman. He wants to alight and make her acquaintance but he berates himself for his timidity when he does the sensible but boring thing and stays on the train.

A common theme in Hardy's novels is his concern about the impact of the railways on communal life in the countryside. In *Under the Greenwood Tree*, (1872), he describes the anger felt by villagers who, with their ancestors over generations, have sung and played the music accompanying services in the parish church. They are deeply distressed when they find out that they are going to be replaced by a new-fangled organ. This organ, or at least its component parts, would have arrived at the local station.

Fanny Kemble

Fanny Kemble made a curtain-stopping stage debut in *Romeo and Juliet* in October 1829. She was propelled to instant celebrity but, unlike many other celebrities, she actually possessed talent and was welcome wherever she took herself. In August 1830, she managed to gain admission to the austere footplate of a steam locomotive on the Liverpool & Manchester Railway. Defying female stereotypes of the time, she then had a ride on the locomotive which was driven by none other than George Stephenson. Fanny was a devoted diarist and has left a delightful account of her experience which shows not only her general vivacity but also acute observational skills. This excerpt is from her *Record of a Girlhood* (1878):

'We were introduced to the little engine which was to drag us along the rails. She (for they make these curious little fire-horses all mares) consisted of a boiler, a stove, a small platform, a bench, and behind the bench a barrel containing enough water to prevent her being thirsty for fifteen miles…She goes upon two wheels, which are her feet, and are moved by bright steel legs called pistons; these are propelled by steam, and in proportion as more steam is applied to the upper extremities (the hip-joints I suppose) of these pistons, the faster they move the wheels… The reins, bit and bridle of this wonderful beast is a small steel handle, which applies or withdraws the steam from its legs or pistons, so that a child might manage it…This snorting little animal, which I felt rather inclined to pat, was then harnessed to our carriage, and Mr Stephenson having taken me on the bench of the engine with him, we started at about ten miles an hour… You can't imagine how strange it seemed to be journeying on thus, without any visible cause of progress other than the magical machine, with its flying white breath and rhythmical, unvarying pace, between…rocky walls…Bridges were thrown from side to side across the top of these cliffs, and the people looked down upon us from them seemed like pigmies standing in the sky…

'Now for a word or two about the master [George Stephenson] of all these wonders, with whom I am most horribly in love. He is a man from fifty to fifty-five years of age: his face is fine, though careworn, and bears an expression of deep thoughtfulness; his mode of explaining his idea is peculiar and very original, striking and forcible: and although his accent indicates strongly his north-country birth, his languages has not the slightest touch of vulgarity or coarseness. He has certainly turned my head.'

Who could possibly hate railways after reading Miss Kemble?

John Bull
The magazine *John Bull* inveighed against railways:

'Does anybody mean to say that decent people, passengers who would use their own carriages…would consent to be hurried along through the air upon a railroad…or is it to be imagined that women…would endure the fatigue, the misery, the danger…of being dragged through the air at a rate of twenty miles an hour, all their lives being at the mercy of a tin pipe, or a copper boiler, or the accidental dropping of a pebble on the line of way?

'We denounce the mania as destructive of the country in a thousand particulars – the whole face of the Kingdom is to be tattooed with these odious deformities – huge mounds are to intersect our beautiful valleys; the noise and stench of locomotive steam-engines are to disturb the quietude of the peasant, the farmer and the gentleman…

'Railroads…will in their efforts to gain ground do incalculable mischief. If they succeed they will give an unnatural impetus to society, destroy all the relations which exist between man and man, overthrow all mercantile regulations, overturn the metropolitan markets, drain the provinces of all their resources, and create, at the peril of life, all sorts of confusion and distress.'

John Bull was perhaps the journal most consistently opposed to the railways and in 1848 said:

'The whole system of railroading is conspiracy. The speculators conspire to buy coaches off the turn-pike roads, in order to ensure exclusive power, in a most disgraceful manner – they conspire to conceal the accidents which occur upon their odious speculations; insolence growing out of growing monopoly, characterises the conduct of their servants; while in the performance of their contracts with their passengers, their constant failures bring the uncertainty of their unnatural speed rather below the level of the good steady ten miles an hour pace of English travelling, which, with good English horses, and good English roads, such as ours were (the pride and envy of Europe), would send any man - except an escaping murderer, or a self-liberated felon – quite as fast across a country as he need to go.'

Punch **Magazine**
Punch first appeared in 1841 and for several generations it produced written and illustrative material which has provided a rich source of evidence for historians, not least for its revelations concerning contemporary attitudes, concerns and insecurities, particularly those of the middle classes who were its target audience.

Punch did not spare the railways. It attacked railway directors and managers for real and allegedly shady financial dealings, reserving special venom for George Hudson, and they lambasted them over their safety record, particularly up to the late 1880s. It denounced them for their destruction of ancient buildings and damage to the countryside and it even attacked them for mistreating their workers. When not engaging them critically, they enjoyed lampooning railways because their activities highlighted so many human foibles and peccadilloes into play.

John Leech was a prolific cartoonist for *Punch* in its early days and his work was perceptive and critical of sharp practice around the 'Railway Mania' and of George Hudson. In *The Railway Juggernaut of 1845* he has a locomotive named 'Speculation' destroying families whose paterfamilias have been foolish enough to invest in fraudulent railway schemes. In 1845, *Punch* published his cartoon showing a concerned Victoria pleading with her distracted-looking consort to admit whether he has any railway shares. He made great fun of Colonel Sibthorp, albeit without the slightest malice and in *A Dangerous Character* (1847) he had Hudson as a criminal locomotive being arrested by 'Policeman Sibthorp'.

Many of the middle-class readers of *Punch* were just the kind of people who would have lost money during the 'Railway Mania'. The magazine was keen to harness the consequent not entirely rational sense of grievance against railways as a whole and it found a rich seam in railway accidents. These were frequently ascribed to the desire for profit having priority over the expenditure involved in measures to promote safer operations. This approach enabled *Punch* indirectly to pursue its ongoing campaign against the directors and managers of the railway companies. Typical of its approach was *The Railway Nursery Rhymer*, which took the tune of *Hush-a-Bye, Baby* and part of which went:

'Rock away, passenger, in the third class,
When your train shunts, a faster will pass.
When your train's late your chances are small,
Crushed will be carriages, engines and all.'

In 1857, *Punch* vented its spleen against railway directors on the question of safety with a cartoon depicting a seat placed on the front bufferbeam of a locomotive. This seat was to be occupied by a director who clearly was likely to be first in line to be slaughtered in the event of a head-on collision. The implication was clearly that if directors were subjected to such exposure they might be keen to spend more money on accident prevention. This simple device *Punch* called *The Patent Safety Railway Buffer.*

Alfred Henry Forr, known as 'Alfred Crowquill', was a prolific caricaturist and illustrator who, in 1849, devoted an entire cartoon pamphlet entitled *How he Reigned and How he Mizzled, a Railway Raillery,* to savagely lampooning George Hudson and, by the standards of the time, it was a best-seller.

Bradshaw frequently found itself the butt of *Punch's* humour but in a more good-natured way as it drew attention to the dogged determination and patience needed to locate a train suitable for the traveller's requirements. The necessity for these attributes was compounded by the difficulties likely to be encountered when trying to make sense of the voluminous footnotes. These then had to be analysed minutely in order to ensure that the train identified did not run only on the local market days or never in months containing the letter 'r' or some similar trap designed to catch the unwary.

There was nothing good-natured about *Punch's* attack on the growing tendency towards mergers and regional monopolies or its attitude towards the failure of the banking house of Overend and Gurney in 1866-7, which contributed to the inevitable collapse of numerous ill-considered railway projects. A cartoon by John Tenniel showed a desperate shareholder of a company caught up in the affair declaring that the directors of the company may be going to trial, but he is sentenced to life.

In the twentieth century, *Punch* found less to attack around railways. Frederick Rowland Emett was one of the magazine's most loved artists, his cartoons appearing from 1939. He possessed a unique, loosely 'Gothic' style which was suffused with affection for the railways. His cartoons were fantasies with a strongly nostalgic flavour and drawn in an inimitable style. They were hugely popular. Even when he was dealing with nationalisation, a development to which he was very hostile, he did not moderate the quirkiness of his approach. Three trains are shown in one of his cartoons, drawn respectively by *Bard of Avon, Robert the Bruce* and *Owen Glendower* and represent a gentle mocking of nationalisation.

William Heath Robinson produced a more limited number of cartoons for *Punch*. Like Emmet, his work consisted of inimitable flights of fancy which frequently featured pseudo-mechanical

Despite having been the butt of ribald comments for generations, there was genuine sadness when it was announced that publication of *Bradshaw* would cease. This is the front cover of the very last edition of the guide. It covered the period from 1 May to 11 June 1961 and this valedictory edition marked the end of an era and of an institution.

There is an interesting contrast between the advertisement for the fairly upmarket hotels and that for the old stalwart of Bovril. The idea of beef tea might have seemed outdated even then but while Bradshaw may have gone, Bovril continues to have its devotees. (Authors' collection).

devices of quite madcap ingenuity. His most famous collection of illustrations were brought together in a collection called *Railway Ribaldry* which was among a mass of publicity material produced by the Great Western Railway for its centenary in 1935. The human figures that populate his work are deliberately understated and give the appearance of an insouciance starkly at odds with the ridiculous activities in which they are engaged.

The Euston Arch

This former icon of the Railway Age was not an arch at all but a portico or propylaeum. It was built to impress and to suggest that Euston was the grand gateway to the north. While it may indeed have impressed many, its neo-classical features certainly did the opposite for Augustus Welsby Pugin, doyen of the supporters of the Gothic Revival. He described it as 'a piece of Brobdingnagian absurdity'.

A contemporary but more favourable observer wrote:

'Objections have been made, and with some appearance of reason, to the great expense of this ornamental entrance in reply to which, it may be said that, the railway is a great national undertaking, and that the national character is, in some respects, involved in the execution of the whole.'

The monumental 'arch' of the original Euston Station which symbolised the gateway to the north. It represented the enormous optimism felt by the promoters of the London & Birmingham Railway who felt that they would not only be enriching themselves but advancing the world. Not everyone shared this enthusiasm, some aesthetes thinking it was an overblown monstrosity. Its appearance was controversial as, indeed, was its eventual disappearance. (Authors' collection)

St Pancras Station and the Midland Grand Hotel

Over something that was really 'only' a question of taste, the Midland Grand Hotel and St Pancras Station showed a remarkable ability to generate controversy and barbed criticism at the time they were built. The hotel was designed by George Gilbert Scott, a prolific architect indelibly associated with his very own eclectic version of the style loosely known as the Gothic Revival. An edition of the *Quarterly Review* for 1872 contained an anonymous review of a number of books on architecture. It included a full-blooded attack on a number of contemporary architects and their works. The author excoriated St Pancras Station and it is worth quoting from the review to give a sense of the derision with which Scott's work was regarded:

'...The building inside and out is covered with ornament, and there is polished marble enough to furnish a Cathedral. The very parapet of the cab road is panelled and perforated, at a cost that would have supplied foot warmers to all the trains for years to come...the noble art of building has been treated as a mere trade advertisement. Showy and expensive, it will, for the present, be a striking contrast with its adjoining neighbour. The Great Northern terminus is not graceful, but it is simple, characteristic, and true. No one would mistake its nature and use. The Midland front is inconsistent in style and meretricious in detail; a piece of common "art manufacture" that makes the Great Northern front by contrast positively charming. There is no relief or quiet in any part of the work. The eye is constantly troubled and tormented, and the mechanical patterns follow one another with such rapidity and perseverance, that the mind becomes irritated where it ought to be gratified, and goaded to criticism where it should be led calmly to approve. There is here a complete travesty of noble associations, and not the slightest care to save those from a sordid contract. An elaboration that might be suitable for a Chapter-house, or a Cathedral choir is used as an "advertising medium" for bagman's bedrooms and the costly discomforts of a terminus hotel, and the architect is therefore a mere expensive rival of the company's head cook, in catering for the low enjoyments of the great travelling crowd. To be consistent, the directors should not confine their expression of artistic feeling to these great buildings only. Their porters might be dressed as javelin men, their guards as beefeaters, and their

St Pancras Station was opened in 1868 and with its massive single span overall roof, it had a great visual impact which was only exceeded when it was given a façade consisting of the Midland Grand Hotel. This was designed by Sir George Gilbert Scott and opened in 1873. It still rears a somewhat dominating if not browbeating presence over the eastern end of Euston Road.

It had 400 bedrooms, was exceptionally luxurious and palatial and enjoyed several decades of success but it was closed down by the London, Midland & Scottish Railway in 1935 largely because it was considered prohibitively expensive to refurbish it to meet the different expectations of twentieth-century travellers. Used as offices for some years, it has been expensively refurbished and is now an integral of the international transport hub that St Pancras has become. (A. Brooke) station-masters don the picturesque attire of Garter-king-at-arms. Their carriages might be copied from the Lord Mayor's Show, and even the engine wheels might imitate the Gothic window near their terminus at York. These things, however, will eventually come: the water tank, we see, is moulded in the Gothic style...'

Other opprobrious comments were made including one which described the hotel as 'Scott's tawdry masterpiece'.

In fairness, it should be said that the reception to the hotel and station was not wholly one-sided. A leading newspaper article about Scott's achievements declared:

'...the architect of a railway station does not generally aim very high, but Sir Gilbert Scott certainly produced in the Midland station at St Pancras the most beautiful terminus in London, remarkable alike for its convenience and its inspiring effect.'

John Betjeman

John Betjeman was more than just a slightly quirky, likeable old buffer who was able to convert the mundane and diurnal into accessible poetry and prose containing perceptive and wry social comment. He fought passionately against the bureaucratic philistines who decreed that Britain's new railway should go ahead without the Euston Arch and who also wanted to pull down the Midland Grand Hotel and St Pancras Station. He was instrumental in bringing about a much greater appreciation of the architectural and other achievements of our Victorian ancestors. In felicitous prose concerning the Euston Arch, he wrote:

'...a mighty understanding like the London to Birmingham must be symbolised by a monumental entrance'. The arch was: 'a gateway from England's capital and heart, London, to her stomach and toyshop, Birmingham.'

By the time he wrote these words, the Arch had vanished and he turned his attention to the replacement for old Euston. This time he wrote no less felicitously but there was controlled anger in what he wrote:

'What masterpiece arose on the site of the old station? No masterpiece. Instead there was a place where no one can sit, an underground taxi-entrance so full of fumes that drivers, passengers and porters alike hate it. A great hall of glass looks like mini-version of London Airport, which it seems to be trying to imitate.'

Euston was and remains, one of the UK's most disliked stations.

Betjeman used his skills to combat other examples of the planning nihilism which was such a feature of the 1960s, for example helping to prevent the demolition of the railway village built by the Great Western Railway close to Swindon Station. He was a leading light in the formation of the Victorian Society which contributed to the creation of a new climate in which it has become less likely for further acts of crass architectural vandalism to take place. In films like *Metroland* he blended love for the railways with nostalgia, whimsy, affectionate mockery and insights into human character. There was no affection when he wrote about the destruction of the Euston Arch.

55, Broadway, London SW1

The Underground Electric Railways of London (UERL) was created in 1902 to fashion a system out of the collection of uncoordinated deep-level tube railways that was developing in London. The only such line not included was the Waterloo & City which was absorbed by the London & South Western Railway in 1907. As the UERL grew, it was felt that it needed a prestigious new headquarters. It created new headquarters at 55, Broadway with an eye-catching and imposing new block, at 175 feet then the tallest office building in London. It was designed by Charles Holden and opened on 1 December 1929. The building was controversial from the first. Many disliked its monolithic and austere appearance and so Frank Pick, the Managing Director of the Underground Group and Holden himself decided that it needed some external adornment. Several pieces by well-known and rather avant-garde sculptors were mounted high up on the façade and out of easy public view. However, two much lower pieces just above the ground floor windows attracted withering comment as soon as they were unveiled. These were by Jacob Epstein, some of whose previous works elsewhere had already gained notoriety among critics of a fastidious nature. One figure, facing north, represented *Night* and the other was *Day*, this facing south-east. This had a naked body and provoked a cacophony of criticism on moral, artistic and aesthetic grounds. Certain modifications were made to the figure and the brouhaha died down.

Perhaps we should not be surprised that William Morris, the designer, writer, socialist and leading light of the Arts and Crafts Movement, was horrified by the appearance of the Forth Bridge. He described it as 'the supreme specimen of ugliness'. It evokes awe in most who view it.

CHAPTER THIRTEEN

Examples of support for Railways

John Bright, the radical politician associated particularly with the Anti-Corn Law League, said, 'Railways have rendered more services, and received less gratitude, than any other institution in the land.'

Thomas Roscoe published a book about the Grand Junction Railway in 1839. We are left in no doubt that here was a man who unequivocally welcomed the coming of the railways. He wrote:

'The Grand Junction Railway will ever maintain its importance in the great undertakings of this country. It can afford to smile with complacency upon schemes of more gigantic comprehension or costly expenditure, while it points to the complete demonstration it has afforded to science…and the almost boundless impulse it has mainly contributed to give to the talent, industry, enterprise, and inventive faculties of the world.'

A similar paean was penned in the *Quarterly Review* in 1830:

'We see in this magnificent invention, the well-spring of intellectual, moral and political benefits, beyond all measurement and price – the source of a better physical distribution of our population – a check to the alarming growth of cities, especially of manufacturing towns, and of this Babylon in which we write – and the source, above all, of…a diffusion of intelligence over the whole country.'

Many people saw railway trains and the big viaducts and imposing stations as the new wonders of the world. They were filled with admiration, awe and perhaps a dash of delicious fear. No machine created by man had ever moved so fast before and the power that had been harnessed was encapsulated in the fire-breathing monster at the head of the train. The steam locomotive was, and remained, the cynosure of all eyes. When a new line opened, people might walk what seem to us vast distances just to watch, transfixed, as one of these creations went about its business. If mysterious tunnels, deep cuttings, steep gradients or towering viaducts were also involved, so much the better because the spectacle was even more astounding and sublime.

A German visitor in 1842 captured some of the awe these structures inspired:

'If England were not so rich in wonders of the same kind, the stranger might fancy the appearance of Stockport unique in the world. The houses of Stockport rise up the deep sides of a valley watered by the river on which the town stands. Over the whole gulf, right over the town and river, from height to height, stretches a gigantic viaduct, across which passes the railway to London... Even in England this is a striking and magnificent work.'

This dramatic new form of transport impacted on a world where, previously, the highest speeds on land were those of the horse. The limits of the horse's capabilities had long been reached. Before the arrival of the railway, most people simply did not travel, other than for local purposes. Even many 'carriage folk' often went little further than the local market or country town. The concept of travel for pleasure and edification scarcely existed for most people. Travel was an expensive, difficult and often dangerous experience. Railways presented a considerable challenge to what by later standards was a nation where many communities were isolated and, by necessity, had a degree of self-containment that was about to be broken down for ever. We have examined various examples of opposition to railways and the changes they brought with them. Here we consider some examples of how railways were welcomed, even if those doing the welcoming were often blissfully unaware of the impact that railways and everything associated with them were going to have on their lives and those future generations.

Sydney Smith, the well-known Victorian wit and essayist, greatly approved of this new form of transport:

'Railroad travelling is a delightful improvement of human life. Man has become a bird: he can fly quicker and longer than a Solan goose...Everything is near, everything is immediate – time, distance and delay are abolished.'

Certainly, many people revelled in the speed offered by railway travel, although there were those of a more timorous nature who

This picture purports to show the first train of the Manchester, Sheffield and Lincolnshire Railway to serve Grimsby. Licence has been employed by the artist but an impression is given of the response of ordinary people to the new railway in their locality. (Authors' collection)

obviously did not do so. A somewhat jaundiced passenger on the Liverpool & Manchester Railway in 1831 commented in *Notes and Queries* in 1868; '...the speed was too great to be pleasant, and makes you rather giddy, and certainly it is not smoother and easier than a good turnpike road'. However, many people approved the reduction in journey times. This might make an out-and-home trip possible in a single day, obviating the need for overnight accommodation. Faster travel also reduced the need for food and drink en route. Travellers were pleased by the reduced cost of travel because, at least in theory, the tips that were expected from all quarters during coach travel were not exacted from those going by train. Booking in advance was the norm with coach travel and passengers quickly appreciated what we would now call the 'walk-on' facility for buying tickets that was offered by the railways.

T.H. Huxley, the eminent zoologist, appreciated railways for making the country's best scenery accessible to all. He was particularly impressed by the stretch of line operated by the Workington, Keswick and Penrith Railway where it ran along the side of Bassenthwaite Lake.

Ernest Foxwell in *English Express Trains: Two Papers* (1884) praised railways for breaking down what he regarded as the debilitating effect of parochialism. As the title of the book might suggest, he was a particular admirer of express trains. He felt that by promoting speedy travel they encouraged the kind of interaction across the country that made for a more intellectually stimulated society.

By 1850, railways were firmly established as the preferred option for inland travel, yet they had been and continued to be the target of criticism, fair and unfair. They were attacked for creating monopolies and exploiting the economic advantages monopoly created even if it was against the public interest. While many towns were still desperate to gain one or more railway connections, there were traders and businesses in towns served by railways who were complaining that railways were ruining their trade. Railway accidents (of which there were too many) were reported in gory detail in the newspapers because they were more cataclysmic and tended to affect larger numbers than those which had frequently occurred in the days of the stage coach. Doubtless some editors welcomed accidents especially on what would otherwise be slow news days.

Bring out the Bunting!

We have given examples elsewhere of towns that were opposed to the coming of railways. Some later relented and embraced the railway while a few were to regret the opposition they had put up in earlier times as they were left off the railway map altogether. Here we give some examples of the welcome that was accorded when work began on a railway scheme or when a line officially opened to the public.

Rather as happened with the launching of a ship, a woman, supposedly of some note, was often invited to perform the ceremony of cutting the first sod. A specially made spade engraved with details of the occasion was usually employed as was a specially crafted wheelbarrow into which the sod and some token soil was tipped. A band would be present and the usual civic dignitaries, directors, investors and general hangers-on would be standing around posing self-importantly. A priest would often be on hand to call down God's blessing on the venture.

On 11 June 1846, Ipswich was *en fête* to celebrate the opening of the Eastern Union Railway. Shops, businesses and workplaces

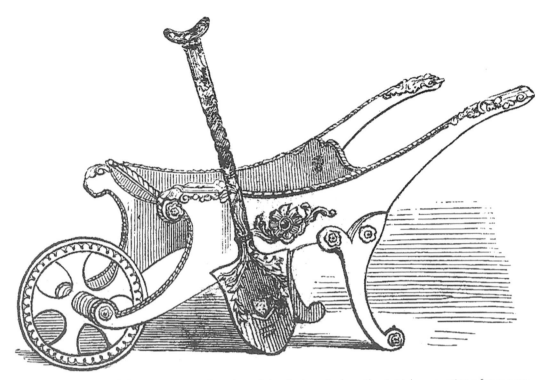

Much was made of the ceremony of cutting of the first sod when the initial excavations for a new line were being carried out. It was common to provide a specially made and largely ornamental spade and barrow which was often then preserved. These were made for the ceremony when work commenced on the Bristol and North Somerset Railway in 1863. (Authors' collection)

were closed. The first train was a special which conveyed directors, favoured guests and other bigwigs. When it arrived, guns were fired, church bells were rung and happy, cheering crowds flocked the streets. Those who had been on the special train were treated to lunch followed by a river trip down the Orwell to Harwich and back before sitting down to a sumptuous dinner in the town's Assembly Rooms. The dinner lasted five hours. The opulence of the surroundings and the quality of the fare then cascaded. Junior management and supervisory grades were treated at the *Golden Lion,* sub-contractors at the *Coach and Horses* and the navvies at the *Railway Tavern.* The celebrations continued into the evening with a balloon ascent and a firework display.

On 5 August 1850, the directors of the Great Northern Railway and selected guests boarded a special inaugural train run to mark the completion of an important component of the company's main line to the north. It left from a temporary station at Maiden

Lane near King's Cross and its destination was Peterborough. The press were on board and favourable publicity was gained by a special stop at Southgate to view the new 'lunatic asylum' being built there and a further stop was made to allow passengers to view the spectacular viaduct over the River Mimram at Welwyn, from ground level. No attempt was made to put the train through its paces because, including these stops, it took well over four hours to reach Peterborough. A meal of the sort described in those days as a 'cold collation' was provided for the passengers at Peterborough.

2 June 1845 was the day of the opening of the London & Birmingham Railway's line from Blisworth and Northampton to Peterborough. Crowds turned out along the route to cheer the official first train on its way and a huge crowd gathered to welcome it on its arrival at Peterborough. A formal banquet was held at the *Angel Hotel* at which invited bigwigs made grandiloquent speeches about how the railway would bring a new era of prosperity to all the settlements along the route. The wine flowed in copious quantities which probably accounted for the reference in one speech to the slow and generally unpleasant nature of travel by road. This caused a rumpus as a group of guests stormed out of the room. Apparently they were stagecoach proprietors who understandably had taken umbrage at the disparaging references to the services they provided. Less understandable is why they were at a banquet celebrating the coming of the railway! The wine had clearly had its effect because some of the revellers had to be coaxed down after insisting that they would prefer riding on the roof as they took the return train!

The first line to Lincoln was that built by the Midland Railway from Nottingham and it opened on 3 August 1846. For the day, most shops and businesses closed and people from surrounding villages poured into the city in their Sunday best. The bells of the cathedral and the various churches pealed out, a band of the Guards played, flags and bunting flew, crowds cheered, pickpockets garnered a rich harvest, people got drunk and fights broke out. In the evening, the *Durham Ox* hosted a banquet at which George Hudson presided and fulsome speeches were made about how Lincoln was on the cusp of untold prosperity because of the arrival of the railway. Many speeches were delivered and they tended to become more incoherent as the evening wore on and the drink flowed. Clearly, there was a sense that this was a key day in the history of the city and its district and that to be on the railway map was a necessity for a community's economic well-being.

When the South Wales Railway officially opened, *The Times* (18 June 1850) was duly impressed:

> '…at every station on the line bands of music…and the cheers of the people were heard…immense multitudes of ancient Britons [sic] assembled on the margin of the new railway…ships in the several ports of Chepstow, Newport, Cardiff, Port Talbot, Neath and Swansea were decked out; at each of these places the bells gave forth many merry peals, and the roaring of cannon saluted the travellers. At every station on the line wreaths of flowers and evergreens abounded.'

The first train on the West Somerset Railway pulled into Williton on 31 March 1862. Across the main street, a banner proclaimed, 'Hail, Steam the Civilizer!' The *West Somerset Free Press* described how even the local workhouse sported a banner made by the inmates simply inscribed, 'Accept our Best Wishes'. There was a clear belief that the coming of the railway was synonymous with progress. Few places wanted to be regarded as a backwater lacking the most modern means of communication. In more material terms, the railway was expected to bring cheaper coal and a greater range of domestic goods while providing the possibility of widened markets for local farmers and manufacturers. Places that were previously remote soon had the high-speed forms of communication that accompanied the spread of railways – the penny post and the electric telegraph. A communications revolution was emerging with immense social and cultural implications.

The Hull & Barnsley Railway was a comparative latecomer and something of an oddity in that, when completed, it never reached Barnsley. The first sod was cut at a ceremony in January 1881 when no fewer than 7,000 people were present to celebrate the occasion. Sir Gerard Smith, Chairman of the Company, cut the first sod which was then delicately divided into thin slices. Each of the slices was then placed in a silver container and presented to the directors and certain specified 'friends'.

The Lancashire & Yorkshire's short branch to serve Salford Docks opened on 28 March 1898. An inaugural train was operated with the great and the good on board arriving at the docks after having safely negotiated the steep downhill gradient. Its appearance was greeted with a cacophony of exploding detonators, ships' sirens, cheering crowds and the display of much celebratory bunting. The guests then embarked on a small vessel for a short trip along the Manchester Ship Canal and back. All this for a line given over exclusively to freight traffic! The enthusiasm was not misplaced. Manchester greatly benefitted from the canal, the docks and the railway connections.

They did things a bit differently at Fort William. The West Highland Railway from Glasgow opened in August 1894. A large crowd turned out to greet the inaugural train. Nothing unusual about that but a temporary platform was erected just outside the town and the train drew to a halt there. A decorated triumphal arch of wood was erected over the railway with two gates, symbolically closed, across the line. As two pipers gave it their all and the crowd cheered and threw their hats in the air, a gold padlock on the gates was ceremonially unlocked, the gates were opened and the train steamed majestically through to arrive at Fort William Station proper, a few moments later.

Another place where they eschewed the norm was Elsenham in Essex. A light railway was promoted from Elsenham, on the Great Eastern Railway's London to Cambridge main line, to the declining small town of Thaxted. The first sod was cut on 25 July 1911 by Sir Walter Gilbey of the gin-distilling family, a local man who had pushed hard for the line to be built and was one of its directors. It was Sir Walter who did the digging with the customary ceremonial spade. So far so good but then things took an unusual turn. Sir Walter was persuaded to take a seat in the ceremonial wheelbarrow along, presumably, with the sods that had been cut, whereupon he was pushed some distance along the formation of the line by his fellow directors. It is interesting to note that Sir Walter, when making the expected speech on this occasion, said that he hoped he would never live to see the nationalisation of the railways.

The Lynton & Barnstaple was a quirky and delightful narrow gauge railway which opened to the public on 11 May 1898. The flags were out in Lynton and the bands played merrily. The railway company lashed out on sticky buns for the happy crowd although some in the throng must have been less happy that mineral water was the only liquid refreshment freely available. Not everyone was in celebratory mood, however. A small contingent consisted of local residents unhappy about the opening of the railway because they thought that it presaged floods of tourists who would threaten the quiet seclusion for which they had paid a lot of money. This little line was an early victim of economy cuts, being closed to passengers in September 1935. It was sadly typical that the number of passengers on the very last train greatly exceeded the total of passengers on all trains in the preceding week. People had a sentimental attachment to trains which did not necessarily extend to using them.

Seldom has more florid verbiage been expended on a sod-cutting ceremony than that recording the events that occurred at Blandford in Dorset on 13 November 1856 concerning the Dorset Central Railway. The *Illustrated London News* (13 November 1856) gave a sense of the kind of welcome that could be extended to a railway project:

'On Thursday, the 13th inst the first turf was cut at Blandford St Mary, by the lady of Sir John James Smith, Bart, of the Down House, in the presence of a vast concourse of people from the surrounding district, graced by a brilliant array of rank and fashion…From an early hour in the morning the town of Blandford had all the appearance of a fete day – carriages of all descriptions, from the barouche and four – to the market cart, brought in their load of holidaymakers, and at noon the Corporation of Blandford received Lady Smith, the High Sheriff of the County, and several of the nobility and gentry; the Mayors and Corporation of Poole and Glastonbury; the directors and officers of the Dorset Central and Somerset Central Railway.

'These all formed in procession, headed by the local schools and benefit societies with banners, navvies bearing spades and picks, and two wheeling in barrows barrels of strong beers. The field of operation was very tastefully decorated under the direction of Mr M.K. Welsh of Poole, with banners, triumphal arches, etc.

'The barrow is of polished mahogany, with bunches of corn and poppies carved on the panels and the handles carved as Indian corn. The blade of the spade is of polished steel, the ornamentation is very beautiful and the handle of tulip wood, carved with ivy leaves.

'Lady Smith cut the turf in a most businesslike manner and caused great admiration in the minds of the navvies when she tipped the barrow, turned the barrow between the handles and drew the barrow back behind her along the planks.

'Three hundred of the company afterwards sat down to an excellent *dejeuner a la fourchette* in the Assembly Rooms, supplied by Mr Eyres of the *Crown Inn*.'

A charming account was given in the *West Sussex Gazette*, 10 October 1859 of the reception accorded to an early train arriving at Horsham on the Mid-Sussex Railway of the London, Brighton and South Coast Railway:

'The people, when they were seen, looked scared at the appearance of the steam engine, as also did the horses, beasts, turkeys and other things, which ran from us in the greatest terror. Some of the natives, as soon as they heard that "Puffing Billy" was coming, were induced to leave their cottages; but they all seemed to keep at a distance of about fifty yards from the train, fearing that "he" might go off…'

Triumphal arches and the ringing of church bells were common features of the welcome accorded to the opening of many railway lines. It was almost obligatory for a band to play *See the Conquering Hero Comes*. At Chard in Somerset a branch line was opened from the Salisbury to Exeter main line of the London & South Western Railway. The first public train ran on 8 May 1863 and it was reported that the navvies were treated to hot beef, potatoes and beer at the Red Lion in Chard and the bigwigs with a less boisterous collation at a marquee at the station. According to a local paper, the 'common folk' then gave themselves up to 'dancing, kissing in the ring, jumping in sacks, football, etc.'

By the early 1850s, the small town of Launceston in Cornwall was in the doldrums having failed to be connected to the railway network. Much to the chagrin of the local populace, in 1861 a scheme for a line which would have passed through the town was defeated in parliament. Shortly afterwards, another scheme was proposed. This was for a 'Launceston & South Devon Railway' which would have joined up with the broad gauge South Devon Railway at Tavistock. It was opposed by the War Office which had no truck with the broad gauge for strategic reasons, and by a number of local landowners. The attitude of the Duke of Northumberland, the most influential local magnate, was unclear until the last minute. A Bill was drawn up but local activists decided to apply added pressure and to send a petition in support of the Bill to the House of Lords. A meeting was to be organised at which the petition would be signed and the biggest possible turnout was needed. The organisers circulated a handbill which was a masterpiece of hyperbole:

> 'Our Railway! Come to the meeting tonight!! Citizens: The enemy is in the field. Arouse Ye! Arouse Ye! And do battle to the enemies of your sacred rights. Having pledged yourselves at two public meetings to support the Launceston & South Devon Railway, now, in the hour of trial, stand forth as a Samson to crush tyranny and despotism! Now or never!! But be a united band, and act on the Cornish motto – "a long pull, a strong pull, and a pull altogether"- and the victory will be yours!!!'[1]

Although they inflicted severe injury on the beautiful English language, the supporters of the railway managed to win over the duke whose support was essential. The Bill became law and the line opened on 1 June 1865.

We have seen how opening ceremonies were characterised by the favoured guests being treated to formal dinners accompanied by copious quantities of drink. Such junkets could be expensive but most companies wanted to put on a good and generous show even if they were cash-starved. Few were more financially challenged than the grandly named Dursley & Midland Junction Railway. The penury of this company was demonstrated when, at the opening ceremony, the invited guests had to pay for their own dinners!

So it is clear that the opening of a railway was made into an excuse for a jamboree and that most people welcomed the event. Stirring ditties were even penned to mark these events and here is an excerpt from one such:

A PENNYWORTH OF FUN
'If you will listen to my song
I'll not detain you long.
On the Ist of May the folks did throng
To view the Oxford Railway.
And to have a ride – what a treat,
Father, mother, son, and daughter
Along the line like one o'clock,
By fire, steam, and water.

EAST GRINSTEAD.

OPENING THE
RAILWAY!

On the arrival of the quarter-past One o'Clock Train,
the Officials will proceed to the Crown Inn, headed by a

BAND OF MUSIC,

WHERE A

COLD COLLATION WILL BE PROVIDED.

CHAIR TO BE TAKEN AT HALF-PAST ONE O'CLOCK.

TICKETS, 2s. 6d. each, to be had at the Bar.

☞ The INHABITANTS of the TOWN and NEIGHBOURHOOD are
especially invited to be present.

A PROFESSIONAL SINGER,

FROM LONDON, IS ENGAGED FOR THE OCCASION.

Refreshments will also be provided on a piece of Ground near
the Railway Terminus, by Mrs. Head & Son.

EAST GRINSTEAD,
JULY 5TH, 1855.

PRINTED AT THE OFFICE OF J. SMITH, EAST GRINSTEAD.

East Grinstead is an ancient market town in West Sussex. It joined the railway network courtesy of the London, Brighton & South Coast Railway which in 1855 opened a branch line from Three Bridges on the main line from London to Brighton. This handbill gives a flavour of how localities gave a welcome to the coming of the railway. Compared to some other places, East Grinstead's welcome seems quite restrained. (Authors' collection)

Chorus:

'Rifum, Tifum, fun and mirth.
Don't you wonder how it's done,
Carriages without horses run
On the Hampton and Oxford Railway.'[2]

The Opening of the Branch to Windermere

The idea of a railway penetrating the Lake District may have elicited the wrath of William Wordsworth but people of less aesthetic sensitivities who lived locally gave the line to Windermere from Oxenholme and Kendal an enthusiastic welcome. It opened on 20 April 1847. The first edition of the *Windermere Gazette* after the opening devoted much of its content to an enthusiastic description of the celebrations which took place on the opening day and of the sights that could be seen from the train window. The plaudits offered to the railway on this occasion contrasted sharply with the morbid relish underpinning a report in the next edition concerning a number of recent fatalities and serious injuries sustained by people using railways elsewhere. The journalist concerned exhibited a trait common to those in his profession when it came to dealing with railways. He did not allow total ignorance of the subject to impede his writing of the article and the conveying of his opinions as if they were facts. Many journalists are not only totally ignorant about railways but seem innately hostile to them. Over the years they must have inflicted considerable damage on readers' perceptions of the railways. This is called power without responsibility.

Then, as now, some local newspapers invited people with pretensions to be poets to submit samples of their work for publication. The intention may be to provide their readers with some cheap laughs but the opportunity has been too good for some people whose egos are immeasurably greater than their poetic skills. Here is an excerpt from a celebration of the opening of the line to Windermere.

'Come let us hie to the Lake and its scenery!
Gliding as if on the wings of the wind, my dear,
And see how the rugged, dark mountain tops meet your eye
While on the smooth waters the isles seem to greet your eye
Those tell of the regions where dwell the sublimities,
Those of th' abodes of some earthly divinities,
Lo! From the hives of industry how thick they come!
Eager to gorge on the fairyland wonderments:

Pouring from East, West and South too how quickly they come!
Transferred from the rail we embark on the glassy lake;
And crowding the steamer a fresh-water passage take.
Moving majestic we leisurely view the sight,
Fraught with enchantment that yields ever new delight!'

There is more but the authors are not sadists.

Early Railway Excursions

Early railway promoters were not a little surprised and certainly very gratified when they discovered a hitherto unexpected demand for passenger travel. This consisted not only of people going by train for business reasons but a sizeable market in what we would now call 'leisure travel'. At first some of this may have been for people to sample this revolutionary new form of travel; for them simply to be able to say they had been on a train. It soon became obvious, however, that an unsuspected demand existed for people to travel for the pleasure and broadening benefits that this high-speed form of transport conferred.

Industrial development from the eighteenth century required vast supplies of manpower. Jobs in agriculture were in decline. Massive migration to the industrial districts took place. Working, housing and general environmental conditions in the industrial towns were frequently appalling. Wages, however, tended to be higher in industrial areas. Enterprising railway companies quickly discerned that money could be made running special trains or providing discounted fares for pleasure-seekers wanting to get away from their squalid surroundings. Railways were welcomed as a way of allowing town dwellers a means of temporary escape.

Possibly the first-ever excursion train was that operated late in 1830 by the Liverpool & Manchester Railway so that its passengers could alight at the right spot to clamber down the embankment and view the Sankey Viaduct from ground-level, the viaduct then being regarded as one of the wonders of the modern world.

The first seaside excursion train may have been that put on by the then London & Brighton Railway on Easter Monday 1844 which ran, predictably, from London to Brighton and back. It was well subscribed because, after making a couple of intermediate stops, it arrived at Brighton consisting of no less than fifty-seven 4-wheel carriages hauled by six locomotives and containing about 1,000 passengers. It established something of a precedent by being about half-an-hour behind time. Its average speed was about fourteen miles per hour but we can assume that, given an average speed of around five mph for a road coach, the excursionists would have been very impressed.

The rather obscure Bodmin & Wadebridge Railway in Cornwall was quick off the mark in identifying a specialist niche in the travel for pleasure market. On 13 August 1840, it ran three special trains conveying almost the entire population of Wadebridge to Bodmin to watch the public hanging of the notorious Lightfoot Brothers outside the prison. Such spectacles were guaranteed to draw large crowds until the abolition of public hanging in 1868 and railway companies were not averse to exploiting the widespread desire to view the final sufferings of condemned felons. By the 1840s, opinion formers were concluding that such events were undesirable, not so much for humane reasons but because the large crowds they attracted often threatened law and order. Thus, we have the *Daily News* in 1849 excoriating the provision of a special train from London to Norwich for the purpose of witnessing a public hanging:

'The squalid inmates of the lowest haunts of lazar infamy, may, thanks to the reduced fares, enjoy tomorrow's spectacle at Norwich. The raffish finery of the swell mob, male and female, will impart a shabby splendour to those pilgrims to the shrine of callous curiosity…'[3]

We might once have said 'as every schoolboy knows' that the first railway excursion was that organised by Thomas Cook on 5 July 1841 conveying a party from Leicester to and from a temperance meeting in Loughborough. It was definitely not the pioneer excursion but it did involve a new concept. Cook, who abstained from alcohol, was an enterprising young employee of the Midland Counties Railway who hired a train from his employer for which he provided the passengers. They travelled at half the ordinary fare and both the company and Cook made a profit. Perhaps Loughborough did not normally attract many excursionists because most of the local population turned out, cheering and waving flags. Not far from Loughborough is the small town of Ashby-de-la-Zouch which also did not normally attract many visitors. The line through Ashby opened in 1849 and the town's first excursion was in 1850. Organised by Cook, it gave people from Leicester the opportunity to explore Ashby's varied delights. The people of the town seem to have been very pleased to welcome the excursionists. Large cheering crowds turned out, bands played martial music and a variety of entertainments was put on. Shopkeepers and other local businesspeople at Ashby and elsewhere were quick to welcome railway excursions because, although the individual trippers did not usually have much money, the collective spending of, say, three hundred trippers might give the local economy a useful quick boost.

Cook went from strength to strength and his proud claim a few years later was that he had organised special trains carrying 165,000 people to and from the Great Exhibition in Hyde Park in 1851. This obviously constituted good business for Cook but he was particularly gratified because the organisers did not allow the consumption of alcohol on the premises. This was much to the chagrin of many of the visitors, but it has to be said that the whole event was a huge success and passed off without any of the antisocial behaviour that drink might have caused.

The Metropolitan Police were among those who welcomed excursions taking large numbers of Londoners on day trips to Brighton. On those days, crime fell markedly in the capital. We are left to speculate on the comments made on the same issue by their counterparts in Brighton. We get some flavour of how one particular seaside resort viewed an invasion of excursionists from this excerpt in a Weston-Super-Mare newspaper:

'A horde of savages making an excursion on a civilised settlement is the only figure we can imagine as fitting to express the general feeling held by our townspeople in regard to them. A mass of boys and girls, and young men and women, comprising the lowest dregs of the more disreputable neighbourhoods of Bristol, who swarmed every avenue and invaded every nook; the song of the birds were hushed by oaths of blasphemy, the ears of innocence shocked by the accents of obscenity…drunken boys were to be seen staggering through every thoroughfare, fights were of frequent occurrence in the streets of the town, and scenes of lewdness met the eye of day.'[4]

The case of Weston may be an extreme case. Early railway excursions helped to transform the leisure experience of vast numbers of working people. 'The railway excursion changed the holiday from a home-based celebration to an activity away from home, often at the seaside…'[5] Previously, for example, some factory workers and their families from Lancashire industrial towns travelled on foot or by cart to seaside locations relatively nearby and people might travel to local fairs but the demands of everyday life, normally met within local communities, meant that there was little need for longer-distance travelling and only the haziest notion that such travel could be a rewarding experience. There was usually little leisure time anyway and on saints' and other festival days there would be all manner of jollifications provided within the local community. Now the railways enabled large numbers of ordinary people to travel *en masse* to a more distant destination in pursuit of pleasure and recreation.

The provision of cheap excursions tapped a hitherto unsuspected market and provided a liberating experience which was available to be enjoyed by all but the very poor. Those who made use of such excursions greatly welcomed the life-enriching experience but it was only to be expected that there were sections of their censorious 'elders and betters' who were concerned about working people gathering and moving about in the large numbers for which excursion trains were able to cater. There was a deeply rooted fear among the middle-class and better-off sections of Victorian society concerning the behaviour of the 'lower orders'. They considered them vulgar, potentially violent and criminally inclined, insufficiently deferential and easily persuaded by unscrupulous rabble-rousers who wanted to overthrow the established order. Excursion trains therefore faced them with a dilemma. Could the desire of the masses to travel for leisure purposes be controlled by being channelled into 'acceptable' ways of behaviour and spending leisure time? The notions of 'social control' and 'rational recreation' developed, whereby value judgements accorded respectability to certain activities and frowned upon others. Either way, the perceived wisdom was that working-class activities needed to be monitored and controlled.

Those who sought to control the leisure hours of the working class were largely from the middle class. Activities approved of included visiting museums and art galleries and excursions to places of beauty, historical interest, the seaside or a source of wonderment like the Great Exhibition. It was evidence of the sense of awe that could be drawn on that large numbers of excursion trains ran to Holyhead in October 1859 to view Brunel's monster ship the *Great Eastern*. To be deplored and discouraged were drinking, physical sports largely without rules, cruel sports (at least those largely involving working-class participation) gambling and street games. Even here those wanting to impose their values on the masses were divided. Sabbatarians, for example, who wanted Sunday to be given over to public worship and quiet leisure time, clashed with others who wanted the provision of rational recreation, including excursions on the Sunday, despite the fact that catering for excursionists involved employment on the Sabbath, this being anathema to an influential minority. Attempts had been made to prevent the operation of Sunday trains in the bills seeking parliamentary sanction for certain railway schemes.

Working people saw Sunday as the only day away from the tyranny of the workplace and did not want this time also to be 'controlled', especially by the same kind of people as their employers.

A range of religious organisations, temperance societies and mechanics' institutes played a major role in making use of early railway excursions. In doing so, they tended to be endorsed by the middle class who saw them as examples of the edifying and respectable use of leisure time by the working-class people who tended to make up a large proportion of the excursionists. The organisers of excursions by such earnest bodies found them useful for bonding among the members but also regarded them as a kind of mobile advertisement for the virtues of sobriety, diligence and religiosity. Unfortunately, it was not entirely unknown for shameless miscreants who neither belonged to nor supported the aims of such organisations, to take advantage of the cheap fares on those excursions open to the public and use them in order to enjoy a pub crawl at the destination. The 'respectable' view of railway excursions as expressed in *Herapath's Journal & Railway Magazine* on 12 October 1850 was that they had 'a very sensible effect on diminishing the consumption of wine and spirits…Here is a good plainly and positively produced by excursion trains, the diminution of intemperance'.

Perhaps ironically, the most impressive railway excursions of the late Victorian period were those organised by Bass, the brewers of Burton-on-Trent. These were known as the 'Bass Railway Trips' and they began in 1865 continuing until 1914. These were for their employees, relations and friends and the peak was reached in 1900 when seventeen trains conveyed 11,241 excited excursionists to Blackpool. No drunkenness or improper behaviour among the trippers was tolerated. The host towns for these trips, mainly seaside resorts, knew this and welcomed the influx of well-behaved visitors and their considerable cumulative spending power. Bass believed that these excursions encouraged gratitude and loyalty in their workforce.

The Victorian period was riddled with issues around class. Much as those with sufficient needs looked down on 'parliamentary trains' for example, so it became fashionable in similar circles to deride excursion trains on which the fares might be as little as a quarter of those on regular trains. Their low standing even in the eyes of the railway companies was shown by the way in which they were frequently shunted aside to allow more prestigious regular trains to pass and by the disdain extended by some locals and regular visitors to these trains and the working-class cargo they deposited at the town's station. Queen Victoria, for example, had made much use of the delights of fashionable Brighton. When excursion trains full of boisterous Londoners began to operate regularly to the town, she decided that they conveyed the kind of subjects with which she had no wish to hobnob and she left Brighton, never to return, moving to seaside locations more difficult for ordinary Londoners to access.

Whatever moral judgements could be made concerning railway excursions, they brought welcome revenue for the railway companies and to the seaside and other towns, places and events which provided their destinations.

Early Railway Guidebooks

Nature abhors a vacuum, so they say, and no sooner had one vacuum been filled by the invention of railways than another was created and duly plugged by the invention of guidebooks for those using them.

James Scott Walker got in on the act with commendable promptitude. His was perhaps the earliest guidebook and it was published to coincide with the opening of the Liverpool and Manchester Railway on 15 September 1830. Walker was a Liverpool journalist who clearly had an eye for the main chance. He promoted his publication as an account of the building of the line and a description of what could be seen by a traveller on it. It was moderately priced and employed a type which made it easy to read when the train was in motion. Despite the ponderous title: *An Accurate Description of the Liverpool and Manchester Railway; The Tunnels, the Bridges, and other Works throughout the Line,* it sold and well and went into four more editions by 1832.

A new market had been found and it grew as the railway network expanded and more people made use of trains to travel for pleasure and education. Among the best-known early travel guides were those written by George Meason. His first had the grandiloquent title *Official Illustrated Guide to the Great Western Railway and its Branches.* It included information about the GWR

This is an example of the cheap guides for travellers produced by Martin & Co. of London. With a recognisable representation of King's Cross on the front, this guide regaled the traveller with written and pictorial information about places through which the East Coast Main Line, for example, passed. It is implied that this publication is associated with the Great Northern Railway but scrutiny will reveal that most of the places mentioned were not actually served by that company. For all that, this is a fine list of places worth visiting! (Authors' collection)

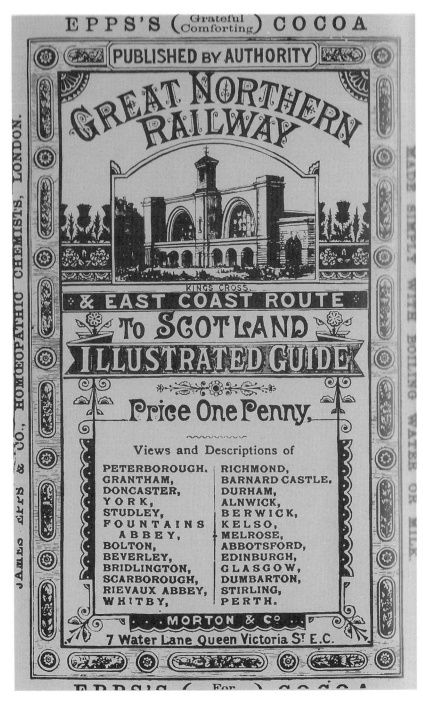

and a description of the lines it was operating. It was illustrated with fifty wood engravings based on original drawings by Meason himself. This was followed by more guides from Meason and a number of imitators, most of whom adopted the word

'Official' in their titles without any evidence that they enjoyed sponsorship but they did, however, tend to contain a somewhat obsequious dedication from the author to the chairman and directors of the particular company. These publications sold well and provided a useful service in encouraging train travel and a greater interest in British history, topography, architecture and folklore, for example. It is difficult to fault the research that went into these publications. Meason's guides were perhaps the best and they often dealt in considerable and accurate detail with the manufacturing activities of the places they described. This information might deal with specialised industries local to these places and provide them in effect with free publicity and, when those who bought the guides visited the places, the possibility of sales. Often the guides contained advertisements from prominent local businesses so Meason gained income while the advertisers hoped to attract custom from visitors attracted to their locality by the guides.

A new market had been identified and publishers gratefully went on to produce a stream of guidebooks or 'companions' as they were often called. Some of these carved out a niche for themselves, others soon fell by the wayside but they were all grateful to the railways for their inspiration and providing such a business opportunity.

Bradshaw's Guides

A rather different guide was that which appeared for the first time in 1838. This was the work of George Bradshaw and he gave it the heavyweight title *Bradshaw's Railway Time Tables and Assistant to Railway Travelling*. In 1842, it changed its name to *Bradshaw's Monthly Railway and Steam Navigation Guide*. A legend in British cultural history was in the making.

Bradshaw owed the considerable fortune he acquired to railways and to his own inspired leap into the dark in the hope that there might be a market for people who wanted a comprehensive, up-to-date compendium of train times. His initiative was not welcomed by all the railway companies, however. Some of them complained bitterly that because his publication listed the times their trains ran, they would be forced to run them at the times indicated. One early railway magnate answering criticism that his trains ran later than indicated in 'Bradshaw' proudly boasted that the number of trains that ran late was balanced by those that ran early! The hostility of the railway companies gradually wore off and the companies began to be thankful to Bradshaw, whose publication in effect provided them with free publicity for the trains they operated. Significantly, even today passenger trains that run but do not appear in public timetables are described as 'unadvertised'.

Bradshaw established a unique place for itself in the British way of life but attitudes to it were curiously ambiguous. Among those who enthusiastically embraced its use were those kinds of people who would probably nowadays be described as 'timetable anoraks'. They would be able to navigate easily through what for others was the indigestible mass of information it contained and would unfailingly be able to give a quick and accurate answer to a question like, 'What would be the best trains to catch to travel on a weekday from Cromer to Aberystwyth without passing through a tunnel?' These people gorged unashamedly on such minutiae but far more people found Bradshaw almost incomprehensible with its minute type and footnotes of byzantine complexity. 'Bradshaw' and 'railway timetables' may have become synonymous but Bradshaw could never have been described as 'user-friendly'.

Not everyone needed a publication which gave details of train times across the whole of Britain. For those whose travelling requirements were more geographically limited, enterprising businessmen, usually printers or stationers, began publishing books of timetables related to particular localities or regions. An early example was *Gadsby's Railway List, containing the Times of Departure of al the Trains connected with Manchester*. The first issue appeared on 1 January 1840.

Bradshaw's success encouraged imitators. It became common for publishers of regional guides whose works were obviously less comprehensive than Bradshaw to have a dig at the complex task involved in deciphering and abstracting the required information from that publication. Thus the Bristol firm of Evans and Arrowsmith, when advertising their West Country guide in 1854, declared:

'We have the greatest confidence in stating that our Time Tables will be found the most lucid, simple…of any that have ever appeared. This desideratum, we feel assured, will be fully appreciated by the Public who must have met with almost insuperable difficulties in pondering over some of the cumbrous budgets [sic] which are monthly issued from the press.'

It was probably inevitable that the information crammed into Bradshaw and the publication itself would incur some gentle ridicule. It was also likely that the ubiquitous Charles Dickens would have something to say about it. In *Household Words* (1851) he has his hero, an ingenuous tradesman, trying to make his way from London to Worcester. Unfortunately for him, he recruits Bradshaw to aid him and, owing to its incomprehensibility, he finds himself making the acquaintance of Scotland and the Isle of Man before somehow arriving back at his starting point, having missed Worcester completely. Anthony Trollope joined in the fun by declaring that he had neither the strength nor the mental ability to tackle Bradshaw when he wanted to make a long-distance journey. *Punch* (Vol.27, 1854) for its part declared, 'It has long been agreed on all hands that nobody can understand a railway timetable'. *The Railway Traveller's Handy Book* endorses this approach when it informs its readers:

> 'This work contains a mass of information compressed into the very smallest compass, but on that account, and by reason of various signs and symbols having to be made use of, it is not as easy of interpretation as it might be. This fact has given rise to innumerable witticisms on its unintelligibility…although we are acquainted with a few of the initiated to whom Bradshaw is as easy as A B C, we have never yet met with a lady who did not regard it as a literary puzzle, while the majority of the sterner sex have failed to master its intricacies.'[6]

Punch suggested that tuition in reading and understanding railway timetables should be a part of every school's curriculum. Was this a semi-serious suggestion?

It is evidence of the role that Bradshaw was carving out in the nation's consciousness and culture that at some time in the mid-nineteenth century, writers and commentators when referring to it began omitting the inverted commas on the basis that everyone knew what was being referred to when Bradshaw was mentioned. *Punch* could not resist poking fun at Bradshaw but paid it a genuine compliment when it declared somewhat ponderously:

> 'Seldom, if ever, has the gigantic intellect of man been employed upon a work of greater utility or upon one of such special

application and general comprehensiveness as on the projection, completion, publication and sustentation of the now familiar "Bradshaw".'

Bradshaw never lost its reputation for opacity but there was a genuine sense of the loss of a loved and entrenched national institution when the last edition was issued in May 1961.

Superlatives

Those Victorians who reflected on their own times were frequently very excited by the sense of progress and achievement, of the increase in man's knowledge and control of the world around him. The spread of railways was an example of this process and many references to them contain superlatives.

A handbook published for travellers on the London & Birmingham Railway described the Doric portico at Euston as the largest in Europe, if not the world. The cutting at Tring was one of the most 'stupendous' in the kingdom. A skew bridge at Box Moor had 'no previous equivalent'. Another publication described the London & Birmingham as: '…the triumphant invention of Science, trained and disciplined under severe study, and gathering accelerated strength from the successful experiments of each successive year'.[7]

Some of the men associated with the Railway Age got the treatment. The Stephensons, father and son, Isambard Kingdom Brunel, Daniel Gooch, Joseph Locke and others were elevated to the ranks of celebrities, albeit with considerably more justification than the vast majority of today's so-called 'super-stars'. Samuel Smiles engaged unashamedly in hagiography in works like *Lives of the Engineers.*

In the burgeoning of wonder at what had been and could be achieved by science and technology, many towns established Philosophical and Learned Societies and Mechanics' Institutes. To cater for the desire among earnest artisans and craftsmen for self-improvement around the theme that 'Knowledge is Power', the *Mechanics' Magazine* was launched in 1823 and this became an ardent supporter of railways for epitomising human advancement through science and technology. The magazine revelled in providing its readers with statistics about the achievements of the railways. One issue of 1836 informed its rapt readers that the ten most efficient engines on the Liverpool & Manchester Railway were averaging no less than 538 miles per week, this being evidence of how railways were annihilating both space and time.

Affection for Rural Railways

Richard Wyndham in 'South Eastern Survey', wrote:

'The track, as green and beautiful as a chickweedy disused canal, finds its way through hedges of willows which rap and brush the carriage sides, or across Bodiam marshes where herons stand by the line – no longer perturbed. There are few roads through this stretch of country, which remains much the same as when the peasants first complained about the iron monster which has desecrated their land...Northiam appeared to be an important station: I was joined by a passenger with a perambulator; and some endless shunting was done. The guard-pointsman could give no fixed time for departure, but he would hold the train for me, of course, if I wished to walk up to the village for a glass of beer...'

Was there ever a more affectionate evocation of a rustic branch line?

Railway Enthusiasts

We have given examples of places which went into festive mode when they joined the railway map. Perhaps many in the jubilant cheering crowd were attracted by the novelty of the occasion and then lapsed largely into indifference once the railways had become embedded in everyday experience. It is clear that many people were awestruck by the sight of steam trains in motion and by some of the more eye-catching civil engineering works such as viaducts. It was impossible to be in the middle of Stockport, for example, and not to be aware of the dominating presence of the railway viaduct. A host of early writers put pen to paper describing the experience of train travel, some almost eulogistically; some with reservations and others with forthright loathing.

Small boys made heroes of the drivers of the crack mail and stage coaches and they swore that when they grew up they in turn would be the 'kings of the road' and emulate these Olympian figures. How capricious was their adulation! No sooner had the Liverpool & Manchester Railway opened than every young shaver wanted to be there on the footplate in charge of a machine with power and speed so evident when compared with the snail-like progress of a team of horses.

It seems that we have to wait until the late nineteenth century for the emergence of anything quite recognisable as railway enthusiasm in terms of a hobby or pastime. Two events are probably seminal. One was the founding of the *Railway Magazine* in 1897; the other the creation of the Railway Club also in 1897. Both proved long-lived and indeed the magazine is still with us. No one could have expected the extraordinary growth of enthusiasm for railways, particularly in the form of train spotting after the Second World War. This was both the creation and the product of Ian Allan's shrewd publishing of lists of locomotives and the depots at which they were allocated. From the late 1940s to the end of regular steam on British Railways in 1968, literally hundreds of thousands of mainly male youngsters were struck by the 'railway bug', particularly the desire to collect numbers. Major stations like Crewe would be invaded by hundreds of spotters on Saturdays and at holiday time. Many of them would

Although much initial opposition to railways has been identified, it did not take long before there was evidence that they had evoked widespread affection as well. Many mementoes and everyday artefacts provide evidence of the developing awareness of railways as part of the fabric of life. (Authors' collection)

also have toy train sets. As they grew older, they might progress into serious layout and model-making from scratch or a lifelong and rewarding interest in one or more aspects of railway activity.

The hordes largely left the platform ends after 1968, but railway enthusiasm was far from dead and buried with the end of regular main line steam traction. The preservation movement swung into action and now the UK has more museums and restored heritage working lines than any other country in Europe. Volunteers have spent millions of hours producing highly authentic recreations of the earlier railway scene. There are even the resources to build brand new examples of types of locomotive that were previously rendered extinct. *Flying Scotsman* is a celebrity feted wherever it goes and drawing mass audiences.

Railway enthusiasts have not had a good press in the last decades, frequently being written off as socially inept, asexual introverts. Those given to making disparaging comments and describing railway enthusiasts as 'anoraks' are not always themselves people leading a particularly rich and enlightened existence. Those enthusiasts who graduate from spotting numbers frequently found that their interest in railways expanded into an involvement in other associated areas such as economic and industrial history, civil and mechanical engineering, architecture, geography, topography and much else, any of which can provide stimulating and enriching experiences.

Dr Charles McKay

A minor Victorian poet, Charles McKay, leaves us in no doubt of the debt we owe railways:

'Lay down your rails, ye nations, near and far;
Yoke your full trains to Steam's triumphal car…
Peace and improvement round each train shall soar,
And knowledge light the ignorance of yore…
Blessings on Science, and her handmaid, Steam!
They make utopia only half a dream'…

CHAPTER FOURTEEN

Hostility continues

The period from 1830 to 1914 has been called 'The Railway Age' and during those years the railways held an unassailable dominance of inland transport. The network reached its peak in 1914, by which time very few new lines were being built other than some extensions to the London Underground system. Britain now had a railway network of great density. It was soon evident that there would be a price to pay for the overprovision that resulted from earlier government encouragement of railway competition. In the 1920s, it became clear that the network was over-extended as road transport started skimming off the traffic with which it was better equipped to deal. A few lines and individual stations had closed before 1914, often facilities that arguably should never have been opened in the first place. During the war, a number of stations and a few lines closed, theoretically as an economy measure for the duration. Some never reopened.

Lorries and buses proliferated after the war, frequently offering a more convenient, cheaper service than the railway. A 'road lobby' emerged by the end of the First World War. Prominent components were the Automobile Association, the Royal Automobile Club, and the Society of Motor Manufacturers and Traders. The next sixty years was to see huge growth in the ability of this lobby to influence government action and public opinion on measures favourable to the road interest while undermining the interests of the railways. The road lobby managed to get the twenty mph speed limit abolished in 1930. The incidence of road accidents escalated and although a record 7,343 people were killed on the roads in 1934, governments rejected calls for a return to the previous limit.

Passenger miles per annum increased in the inter-war years but while those made on railways remained virtually static, travel by bus and coach grew rapidly. Railways have fixed costs which remain even when traffic falls and this was making an increasing number especially of rural branch lines marginal or loss-making. 1930, an economically troubled time, saw no fewer than 903 route miles of passenger services withdrawn, a sizeable figure forgotten in the furore around the

Beeching Plan in the 1960s. Between 1923 and 1938, over 1,250 route miles lost their passenger services. No legal procedure was laid down to handle objections to closures. Such objections were mostly low-key and in 1931, for example, when a local authority tried to persuade the Cheshire Lines Committee not to close the passenger service to Winsford & Over, the committee simply told them that it was not its job to maintain an unprofitable service.

There was criticism even before 1914 about the waste in capital and manpower which had come about because of the unplanned way in which the railway network had been allowed to develop. Government preference for encouraging competition had led to an excessive duplication of facilities. Writing in 1936, H.G.Lewin somewhat ruefully commented:

> '...we now have to pay for the waste of capital in fruitless Parliamentary contests, uneconomic branch lines, and futile competition which might have been greatly diminished, if not entirely avoided, by the existence of a wise and discriminating Board, such as Gladstone visualised, whose duty it had been to direct our railway development on lines alike compatible with national interests and economic considerations.'[1]

Lewin was referring to the short lived 'Lord Dalhousie's Board' established in 1844.

The railways had come under direct government control during the First World War, indicating the vital importance they were seen as having for the war effort. This implied that private ownership could not be entrusted with the stewardship of the railways at such a critical time. The government formed the managers of the twelve leading companies into a Railway Executive Committee (REC). This required the railways to work within laid-down military and strategic guidelines but with some everyday operating flexibility. Indirect control was preferred to outright nationalisation. In return, the government guaranteed the companies the net revenues they had received in 1913 which had been a good year. Additional payments were made to offset the exceptional wear and tear suffered as the result of the demands of war. The railways had to carry fifty per cent more goods traffic through the war years than they had been carrying before 1914.

Nationalisation was talked about after hostilities ceased but that was a step too far even though political thinking had moved some distance from the *laissez-faire* that was so characteristic of Victorian political economy. It was generally accepted that there could be no return to the wasteful competition which was a feature of the railways before 1914. In the event, the work of the REC continued for two years after the cessation of hostilities. This gave the government a breathing space in which to consider the options for the industry. In 1919, a Ministry of Transport was established. Quickly, a pro-road group of MPs and a growing extra-parliamentary pro-road lobby were determined to ensure that a national plan for co-ordinating all inland transport was a non-starter. This view conflicted with that of the Labour Party. This had MPs including railwaymen who thought that the railways needed to be in state hands and that coordination was necessary.

The private companies did not want a state takeover so, instead of nationalisation, a regional grouping of companies was controversially proposed. Each of these would have a monopoly of its district thereby eliminating competition, at least in theory. The Railways Act of 1921 set up the 'Big Four' regional companies. They were the Great Western (GWR); the Southern (SR); the London & North Eastern (LNER) and the London, Midland & Scottish (LMSR). This 'Grouping' came into legal effect on 1 January 1923.

The 'Big Four' were saddled with the legal obligation to accept all traffic offered for conveyance and to publish details of the charges made for carrying each type of goods. This was to become an increasing burden as road transport, which had no such legal responsibility, began over the next few years to extract from the railways large amounts of merchandise traffic for which they were well suited. The railways were left with an increasingly unattractive residue which could not be charged at commercial rates but which they were legally required to handle. In 1933, the Road and Rail Traffic Act had extended the licensing system to cover all road freight vehicles. Although some relaxation of freight rates was allowed for the railway, the Act was not good news for the railways because firms could now be granted 'C' licences to carry their own goods in their own vehicles. The railways had hoped that this would involve only short-distance collection and delivery but soon many 'C' licence operators were engaged in long-distance haulage.

Large-scale economies which had been hinted at as a result of grouping proved hard to achieve. Not least of these was the difficulty in reducing the vast numbers of non-continuously-braked privately owned wagons of uneconomically small capacity for many of the kinds of load for which the railways were better suited than road haulage. Railway management failed to anticipate the exponential growth of road haulage and the fact that for many kinds of consignment, the roads offered a cheaper and considerably more flexible and convenient service. Although a supposedly free market economy was in existence, the railways were subject to regulations which prevented them altering their rates to compete more effectively with the road haulage industry. The railways launched a 'Square Deal' campaign in 1938, arguing that the railways were not allowed to run their business on commercial and sensible lines. Unlike other businesses, the railways were compelled to comply with laws and restrictions which were obsolete and should have been abolished long before.

The railways also suffered from the decline of heavy industry and mining, areas of business around which they had been built and which they were well equipped to serve effectively. Road transport was better suited to provide the haulage needs of the new light industries expanding at this time. The operating ratio indicating working costs expressed as a percentage of revenue which had been sixty-two in 1900-4 ominously continued moving in the 'wrong' direction to eighty-one in 1934-8.

Evidence of changing governmental attitudes was the development in the inter-war years of statist organisations such as the British Broadcasting Corporation, the British Overseas Airways Corporation and the London Passenger Transport Board. The latter showed how road and rail could be co-ordinated and services improved with state intervention. However, the state could have played a much more positive role in confronting and controlling the competition between road and rail which benefitted neither the rivals nor the public. Governments consistently allowed themselves to be overawed by the growing pro-road lobby.

The railways, in seeking a square deal, did have reasons for considering themselves hard done by. They still had to pay passenger duty on first class tickets, this requirement being based on legislation drawn up as far back as the 1840s. A major grievance was that they had to pay rates to the local authorities where they had their installations. Some of the rate income received by local authorities from the railway companies might be spent on municipally owned tram and bus systems. This meant that the railways were effectively subsidising a competing form of transport. The railways also argued that the cost of the damage done by road vehicles was not reflected in the rates their operators paid, giving them an unfair advantage. Also, unlike railway companies, road hauliers were not required to publish their charges. This enabled them to pick and choose the kinds of consignments which suited them best, unlike the railways who were still legally obliged to convey any consignments offered, irrespective of whether they were profitable or not. The 'Big Four' considered themselves burdened by a mass of restrictive government regulation whereas the road haulage industry was subjected to far less control.

Lessons had been learned from the experience of the First World War and were quickly applied with the outbreak of the Second World War. A revived REC was set up under the Emergency (Railway Control) Order of 1 September 1939. The Minister of Transport, acting through the REC, now had complete control of Britain's railway system. The railway managers assured the minister that with their excess capacity before the war, they would have no difficulty absorbing the increased traffic that would result from the demands of hostilities. They were gravely mistaken. If 1944 is compared with 1938, railway freight traffic rose by nearly fifty per cent and passenger traffic by sixty-eight per cent. The consequence was that rolling stock and other equipment and manpower resources were strained to breaking point and beyond. The railway companies were forbidden to raise their rates and charges to offset the rising wartime costs of labour and materials. Also they were inadequately compensated for the damage sustained from enemy action. Given that investment had been limited in the difficult inter-war years and the system subjected to such excessive demand during the war, Britain's railways were in a very poor state to face the challenges of the second half of the twentieth century. In the post-war world of shortage of raw materials and investment, neither Labour nor Conservative governments gave them any degree of priority. Somehow the network, as British Railways, managed to keep going but was in no state to face the interconnected challenges posed by the huge post-war increase in motor transport and wide-ranging economic and social change.

The Nationalisation Issue

The question of nationalisation first came on to the political agenda in the 1840s as a response to experience gained from the early decades of railway operation. It was clear from earliest times that legal structures were needed to control certain aspects of their activities. The process began whereby they were subjected, largely unwillingly, to increasing amounts of government regulation. Behind this regulation was the perennial question as to whether the pursuit of railway business for private profit was compatible with the provision of services that best met public need.

Nationalisation came onto the political agenda with some force around the turn of the century. The unions in the industry and the nascent Labour Party favoured nationalisation. Private members' bills for nationalisation were introduced each year from 1906 to 1909 and again in 1911 but none obtained a second reading. The issue was forcibly thrust into the limelight as a consequence of the vital role played by the railways in the two world wars. As we have seen elsewhere, the government after 1918 saw outright nationalisation as a step too far but the issue continued to rumble on, there being a widespread feeling that greater government control would be in the interests of both industry and the consumer. The creation of London Transport in 1933 quickly demonstrated the very beneficial impact it had on public transport in the city and it was used by those who favoured nationalisation as an example of the benefits of comprehensive consolidation within the public sector. It gave strength to the growing feeling in some circles that a unified and state-owned railway system would be able to draw on more resources for much-needed modernisation and investment.

During the Second World War, the possibility of nationalisation again began to be voiced, much to the alarm of the 'Big Four' railway companies. From 1943, they started publishing propaganda concerning the improvements they intended to make once peace returned. A campaign was launched against nationalisation but it was somewhat toothless since little common ground appeared to exist between the companies other than hostility to state ownership. The railways and their employees made heroic efforts during the war, only for the industry to emerge in 1945 hopelessly run down with huge arrears of maintenance and in dire financial straits. Urgent restorative action was essential.

In 1946, the 'Big Four' joined with their traditional enemy, the Road Haulage Association, many of whose members were also concerned about nationalisation threats, to challenge the purpose and alleged value of state ownership. They argued that the Labour government was driven by 'socialist dogma'. This government did indeed call itself socialist and it had decisive electoral support for policies intended to bring about comprehensive economic and social change. Its manifesto had made clear its intention to bring the railways under state control. It was also committed to introducing the National Health Service and the Welfare State and nationalising a number of other industries which were vital to the effective operation of an economy that would still be dominated by private enterprise. The use of the word 'socialism' was a jibe suggesting similarities with a collectivist state like Russia but Labour had no intention of proceeding to take over the 'commanding heights' of the economy. It was always firmly wedded to the idea of the 'mixed economy' where private enterprise remained dominant.

There was little effective opposition to the nationalisation of the railways. 1945 was a unique time when a number of factors came together to underpin a widespread public demand for radical new ways of doing things. The post-war world was on no account to see a return to the bad old days of the 1920s and 1930s. The Conservatives under Churchill had been widely expected to win the election of 1945 but Labour gained its decisive and unexpected win because it managed to encapsulate this transient but very real mood. Having put the war behind them, people thought that all the privation they had experienced was only justifiable if a new kind of society was forged where the state intervened to create greater social equity and equality of opportunity. Extensive state intervention had been vital for the war effort and voters had seen that collectivist measures were not necessarily bad.

The propaganda of the 'Big Four' rightly emphasised the vital role of the railways in the war effort and the resulting state of exhaustion and decrepitude in which they had emerged from hostilities. They argued that the dead hand of governmental bureaucracy would descend on the railways, destroying their expertise, flair and initiative (qualities which had not always been too obvious). The popular perception, however, was that government control of the railways during the war was a proven success and that nationalisation was a positive move.

The opposition put up by the railway companies was somewhat half-hearted, perhaps because they knew they did not have the resources to implement the improvements they talked about or because they had received intimations about the compensation that would be offered to shareholders. The senior directors of these companies had considerable influence and were able to negotiate and obtain very favourable terms. The former shareholders were compensated to the tune of over £1,065 million which saddled the newly created British Transport Commission (BTC) with an enormous initial debt. The compensation was seen in some quarters as excessively generous. Servicing the interest on the money borrowed to pay compensation used resources that could have been better used by being invested in improvements on the railways themselves.

Disillusionment with the form of nationalisation that was put in place soon set in when it became clear that it was not the magic bullet that would produce a modern, efficient railway system. It did not help that many of the people who had senior management roles in the private railways and who were hostile to the concept of nationalisation took similar posts in the nationalised railway. Some members of the workforce had entertained hopes that employees would be involved in the management of the state system but talk of that possibility proved to be no more than talk. Earlier public corporations such as the BBC and the Central Electricity Generating Board had governing bodies composed of people supposedly chosen for their suitability by senior ministers. Sectional interests such as the trade unions had no automatic right to be represented on these bodies. It added insult to injury that those who were appointed to the British Transport Commission and were, in effect, the railway workers' bosses, did not necessarily have any experience in the railway industry.

It is not unfair to say that Britain's nationalised railways gained a somewhat undeserved reputation for bureaucratic inefficiency once the initial enthusiasm for a more collective society had waned. The railways and other nationalised industries were a small island of state control in an ocean of private enterprise and the political culture quickly moved to the right and against the concept of nationalisation. The Labour Party proved incapable of making a robust defence of nationalisation when privatisation came up for discussion some decades later.

Nationalisation of the railways after the Second World War was initially envisaged as part of a scheme to create a nationwide integrated transport system. This never came anywhere implementation.

Anti-Railway Culture in the Post-war Years

Since the Second World War, the railways have been subjected to continuous politically motivated interference by governments of both main parties. This means that they operated in an uncertain climate, subject to the whims of their political paymasters. Vast amounts of time, energy and money were spent responding to some possible vacuous government directives which would have been far better used in implementing modernisation and improving efficiency. For much of this period, railways existed in a largely unfavourable economic and political culture. Despite having implemented their nationalisation, Labour governments were not markedly more sympathetic to railways than Tory administrations. Both main parties regarded railways as a financial liability, run-down and in decline. No sooner was the war over than the British Road Federation and the Society of Motor Manufacturers & Traders put pressure on the government to pronounce in favour of a motorway-building programme. Legislation concerning the construction and use of motorways was passed in 1949 but austerity conditions delayed the implementation of the programme.

As always, politicians from all parties had their own purposes and priorities. Often their primary concern is to advance their own careers. Governments normally give priority to attempts to ensure their own survival and ultimate re-election. Parties in opposition seek to promote their own electoral success, not least by trying to bring governments to account for their actions. None of these activities necessarily accords with what is best for the economy, the electorate in general or railways in particular. Ministers of State may come and go very quickly, taking on a portfolio at short notice and often being moved elsewhere without having become fully conversant with the specific requirements of the job. Some have not even wanted the Transport portfolio, it not being among the coveted jobs. In a generally anti-railway culture, few politicians felt it was in their career interests to be seen as seriously pro-railway. Chancellors of the Exchequer, in reviewing public expenditure, looked askance at the losses made by the railways and sought to restrict the cash provided for their support. Ministers and senior civil servants seemed unwilling or unable to identify a clear role for the nationalised railway industry. In rounded terms, the 1950s to the 1980s was a period of disinvestment in Britain's railway network despite the modernisation that took place. It was also a period of disillusionment for many railway employees and railway supporters, despite occasional rays of hope.

As a state responsibility, the railways became a political football and not masters of their own fate. British Railways in 1948 became part of the British Transport Commission which controlled most inland transport. It was required to develop an integrated transport system and to balance its books, including those of the railways. This never happened. From the start there was confusion as to the roles of and relationship between the BTC and the Railway Executive, one of what eventually became six subsidiary Executives with different areas of transport jurisdiction. These Executives never worked together to provide the co-ordination necessary to compete with the growth of road traffic. At the next level down there was friction between the Executive and the managers of the six regions into which the railways were divided. The Executives were, in effect, competitors and even the regions did not necessarily work well with each other.

The railways were not given the tools with which to tackle the job effectively. They were not, for example, permitted to raise their fares and rates to generate the extra income needed for vital modernisation projects. Politicians knew that increased fares were unpopular with the voters and so political expediency all too easily took precedence over what was best for the nation and its railways. Ironically, before the Second World War, the Conservatives had approved of government support for the private railways on the grounds that they were providing an important public service. Post-war, the Conservatives were generally hostile to providing extra money for what was now a nationalised railway system. Nationalised industries always sat uncomfortably in a so-called 'free-market' economy.

It was somehow typical that the Bill that eventually, even painfully, became the Transport Act was plagued in its progress through parliament not so much by debate about how governments could ensure the creation of an economic and efficient railway system in post-war Britain as with wrangling over the terms of compensation to be paid to former railway shareholders.

When nationalisation of the railways took place, there were about 20,000 route miles of passenger services. There was a healthy demand for passenger travel of all kinds after the war but bus and coach usage increased considerably faster than railway patronage. In 1952, petrol rationing ended. With the rising real incomes for many that were a feature of the 1950s and 1960s, car ownership and use started to escalate. Two million cars were owned in 1938. In 1978, that figure had risen to 14.4 million. Car ownership rose markedly faster in rural than in urban areas. Demand for travel went up but private rather than public transport expanded to meet that demand. 1,266 million railway journeys were made in 1946, a figure which fell to 724 million in 1978.

Although freight traffic was being sapped away from the railways by road haulage as early as the 1920s, much of the road haulage industry was nationalised after the Second World War with the intention of integrating it into a coordinated and efficient inland transport system. The Conservative government which gained office in 1951, under pressure from the road lobby denationalised British Road Services in 1953, which by that time was making healthy profits. This denationalisation meant virtually unrestricted competition for certain types of traffic, some with which the railways were very poorly equipped to deal. All talk of a genuinely integrated inland transport system was quietly dropped.

British Railways had some positive achievements during the first five years of nationalisation. By 1952, with a substantial reduction in locomotives and wagons, they were carrying twelve million tons more merchandise than in 1938. Advances were made in productivity and standardisation of equipment. The predominant impression given by much of the system was, however, that of nineteenth-century infrastructure and methods of operation looking increasingly unable to deal with the challenges presented by economic, social and technological change and the inexorable rise of road usage. The cost of providing essential new equipment such as diesel and electric locomotives and multiple-units, colour light signalling, long-welded rails and larger-capacity freight and mineral wagons fitted with continuous brakes, was absolutely daunting. The failure of the BTC to obtain the necessary funding was not necessarily its own fault but took place against a background in which governments did not see railway modernisation as a priority among many other calls for public expenditure. The proportion of UK capital investment given over to railways fell from 4.4 per cent in 1948 to 3.3 per cent in 1951.[2] Far more investment was being made in road building. In 1952, just over £300 million was invested in road transport and around £950 million in 1960 whereas railways received about £40 million in 1952 and £175 million in 1960.[3] Additionally, in the post-war years the railways were starved of their share of the admittedly frugal supplies of steel, much of which, with government encouragement, went to the motor industry when it was still exporting vigorously. It was significant that in 1949 a body was set up to identify loss-making lines and implement closures. While there was dead wood that needed to be lopped, the existence of such a body suggested negative perceptions of railways and their future. It has to be said that there was 'an enemy within' of senior railway managers who were enthusiastic about reducing the size of the system and fitting in with the unfavourable perceptions of railways evident from successive governments. There were also local authorities who, as early as the 1960s, seem to have written the railways off as useful providers of transport. One such authority was Blackpool which gleefully converted the vast site of the closed Central Station into a car and coach park.

In 1953, the Conservative government abolished the various Executives and reorganised the BTC. Its membership was increased but, perhaps significantly, it now contained only two who were career railwaymen. A degree of power was now devolved to the regions, theoretically to encourage more local initiative but the BTC had more direct control than before the Railway Executive was abolished. British Railways was divested of the long-term burden of having to publish its freight charges but the Transport Tribunal and the minister could still veto proposals to increase charges. A nightmare top-heavy bureaucracy was created but as lines and stations closed, the number of hands-on railway workers fell.

The pace of closures of passenger and also of some freight operations stepped up and piecemeal contraction continued at an expanded rate. Between 1950 and 1962, 4,236 route miles closed. The operating methods, often the locomotives, rolling stock and other equipment and even the staff of many branch lines looked as if they had been there since the turn of the century. Sometimes they actually had. Branch lines whose time-hallowed ways of doing things sent certain kinds of railway enthusiasts into transports of delight frankly had no place in the world of the 1950s and 1960s where 'modernisation' was the buzz-word. Railways looked outdated. Churchill, Conservative Prime Minister in succession to Labour's Attlee, believed that railways were inevitably going to play a diminishing role in the country's economy.

In 1951, the Railway Development Society was established. Initially, its main concern was to persuade the BTC to look seriously at introducing economies on branch lines with cheap-to-run diesel trains, for example, rather than simply viewing such lines as liabilities to be disposed of, if necessary after deliberately altering services to inconvenience users. Having changed its name to the Railway Development Association (RDA), in 1953 battle was joined with the Railway Executive over proposals to close most of the system in the Isle of Wight. This was perhaps the first time in which very serious doubt was cast on official figures regarding alleged losses made by specified services. The important factor of 'contributory revenue' was omitted by the Railway Executive in its figures. This was the value of the revenue earned by traffic going to but not originating on the island. Since the Isle of Wight was a very popular holiday destination at this time and most visitors came by rail to the mainland ferry ports and then moved to their destinations on the island by rail, it clearly gave a very misleading impression of the revenue that was generated as a result of the island having its railway system in the first place, even if admittedly it was underused outside the holiday season. Officialdom had no legal requirement to make public the methods employed in its accounting procedures. The protestors demonstrated beyond reasonable doubt that the 'books had been cooked' in order to support the case for closure and not all the closures were immediately implemented.

A constant propaganda war was being waged against the nationalised railway system by the road lobby. It developed very close links with the Conservative administration that gained office in 1951 and with senior officials in the Ministry of Transport. It succeeded in securing denationalisation of road haulage and maintained constant pressure for motorway building and higher speed limits for lorries. Even *The Times* newspaper commented that the road lobby was receiving favoured treatment which contradicted the concept of a serious planned and rounded approach to inland transport. In 1953 there were 5.3 million motor vehicles and in 1962, 10.8 million. Given the exponential growth of road traffic, railway usage inevitably suffered and the BTC plunged into growing debt during that time.

Between the wars, the Southern Railway had embarked on a substantial programme of electrification around the southern Home Counties and down to parts of the south coast. This scheme was generally adjudged successful, being associated with frequent, clean and modern trains. Elsewhere, a few not entirely wholehearted experiments were made with diesel locomotives but it was 1954 before the soon-to-be almost ubiquitous diesel multiple-units were introduced. The operation of these not only effected useful economies but in many cases attracted increased usage, not least because they were clean and had an up-to-date image. Growing numbers of small diesel shunting locomotives came into use but in 1955, steam still accounted for eighty-seven per cent of train haulage with electric trains at ten per cent and diesel at just three per cent.

A Modernisation Plan was indeed published in 1955 which, among other objectives, proposed the elimination of steam locomotives, a nightmarish prospect for much of the sizeable railway enthusiast fraternity. The end of steam was achieved in 1968 but, almost incredibly, new steam locomotives were still entering service as late as 1960. Senior railway managers had taken a long time to be convinced that steam had to be replaced. Once they were convinced, steam locomotives were scrapped with indecent haste and, at least in the case of the newer ones, with scandalously short lives.

The Plan envisaging an expenditure of £1,240 million over fifteen years was proposed. The Plan attempted to tackle the deep-rooted issues of a wide economic and social nature which impacted on the railways by the use of technical means. It seemed to be based on the dubious premise that traffic could be retained or even increased if the system could only be extensively modernised and made more efficient. Steam locomotives of course had to go but what was also needed was a thorough review and overhaul of wider operational methods and commercial practices in light of the radical changes occurring in the post-war boom world of the 1950s and 1960s. Even on lines where diesel multiple-units were increasing passenger patronage, freight services were still almost exclusively steam-hauled and operating methods and staffing levels scarcely different from those of the late Victorian era. In other words, some modernisation would be grafted on to a largely ageing, creaking infrastructure and without serious consideration being given to the growing impact of competition from road transport. Little attention was paid to increasing productivity even where partial modernisation had taken place.

In the heady atmosphere of the then booming economy, it was thought that a modernised railway network might be able to play a useful role in the increased traffic resulting from industrial expansion and growing consumer spending power. Demonstrably, modernisation could bring substantial benefits. Following completion of the electrification throughout from London to Crewe and on to Liverpool or Manchester, services were greatly accelerated, passenger receipts went up by fifty per cent and passenger journeys by sixty-five per cent, custom being won back from the airways.[4]

British Rail runs out of steam

Last steam train makes historic special farewell journey Sunday August 11th

Liverpool/Manchester to Carlisle & back

This will be the very last train to operate on
standard gauge track headed by a B.R. steam locomotive. 314 nostalgic miles, 10¼ happy hours, with
luncheon, high tea, other refreshments, souvenir
ticket and souvenir scroll. 15 guineas.
Liverpool Lime Street Dep 09.10 – Arr 19.50
Manchester Victoria Dep 11.06 – Arr 18.48
For Tickets, Write quickly to Passenger
Marketing Manager, British Rail, London Midland
Region, Euston House, London NW1. Mark your
envelope Personal and enclose £15.15 per ticket
required. Money immediately refunded if the 470
seats have already been sold.

British Rail

Publicity for the so-called '15 Guinea Special' which British Rail operated on
11 August 1968 to mark the end of regular steam-hauled trains on its standard
gauge tracks. The fare was considered a rip-off at the time but the train was
inevitably over-subscribed and huge crowds turned out along the route to
witness the event. No one could have foreseen the renaissance of innumerable
special steam-hauled trains on many parts of the nationalised and then the
privatised railway network given the almost indecent haste with which British
Rail had rid itself of steam traction from the mid-1950s. (Authors' collection)

This was positive but the reasoning behind the Plan seemed to forget that orthodox methods of railway freight operation could not match up to the more convenient door-to-door service provided by road transport for many kinds of traffic, particularly that associated with the light industries and service economy which was replacing Britain's heavy industry for which the railways were well-suited. Predictions that modernisation would turn the economic fortunes of the railways round seemed to be based on an assumption of wage and price stability. Inevitability this was not to be after the Guillebaud Committee had recommended an immediate and substantial increase in railway workers' pay. Better pay and conditions were overdue but what was now set in motion was a merry-go-round of wage increases being chased by largely impotent efforts to cover them by raising fares and charges.

Whatever enthusiasm the Modernisation Plan generated in politicians' minds soon ebbed in the face of the unremitting pressure of the pro-road lobby and the massive growth of road traffic. Just two months after the Modernisation Plan was published, the government announced plans for a huge motorway-building programme only for the British Road Federation to grumble that it was not enough. Also in 1955, the Society of Motor Manufacturers & Traders established a Roads Campaign Council to co-ordinate the activities of the various road lobbies and campaign for more motorways and upgrading of trunk roads. The railways were seemingly regarded as a financial black hole into which ever-increasing amounts of taxpayers' money were poured without any apparent benefit. Those who used the roads did not pay the full cost of road infrastructure and services while the railways were expected to finance their own maintenance from receipts rather than taxation. Motorways were extremely expensive to build. The cost of their construction and maintenance effectively meant less money available for railways. A burgeoning motorway programme showed that governments saw roads as the predominant inland transport mode of the future.

Even an enthusiastically pursued modernisation plan supported by adequate financial resources would have taken years to demonstrate its benefits. Governments were not prepared to give it the funding or the time. The cost of modernisations was revised upwards to £1,660 million in 1957. The scepticism with which the Plan was regarded in official circles is perhaps evident in the fact that that it was reappraised by the BTC in 1956 and 1959. Since the railways were now firmly on the political agenda, what had to be decided was whether governments were prepared to underwrite unprofitable operations on the basis that they met essential social need or whether British Railways should be allowed to operate without commercial restraint. A reluctance to commit major resources to thorough modernisation was shown by the shilly-shallying over electrification of the London to Manchester and Liverpool routes and the long-term postponement of the electrification of the East Coast Main Line.

Commercial Motor on 28 January 1955 dismissed the Plan as 'a waste of resources which would have been better spent on Britain's roads'. We would disagree with this comment but have to say that a real hash was made of the process of ordering expensive diesel locomotives to act, theoretically, as a stopgap until comprehensive electrification took place, some time in the undefined future. Far too many types were introduced. Many were ordered straight off the drawing board without the testing of prototypes and some classes were withdrawn after very short lives as hopelessly unfit for purpose. For example, the North British Locomotive Company was favoured with many contracts at least partly to allay unemployment in Glasgow's East End but despite a proud history of steam locomotive construction, they could not adapt successfully to the demands of the new technology. Huge amounts of public money were spent on building vast marshalling yards for wagonload freight traffic that was already ebbing away. These yards were never used to full capacity and most closed very quickly. The Modernisation Plan was ill thought-out and incompetently executed. As Gerard Fiennes (2015), a very senior railway manager said in a book that got him sacked, 'We had made the basic error of buying our tools before doing our homework on defining the job.'

Even though the Modernisation Plan brought about increased productivity and efficiency, the culture in parliament and among most of the media remained largely sceptical of, or actually hostile to railways. Their losses continued to mount, seemingly out of control despite diesel multiple units attracting much new passenger traffic. Governments wanted profitability without being prepared to provide the resources to achieve it, even had it been possible. Admittedly, volatile and unpredictable international events destabilised the British economy and created an aura of uncertainty in which heavy investment in railways was seen as a low priority. In 1959, a Conservative government under Harold Macmillan came into office imbued with a 'rubber tyres on tarmacadam good, steel wheels on rails bad' philosophy. In 1960, the Conservative Minister of Transport, Ernest Marples, appointed the Stedeford Group to examine the industry and identify the role to be played, if any, by the railways in the British inland transport system of the future. Stedeford himself came from the motor industry. The group contained no representatives of the railway industry but it did feature Dr Richard Beeching from ICI, soon to achieve national notoriety. The findings were never actually published but it seems likely that these 'experts' from the world of industry and commerce confirmed what the government wanted to hear; that the railway's role was a declining one. Such secrecy surrounded the group's findings that Barbara Castle when Minister of Transport never had access to it and years later Margaret Thatcher as prime minister claimed the documentation could not be located.

It is hard to view Marples as an honest broker given his business interests in a sizeable road construction company. When quizzed about a possible clash of interests, he was at pains to point out that, on appointment, he had rid himself of his shares. He omitted to point out that he had put them in the hands of his wife. He was insistent that the railways should be self-financing and it is likely that had he remained in office longer he would have been prepared to use any methods in an attempt to achieve that end. Why should money be spent modernising an inefficient transport system rooted in Victorian times when new motorways and improved road systems could handle the country's transport needs far more effectively? And enrich him at the same time. In government circles, the received wisdom was that the income generated by roads greatly exceeded the cost of road building and maintenance. Coyly omitted from consideration was the cost of the pollution, congestion, policing, accident damage, litigation and medical bills that were inescapable as road traffic increased year by year. Yet the juggernaut continued to roll on, literally. The venom directed at the railways was made clear in an article in the April 1960 copy of the Road Haulage Association's journal:

'We should build more roads, and we should have fewer railways. This would merely be following the lessons of history which shows a continued and continuing expansion of road transport and a corresponding contraction in the volume of business handled by the railways…A streamlined railway system could surely be had for half the money that is now made available…We must exchange the "permanent way" of life for the "motorway" of life…road transport is the future, the railways are the past.'[5]

The priority given by the Ministry of Transport to road affairs over railway matters was evident because by 1966 at least eighty per cent of its staff dealt with road business while the railways' share was just one per cent. At senior level, roads were allocated eleven under-secretaries while railways enjoyed the services of one. A worker for the Ministry who wanted career advancement needed unequivocally to be pro-road.

Many of the station closures which had already occurred were of rural wayside stations on main lines, these often having a very limited service. The stops involved frequently generated little usage but impeded the passage of faster passenger and other traffic which generated greater income. The East Coast Main line, for example, lost many such wayside stations in the 1950s and 1960s. Most of these closures and those of entire branch passenger services took place without arousing much protest, despite the fact that after stopping services had been withdrawn, the trains rushing through no more served the local community than did a passenger aircraft flying overhead. Little-used many of them may have been but the fact that they had closed acted as a disincentive to rail travel for local people who now, instead of driving to the nearest railhead, might decide that it was simply easier and more practical to use the car for the whole journey. The closure of a little-used passenger station here or an entire passenger service there may have saved some money but it contributed to a growing perception that railways were on their way out and that private transport was a more flexible, convenient and often quicker and cheaper means of getting from A to B.

After the nationalisation of the railways, successive governments seemed to view the railways as a financial millstone. Many of their operations, some of which they were still legally required to carry out, and others, were now hopelessly unprofitable given the rise of private motoring and road haulage. The Treasury desperately wanted to reduce the drain on the public finances needed to support the railways. Both passenger and freight traffic were leaching away in the 1950s while costs were increasing in real terms. Meanwhile, those few politicians who were not openly hostile to railways remained wedded to the idea that at some stage, a miracle would occur and the economic fortunes of the railways would be turned round.

The twentieth century was not kind to Britain's railways. The infrastructure and technology necessary for even the simplest railway operations have fixed costs not simply proportional to the volume of usage. Income began ebbing away once road transport became an effective competitor for certain kinds of traffic after the First World War. This made lightly used lines and stations proportionately more costly to operate and often loss-making. Even in the 1920s, it was becoming obvious that Britain's railways were over-extended and contraction began. They had been taken to the limit and beyond by the demands of the two world wars and in 1945 were in a state of near-collapse. The huge expansion of private motoring, changing social habits and the decline of the heavy industries which had provided much of their staple business hit them hard in the 1950s and 1960s. The decline of heavy industry and the use of alternative fuels reduced coal and coke traffic, for so long an essential part of the railway's business. Those industries whose fortunes were buoyant frequently found road transport more appropriate to their needs. No other European railway lost such a large proportion of its freight traffic in the 1950s and 1960s as British Railways although this has to be seen in the context of wider economic and industrial change.

Nationalisation came with strings attached and led to the railways becoming a football kicked hither and thither dependent on the very capricious whims of their political masters. No one begrudges railway workers decent wages but the wages bill rose rapidly while rates and fares increased, although relatively less. In 1955, revenue no longer even covered operating costs. With railways making growing losses, they were accused, not necessarily without some justification, of being incompetently managed and subjected to a constant barrage of abuse in the media to the effect that they were inefficient, out-of-date and an intolerable drain on taxpayers' money. It was clear that most politicians supported road against rail transport.

Anguished debates took place about the kind of traffic, if any, for which railways were best suited, about what criteria should be used to assess the costs and benefits of railways and particularly how these could be compared with those of the roads. If it was accepted that the world in which railways operated was changing, were there ways to modernise their activities to make them more efficient and competitive even if the size of the system was reduced. Should there be a concept of 'socially necessary' services which could not conceivably be profitable from an accountant's point of view but which could be shown to serve real social need?

The Conservative government of 1959 set about reorganising nationalised transport undertakings under the Transport Act of 1962. This abolished the British Transport Commission and replaced it with the British Railways Board (BRB). What was now 'British Railways' saw the writing-off of much of its predecessor's debts. The principle underpinning the government's approach was that the BRB must be run on commercial lines. The long-standing and very burdensome common carrier obligation of the railways was abolished and the BRB was given almost total freedom to fix passenger fares and freight rates and choose the freight traffic it wished to handle according to the perceived dictates of the commercial market. Any vestigial idea of a co-ordinated national public transport went by the board. The chairman of the British Railways Board was Dr Richard Beeching. He was soon to become a reviled man.

Of concern to the growing band of people not prepared to stand by and watch the decimation of the railways were changes made under the 1962 Act to the powers of the Transport Users' Consultative Committees (TUCCs). They were now told that issues around the wider social and strategic implications of closure were irrelevant to their deliberations and that their only concern was to consider claims of hardship when closure proposals were being examined. Debates were not to be allowed and the TUCCs were to report their findings directly to the Minister of Transport. They were not permitted to make recommendations. The possibility that a line being proposed for closure provided considerable contributory revenue was not germane to a TUCC's deliberations. The government was loading the dice in favour of closure. Every time a line closed, some traffic transferred to the roads. It is hard not to think that this was the desired outcome. Politicians at this time knew that there were more votes to be garnered from policies encouraging road usage than from those favourable to railways.

Beeching

In 1960, British Railways had an operating deficit of £67.7 million; in 1961 one of £87 million and a nadir was reached in 1962 with £104 million. The Conservative government under Harold Macmillan decided that drastic action was needed. The Transport Act of 1962 was swiftly followed up in 1963 by the publication of *The Reshaping of British Railways,* commonly known as the 'Beeching

Report'. This had a stunning impact with its long list of services and individual stations identified as loss-making after a traffic survey over one week ending 23 April 1961. It came as a great shock when the Beeching Report revealed that half the route miles of the network carried just four per cent of the traffic. Five thousand route miles and 2,363 stations out of a total of about 7,000 were recommended for closure. The report's author, Dr Richard Beeching, became a household name overnight. He had been a member of the Stedeford Group and was a metallurgist, physicist and director of ICI with no specific knowledge of transport, let alone of railways. This immediately alienated career railway workers at all levels. The Labour Party was noisily critical of his appointment but after a Labour government was elected to office in October 1964 it cannot be said that there was any very sharp break from its predecessor's attitude to the railways or the Beeching Plan itself.

Beeching worked to the remit of the BRB, which was to create a system that balanced its books. This meant that loss-making services needed to be culled while investment should be directed into operations that offered good profits – mainly inter-city passenger services and trainload freight traffic. Perceptions of the report and its recommendations were shown by the common use of the term 'Beeching Axe', employed as if it was synonymous with butchery. *The Times* (16 March 1961) commented tartly that Beeching had been appointed by the government to sort out its greatest loss-maker and report to a Minister whose interest lay with redirecting resources into road transport.

Reviled Beeching may have been but he did the job he was given, which was to produce recommendations that, if implemented, were intended to make radical improvements to the economic state of the railways. He could be criticised for the theory underpinning the recommendations he made but the implementation of those recommendations was not within his remit. Beeching did not have the power to close railway lines. A pertinent question, however, was how to reach an objective means of ascertaining the costs of running any particular stretch of railway since every line was part of the national network. No line ran in glorious isolation and all took their share of the pool of resources allocated to the railway network as a whole. Doubt always existed about the validity of the statistics contained in the report.

In all, the passenger-carrying mileage contracted by 5,700 route miles from 1962 to 1970. Sizeable parts of the country were deprived of access to rail transport. Some would say that this was a victory for the pro-road lobby, battering away constantly promoting an anti-railway culture. No attempt was made to subject the cost of the congestion, injuries and death on the roads, the physical damage done by heavy goods vehicles or the impact of environmental pollution created by road vehicles to similar quantitative scrutiny. Jeremy Thorpe for the Liberals warned the House of Commons against the danger of examining railways policy in isolation from transport problems in general. This, he said, would be 'like a judge making up his mind on the evidence of one expert witness'.

Beeching, who was presumably chosen for an analytical mind combined with scientific and business experience, could sometimes give the impression of considerable naivety. Only this could account for his bland claim that the passengers whose railway services were being closed would happily switch to bus replacement services. He was 'away with the fairies' when he stated:

> 'People who can afford to choose won't motor between the main centres of population. They don't now and they won't in the future.'[6]

Where 'bustitution' took place, the replacement services rarely lasted long, there being no statutory requirement for their continuance. Those whose passenger trains were taken away largely rejected buses, bought cars and turned their back on the railways.

Writing in 1965, G. Freeman Allen in his assessment of the man stated:

> 'The Beeching regime did far more than lop off the British railway network a good deal of miserably under-utilised, rural network. Dr Beeching's outstanding achievements are: first, to have driven the British public to face the fact that retention of a national railway system on its historic scale deep into the motor age will cost them an increasingly frightening and unnecessary fortune; and, second, to have comprehensively re-educated the management of an industry that before his arrival was shackled from top to bottom by time-hallowed methods and techniques of running and selling its product. In brief, he transformed a browbeaten, rather aimless social service into the making of an aggressive modern industry.'[7]

This may be true, but a very pertinent criticism of the report was that railways were examined largely in isolation from other forms of transport. A holistic approach would have taken into account all forms of transport on a national basis in an attempt to identify which modes were best suited for each purpose and then to plan accordingly against the background of the overall needs of the economy. Instead, by isolating the railways in this way, it looked as if they were being picked on by a government seeking to justify its own anti-railway bias. The narrowness of the report's vision also meant that, for example, lines were proposed for closure serving areas where New Towns had been designated. There were even branch lines closed where adequate bus replacement cost more than maintaining the passenger service on the railway. An example was the Yatton to Clevedon Branch in Somerset.

The entire thrust of the report was about curtailing the network. It was not in the report's brief to suggest cost-saving measures that might have reprieved some marginal lines. Whether or not by design, the traffic survey on which it was based took place at a time of year which gave a highly misleading impression of passenger usage, especially to holiday destinations such as seaside resorts. The line to Skegness, for example, might be used to saturation point at times in the summer but would be relatively little-used in April.

The much less-known Part Two of the Beeching Report, *The Development of the Major Trunk Routes*, identified those lines in which investment was considered worthwhile. Implicit in this was that the rest were not seen as having a long-term future. Beeching did, however, envisage a future for express passenger services, block freight trains and 'liner' or what would later be called bi-modal container trains. Part Two did not receive the attention accorded to Part One which is perhaps surprising seeing that it envisaged no long-term railway west of Plymouth or Swansea, for example. This report was not published until 1965 by which time a Labour government had replaced the Conservatives. In June 1965, Dr Beeching returned to senior management at ICI. He left the railway scene, seemingly unfazed by the hornets' nest he had stirred up. He predicted that the changes he had proposed, if fully implemented, would enable Britain's railways to make 'a good profit'. He was chasing a chimera.

The impact of Beeching was all the greater because for the first time, the issue of closures was being examined on a nationwide basis. Before, closures had seemingly been random. The branch line from Yelverton to Princetown in Devon was a typical example of a line which succumbed to closure well before the 'Beeching era'. It carried convicts to Dartmoor gaol, ramblers in good weather and not much of anything else. It closed in 1956, despite the knowledge that many roads on Dartmoor were impassable in winter and that the line undoubtedly had a potential for far more tourist traffic. As with so many other closures, no serious attempt had been made to mix judicious modernisation with greater efficiency and cost-cutting. Rather, a negative approach was often implemented whereby the level of service was reduced to the extent that it became a deterrent to travel. Fewer trains were used by fewer people and official utterances that 'the line doesn't pay' became a self-fulfilling prophecy. The oldest, most decrepit rolling stock was decanted to many branch lines and while railway enthusiasts may have revelled in the experience of travelling in a vintage carriage, most passengers received the negative impression of an outdated, inefficient and inconvenient mode of transport.

It had come as a serious shock in 1957 when rumours began to circulate that the authorities wanted to close the bulk of the former Midland & Great Northern Joint Railway system. It was argued that most of the system ran at a loss, that the rural nature of its territory meant little potential for new traffic, that much traffic had already been lost to the roads and that extensive repair work was needed, the expense of which could not be justified because of the losses. On summer Saturdays, heavy holiday traffic still ran to and from the Norfolk Coast but it was declining and could be handled by alternative routes. The fact that the line was used to capacity on those Saturdays with crowded trains gave a specious appearance of prosperity and permanence but trains ran largely empty for much of the year. The closure proposal went through the statutory process and many objections were heard from seaside hoteliers, for example, but it was indisputable that this system was playing a rapidly decreasing role and most of it closed in 1958. It was a wake-up call that the world which created Britain's intensive railway network was changing and that large parts of the latter were vulnerable especially in the face of the seemingly inexorable rise of the family car and changing social habits. This was an uncomfortable reality which hit home much harder when the 'Beeching Report' was published.

The closure proposals in the Beeching Report in general met with considerable opposition, and some were particularly contentious.

Among these were the Dumfries to Stranraer and Whitby to Scarborough lines and it seemed incredible that it was proposed to leave a town the size of Mansfield without passenger services. Questions were asked about how the statistical evidence on usage had been compiled and many people believed that it was not an objective analysis but the product of a fundamental anti-railway mindset. This portrayed railways as a drain on financial resources because so much of the system lost money while, by contrast, money going to roads was seen as an investment. It was also criticised for ignoring wider social and economic issues than simply the financial viability of this or that station or line. It called into question whether any national railway network could be financially self-sustaining in the second half of the twentieth century. With the rapid growth of road traffic that was all-too apparent, voices were raised about what would happen when the road system reached gridlock. The almost contemporary Buchanan Report, *Traffic in Towns*, had made it clear that this was indeed a possibility but closures went ahead despite such warnings. It seemed almost incredible that electrified, heavily used but apparently loss-making lines in densely populated urban areas such as those from Liverpool to Southport or Manchester to Bury were being proposed for closure. In the event, neither of these did close. While it seemed that many people seemed comforted by knowing that that the railways were there while never actually using them, it was only to be expected that there would be a hostile reception to the report which, for example, with complete insouciance proposed to rob a city the size of Nottingham of many services to London. Anti-closure protests were becoming more professional and some services such as that from Manchester to Buxton were reprieved after robust submissions before the relevant TUCC.

The method of crediting income only to the stations where traffic originated was widely criticised. This meant, for example, that Birmingham Snow Hill would garner all the income from the considerable number of passengers booking there to travel for holiday purposes to, say, Aberystwyth or Barmouth. These stations would be credited with none of the income.

Bernard Hollowood, writing in *Punch* (23 August 1967) made clear his opinion of Beeching:

'Lord Beeching is praised by many for his ruthlessness. He was given a job of making the railways pay, and to this task he applied precisely the same tools that he would use to make a cosmetics company pay its way. His recipe was to cut out all uneconomic lines. Simple, but utterly naïve and in callous disregard of the convenience of millions. He could make the hospitals or schools pay by similar methods.'

Given that the BRB was told to make the railways break even, its priority became the most obvious form of cost-cutting which was closures. Of course there were routes which had little or no potential for developing new traffic but many considerable economies could have been made along the lines of the 'basic railway' advocated by Gerry Fiennes and applied successfully to the East Suffolk Line between Ipswich and Lowestoft. Railways had a long tradition of being highly labour-intensive and although the workforce had been decreasing continuously for decades, falling traffic meant there was overstaffing. With a basic railway there was an unhappy balance between passenger trains still running but the stations at which they called mostly becoming little more than an unstaffed platform with a bus shelter; creating potential insecurity among users and a negative perception of rail travel. This could be a disincentive to use trains, giving the impression of nasty, if not cheap, travel and an industry in decline. Over time, people became used to the basic railway. They may not have liked it but it was better than no railway at all.

British Railways looked as if it was determined to close certain lines at any cost. Selective culling of trains might render the services on a line inconvenient or virtually useless and as usage inevitably fell away, it would be triumphantly declared that the line did not pay. Sometimes routes marked for closure but not yet considered by the Transport Users' Consultative Committee would be omitted from public timetables. This was officially described as an 'oversight' but no one believed it. Some lines passed through two or more regions, each of which advertised in its timetables only that section of the route lying within their region. For those not in the know, the inter-regional nature of the service might not be apparent.

The procedure was for the proposal to close a particular passenger service to be adjudicated on by the appropriate regional Transport Users' Consultative Committee if objections were raised. The case would be considered and a report made which would be submitted to the Minister of Transport for a decision. The system was loaded in favour of the closure proposal because objectors were not allowed to question the financial figures submitted by British Railways nor how those figures had been reached. There was no requirement to 'open the books' even when opponents of closure managed to point out inconsistencies in BR's figures, a not uncommon occurrence. The TUCC had to decide whether genuine hardship would follow a service closure. Mere inconvenience was not enough. They also had to decide whether buses could provide an effective substitute service. They rarely did. Each regional TUCC submitted its findings as a recommendation to the Central TUCC but the final say was with the Minister of Transport. The Minister was perfectly entitled to close a line even if the TUCC had submitted evidence that hardship would be caused.

Another source of disgruntlement was that British Railways did not have to refer proposed closures of freight services and depots for adjudication to the TUCC or anyone else. Where freight services were withdrawn, the passenger services were left to bear the entire cost associated with keeping the line open. In most cases, this would tip marginal passenger services into the red. It seemed that here was a nationalised industry which was virtually unaccountable to the public. Both main parties had accused nationalised industries of being bureaucratic monoliths. Now they were demanding the elimination of much of the railway network and supporting the lack of transparency around the figures submitted as justification for closure proposals.

The report emerged just at a time when a feeling was developing that the uncontrolled growth of road transport and expansion of the road system were generating serious environmental problems. The brief that Beeching worked to required him to identify those railway operations that made money and for which railways remained effective providers and also to highlight those for which railways in the second half of the nineteenth were ill-suited. Many stopping passenger services, wagonload traffic and underused minor lines were little better than basket cases. However, his recommendations seemingly failed to consider the fact that branch lines fed traffic into main lines and that when branch lines closed, the odds were that their former passengers would not drive to the nearest railhead. Instead they would use their own cars, create pollution and almost certainly be lost to the railways. Beeching's job was only to recommend. It was inevitable that he would be made to look like the villain, intent on closing the railways down.

His brief was to deal with the contemporary situation, not to predict future developments which might make closures and cutbacks short-sighted or worse, as so many have proved to be. His brief did not include consideration of wider environmental factors. The Beeching Plan did not rescue the railway's finances. It was flawed thinking even to consider that it might do so.

Governments themselves were inconsistent and unprincipled. They refused to close such grossly loss-making lines as Glasgow and Girvan to Stranraer and the Central Wales line (now the Heart of Wales Line), seemingly doing so for reasons of political expediency. Such lines often ran through marginal constituencies and politicians did not want to be associated with closures at times when elections were in the air. Railways were therefore pawns in the dirty game of politics. Before the general election of 1964, Harold Wilson had promised that if Labour won then it would halt closures and set up a national transport survey. Labour did win and the incoming government reneged on its promise. No survey and a new Minister of Transport, Tom Fraser, notable only for his aversion to railways.

Given the number of station and even line re-openings in recent years, the rise in passenger usage and the ever-increasing congestion on the roads, it is very clear that the thinking behind the Beeching Plan was a short-sighted, kneejerk reaction to the ever-mounting losses being made by Britain's railways and the pressure of a deeply rooted pro-road culture at government level. The vicissitudes of so-called market economics can make long-term planning very difficult but this was short-termism at its worst. Assets were destroyed, the loss of which was quickly regretted. One service, that connecting Peterborough to Spalding, was restored with local authority financial support within a year of initial withdrawal. The current plans regarding HS2 involve a state-of-the-art partial replacement of capacity destroyed during the 1960s and 1970s as the result of the machinations of politicians who could not see beyond their anti-railway prejudices. The taxpayer, as ever, pays the bill.

Although its run-down began before the Beeching era, the case of the former Great Central Extension from the East Midlands to London was an example of the squandering of assets which, had they survived into the twenty-first century, could have proved invaluable. The London Extension was built as a superbly engineered line, designed for high-speed and with a generous loading gauge. It had few junctions but those it did have enabled the operation of interesting freight and passenger services from the North-East, Yorkshire and Humberside towards the South Coast, the South-West and South Wales. It was never a particularly lucrative line but its problems really began when it was transferred from the Eastern to the London Midland Region (LMR) in 1958. The LMR saw it as a competitor, particularly with the Midland Main Line, and they began to run it down. Long-distance expresses from Manchester and the West Riding were withdrawn in 1960, wayside stations were closed, freight traffic diverted as were the cross-country trains and then the Nottingham to Marylebone semi-fast trains were taken off. The run-down of this latter provision was almost criminal. Trains were few and far between and ran at times which made a mockery of anything approaching a useful service. The line was made the dumping ground for the LMR's most decrepit hand-me-down former express steam locomotives. These broke down with great frequency and the service became notoriously unreliable, so much so that the region was able to say, perhaps with an air of studied amazement, that no one was using it. A vestigial Rugby to Nottingham local service was withdrawn in 1969. Outer-suburban services still ran into and out of the London terminus at Marylebone but as mentioned elsewhere, there were even proposals to rip up the track and use it as an approach road to Marylebone, converted into a coach station. The Great Central was by no means the only line that was purposely run down to make it unattractive as a travel option.

Chiltern Railways have made a considerable success of sections of the route to serve parts of the Home Counties, the West Midlands and, more recently, Oxford, doing so in competition with existing routes and no longer viewed negatively as a duplicate facility. To some extent, the Great Central was the victim of inter-regional jealousies at senior management level but there was no mood among civil servants and ministers to save or even mothball it on the grounds that it might be useful in the future. The capacity that it represented would have proved invaluable given today's congested railways and might have rendered the idea of a brand new High Speed Line unnecessary.

Perhaps the implementation of much of the Beeching Plan can be seen as a victory for the anti-railway lobby but events have shown that it was a pyrrhic victory.

Campaigns against the Closure of Lines

We have considered various kinds of opposition to and criticisms of railways and their activities in the nineteenth century. We will now look briefly at the time during which the wheel turned full circle and vehement arguments and a diverse range of reasons were put forward as to why railways should not be closed. Especially in the period from the 1950s to the mid-1980s, the tide seemed to be flowing against the railways but as the pace of proposed closures accelerated so the opposition to closures became more organised and professional. Some of the closure proposals that generated the greatest opposition were of lines that had not even been earmarked for closure in the Beeching Plan.

Among the groups fighting the corner for the railways was the Railway Development Association. It was concerned about the attitude of governments and the general public towards railways and the unfavourable light in which they were frequently seen. They wanted to combat the closure of branch lines and claimed that many were being deliberately run down and starved of investment. Another was the Branch Line Reinvigoration Society which changed its name to the more proactive 'Railway Invigoration Society' and then, in 1972, Transport 2000 was set up. Organisations like these often had members who were professional economists or statisticians who were able to use their skills to good effect. Pro-closure railway managers regarded them as a perishing nuisance and sometimes wondered whether the savings made by closure were actually worth all the time, money and effort put into securing them.

The British had long developed a sentimental attachment to their railways even if by the 1950s they increasingly seldom used them, finding buses and especially the private car more convenient. This affectionate regard for railways is exemplified by the charmingly eccentric drawings of 'Emett', or in the film *The Titfield Thunderbolt* and it applied particularly to branch lines in rural areas. Unfortunately, it was often such lines that had by then become hopelessly uneconomic to operate. When threats of any particular closure were first mentioned, protestors would emerge to challenge the anonymous apparatchiks who dared to decree that a particular branch line had to produce an operating surplus. Here we examine a number of closure proposals and some of the objections that were lodged against them.

The railways of the Isle of Wight were a system in miniature. The east of the island was well provided, indeed overprovided, with lines but only one line struck out into the west of the island, that from Newport to Yarmouth and Freshwater. The south-west of the island was always bereft of railways. By the 1950s, the railways of the Isle of Wight were running at a considerable loss. Burdened with overcapacity out of the holiday season, summer Saturdays in particular stretched the system to crisis point and beyond as tens of thousands of holidaymakers set off for home by train and ferry only to be met with similar hordes of arriving holidaymakers. Early in 1953, proposals were put forward to close down much of the island's railway network and the arguments put forward for closure and against closure gave a foretaste of some of the epic battles that were to be fought against the closure proposals put forward in the Beeching Plan. The main case of British Railways was that the island's railways were loss-making, which was undeniable, and that substantial savings could be made by closing the most unremunerative lines. Opposition was led by the Isle of Wight Chamber of Commerce and the County Council whose main argument was that the local economy, so dependent on tourism, would be ruined by closures and that the suggestion that buses should replace trains on those lines slated for closure was simply unrealistic in terms not only of moving the passengers but also their luggage, prams and other paraphernalia. The roads of the island were narrow, winding and ill-equipped to handle most traffic. The problems stemming from the fact that the vast majority of visitors arrived and left from Ryde were accepted and it was suggested that ways be found to encourage greater use of the alternative ferry routes although they recognised that problems also existed with these. Additionally, it was contended that British Railways was over-centralised and had little knowledge of, or interest in, issues that were local and unique to places like the island.

One factor in the closure proposals that was called into question then and often later concerned the methods used to arrive at these proposals. How could the public question, let alone verify, the financial figures that British Railways used in support of their case for closure? The TUCC produced a report in which it argued that whatever savings were made, the island's railways were bound to run at a loss. While they were intrinsically loss-making, they met essential economic and social needs. Whatever the virtue of this argument, the Isle of Wight railway system was in the process of contraction. Merstone to Ventnor West had already closed in 1952. 1953 saw the end of the Newport to Freshwater and the Bembridge services and Newport to Sandown lost its services in 1956. The system now consists of just the Ryde to Ventnor route.

The branch line from Wivenhoe to Brightlingsea in Essex was the creation of an impecunious local company which needed financial support from the Great Eastern Railway. The latter operated the services in return for a percentage of what were always frugal takings. The line opened in 1866. In 1953, the line was said to be losing £8,000 annually. It was proposed for closure in that year after the line had been severed in the infamous East Coast floods of that year. The local TUCC handled the case for closure and also the objections. Among the issues raised was that the town, being a minor seaside resort, would lose trade from day-trippers if the line closed. In fact even as early as 1953, most of those visiting Brightlingsea for the day already came by car or coach. It was claimed that the branch had a poor service but there was actually a generous provision of well over a dozen trains in each direction. Outside holiday times, only about 130 people used the trains daily. It was suggested that cheaper fares would encourage greater use. British Railways argued that the line made a loss but did not provide figures relating to actual usage. However, they claimed that passenger figures would have to rise to unattainable levels if the line was to become profitable. It was pointed out that proposed replacement buses would be slower and more inconvenient. Similar objections were frequently made when proposals were put forward for passenger services to be withdrawn but some arguments were unique to the Brightlingsea case. It was argued that the line must be retained for the transport of sprats. Sprat numbers were notoriously unpredictable but had been falling for some time and it was clear that the line could not be kept open in the hope that the sprats might decide to return in commercially viable numbers. Reference was made to the local trade in fresh oysters. This was ongoing but the oysters were already going to market by road. It was claimed that the line had been of strategic importance in the last war and should be retained against the possibility of another war. The line was then reprieved and services continued but even with diesel trains, patronage remained poor. It could be argued that British Railways did nothing to improve services but beyond the use of diesel trains it is hard to know what could have been done. No sensible case could have been made for electrification. Closure came, inevitably, on 15 June 1964.

The Southern Railway opened a line to Allhallows-on-Sea on the Isle of Grain in north Kent in 1932. The Southern had high hopes that Allhallows would develop into a popular resort. It was not to be. Beyond a pub and a parade of shops, Allhallows scarcely developed. It was a bleak, dreary place with acres of Thames mud and it never became the hoped-for hugely popular destination for pleasure-seekers. The first proposal to withdraw passenger services from Gravesend to Allhallows came in March 1960 but it was rejected by the TUCC largely on the grounds that the proposed bus replacement services would be inadequate. The local roads were notoriously poor. Licking its wounds, British Railways then produced figures showing how usage was in steep decline and losses building up. No effort was made to effect economies and the usual 'dirty' tactics were employed such as cutting out late evening trains making the service less attractive. Another closure proposal was lodged. Objectors were very suspicious of the methods British Railways had employed to produce figures as evidence of the losses being made but there was no obligation to demonstrate how the figures were reached. It was, however, shown that they did not include special summer excursion trains some of which carried as many as 1,000 passengers. It was clear that British Railways was intent on closing the passenger service and duly did so from 4 December 1961, causing considerable hardship and ironically at a time when the line's oil and aggregates traffic was building up.

A speedy through railway link between Oxford and Cambridge would seem to be a natural winner but such a link has never existed. From its inception under the auspices of the London & North Western Railway, the route had been operated in sections, the only part with a relatively intensive service being that from Bedford to Bletchley. There were very few through services. Trains dawdled along calling at any number of wayside and generally ill-frequented stations. The best services took at least three hours. It was hardly surprising that most passengers travelling between the two university cities elected to go via London. This was more expensive and not necessarily much quicker, given the need to get from Paddington to King's Cross or Liverpool Street for Cambridge trains. Managed as a whole and imaginatively, the route might have been invaluable given that it could also have made connections into the East Coast, Midland and West Coast Main Lines. No serious attempt was ever made to exploit these links, enhance the service or even effect economies. As it was, in British Railways days, it was under the jurisdiction of two and sometimes three different regions and consequently it was nobody's baby.

The service was not proposed for closure in the Beeching Report of March 1963 but a few months later, British Railways added it to the list of passenger services it wished to withdraw. No sooner was the possibility of closure mentioned than opponents appeared who made much of the wasted potential of the route, pointed out how reductions could be made to running costs, highlighted the existing and planned population growth of places along the route and suggested that the potential usefulness of an upgraded service could be enhanced by extending trains at each end to Norwich and Swindon or Cardiff, for example. It was pointed out that the line could have a vital role contributing to the facilities offered by the designated new town of Milton Keynes. The area through which the line ran was one in which large-scale population growth was expected. All this was of little interest to British Railways, while the brief of the TUCC was not to propose better services or predict future increased use based on economic and demographic factors but to consider objections to the withdrawal of the existing service, judge the extent of hardship that closure would create and make recommendations based on that evidence alone. Much suspicion was levelled at the figures produced by British Railways regarding the losses it claimed were being made but while the rules allowed such figures to be presented by British Railways in its case for closure before the TUCC, objectors were, of course, not permitted to inquire about how these figures had been reached. Ministerial assent to the closure of this service was given on 8 July 1965, subject to the provision of replacement bus services. When it came to apportioning blame for such a closure, ministers claimed that they were only reacting to the case made by rail management and that closure was therefore the latter's responsibility. Managers in turn claimed that they had to work within cash limits imposed on them by the government which meant that their hand was forced.

From 1968, the only component of this route which retained its passenger service was that from Bedford to Bletchley. The Bedford to Bletchley Rail Users' Association fought for the retention of this service and has continued with other bodies to defend and promote the service ever since. The question of reinstatement of what is now seen as a key east to west rail link has never been allowed to go away. It could be argued that the line should never have been closed but it was a victim of the powerful and totally myopic anti-railway culture of the time. Currently, consideration is being given to the possibility of private capital being used to build a new link between the two cities.

By the late 1950s, the Dunton Green to Westerham branch in Kent was becoming an isolated pocket of steam passenger operations in an area where the Southern Region of British Railways was pushing ahead vigorously with the electrification of passenger services. The branch was not earmarked for electrification and indeed, in 1960 it was proposed for closure. Passenger usage was low and British Railways claimed that an annual saving of £11,000 could be made if the line closed. A campaign against closure was quickly set up in the form of the Westerham Branch Railway Passengers Association. They were able to show that vital financial information had been withheld by the Southern Region when the case for closure appeared before the local TUCC. They also publicised the embarrassing fact that much of the track had only recently been renewed. The longstanding dark joke among railway workers was that when an inspection saloon toured a line followed by stations being repainted and track renewed, then you knew that closure was in the offing. Despite a vigorous case being made against closure, the Westerham line closed on 28 October 1961. Parts of the formation were used for the M25.

An example of a line built under the auspices of the Light Railways Act of 1896 was the Fraserburgh to St Combs branch of the Great North of Scotland Railway. The boost that the much earlier line from Aberdeen to Fraserburgh had given to the latter's fishing industry had been noted and the small villages along the short line and St Combs itself hoped that a basic railway would provide them with a similar shot in the arm for their fishing ventures. The line had opened in 1903. No miraculous growth occurred with the local fishing industry but the passenger trains were well-used. This did not prevent the line being earmarked for closure in the Beeching Plan. The line from Aberdeen to Fraserburgh was also slated for closure and the locals believed that their line to St Combs was still a paying proposition but was being sacrificed because of the proposed closure of the 'main line'. It was obvious that British Railways would not keep an isolated piece of line open if the line from Aberdeen closed. They demanded statistical proof that the St Combs line was making losses but of course, BR was under no obligation to supply this information and the St Combs branch closed on 3 May 1965.

One of the worst examples of bad faith on the part of British Railways related to the 'Bluebell Line' in Sussex. The Lewes & East Grinstead Railway Company was incorporated in 1877 and absorbed into the London, Brighton & South Coast Railway (LBSCR) before it opened on 1 August 1882. It passed through delightful pastoral countryside and possessed some disproportionately grandiose wayside stations, mostly remote from the communities they purported to serve. Passengers were never particularly numerous but that did not prevent the LBSCR from providing a refreshment room at rustic Newick & Chailey, supposedly because there was no pub near the station. The communities along the route did not grow significantly after the coming of the railway and first the Southdown bus company and later the spread of private car ownership abstracted most of the line's users. The Southern Region proposed the line for closure, scheduled to take place on 28 May 1955. The authorities, however, had not bargained on Miss R.E.M. Bessemer. This formidable woman who lived at Chailey discovered that the closure was illegal under the terms of the line's incorporating Act. She had a flair for publicity and quickly got the media involved in a campaign to restore the passenger service. Grudgingly, the Southern Region was forced to restore a service of sorts. A skeleton timetable was operated with four trains in each direction daily, operating at inconvenient times and carefully missing possible connections at Lewes or East Grinstead. Passengers from intermediate stations could not book tickets for stations beyond East Grinstead or Lewes. Barcombe Station had not been included in the original Act. It was the best-used station on the line but the 'grumpy' trains as they were quickly nicknamed did not call there. Even the trains were mean – a locomotive and one carriage – the scruffiest that could be found. British Railways pulled out all the stops to gain the repeal of the original Act and the last trains ran on 16 March 1958. There would be no return this time but the whole episode put BR in a bad light.

Another example of bad faith on the part of British Railways occurred when it was revealed that in their case for the closure of the Darlington to Richmond Line they had 'overlooked' the contribution made to the line's finances by traffic to and from the army camp at Catterick.

The Helston Branch in Cornwall lost its passenger services in November 1962, again after detailed querying of BR's facts and figures about the line's traffic figures. No one was denying that the line lost money but was it as much as BR claimed and why had there been few, if any, attempts to implement economies?

The pioneering electrified main line from Manchester to Sheffield via Woodhead was recommended for development in the second and less well-known part of the Beeching Plan titled *The Development of the Major Trunk Routes*. This presented a case for increasing the number of freight and mineral trains along this route to a potential 200 daily in each direction. Passenger services would be diverted to the Hope Valley Line, albeit with an increase in journey times.

BRITAIN'S FIRST ALL-ELECTRIC MAIN LINE

The main line of the former Great Central Railway from Manchester to Sheffield was electrified and energised on 14 June 1954. It was a huge investment and was viewed as a harbinger of a future greatly expanded overhead electric railway network. It was not to be. Governments prevaricated. When modernisation was announced, stopgap diesel locomotives were introduced, many of them very expensive failures. Once electrification of the West Coast Main Line was completed, the Manchester to Sheffield system found itself isolated and incompatible. Bit by bit it was run down and most of the route was closed in 1981. Although the coal traffic which was its lifeblood was bound to decline, closure was extremely short-sighted and was quickly regretted. (Authors' collection)

The passenger service was duly withdrawn. Then official noises started to be made about total closure because of the expense of renewing the electrical equipment. In what by now had become the usual manner of obfuscation, British Rail was less than forthcoming on how it reached the figures it presented in its case for closure. Since there were no passenger services involved, the closure proposal did not need to go before a TUCC. Despite considerable protests by the railway unions, the line closed on 20 July 1981.

Vigorous, well-organised opposition was launched successfully against the proposed closing of the Manchester to Buxton, Birmingham to Redditch, Machynlleth to Pwllheli, mid-Hants and East Suffolk Lines among others. Birmingham to Redditch, incredibly, was mooted for closure precisely at a time when massive expansion was planned at the latter town. It took a long time for British Rail to secure the closure of the Liverpool Central to Gateacre line which might have been a considerable success had it been brought into the electric rail network on Merseyside and been used to relieve road congestion. Among many other lines that were closed but would now probably be playing a very useful role in the national rail network were the Exeter to Plymouth line of the former London & South Western Railway; Cheltenham to Honeybourne and Stratford; Harrogate to Ripon and Northallerton; Carlisle to Stranraer and the former Colchester to Cambridge line beyond its present terminus at Sudbury. It has to be said that in some cases the cessation of services was followed by dismantling of the track and other infrastructure with almost indecent haste. It seemed that the demolition of bridges and the selling of parts of the formation were intended to ensure that once they closed, lines remained closed.

Perhaps the *cause célèbre* was the tussle between British Rail and a coalition of pressure groups, local authorities and other interested parties to close the Settle & Carlisle Line. In *The Line that Refused to Die* (1990), Abbott & Whitehouse treat the reader to a blow-by-blow account of the successful campaign not only to save the line but to boost its revenue. It shows the devious but actually rather incompetent methods attempted by British Rail to force through the closure of a line they clearly wanted to get rid of. However, there were by now were many seasoned campaigners against closures. They knew how to use BR's statistics against them and were fully conversant with the tactics required to fight to the finish. The Settle & Carlisle lives on – gloriously!

Direct Action against Railway Closures

The British have long displayed a curiously ambivalent attitude towards railway closures. We know from contemporary illustrations and written witness accounts that ordinary people turned out in jubilant crowds to celebrate sod-cutting ceremonies and then to greet the first trains to run on newly opened lines. Where some of the local landowners and other bigwigs may, at least initially, have been hostile to a proposed railway because it conflicted with their particular interests, ordinary people seem generally to have welcomed the coming of a railway as benefitting the localities in which they lived and 'putting them on the map' as it were. The real ambivalence comes out when railway usage begins to decline. There might be low-level grumbles about the closure of a line or there might be more formal protests but there are numerous records of large crowds cheering as the last train steamed out of their local station. Hundreds of local people who had not used the trains for years might cram into the trains running on the last day. Railway management recognised this possibility by frequently adding additional coaches to the normal formation. Also present on these occasions might be those who made a habit of travelling on last trains and, sometimes the same people, those who competed to buy last-day tickets issued at stations on the line, even if they used cars to reach these stations. There was something slightly ghoulish in the way they homed in on doomed lines and stations. The tickets bought might, of course, accrue a value for collectors. There were also others of a light-fingered persuasion who were eager to obtain 'souvenirs' and would remove anything that was not nailed down if they thought they could get away with it. It is stretching definitions to describe such people as genuine railway enthusiasts. Also likely to be present at the last-day rites would be some genuine protesters. They would be making clear their feelings concerning railway management's attitude towards services that they did not want to maintain and also the aversion to railways apparent among most of the country's political leaders and decision-makers.

Most of the early inter-war years closures seem to have gone off without incident but a line which had already won a devoted fan club if not a large regular travelling clientele was the narrow-gauge Lynton & Barnstaple which closed on 29 September 1935. The final train was packed and crowds of locals turned out to wish it well as if it was an old friend, albeit one that they rarely, if ever, used. There was cheering from many as it passed along the line, tears from others, saddened that this was the end of a familiar if largely unused feature of the locality. There was also a contingent, some local and others from further away, who were angry with the Southern Railway and what they thought was the high-handed attitude and insensitive manner of its distant management which had decreed the closure of the line, loftily dismissing issues of local importance. A band enlivened events on the last night, establishing what became a common practice at these rituals and giving an upbeat air when dirges might have been more appropriate. The Lynton & Barnstaple has recently undergone a rebirth.

In later years and particularly during the cull of lines associated with the Beeching Report, large crowds often turned up out especially for the very last train, more often cheering than jeering. The rake of coaches would be augmented and still be packed. Locomotives might be adorned with wreaths and graffiti often featuring the letters 'R.I.P.' and an effigy of Dr Beeching might be present, sometimes being ritually burned. Detonators were frequently placed on the line and it was not uncommon for the communication cord to be pulled. Little attention seemed to be paid to the fact that this was the last day of employment for many of the staff. It was also, of course, the last day of what had become a familiar if somewhat neglected part of the local way of life. The usually good-humoured manner in which these events went off suggested that most of the participants had a sentimental attachment to the line but were not expecting that its closure would cause major hardship or inconvenience in the locality.

Trains started running from Carlisle to Silloth in August 1856. The line was leased by the North British Railway in 1862. As with so many lines, traffic began to fall away seriously in the 1950s. The line ran through sparsely populated country, generating little traffic, although on sunny summer days trains could be packed with excursionists intent on enjoying the simple estuarine delights of Silloth. The Beeching report claimed that the line was losing £23,500 annually and required repairs costing £31,500 which could not be justified. Transport Minister Marples approved closure, scheduled for 6 March 1964. Huge numbers turned out to watch or travel on the last trains.

As the very last train from Carlisle approached Silloth it found its path blocked by a sit-down protest of over 1,000 demonstrators. A substantial force of police was on hand in anticipation of trouble and they eventually cleared the way for the train to enter Silloth

Station but not before verbal insults and a few punches had been aimed at the law-enforcers. This demonstration had been well-planned. A folk group was on hand giving a rendition of their own composition 'The Beeching Blues' while there were periodic choral outbursts of Lonnie Donegan's 'Last Train to San Fernando'. The TUCC had accepted that the closure would cause genuine hardship particularly at Silloth and it was clear that many of the demonstrators did not believe that the closure would have gone ahead under a Labour government. Several 'Vote Labour' banners were to be seen. The communication chord was pulled several times as the train returned to Carlisle.

Emotions were running particularly high because it was felt that the closure should have been postponed. Recently a steel company had proposed opening a sizeable scrapyard at Silloth promising considerable traffic for the line from Carlisle. The company concerned had even mentioned the possibility that it would consider subsidising a restored passenger service. There were mixed feelings – anger that the closure had gone ahead but a hopeful feeling that a reopening was in the offing. British Railways was having nothing of this and took the unprecedented step of disconnecting all signal boxes and point rods along the line within hours of the passage of the last train. Even if the new Minister of Transport who came into office after Labour's victory in the 1964 general election had wished to do so, he had no powers under the Transport Act of 1962 to overthrow a decision already made to close a railway. Some doubt was cast on this claim by a speech reported in *Hansard* for 27 May, 1965 when a former Under Secretary at the Ministry of Transport told the House of Lords:

'My right Hon. Friend [Mr Fraser, the then Minister] is fully satisfied that if it became necessary to reopen a line, where in fact a consent had already been given, he could negotiate with the Railways Board for it to be reopened.'

Another closure which saw feelings running high was, by coincidence, that of the nearby ex-North British Railway 'Waverley Route' from Edinburgh to Carlisle. This was a main trunk line carrying Anglo-Scottish traffic and heavy freight movements if not much local business because of the relatively small towns it served and the sparsely populated and wild country through which it passed. It presented many operating difficulties and British

Railways saw it essentially as a line that was expendable because the bulk of its traffic could be diverted to other routes and extensive savings made. This was all very well from an accountant's point of view but genuine hardship would be caused to those who wanted to use the train from intermediate stations between Hawick and Carlisle, which was the stretch of the line generating the least local usage. There were genuine grounds for protest but some were verging on the ludicrous. For example, the South of Scotland Budgerigar and Foreign Bird Society made a written protest in which it claimed that the closure would '…spell the death warrant of all bird societies in this area.'[8]

Two of the last trains were delayed by bomb scares and attempts were made to board one of them with a coffin inscribed 'Waverley Line, Born 1849, Killed 1969'. The very last train of all was the sleeper for London which left Edinburgh Waverley at 21.55 on 5 January 1969. When this train arrived at Hawick, the coffin, which was addressed to the Minister of Transport, was loaded into the brake-van and there was an ugly mood among people seeing the train off. Near Riccarton, the communication cord was pulled and the train stopped. At Newcastleton the train was forced to stop again. Here, the level crossing gates had been padlocked against the train and an angry crowd of locals led by the local minister delayed the train for an hour. This episode was evidence of local feelings running very high. With local roads being so poor and bus services so infrequent, people without cars were immediately plunged into an isolation every bit as real as it would have been in the Middle Ages, and this despite modern high-speed communication media such as television.

Barbara Castle at the Ministry

Labour's Tom Fraser who was Minister of Transport from 1964 to 1965 was no friend of the railway, being eager to implement closures and impatient with the slow advance of this process. His replacement, Barbara Castle, took office late in 1965 and was an exception to the tendency for Transport Secretaries to be indifferent to or actually hostile to railways. She was concerned that road traffic was reaching saturation point in places. In 1967, she identified the concept of a 'Basic Railway' of about 11,000 miles of which 9,500 miles would have passenger services and she saw this as the minimum necessary to meet long-term transport needs. In 1968, she launched the idea of Passenger Transport Authorities and Passenger Transport Executives. The Authorities would plan and oversee the creation of efficient integrated public transport systems which met the needs of the major provincial conurbations and the Executives would manage their operations. It was accepted that some of the services involved would need to be subsidised by the taxpayers. Without this initiative it is likely that most suburban trains outside London would have disappeared.

Castle was a feisty character and tough-minded as she needed to be because, as she said in her memoirs, the permanent officials at the Ministry of Transport were 'closure mad'. She wanted to slow down the rate of rail closures and encourage the retention of a larger network than Beeching had envisaged. The public mood was changing and widespread closures were no longer so acceptable.

Castle was unusual as a Transport Minister for two other reasons. Firstly she had the view that transport needed to be planned and treated on a national basis and as a unity rather than its component parts being viewed in isolation. Secondly, and this was ground-breaking in the context of the times, she argued that subsidies were required for parts of the system which could never be made to pay but which met essential social needs. 'Socially necessary' was the phrase. She understood that passenger railways constitute a social service which cannot be viewed in isolation from the wider political context in which they operate.

The 1968 Transport Act inaugurated the concept of the 'socially necessary' railway supported by public funding. It was becoming obvious that service closures were not a magic bullet that would solve the loss-making tendency of much of Britain's railway network. A radical new approach was implemented. This involved making public funds available for particular lines which lost money but were adjudged to meet social need, thereby relieving the railways of the requirement of achieving the impossible target of breaking even or even making a profit. Castle wrote off the debt of £153 million which had been accumulated by the railways. There were, however, still senior civil servants who wished to see further closures.[9] Her Permanent Secretary, Thomas Padmore, was notoriously hostile to railways. The idea of railways operating loss-making but necessary services was anathema to politicians and civil servants with pro-road sympathies. Castle stood up to the pro-road lobby which resulted in her eventually being given a new portfolio where she would cause less controversy.

Barbara Castle was arguably the most prominent female Labour MP. During her tenure as Minister of Transport from December 1965 to April 1968 she was both execrated for enacting many of the proposed closures in the Beeching Report and lauded for introducing the concept of government subsidies for socially necessary but loss-making railway passenger services. (Authors' collection)

The harsh realities of the costs of road congestion and traffic accidents could not be entirely ignored even by the most case-hardened mandarins and their political masters. The public mood was beginning to turn against closures assisted by loose coalitions of railway unions, progressive railway managers, environmentalists and pro-rail lobbies. The Transport Act of 1974 replaced grants for socially necessary services by a block grant to the British Railways Board for passenger services, this being known as the Public Service Obligation Grant (PSO) and it was required under European law. It was not long before the flow of closures slowed to a trickle and eventually virtually stopped. The pro-railway lobby had accumulated experience and civil servants and senior railway managers were thoroughly fed up with the complications and expense entailed in attempting to implement closure proposals in the face of concerted opposition. For that reason, a new kind of 'parliamentary train' has appeared. This is the skeleton service exemplified by the derisory one train per week that runs from Stockport to Stalybridge without a return working. It was everything short of actual closure but avoided the potential obstacles of the legal closure process. A few grant-supported services did close, however.[10]

In 1974 a 'No Rail Cuts' campaign was launched by a coalition of railway unions and various pro-public transport organisations under the umbrella of Transport 2000, now the 'Campaign for Better Transport'. It owed much of its success to engaging the support of influential newspaper editors who were encouraged to place issues concerning the role of railways in modern Britain at the forefront of public debate.

Despite some positive moves for the railway industry, this was very much the 'Road Age'. Preliminary work on a railway Channel Tunnel was cancelled by the Labour Government in 1975. In the same year, 1,100 miles of motorway opened. Between 1960 and 1975, the number of road vehicles had increased by 149 per cent.

Whereas in 1958 seventy-seven per cent of households were without a car, by 1975 that figure had fallen to forty-three per cent. The freight ton-mileage carried by road increased over seventy per cent between 1962 and 1975. Lorries became longer, heavier and faster. This meant that they inflicted increasingly expensive damage on the roads. The road lobby retorted with the totally spurious argument that permitting larger lorries meant fewer lorries and therefore less damage. Every time governments surrendered to their demands for larger vehicles, the road lobby was encouraged to come back with demands for even larger ones. The number of juggernauts browbeating their way along Britain's highways simply continued growing. The railways operated in a transport system dominated by the roads. They also were operating in a period of severe economic difficulties which affected all industries. The oil crisis of 1973 had been followed by excessive inflation, cash limits, restrictions on investment and troubled industrial relations.

Overall, the railway industry could be said to have done well to cope with constant imposed change. The British Transport Commission was replaced in 1963 by the British Railways Board helping to create a sense of insecurity and defensiveness in many senior railway managers. They rarely enjoyed good relationships with civil servants and relevant ministers who frequently saw them as inward-looking and opposed to change. For their part, the managers thought the politicians and civil servants were interfering, ignorant and dismissive of many of the issues relevant or even unique to the railway industry. They would have liked to be able to get on with the job of running the railways without interference on key issues such as pricing, investment and pay but this was a non-starter under nationalisation. Ever-present were the stresses that resulted from the seeming impossibility of reconciling public service and commercial viability. Generally, the railways did not enjoy a good press and for that substantial section of the population that was totally car-oriented, they were largely seen as an outdated and expensive irrelevance. It was perhaps not surprising that many career railwaymen were seen as bloody-minded when they knew they were operating in a culture firmly biased towards the private car, road haulage and road-building programmes.

Much of what can be said about official attitudes to British Railways could also be said concerning the London Underground – persistent interference and abrupt about-turns of policy as governments changed. In 1970, the Greater London Council, the successor to the London

County Council, took over responsibility for London's local transport. The Underground was suffering from decades of under-investment with official policy promoting private motoring rather than public transport. Now, the writing off of London Transport's debt and the provision of grants for capital expenditure seemed to promise a better future. Useful investments were indeed made but control of the GLC swung to and fro between Conservative and Labour with almost four-year regularity and with consequent disruptive zigzags in policy.

In the 1970s, it was becoming evident that the private car was strangulating surface transport in the capital and that there was a substantial cost in the congestion and pollution that it created. Labour won the GLC election in 1981 and controversially under its 'Fares Fair' policy drastically cut fares in an attempt to reduce private motoring in London. Usage of the Underground rose rapidly, resulting in some beneficial reduction in road congestion. Of course Londoners paid for the fare cuts via their rates and they were not unanimous in thinking that 'Fares Fair' was fair. Bromley was a Conservative-controlled outer-London borough whose council provocatively challenged the GLC's legal right to cut fares so drastically and subsidise the shortfall in income via rate increases. The case went to court and the GLC lost. The latter then concluded that to comply with the law they needed a substantial fares increase. Inevitably, usage of the Underground fell away and road congestion was king again. An uneasy compromise was reached which cut fares but eased the burden on the ratepayers. The GLC had proved clearly that demand for underground travel was elastic, responding both to fare rises and falls and that traffic congestion could be eased by fare reductions.

Mrs Thatcher liked cars and private transport and did not like trains, even underground ones in congested London, did not like a Labour-controlled GLC and especially did not like its maverick leader Ken Livingstone. What she did not like she tended to destroy. The GLC's days were numbered.

A Heritage Interlude

Although, as we have seen, by no means everyone welcomed the arrival of the railways, this new and revolutionary form of transport encapsulated the dynamic of the period with its application of human ingenuity to science and technology in order to push back the boundaries of what was possible. The railways were changing the world and some railway companies that could afford to do so, as well as others that could not, thought it appropriate to make grandiloquent statements in some of their big city stations and other installations. No one who stands on the south side of Euston Road and looks across at the Midland Grand Hotel façade to St Pancras Station and its near neighbour of King's Cross can have any doubt that the Midland Railway was making a statement. The Midland was comparatively late in building its own independent line into London but now it was saying 'we have arrived'. The station was opened in 1868 and the hotel in 1876 and both were on a scale clearly intended to overawe the much humbler but dignified premises of the Great Northern 'next door'. As we have seen, severe criticism was voiced at the time about the massively intrusive presence of the hotel

Even as the grand new stations and imposing bridges and viaducts were erected, some people, perhaps with an excess of enthusiasm, were comparing them with the great cathedrals, monasteries and parish churches built in medieval times. They chose to ignore those railway buildings that had little grace but much meanness and ugliness and of which there were plenty. The industrial towns that expanded so rapidly in the nineteenth century were filthy and squalid but the local bigwigs were fond of vanity projects in the form of grandiose public buildings such as town halls and market halls. Railway companies responded by sometimes building stations that were as grand as, or grander, than any other buildings in the town or city concerned. Good examples are Newcastle Central, Huddersfield and, on a smaller scale, Monkwearmouth. Early railways came in for all manner of criticism and the railway companies were engaged in a public relations exercise, wanting to make their major stations look solid and secure while flattering local vanity. In some cases where the municipal authorities felt that a station did not do justice to the importance of the town or city it served, complaints would be made. An example was the rebuilt station in Sheffield. Pond Street Station, later Sheffield Midland, was comprehensively rebuilt in 1905 but not on a scale sufficiently grand to satisfy the local authority or the local newspapers.

Everything undergoes a continuous process of change, not least perceptions of the architectural and historical merit of buildings. Abuse of St Pancras Station and the Midland Grand Hotel in particular in the 1870s turned into fulsome praise and spirited defence from the 1960s when these and other major monuments of the Railway Age were threatened with destruction either because of modernisation or closures. It is worth remembering that the

'Euston Arch' was destroyed in 1962 with the endorsement of *The Times* newspaper. This was an era that saw a sustained campaign of official vandalism aimed at destroying many buildings of the Victorian period and replacing them with erections of quite extraordinary ugliness and banality, many of which have already, and rightly, been razed to the ground. As Marcus Binney and David Pearce (1979) wrote:

> '...since its establishment in 1947 British Rail has acquired for itself an all too deserved reputation as the biggest corporate vandal and iconclast Britain has seen since the Tudor dissolution of the monasteries.'

The Euston Arch's misfortune was that it came under threat just before a reappraisal of taste in favour of Victorian achievements developed into a potent force. Perhaps its destruction had a salutary effect leading to the emergence of a much more enlightened attitude to the preservation and conservation of examples of buildings of the early modern age. In the 1960s, such buildings as the Euston Arch and St Pancras and its hotel came to be seen as worthy of preservation despite the Arch having been described as a 'piece of Brobdingnagian absurdity' by the aesthete and art critic John Ruskin at the time it was built.

Those who thought they knew best decided that Euston Station had to be totally rebuilt to be an appropriate London terminus for the modernised and electrified West Coast Main Line. The old Euston had developed piecemeal over the years and was an operating nightmare in the modern age but means could have been found to enable it operate more efficiently while retaining its historic core features. However, it was out with the old and in with the new. Nothing was to be allowed to stop the bulldozers. Planning permission was required to demolish the Arch as a listed building and initially permission was given on condition that it was re-erected elsewhere. The contractor involved refused on the grounds of cost and the supposed absence of a site on which it could be rebuilt. Demolition was completed in 1962.

Just as people of aesthetic sensibilities had deplored the intrusion of the railways into places of great natural beauty back in the nineteenth century, so, during the period of large-scale closure of lines from the 1960s to the 1990s, the opposite view made itself apparent. This argued that many railway structures blended into or even enhanced their surroundings and that there was a duty to preserve at least the best of them.

In September 1967, the British Railways Board announced plans for the development of King's Cross, the diversion into Euston of the long-distance services then running into St Pancras and the diversion into Moorgate of the local services from Bedford and Luton and a proposed vestigial semi-fast service from Leicester. This proposal caused many a jaw to drop but it was largely forgotten that back in 1936, there had been discussion about the merits of closing one of the major termini along the Euston and Marylebone Roads. At that time, the most likely candidate was identified as being St Pancras. In 1967, the debate centred less about the viability of the proposed diversions as a defence of the station and the hotel on architectural and aesthetic grounds.

Railway Preservation

Serious railway preservation by amateurs was a creation of post-Second World War Britain, the threat to a substantial part of the network posed by the decline of traffic, unprofitability and the imminent end of regular steam locomotive operation. It is not to decry the extraordinary achievements of the multi-faceted preservation movement to say that much of its activity produces a highly selective and sanitised version of past railway practice – historical reconstruction but with the nasty bits taken out. These included low wages, dangerous and dirty working conditions, draconic discipline and antisocial hours. Whole branch lines have been painstakingly restored and preserved in idyllic aspic, a kind of model railway but full scale, a sentimental reconstruction of a prototype that was never actually like that.

Preservation has become a significant part of the heritage industry bringing money into many a local economy. It is likely that the movement contains an element of protest that hostile politicians and faceless bureaucrats callously took away things that we knew and loved, all in the name of progress. People did not want simply to stand back and let these iconoclasts do their worst.

The sheer number of working railways and static museums is evidence of the nostalgic affection with which railways are regarded and especially their most iconic feature which is, of course, the steam locomotive. Brand new steam locomotives have been and continue to be built. They usually represent classes whose original members were all scrapped. Valuable engineering skills are employed in such exercises and the fact that such projects exist at all is indicative of the determination of the enthusiasts involved and the resources they can muster.

Railway to Road Conversion

An idea which has raised its head periodically is that of converting railways to roads. It is usually voiced by the anti-railway lobby but its first manifestation was actually by the London & North Eastern Railway in 1932. They produced an internal report examining the possibility of saving money by converting two rural branch lines into roads for the exclusive use of railway-owned buses. The lines concerned were the Wivenhoe to Brightlingsea Branch in Essex and the Mid-Suffolk Railway which meandered inconsequentially through the depths of the Suffolk countryside before petering out some distance from the village of Laxfield. The report concluded that any savings made would be absolutely minimal.

The Railway Conversion League, dating from the 1950s, was created to advocate the conversion of the UK's railways into 'reserved roads'. These would be open only to fast, thoroughly roadworthy and competently driven vehicles. Overtaking and 'dawdling' would be prohibited. Its best-known advocate was Brigadier T.I. Lloyd. The league and Lloyd in particular were generally regarded as somewhat batty. The conversion issue raised its head again in the early 1980s during Mrs Thatcher's premiership when it was given vocal support by Alfred Sherman, Director of the Centre for Policy Studies and one of the prime minister's closest advisors. A detailed examination of the issue concluded that the idea was largely impractical and it was quietly abandoned.

An example of a line closed not because it was necessarily loss-making but because the powers-that-be had decided that much of its course should be used for building a major road, the M90, was the former North British main line from Edinburgh and Cowdenbeath to Perth via Glenfarg. It closed in January 1970. Other rail to road conversions in Scotland included the Western Approach Road in Edinburgh which was built along the former Caledonian Railway's line into the city's Princes Street Station and the diversion of a stretch of the A6091 along the old Waverley Route to avoid Melrose.

In the early 1980s, there was a strong move to declare Marylebone Station surplus to requirements. It was proposed to convert it into a new coach station for the capital, the track being ripped up to allow a dedicated approach to central London for the coaches. It was reckoned that Paddington could handle Marylebone's trains. Loud protests met these proposals which were not implemented and died down after 1986.

Almost all the bus services which were put on as replacement for railways failed. Most former rail passengers soon found that buses were generally slower and that they had difficulty in handling luggage, bicycles, prams and pushchairs. They either bought cars or stayed at home. The replacement bus services went the way of the rail services they had, in theory, superseded.

Railways in the days of Margaret Thatcher

Few prime ministers have provoked such strong emotions, either of admiration or aversion, as Margaret Thatcher. She was ideologically driven and she set herself the mission of reversing three post-war decades marked by much consensus and common ground between Britain's two main political parties. She believed that consensus had led to a craven failure to recognise and deal with a number of problems that were contributing to Britain's relative economic decline. On becoming prime minister in 1979, she announced that she was going to eliminate 'socialism' from British politics and, by reversing what she saw as the baleful trend towards collectivism so characteristic of post-war Britain, she would implement an economic and moral reinvigoration of Britain.

She believed that the growth of the state sector had had a debilitating effect by encouraging bureaucratic inefficiency and incompetence and a 'benefits culture', discouraging entrepreneurial 'wealth-creating' enterprise. In the 1980s, therefore, many state-owned industries were sold off to the private sector for the ostensible purposes of encouraging competition, raising money for the Treasury that could be used to pay off some public debt, increasing the quality of management and allowing people to invest in the sold-off industries thereby creating a 'popular capitalism'. It became the received wisdom to argue that nationalisation equated with inefficiency and bureaucratic waste and that private enterprise was a far better custodian of the nation's economic assets. The fact that the taxpayer through the state subsidised many of the activities essential for the functioning of a predominantly private enterprise economy was discreetly ignored. Another of her targets was the trade union movement. She felt that their leaders were unrepresentative of the members' aspirations, that they wielded undue power and that their activities undermined the profitability of much of British industry. She was determined to cut them down to size. Unions were particularly strong in the nationalised industries such as the railways and in other parts of the state sector. Privatisation therefore served to kill two birds with one stone. Railways were not at the top of the list of proposed privatisations but longer-term intentions were clear when, for example, the British Railways Board was instructed to dispose of its shipping and hotel interests to the private sector. Sealink was sold for £66 million, against its stated assets of £108 million, a disgraceful squandering of public wealth for no better reason than political dogma and short-term political advantage. Much similar 'selling of the family silver' was to follow.

Mrs Thatcher disliked railways – the private car was her favoured means of transport and suited her political purposes. People in cars see other road-users as competitors or rivals, encouraging selfish and aggressive behaviour behind the wheel and they drive in isolation, each absorbed in their own little tin box. She may have had an inveterate aversion to railways but Britain's roads were already the most crowded in the world and even an antagonism to railways in the highest government and departmental circles and the continuing remonstrations of the road lobby were not enough to make significant cutbacks on the railways any longer acceptable.

Alfred Sherman was one of a number of right-wing ideologues who had influenced Margaret Thatcher in the period leading up to her becoming prime minister. He was the founder and director of the right-wing think tank, the Centre for Policy Studies. He told her in September 1980 that: 'Rail was an anachronism and had been since the invention of the pneumatic tyre and the internal combustion engine'. Railways could expect no favours.

The Serpell Committee of 1982 was commissioned by Thatcher's government, ostensibly to enquire into railway finances and attempt to identify means for putting them on a sounder long-term base. It was a cynical move because it was a subplot in the drive for eventual privatisation. The losses being sustained by Britain's railways made it unattractive to potential investors. If a core system could be identified that generated profits, an attractive package could be produced and presented for sale. The report, published early in 1983, caused an immediate storm. It produced a series of maps accompanying various 'options' for the size and shape of the future railway system. It was 'Option A' which caused the greatest furore because this consisted of a skeletal model which would have deprived all of Wales except Cardiff of railways, penetrated no further west than Bristol, left nothing north of the central belt of Scotland and in East Anglia only a line to Norwich. The report suggested extensive replacement of railway passenger services with buses. Experience had highlighted the shortcomings of this tactic and it was simply unacceptable. Even with a government hostile to railways, Serpell was too much of a hot potato and it was quietly allowed to slip out of the news. A general election was looming. The government did not want to be on the receiving end of the opprobrium generated by the report for which it was responsible. The tide was turning in favour of railways and it was clear that there was now widespread hostility to railway closures. Even the electrification of the East Coast Main Line was given the go-ahead.

In 1983, a private member's bill put forward by Tony Speller, MP for North Devon, eased the way to the reopening of stations and even whole lines, initially on an experimental basis. This much-needed legislation paved the way for some highly successful restorations such as the 'Robin Hood Line' from Nottingham to Mansfield and Worksop or the line from Bathgate to Edinburgh. More have followed.

By 1989, Britain's railways were not only the most efficient in Europe but in receipt of the lowest public subsidies. The down side was their expensive fares and large-scale job losses. Unmanned and vandalised stations could provide a negative, even threatening, experience for travellers. By the late 1980s, official thinking had moved to the idea of creating a new generation of diesel multiple units, eventually to see the light of day as 'Pacers', 'Sprinters' and 'Supersprinters'. Pacers provided a very poor quality of travel but a service with them was better than no service at all. Further electrification schemes raised the percentage of the whole network that was electrified from twenty-six to thirty per cent. An attempt was made to develop the Advanced Passenger Train (APT), a 155 mph train which would use new technology to tilt round curved track and greatly cut timings on inter-city routes. It was a failure and eventually tilting 'Pendolino' trains were bought, employing Italian engineering know-how. These were employed on the West Coast Main Line. The APT was an attempt to gain much higher speeds without the cost of building a new purpose-built railway. The APT project was abandoned in 1986. From 1976, the High-Speed Trains had been introduced and they eventually proved to be a huge success, helping to change the image of inter-city rail travel. Passenger usage began to increase significantly as did fares but railways had turned the corner and they were now operating in a culture which was very different from that when they had been nobody's baby back in the period from the 1950s to 1970s. Reduction of the railway network was no longer seen as an option. This did not mean that Thatcher's governments were pro-railway. They were still firmly in thrall to motorists and the road lobby with massive resources being allocated for road building and improvements.

Privatisation

Britain's Railways were a victim of the neo-liberal economic policies pursued with such dogmatic ruthlessness by governments from the mid-1980s. A crucial tenet of neo-liberalism was a reduction in the size of the public sector and this involved the selling off of public assets to private buyers, at prices usually way below their market value. Political ideology was involved as privatisation fragmented industries and reduced the power of the trade unions to defend wages and conditions. A neo-liberal mantra informed us that nationalised industries were inefficient bureaucratic monopolies and that privatisation would infuse new life into these businesses because they would now be subject to the robust and dynamic stimulus and challenge of market forces. They would be run more efficiently and provide better value for money. Some doubted this at the time and many more have questioned this claim since. The 'fresh air' of the private sector and its values saw, for example, infrastructure maintenance contracted out and then subcontracted with literally disastrous results. Train Operating Companies (TOCs) were allowed to pocket profits while receiving larger subsidies from the public exchequer than those previously extended to the nationalised system. Labyrinthine and expensive new bureaucracies have flourished.

The words of a former senior railway manager regarding the division of operational activity into sectors in the period following privatisation, are very instructive. He described how young and often inexperienced managers from other types of business were shoe-horned into Railtrack and who misguidedly but arrogantly saw investment in railway safety not as an absolute necessity but only one among a number of 'business options'. The outcome of this blinkered thinking was a number of vary serious accidents.

The public were softened up on the issue of privatisation of the railways by a sustained propaganda campaign against British Rail, emphasising, for example, the age of much rolling stock and slowness in applying necessary innovation and modernisation. That the railway system had never been given the necessary resources was quietly ignored. A continuously repeated canard referred to the 'monolithic' character of Britain's railways as if this was a damning point. Conveniently omitted was any reference to the global corporations that dominated economic activity across the world. If any contemporary business concerns were monolithic and monopolistic, it was these multinationals, some of which had budgets larger than many nation states. The earlier selling off of railway-operated ferries, catering, hotels and engineering were straws in the wind for privatisation. A plethora of 'consultants', accountants and merchant bankers assured the public that privatisation was a dawn of new hope for the railways. Such people had little interest in what was best for the railways and railway users.

An example of the depths to which matters sunk was 'the wrong kind of snow' episode. British Rail's Director of Operations was being interviewed for the BBC's *Today* programme. What he said was seized by a journalist trying to make a name for himself who was not going to let the exact truth get in the way of a good story. There are indeed different kinds of snow. That being referred to was the very light and powdery variety which can easily get into the traction motors of electric trains and immobilise them. It was a reference to this which transmuted into 'the wrong kind of snow'. In this context it implied that senior managers at BR were simpletons making feeble excuses for the inadequacy of their operations and this was only to be expected from an inefficient state monolith. If anyone was to blame, it was successive governments who underfunded the railways. In this case, economies meant that these electric multiple units were not fitted with the comparatively cheap ducts and filters that would have excluded the snow. The ignorance of the media on matters concerning railways is almost bottomless and they constantly present their readers with blatant howlers masquerading as 'facts'.

The privatisation of British Rail was arguably the most contentious privatisation carried out by the Conservative governments that were elected in 1979 and continued in office until the mid-2000s. Already sold off, among others, were telecommunications in 1984, gas in 1986, water in 1989 and electricity in 1990.

Privatisation of Britain's railways was not carried through out of any desire to enhance the system or improve its services. It did not represent a Damascene conversion of Tory politicians to a pro-rail standpoint. It was the product of neo-liberal dogma and a political culture which sought to bring into the private sector any state activities which could be sold off cheaply and made to produce a profit for so-called private enterprise, profits underwritten if necessary by the taxpayer. It was a piece of political dogma, John Major's government being determined to carry it through come what may. Before nationalisation, Major had famously described Britain's railways as inefficient while the reality had been that in the 1980s they had become increasingly efficient, shaping up well against the best in Europe.

There was little enthusiasm in Westminster for railway privatisation, much scepticism about the point or purpose of it and concern about what the outcome might be. Labour MPs were hostile and many Conservative backbenchers not convinced of the case. In fairness, it has to be said that Labour in office in the 2000s refused to take up the issue of renationalisation.

Paradoxically, some senior railway managers welcomed privatisation, believing that it might mean that railways could free themselves of the trammels of the politicians. The opposite turned out to be true. The difference was that privatisation was being promulgated when senior politicians and civil servants had at last accepted, many of them reluctantly, that investment was needed because railways were essential for long-term economic growth. The culture was changing. Investment in railways was now seen as being a generator of economic benefits rather than simply being public money thrown into a bottomless black hole. The public was showing by using them in increasing numbers that they believed that railways were needed even if they were critical of their 'excessive' fares, still complained bitterly when they were late and found numerous other issues to grumble about.

Terry Gourvish (2008) argued that the process of privatisation created an unprecedented fragmentation of what had previously been a highly integrated business, raising issues of safety versus profit and owing as much to political dogma and expediency as to theoretical niceties. It was a fundamental mistake to abolish the vertical integration of the railway's operations and infrastructure.

The fragmentation of the system has led to the collapse of clearly defined chains of responsibility in a culture where each player seeks to offload the blame for things going wrong onto other players. The running of the railway network has been made much more expensive by the proliferation of non-productive bureaucracies.

Christian Wolmar contrasted the privatised railway system with the expansive days of Britain's railways in the nineteenth century when the railway barons were, as he said, 'genuine risk-taking capitalists'. He continued: 'under the present system…a game of "pretend capitalism" is played with the taxpayer always in the background to pick up the tab'.[11]

The then Transport Secretary told the House of Commons on 26 March 2013:

'Traffic has doubled since privatisation from 750 million journeys a year to 1.5 billion now. There are more services and record levels of investment. And our railways have the best safety record in Europe. This hasn't been achieved despite privatisation. It has been achieved because of privatisation.'[12]

Perhaps the Transport Secretary was playing political games here. It was naïve at best to argue that privatisation itself caused a large increase in passenger usage of the railways. That indisputable increase was the product of a complex set of inter-related factors which happened independently of the machinations of politicians bent on implementing neo-liberal policies. The Transport Secretary conveniently omitted to mention that Railtrack had to be nationalised in order to address the appalling record of that privatised company so far as railway safety was concerned. Rail users in parts of the provinces distant from London who had to tolerate the nasty but expensive experience of travelling on 'Pacer' diesel units might wonder where all the investment had been made. It was certainly not on their trains. Passengers trying to get to and from Whitby by train might question the adequacy of the level of service provision.

It cannot be denied that passenger numbers have risen considerably on many parts of the railway network and that innumerable stations and several lines have been reopened, occurrences that would have been largely inconceivable thirty years ago. However, perceptions of railway travel frequently remain jaundiced. Staff numbers have been cut back to the absolute minimum so a driver not turning in for work for whatever reason can lead to cancellation of all the trains for which he was rostered. Passengers rightfully feel aggrieved about cancelled trains. The concept of more frequent but short trains falls down especially on longer journeys which may start out at an off-peak time but then pass through a major hub in the middle of the peak. A two-car unit travelling from, say, Norwich to Liverpool, may provide adequate seating accommodation on most days and for much of the route but be grossly overcrowded at peak times. With rolling stock pared down to the bare minimum, there is no chance of adding an extra carriage or unit. Overcrowding is one of the most frequent causes of complaint. Among the gremlins of modern rail travel particularly on long-distance trains are incessant and frequently inane announcements from the robotic 'on board team'; seats that do not align with windows and seem to have been sadistically designed primarily to cause of discomfort for the occupant; people using phones and other electronic equipment without due considerations for others and the constant passage of bored people to the feeding station and their returning carrying overpriced comestibles with which they proceed to stuff themselves while the unwelcome aroma of their food permeates their surroundings. Fare systems of incomprehensible complexity have been devised. There is a sense that the railways no longer constitute a system. Passengers arriving on a train which is running ten minutes late may find that they have missed a hoped-for connection to a train operated by another company because the latter does not want to incur possible penalties for lateness.

HS1 and HS2

Finally, something needs to be said about High Speed 1 and High Speed 2. When, on 1 December 1990, a French construction worker and an English construction worker shook hands through a hole connecting the two ends of a tunnel driven under the narrow stretch of sea between the European Continent and the UK, the event was of far more than symbolic importance, a fact recognised by the attention paid by the world's media. The Channel Tunnel was the culmination of the biggest civil engineering project in which Britain had ever been involved. Tunnels under, and bridges over, the Channel had been mooted on numerous occasions since the early nineteenth century. Such proposals had always excited heated controversy but had always failed to materialise, precisely because of the disagreements they provoked. These largely centred on nationalist, xenophobic and security issues as well as concerns about the expense involved. Between 1882 and 1950 alone there

Explore

A first-generation High Speed electric unit stands in the part of the remodelled St Pancras Station given over to trains travelling to and from Europe. Many people consider it absurd that HS1 and HS2 will not share the same London station. (A. Brooke)

Sir Edward Watkin was one of the most determined, not to say ruthless of Britain's nineteenth century railway magnates. His realm included the South Eastern, Metropolitan and Great Central Railways. Something of a visionary, he was an energetic advocate of a railway tunnel under the English Channel to France, connecting locations in the north and midlands of England with London and various destinations on the Continent. The Submarine Continental Railway Company actually started work on a tunnel until officially ordered to stop. (Author's collection)

were thirty-five occasions on which the subject of a Channel Tunnel was brought before parliament for discussion and ten of these resulted in Bills being presented, debated and rejected or set aside.

After some abortive initiatives, the first serious attempts to build a tunnel began in 1880 when heavy machines commenced operations on both sides of the Channel. Work stopped as renewed political tensions between Britain and France raised fears, particularly in the former, that a tunnel might be used by hostile invading military forces. A major proponent of this project was Sir Edward Watkin who envisaged a new superbly engineered international main line. This would link Sheffield and cities in the East Midlands with London and Dover and a tunnel under the Channel, allowing the operation of direct through trains to many cities in Europe. It was a grand vision, ahead of its time. It foundered on the security fears so prevalent in the 1880s.

The idea of a tunnel of the length necessary to pass under the Channel was an intimidating prospect given the expertise and level of technology of the time and it was not until the building of London's underground railway that something like the length of tunnel was actually attempted. By 1926, what later became the Northern Line was opened as a continuous tunnel sixteen miles long from Morden to Highgate. This may have been an impressive demonstration of what the latest technology could achieve but there was no will at the time to proceed with a Channel Tunnel project. Doubts continued to be expressed about whether a tunnel was needed while some who supported the idea argued that it should be a tunnel for road vehicles only. Matters remained on hold until interest slowly

Lieutenant General Sir Garnet Wolseley was a soldier of almost reckless courage around whom a cult of immense personal popularity was created in the late nineteenth century. He was one of the most vehement opponents of the Channel tunnel project and is shown in this 1882 cartoon riding the British lion and turning his back on 'Johnny Foreigner', particularly the French who might use the tunnel to effect an invasion of Britain.

revived in the 1950s, but it was not until the 1980s that the French and British governments agreed to go ahead and it is ironic that it was Margaret Thatcher, the most Europhobic of British prime ministers, who was instrumental in pushing through the decision to go ahead with the tunnel. The official opening was on 6 May 1994 and commercial freight services began running in June. Even then, doubts were still being raised that this was a vanity project which would bring little benefit to the country as a whole. In an attempt to placate such observations, parliament gave reassurances that international trains would run from certain major provincial cities as well as London. These promises were like pie-crusts, made to be broken. However, in the UK, with the understandable exception of constituencies containing ferry ports, public opinion was 'not in general anti-link, despite some reservations'.

The tunnel, thirty-one miles long, linked Folkestone with Coquelles, Pas-de-Calais. In 1985, the cost had been estimated at £5.5 billion although the eventual cost reached £9 billion. Not surprisingly, the French made something of the fact that the Channel Tunnel Rail Link on the British side used existing infrastructure. A dedicated link branded HS1 had to wait until November 2007 at which time trains began to operate along a purpose-built route between St Pancras and the Tunnel.

In 2009, plans for HS2 were announced. It was to be a dedicated high-speed rail link from London to Birmingham, Leeds and Manchester on which trains will be able to operate at speeds of up to 250 mph. Liverpool, Sheffield, York, Newcastle, Glasgow and Edinburgh will be linked to HS2 but by trains running over infrastructure that does not allow for such speeds. HS2 will be built in two phases and will involve the building of around 350 new route miles. The projected cost was initially put at £32.7 billion but by late 2017 had increased to £56 billion with every prospect that it will continue to rise further. HS2 excited controversy from its inception and has been described by Simon Jenkins, the author and journalist who has served on the boards of British Rail and London Transport, as 'the most extravagant infrastructure project in Britain's history'.[13]

HS2 will be the first main line railway built to connect British cities since the opening of the Great Central Railway's London Extension from Sheffield to London Marylebone via Nottingham and Leicester in 1899. The massive irony, of course, is that this line, built for high speed by the standards of the time, was sacrificed as a through route after it had been given the black spot in the Beeching Report. Parts of its alignment could have been used for HS2.

No sooner were the proposals for HS2 published by the Labour government in 2010 than strenuous objections began to be heard. These are unlikely to diminish in the future. Those in favour argue that the project is essential if the UK's economy is to grow. Opponents argue that HS2 is unnecessary, too expensive and will have a seriously damaging impact on areas of natural beauty and the ecosystems of which they are a part. Some protestors, mostly close to its projected alignment, have nothing against a high-speed railway as such, so long as it is somewhere else. Of course, it is inevitable that objections will be raised to any scheme for a major new railway but the objections on the grounds of noise are curious.

From a station that was slated for possible closure in the second half of twentieth century, there has been a remarkable transformation in the fortunes of London's St Pancras Station. Formerly a terminus of inter-city and suburban services it is now also a hub handling international services through the Channel Tunnel to Europe. It has undergone extensive remodelling and this shows a High Speed train in the station in 2018. (A. Brooke)

Fast trains on today's modern track are very quiet compared with the sound of traffic on motorways and major roads. This is virtually incessant seven days a week. Perhaps the selective loss of hearing of these objectors is fallout from the pervasive pro-road culture in which we currently live.

Local anti-HS2 groups began to appear, many of them in communities that will be affected by the building and operation of the route. An example is 'MAPA', an acronym for objectors concerned with the impact of HS2 on Measham, Appleby Magna, Packington and Austrey in Leicestershire and Warwickshire. Many local action and protest groups have cohered into national organisations such as 'Stop HS2'. This organisation has co-operated with eighteen councils along the line of the route who in turn set up '51M' named as such for the cost in millions of pounds of HS2 to every constituency in the UK. Among Stop HS2's claims is that estimates of the positive effects of the new line do not take into account the impact that HS2 will have on existing rail services. It has warned of significant reductions in many existing intercity services to and from London and the areas that HS2 is planned to serve. Other national groups opposing HS2 include 'AGHAST' (Action Groups against High Speed Two), 'Right Lines Charter Group' and 'HS2AA' or 'HS2 Action Alliance'.

Anger about HS2 is not exclusive to leafy parts of the Home Counties or rural idylls in the Midlands. A new housing development near Mexborough in South Yorkshire has been threatened with demolition because it straddles the proposed alignment of HS2. Some occupants had only moved into their new homes days before the plans were announced. While residents were attempting to come to terms with the news, the Secretary of State for Transport, Chris Grayling, was reassuring the public that HS2 will bring huge economic benefits across the country as part of government plans to spread wealth beyond London and the South-East. This claim of dubious veracity was scant consolation for those new residents near Mexborough.

A project of the size of HS2 has inevitably raised a multitude of legal issues and conflicts. The *Daily Telegraph* reported in May 2016 that HS2 Ltd had been accused of 'dictator-like arrogance' after demanding that more than 600 groups and individuals including the Attorney General and the Speaker of the House of Commons should be prevented from raising objections to the scheme. Even individuals living within sight and sound of the proposed line but not in its direct path have been deemed as not having a valid reason for protesting. Injunctions have been threatened to prevent anti-HS2 demonstrations. Despite such measures, objectors have managed to extract concessions from the government and HS2. For example, in September 2017, Nick Hurd, MP for Ruislip, acknowledged that successful negotiations with HS2 Ltd to mitigate its impact would not have been possible without agitation and organisation by people in his constituency.

Politicians across the political spectrum have voiced criticisms of the HS2 project. In 2014, ex-Chancellor Alistair Darling and ex-Minister of Transport John Prescott expressed many concerns about HS2 while Lord Mandelson declared that HS2 was 'an expensive mistake' and would come at the expense of 'large numbers of intercity services'. David Davis MP, Conservative, commented that the 'blighted HS2 rail project' should be cancelled while Frank Dobson MP, Labour, described HS2 as a vanity project.

Caroline Lucas of the Green Party criticised the cost and added that it was environmentally damaging and badly thought through. The then Transport Secretary, Patrick McCoughlin, in April 2014 turned on fellow Conservative MPs such as Michael Fabricant who had claimed that HS2 would have a devastating effect on the environment and would not deliver its promised economic benefits. He accused them, somewhat ironically, of acting like the landowners who resisted the railways in the middle of the nineteenth century. Fabricant responded by criticising the expense of HS2 and pointing out that it would neither link with St Pancras or whichever of the London airports would eventually be chosen to have a third runway. While many individual MPs have opposed HS2, they have often done so against the official policy of their party. Generally, the Conservatives, Labour, Liberal Democrats and Scottish Nationalists have supported the project while UKIP, the Greens and Plaid Cymru have been opposed. The Greens have argued in favour of improvements to the existing railway network.

A diverse range of organisations has expressed opposition to or scepticism towards HS2. The Institute of Economic Affairs has called for the project to be scrapped, saying that it would be 'unbelievably costly to the taxpayer while delivering incredibly poor value for money'.[14] It added that government claims that HS2 will transform the North are misleading and possibly completely mistaken. The

Engineering Employers' Federation has argued that the money should be switched to improving the road network while the Institute of Directors has called it 'a grand folly'. The RAC, speaking for its members and motorists in general has described HS2 as a hugely expensive scheme which will benefit a minority of wealthy travellers while doing nothing to solve what it described as the dire transport problems faced by the majority of the population. The New Economics Foundation claimed that HS2 is no substitute for comprehensive regional investment and nationally sustainable transport strategies. The Adam Smith Institute has said: '...there are no significant benefits of HS2; it will cost a lot of money and achieve virtually nothing'.[15] In an earlier editorial, the *Financial Times* questioned whether the value of a shiny new high-speed line outweighed the many other valuable projects that could be tackled with the limited resources available. *The Guardian*, in an article titled 'The Great Train Robbery' drew attention to the advantages that HS2 would bring to businesses in certain parts of the country and predicted that these advantages would be at the expense of other areas. It said:

> 'Parts of Britain...fear that a new zippy railway will create a second tier of cities supplied by fewer and slower trains. High-speed lines, like other regeneration projects, often displace economic activity rather than create it. The advantages, meanwhile, mostly accrue to business travellers...instead of redistributing wealth and opportunities, rich regions and individuals benefit at the expense of poorer ones. Britain still has time to ditch this grand infrastructure project – and it should.'[16]

The decision to make Euston the London terminus rather than to link with HS1 at nearby St Pancras has attracted criticism. Simon Jenkins wrote:

> 'Euston has poor east-west connectivity, as it is not on the tube's District, Metropolitan or Circle Lines. This meant that HS2 would enter London half-a-mile adrift of HS1 and trains to mainland Europe...HS2 was always a project born of political vanity.'[17]

Christian Wolmar addressed the issue of the potential demolition of flats and displacement of businesses around Euston, notably in

Drummond Street. He observed that this is a mixed community with a thriving street culture of small shops and cheap restaurants, one of few left in central London and that its loss was to be regretted. He also spoke of the incongruity of government funding for HS2 at a time of huge cuts in public spending including significant reductions in transport budgets elsewhere.

Among other protestors about the impact of HS2 in the Euston area was the vicar of St Pancras New Church. She told the House of Lords' Select Committee that the developers of HS2 should be forced to justify the removal of every single tree earmarked for destruction in the Euston area. Included in her evidence was the expected loss of part of the ancient burial ground known as St James's Gardens. This is ironic given the serious emotions expressed in 1866 about the impact of the building of the Midland Railway over part of the Old St Pancras Churchyard not far from Euston. The issue then had been the disturbance of human remains and the likelihood that they would not be treated with the respect which was their due. With reference to HS2, exactly the same concerns were expressed about St James's Gardens. Even dumb animals have expressed their opposition through human proxies when it was revealed that central London's only remaining population of hedgehogs is likely to be destroyed following the building of a lorry holding area yards from London Zoo.[18]

The Campaign to Protect Rural England, although not totally against HS2, has some reservations. They acknowledge that one effect of HS2 would be to remove many long-distance express passenger trains from certain lines giving those lines the capacity to operate more local passenger trains and increased rail freight. The Campaign supports HS2 in principle but has severe reservations about the nature of its planning and its likely environmental impact. It argues for significant increased investment in urban and rural railways and against any major programme of road-building. The Royal Society for the Protection of Birds queries claims made for the benefits that HS2 will bring to the economy and warns that it will have a serious impact on wildlife and the environment.

The Wildlife Trusts, with combined membership of thousands, are in favour of sustainable public transport schemes, arguing that they can play an important part in a necessary transition to a low carbon economy, but they want to ensure that any such schemes are not damaging to the natural environment. They have concerns

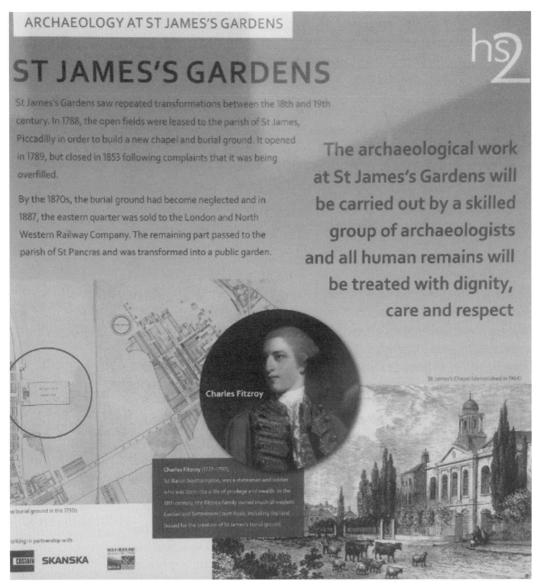

ARCHAEOLOGY AT ST JAMES'S GARDENS

ST JAMES'S GARDENS

hs2

St James's Gardens saw repeated transformations between the 18th and 19th century. In 1788, the open fields were leased to the parish of St James, Piccadilly in order to build a new chapel and burial ground. It opened in 1789, but closed in 1853 following complaints that it was being overfilled.

By the 1870s, the burial ground had become neglected and in 1887, the eastern quarter was sold to the London and North Western Railway Company. The remaining part passed to the parish of St Pancras and was transformed into a public garden.

The archaeological work at St James's Gardens will be carried out by a skilled group of archaeologists and all human remains will be treated with dignity, care and respect

Charles Fitzroy

St James's Chapel (demolished in 1964)

Charles Fitzroy (1737–1797), 1st Baron Southampton, was a statesman and soldier who was born into a life of privilege and wealth. In the 18th century, the Fitzroy family owned much of modern Euston and Tottenham Court Road, including the land leased for the creation of St James's burial ground.

the burial ground in the 1790s

working in partnership with

SKANSKA

There is massive disruption in the Euston area in preparation for the building of HS2. Among the locations close by is St James' Gardens which was originally the burial ground for St James, Piccadilly. Thousands were buried at this spot including the artist George Morland and the demagogue Lord George Gordon, associated with the anti-Catholic Gordon Riots of 1780. It is now a public garden and this board tells the story. (A. Brooke)

about HS2 on that score. The Woodlands Trust while favouring greener forms of transport and not against HS2 in principle sees the latter as a serious threat to specific areas of ancient woodland. The Countryside Alliance is worried about what it sees as the excessive cost of HS2 and its potentially devastating effect on the tracts of countryside through which it will run and the lives of large numbers living close to the proposed route.

Peter Barkham, the natural history author and journalist wrote emotionally about his walk along the proposed route of the first phase of HS2 from London to Birmingham. He recorded the attitudes of local people who would be affected by the route and he described the landscape through which HS2 is to pass and on which it will inevitably have an impact. At one stage he crossed the pretty Leam Valley and cut through South Cubbington Wood. He wrote:

'The ancient woodland was a tangle of honeysuckle and hawthorn; its most charismatic resident a huge pear tree. Reputed to be the second largest in the UK, it boasted five trunks, three colours – green leaves at head height, yellow further up, red at the top and no pears. Last week it was named the Woodland Trust Tree of the Year after 10,000 people voted for it.'[18]

Twenty-first century protests against a projected major railway line would not be complete without an input from aristocratic landowners, albeit not carrying quite the weight of their predecessors of the nineteenth century. Earl Spencer argued that the construction of HS2 would exacerbate problems with rabbits and deer on land which will be bisected by the route's alignment. He called for fencing to be erected to protect his estate. Lord Rothschild was concerned that the Waddesdon Estate in Buckinghamshire, given by his family to the National Trust, would be severely disrupted by the building works associated with HS2 and that visitor numbers might be reduced once the line was in operation. Nicholas van Cutsem, a friend of Prince William, fears disturbance on his property near Great Missenden. It stands a few hundred feet from the route and he sees the area losing its rural tranquillity while he claims that his own family will suffer years of disruption from building operations.

Back in the nineteenth century, as we have seen, many very powerful landowners had voiced opposition to and initiated action against the coming of the railways. They did so in the context of a social system considerably different from that prevailing today. That distant and usually urban business people sought to enrich themselves by building and operating railways and could obtain legal powers entitling them to buy the land they required for this purpose was seen as a gross affront to long-held and precious seigneurial rights and privileges. We can see now that a struggle was taking place between the declining influence of a social elite owing its prominence to landownership and pedigree and an upwardly aspiring and energetic new elite of an industrial, manufacturing and commercial nature. At that time 'old money' was able to use its influence to extract generally very favourable, some would say unduly favourable, economic terms for being forced to sell land to the railway companies. Considerable ingenuity was shown in finding reasons why there should be such generous compensation for the 'inconvenience' to which landowners were put by the coming of the railways.

The controversy around HS2 offers similarities with issues that were raised against railways in the nineteenth century: threats of environmental damage and destruction of precious countryside; the use of seemingly arbitrary legal processes by powerful forces against the interests of individuals; widespread disruption particularly during the construction phase; questions of balancing the gains of railway construction and operation against their negative effects and the issue of who or which groups were most likely to enjoy the benefits, if any. We can now, of course, appreciate the huge impetus for economic, social, political and cultural advance that was provided by the railways in a way that was not possible in the middle of the nineteenth century but even so questions remain as to whether HS2 is really needed in an age where vast amounts of information can be communicated in an instant and face-to-face meetings may be largely unnecessary. Should we simply accept the fulsome promises of economic betterment in which most enthusiastic advocates would have us believe? The railways of the nineteenth century were built during what was a far more expansive period in British history when there was a sense of élan, confidence and optimism that a better future could and indeed was being built. HS2 is being developed in a period of economic austerity and widespread cynicism about the motives and mores of powerful business forces and the politicians who further their interests in parliament. It is also being built at a time when there seems to be little prospect, immediate or distant, of economic betterment for large sections of the population.

It could be argued that the former dominance of the landed interest has been replaced by faceless global corporations with the material resources that largely ensure that governments respond favourably to their economic objectives. In the nineteenth century, before sections of the population were enfranchised but also today, substantial numbers feel politically impotent – that as individuals they have little control over the major decisions affecting their lives. Whether or not something like HS2 is necessary for the common good, many people believe that the decision-makers will go ahead anyway. A balancing factor is that more pressure or interest groups obviously exist now than in the great age of railway expansion. Through involvement in them, individuals may gain some degree of collective power. It is not unknown for such groups to succeed against what would seem to be all the odds. They made a major contribution to saving the Settle and Carlisle Railway, for example.

We have traced aspects of official and private attitudes accorded to railways over two centuries. The British have been very ambivalent about railways. As we have seen, influential landowners often opposed railways, at least initially, whereas ordinary people frequently feted the opening of lines serving their communities. Governments have felt it necessary to apply all sorts of regulatory measures to the railways these ostensibly being in the public interest, often such state intervention conflicting with contemporary priorities of political economy. Private railway companies frequently had to be cajoled into taking measures with regard to safety, for example. Especially since 1945, the railways have suffered from the capricious whims of politicians. Governments and senior civil servants have been in thrall to powerful lobbies consisting of those with interests in promoting road transport. For much of the last seventy years a strong pro-road culture has existed with perceptions that railways were outdated, inefficient and that money spent on them was simply money wasted, whereas resources given to roads brought significant economic returns.

Along with the weather, railways have formed a staple diet for the formidable number of people for whom moaning and complaining provides much solace. They have managed to combine constant griping about the shortcomings of the railways with sentimental, comforting feelings of reassurance that somehow the world is a better place for railways being there, even if they don't actually use them.

However, the last twenty to thirty years have witnessed a transformation in the role of the railways. For reasons not necessarily connected to the privatisation of the network, more people than ever before are using rail transport. From a culture of contraction and closures, re-openings and expansion are now the order of the day. Such a situation would have been inconceivable as late as the 1980s. This is highly encouraging and yet scarcely a day passes without complaints being voiced about unpunctuality, overcrowding, disruption for engineering work, missed connections resulting from a fragmented and uncoordinated network, unnecessarily complicated fare systems and excessive fares combined with handouts from the taxpayer to privatised railway businesses.

Any attempt to implement a closure programme is now a total non-starter. A major political party that committed itself to renationalisation of the railways would surely be on to a winner. We are still left with the legacy of what has been described as: 'the bad planning, dogmatism, political chicanery, ineptitude and lack of imagination that characterised rail policy in the middle of the 20th century'. Those who were looking forward to the electrification of the Midland Main Line, for example, may think that the age of chicanery is not over.

Select Bibliography

Abbott, S. & Whitehouse, A. *The Line that refused to die*, Hawes: 1990, Leading Edge.

Alderman, G. *The Railway Interest*, Leicester: 1973, Leicester University Press.

Allen, G. Freeman, *British Railways after Beeching*, London: 1965, Ian Allan.

Andrews, C.B. *The Railway Age*, London: 1937, Country Life.

Arnold, A.J. & McCartney, S. *The Rise and Fall of the Railway King*, London: 2004, Hambledon and London.

Austin, C. & Faulkner, R. *Disconnected! Broken Links in Britain's Rail Policy*, Addlestone: 2015, Oxford Publishing Company.

Bagwell, P.S. *The Transport Revolution from 1770*. London: 1974, Batsford.

Bairstow, M. *The Sheffield, Ashton-under-Lyne and Manchester Railway*, Pudsey: 1986, Martin Bairstow.

Beckett, J.V. *The Aristocracy in England, 1660-1914*, Oxford: 1989, Basil Blackwell.

Betjeman, J. *Collected Poems*, London: 1979, John Murray.

Biddle, G. *Railways in the Landscape*, Barnsley: 2016, Pen & Sword.

------------ *The Railway Surveyors*, London: 1990, Ian Allan.

Binney, M. & Pierce, D. (eds.), *Railway Architecture*, London: 1979, Orbis.

Bonavia, M. *British Rail: The First 25 Years*, Newton Abbot: 1981, David & Charles.

Bradley, S. *The Railways. Nation, Network and People*, London: 2015, Profile.

Brandon, D. & Brooke, A. *Bankside, London's Original District of Sin*, Stroud: 2013, Amberley.

--------- *Blood on the Tracks. A History of Railway Crime in Britain*, Stroud: 2010, History Press.

Carter, I. *Railways and Culture in Britain. The Epitome of Modernity*, Manchester: 2001, Manchester University Press.

Coleman, T. *The Railway Navvies*, London: 1965, Hutchinson.

Dow, A. (ed.), *Dow's Dictionary of Railway Quotations*, Baltimore: 2006, John Hopkins University Press.

Dyos, H.J. & Aldcroft, D.H. *British Transport. An Economic Survey from the Seventeenth Century to the Twentieth*, Leicester: 1969, Leicester University Press.

Dyos, H.J. & Wolff, M. (eds.), *The Victorian City – Images and Realities, vol.2*, London: 1973, Routledge & Kegan Paul.

Ellis, H. *British Railways History 1830-1876*, London: 1954, George Allen & Unwin.

---------- *Four Main Lines*, London: 1950. George Allen & Unwin.

---------- *Railway Art*, London: 1977, Ash & Grant.

Evans, A.K.B. & Gough, J.V. (eds.), *The Impact of the Railway on Society in Britain. Essays in Honour of Jack Simmons*, Aldershot: 2003, Ashgate.

Faith, N. *The World the Railways Made*, London: 1990, The Bodley Head.

Faulkner, R. & Austin, C. *Holding the Line. How Britain's railways were saved*, Manchester: 2018, Crecy.

Fiennes, G. *I tried to run a Railway*, London: 2015, Ian Allan.

Foxwell, E.E. *English Express trains: Two Papers*, London: 1884, Edward Stanford.

Francis, J.A. *A History of the English Railway: Its Social Relations and Revelations, 1820-1845*, London: 1851, Smith & Elder.

Freeman, M. *Railways and the Victorian Imagination*, New Haven: 1999, Yale University Press.

Gage, J. *Turner, Rain, Steam and Speed*, London: 1972, Allan Lane.

Gilmour, R. *The Victorian Period: The Intellectual and Cultural Content of English Literature, 1830-1900*, London: 1993, Robin Gilmour.

Gourvish, T.R. *Britain's Railways 1997-2005*, Oxford: 2008, Oxford University Press.

------------------- *British Rail 1974-97, From Integration to Privatisation*, Oxford; 2009, Oxford University Press.

------------------- *British Railways, 1948-73*, Cambridge: 1986, Cambridge University Press.

------------------- *Railways and the British Economy*, London: 1980, Macmillan.

Gray, A. *Crime on the Line*, Penryn; 2000, Atlantic.

Grinling, C.H. *The History of the Great Northern Railway 1845-1922*, London: 1966, George Allen & Unwin.

Hardy,R.H.N. *Beeching: Champion of the Railway?* London: 1989, Ian Allan.

Harris, S. *The Railway Dilemma, The Perpetual Problem of Ownership, Costs & Control*, Addlestone: 2016, Ian Allan.

Henshaw, D. *The Great Railway Conspiracy*, Hawes: 1991, Leading Edge.

Hepple, J.R. *The Influence of Landowners' Attitudes on Railway Alignment in Nineteenth Century England*, Unpublished Ph.D Thesis, 1974, University of Hull.

Hobsbawm, E. *The Age of Empire 1875-1914*, London: 1987, Weidenfeld & Nicolson.

------------------- *The Age of Revolution 1789-1848*, London: 1962, Weidenfeld & Nicolson.

------------------- *Uncommon People, Resistance, Rebellion and Jazz*, London: 1998, Weidenfeld & Nicolson.

Hoskins, W.G. *The Making of the English Landscape*, London: 1988, Hodder & Stoughton.

Hylton, S. *The Grand Experiment. The Birth of the Railway Age: 1820-45*, Hersham: 2007. Ian Allan.

------------ *What the Railways did for Us, The Making of Modern Britain*, Stroud; Amberley, 2015.

Kellett, J.R. *Railways and Victorian Cities*, London: 1969, Routledge and Kegan Paul.

Kemble, F. *Record of a Girlhood*, Beccles: 1978, Heller.

Klingender, F.D. *Art & the Industrial Revolution*, London: 1947, Royle.

Kostal, R.W. *Law and English Railway Capitalism, 1825-1875*, Oxford; 1994, Oxford University Press.

Lambert, A.J. *Nineteenth Century Railway History through the Illustrated London News*, Newton Abbot: 1984, David & Charles.

Lewin, H.G. *The Railway Mania and its Aftermath, 1845-1852*, revised edition, Newton Abbot: 1968, David & Charles.

Loft, C. *Last Trains. Dr Beeching and the Death of Rural England*, London: 2014, Biteback.

Major, S. *Early Victorian Railway Excursions*, Barnsley: 2015, Pen & Sword.

Margetson, S. *Journey by Stages*, London: 1967, Cassell.

Marx, K. & Engels, F. *Articles on Britain*, Moscow: 1971, Progress Publishers.

Mather, F.C. *Public Order in the Age of the Chartists*, Manchester: 1959, Manchester University Press.

McKenna, F. *The Railway Workers, 1840-1970*, London: 1980, Faber.

Nock, O.S. *Branch Lines*, London, 1957, Batsford.

Parris, H. *Government and the Railways in Nineteenth-Century Britain*, London: 1965, Routledge & Kegan Paul.

Perkin, H. *The Age of the Railway*, Newton Abbot: 1971, David & Charles.

Pollins, H. *British Railways. An Industrial History.* Newton Abbot: 1971. David & Charles.

Ransom, P.J.L. *The Victorian Railway and how it evolved*, London: 1990, Heinemann.

Reed, M.C. (ed.), *Railways in the Victorian Economy. Studies in Finance and Economic Growth*, Newton Abbot: 1969, David & Charles.

Richards, J. & MacKenzie, J.M. *The Railway Station. A Social History*, Oxford: 1986, Oxford University Press.

Robbins, M. *British Railways, an Industrial History*, Newton Abbot: 1981, David & Charles.

--------------- *The Railway Age*, London: 1962, Routledge & Kegan Paul.

Rolt, L.T.C. *George & Robert Stephenson. The Railway Revolution*, London: 1960, Longmans.

Schivelbusch, W. *The Railway Journey. The Industrialisation of Time and Space in the 19th Century*, Leamington: 1986, Berg.

Simmons, J. *Railways: An Anthology*, London: 1991, Collins.

--------------- *The Railway in Town and Country 1830-1914*, Newton Abbot, 1986, David & Charles.

--------------- *The Victorian Railway*, 2nd edition, London: 1986, Thames & Hudson.

Simmons, J. (ed.), *The Railway Traveller's Handybook*, 1971 edition, Bath: Adams & Dart.

Thomas, D. St.J. *The Country Railway*, Newton Abbot: 1976, David & Charles.

Thomas, D. St.J. (ed.), *How Railways changed Britain*, Derby: 2015, Railway & Canal Historical Society.

Thompson, F.M.L. *British Landed Society in the Nineteenth Century*, London: 1963, Routledge & Kegan Paul.

Turnock, D. *Railways in the British Isles. Landscape, Land Use & Society*, Cambridge: 1982, Cambridge University Press.

--------------- *The Historical Geographer's Approach to Railway History: The Relations between Railways and Canals* in Ambler, R.W. (ed.), *The History and Practice of Britain's Railways*, Aldershot: 1999, Ashgate.

Vaughan, A. *Railwaymen, Politics & Money*, London: 1997, John Murray.

--------------- *Railway Blunders*, London: 2003, Ian Allan.

Williams, F.S. *Our Iron Roads. Their History, Construction and Administration,* London: 1968 edition, Cass.

Williamson, T. & Bellamy, L. *Property & Landscape,* London: 1987, George Phillip.

Wolmar, C. *Down the Tube. The Battle for London's Underground,* London: 2002, Aurum.

-------------- *Fire & Steam. A New History of the Railways of Britain,* London: 2007, Atlantic.

-------------- *On the Wrong Line,* London: 2005, Gardners Books.

-------------- *The Subterranean Railway,* London: 2004, Atlantic.

Wooler, N. *Dinner in the Diner,* Newton Abbot: 1987, David & Charles.

Wragg, D. S*ignal Failure. Politics & Britain's Railways,* Stroud, 2004.

Notes

Introduction
    1. Quoted in Andrews, London, 1937, p.58.
    2. Quoted in Burke, London, 1942, p.118.
    3. Ibid. p.119.
    4. Hobsbawm, London, 1987, p.27.
    5. Rolt, London, 1960, ix.
    6. Freeman, New Haven, 1999, p.19.

Chapter 2
    1. Margetson, London, 1967, p.211.
    2. P.P. *Select Committee for Enquiring into the State of the Roads in England and Wales,* 1840. Vol. XXVII, App.X.
    3. Francis, London, 1851, p.70.

Chapter 3
    1. H.C. 1844, (113), xi, 16 June, p.5.
    2. H.C. 1845, (220), x, 29 May, pp.140-1.
    3. Kostal, Oxford, 1994, xi.
    4. Francis, op.cit. p.171.
    5. Hepple, 1974, p.256
    6. *Herapath's Railway Journal,* 19 October 1872.

Chapter 4
    1. Thompson, London, 1963, p.112.
    2. Perkin, London, 1971, pp.34-5.
    3. Quoted in Beckett, London, 1989, p.244.
    4. Perkin, op.cit. p.49.
    5. P.P. H of L. *Select Committee on Charging Entailed Estates for Railways,* 1863, Report, iii, Evidence, Q.33.
    6. P.P. *Report of the Select Committee of the House of Lords on Compensation for Lands taken by Railways,* 1845, vol. x, pp.445-460.
    7. Marx & Engels, 1971, p.109.
    8. Ibid. p.110.

Chapter 5
    1. Quoted in Bairstow, Pudsey, 1986, p.16.
    2. Robbins, 1962, op.cit. p.104.

3. Kostal, op.cit. p.2.
4. Ibid. p.12.
5. Ibid. p.23.
6. *Railway Gazette*, 20 May 1848.
7. Ibid. 14 July 1849.
8. *Bradshaw's Railway Gazette*, 20 May 1848.
9. HLRO, House of Lords *Select Committee on Railways*, 1846.

Chapter 6

1. Kostal, op.cit. p.144.
2. Ward, *Journal of Transport History*, IV, 1960, p.243.
3. Kostal, op.cit. p.145.
4. *Birmingham Gazette*, 24 January 1831.
5. *Hansard*, LXXX, 8 May 1845, c.280.
6. Quoted in Vaughan, 1997, p.53.
7. House of Lords Record Office, HL 1832, *London & Birmingham Railway, Minutes of Evidence*, vol.16, 3 July, p.197.
8. Thompson, 1963, op.cit. p.144.
9. Hepple, op.cit. p.164.
10. HLRO, HL 1843, *Blisworth & Peterborough Railway, Minutes of Evidence*, Vol.2, 20 June, p.222.
11. HLRO, HC 1845, *Syston & Peterborough Railway, Minutes of Evidence*, vol.2, 20 June, p.56 April, p.193.
12. Nock, London, 1957, p.15.
13. *Stamford Mercury*, 4 April 1845.

Chapter 7

1. Dow, Baltimore, 2006, p.94.
2. Carter, *The Lambourn Valley Railway*, Backtrack, vol.7, no.4, 1993.
3. D. St. J. Thomas, Newton Abbot, 1976, p.15.
4. Hoole, *From York to Scarborough Pt I*, Railway Magazine, vol.106, March 1960.
5. Quoted in Williamson & Bellemy, London, 1987, p.206.
6. Cook, *Brentford Dock and Branch*, British Railways Illustrated Annual, 3, 1994, p.53.
7. Wolmar, (2007) p.182.
8. HLRO, HC 1876, *Westerham Valley Railway*, vol. 42, 22 March, pp.104-106.
9. *Hampshire Telegraph*, 1 July 1845.
10. Simmons, Nairn, 1994, p.60.
11. Quoted in Biddle, London, 1990, p. 90.

12. Hepple, op.cit. p.282.
13. Andrews, op.cit. p.37.

Chapter 8

1. *Hansard*, 2nd Series, 1836, pp.1161-2.
2. Perkin 1971, op.cit. p.109.
3. P.P. *Select Committee on Railways, Second Report* 1839, vol.x.
4. Quoted in Dow, op.cit. p.78.
5. *Illustrated London News*, 24 February, 1864.
6. P.P. *Royal Commission on Railways, Appendices to Minutes of Evidence*, 1867, xxxvii, pt.2, p.583.
7. McKenna, London, 1980, p.38.
8. P.P. *Royal Commission on Railway Accidents Report*, 1877, vol xiv, p.94.
9. *Edinburgh Review*, July 1851.
10. P.P. *Royal Commission on Railway Accidents Report*, 1877, vol. xlviii, Appendix G.
11. Quoted in Harris, Addlestone, 2016, p.22.
12. Perkin, op.cit. p.80.

Chapter 10

1. Carter, *The Lambourn Railway*, op.cit.
2. Hoskins, 1988, p.213
3. Brandon, 2010, p.45.
4. *The Times*, 30 November 1861.
5. *The Times*, 14 July 1879.
6. Richards & Mackenzie, Oxford, 1986, p.94.
7. Maggs, *Railway Curiosities: Passengers*, Backtrack, vol.23, no.7, 2009.
8. Brandon & Brooke, Stroud, 2010.
9. Brandon & Brooke, Stroud, 2013, p.10.
10. Francis, op.cit, p.120.
11. Coleman, op.cit. p.21.
12. Barrett, London, 1880, p.140.
13. Quoted in Ransom, Edinburgh, 2007, p.64.
14. Nisbet, *The Tay Bridge Disaster and the Press*, Backtrack, vol.23, no.12, 2009.
15. Ludlum, *The East Lincolnshire Railway*, Backtrack, vol.22, no.4, 2008.
16. *The Railway Signal*, July 1883, p.242.
17. Mather, Manchester, 1959, p.161.
18. PP, *Select Committee on Railways*, 1844, *Minutes of Evidence, Fifth Report*.

19. HLRO, HC 1846, *Select Committee on London & Birmingham Railway (Birmingham Extension)* 12 June 1863.
20. Kellett, London, 1979, p.327.
21. *The Times*, 2 March 1861.
22. *Illustrated London News*, 17 January 1863, p.83.
23. *The Economist*, 20 July 1844, p.101.
24. Ibid. 7 January 1865, p.2.
25. *Hansard*, LXXVIII, 6 March, c.370.

Chapter 11

1. Quoted in Aye, London, 1931, p.76.
2. Quoted in Perkin, op.cit. pp.87-8.
3. Quoted in Cupit, *The Lincoln Branch of the Midland Railway*, Steam Days, May 1992, pp. 270-1.

Chapter 13

1. Quoted in Robbins, *Railways and Politics in East Cornwall*, Railway Magazine, vol.104, no.682, pp.126-128.
2. Quoted in Andrews, op.cit. p.127.
3. Major, S. 2015, p.85.
4. Ibid. p.147.
5. Ibid. p.7.
6. Quoted in Simmons (ed.), 1971, p.22.
7. Quoted in Freeman, 1999, op.cit. p.67.

Chapter 14

1. Lewin, 1968, Newton Abbot, p.14.
2. *BTC Annual Reports and Accounts*, 1952, p.3.
3. Ditto, 1962.
4. *BRB Annual Reports and Accounts*, 1966, p.3.
5. Quoted in Henshaw, Hawes, 1991, p.20.
6. *BBC Interview*, 27 March 1963.
7. Freeman Allen, G. London, 1965, p.1.
8. Quoted in Gourvish, Cambridge, 1986, p.455.
9. Austin & Faulkner, op.cit. pp.9-10.
10. Ibid. pp. 9-15.
11. Wolmar, 2007. p.311.
12. *Hansard*, vol.560, 26 March 2013, col.1487.
13. *Guardian*, 17 November 2015.
14. *Financial Times*, 25 October 2011.
15. *The Economist*, 3 September 2011.
16. *Guardian*, 7 June,2016.
17. *London Review of Books*, 'What is the point of HS2?' 7 April 2014.
18. *Guardian*, 17 November 2015.

Index